CHARLEY'S WAR

2 June 1916 – 1 August 1916

PAT MILLS
JOE COLQUHOUN

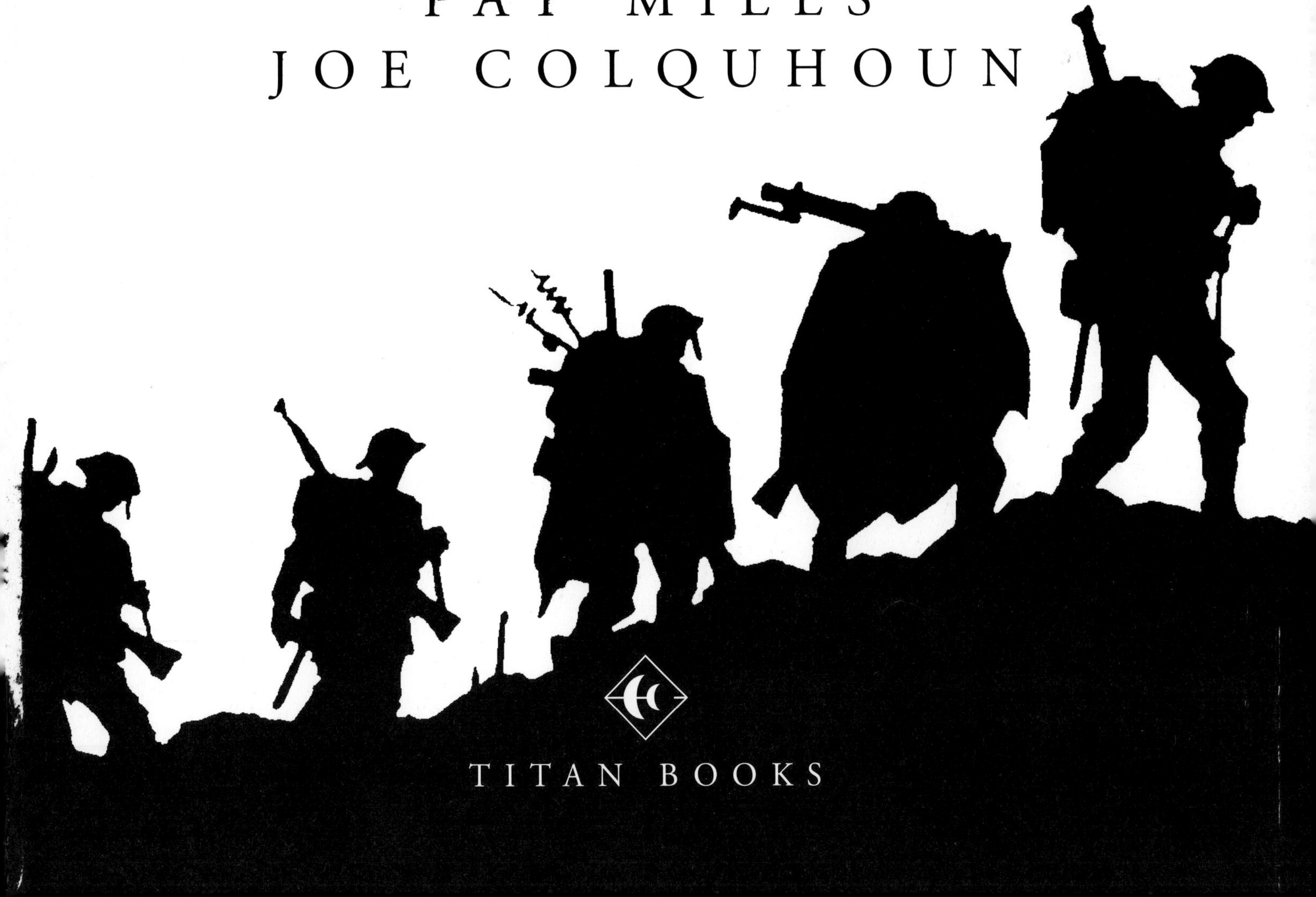

Titan Books

CHARLEY'S WAR: 2 June 1916 – 1 August 1916
ISBN 1 84023 627 2
ISBN-13 9781840236279

Published by
Titan Books
A division of Titan Publishing Group Ltd
144 Southwark St
London SE1 0UP

A CIP catalogue record for this title is available from the British Library.

This edition first published: November 2004
4 6 8 10 9 7 5 3

Printed in Italy.

Also available from Titan Books
Charley's War: 1 August 1916 – 17 October 1916 (ISBN: 1 84023 929 8)

Grateful thanks to Pat Mills, Trucie Henderson, Neil Emery and Yvonne Oliver for their help
and support in the production of this book.

Cover photo used by permission of the Imperial War Museum,
London. Q2756
Poppy artwork © 2004 Trucie Henderson

Introduction & Strip Commentary © 2004 Pat Mills
Into *Battle* © 2004 Neil Emery

Photo credits: Page 109, Malcolm Fairman; page 110, *Collier's New Photographic History of the
World's War* (New York, 1918); page 111, Malcolm Fairman and *Collier's New Photographic History of
the World's War*

What did you think of this book? We love to hear from our readers.
Please email us at: readerfeedback@titanemail.com, or write to us
at the above address.

www.titanbooks.com

INTRODUCTION

by Pat Mills

I'm delighted to see *Charley's War* reprinted after all these years. It's great to see Joe's work reaching a new and wider audience as well as providing a permanent format for the stories so many readers grew up with. For me, Joe is the ultimate comic book artist and there is still no one to match him in this particular genre.

And yet it's a cause for sadness, too, because *Charley's War* is a creative cul-de-sac, a series that actually led nowhere. As the most successful story in the weekly comic, *Battle*, it should have inspired similar stories and brought about a radical redefining of the modern British comic in a way that other successful serials did. Thus *One-Eyed Jack*, the story of a tough New York cop in *Valiant* by John Wagner, led him to develop *Judge Dredd* for *2000 AD*. But it was not to be. And, whilst I greatly appreciate how highly my fellow creators rate *Charley*, it has never influenced, in any meaningful way, other writers to produce similar dramas with such subversive subtexts.

To understand why, it's necessary to peel away the different layers of the story and see what really lies beneath. On the first level it's a humorous, tragic, heavily researched drama with strong characterisation, drawn in mesmerising detail. So the reason why it has never been imitated on this level is simple: it's just too time consuming. Most British or American creators simply cannot afford to produce artwork and story to this detailed standard for a genre that is almost redundant. In saying this, I exclude French and European comics, where the financial rewards are potentially greater, and where there is a stronger comic audience for stories about the lives of ordinary people.

On a second level, here is a story that does not endorse macho hero values. Charley is a hero, but I made the deliberate choice to make him neither particularly intelligent nor strong; he's just a typical 'Tommy'. There is nothing fantastic going on in the usual comic sense of the word and yet – through Joe's genius – there is actually something absolutely fantastic going on. He is making the lives and struggles of our fathers, grandfathers and great grandfathers important and entertaining and worthwhile. That the young readers at the time appreciated this and preferred Charley's adventures to superheroes is a tribute to their discerning eye. But beyond the *Battle* readership, this was not recognised because the UK/US market is still essentially all about fantasy. Important themes are covered with some impressive writing, but always with fantasy sweetening the pill. *Charley's War* is acknowledged as a celebrated curio of its time and then filed away in the archives.

On a third level, *Charley* is an anti-war story, often with polemical comments and footnotes that I deliberately wrote 'head on' so they couldn't be ignored. Such an approach is often criticised; it's certainly no longer fashionable and was more common in the 1960s and 1970s. So, it can also be seen as rather dated and therefore not a style to repeat, although there is one story that did explore the genre – the excellent *White Death* by Robbie Morrison and Charlie Adlard and set in the alpine trench war of 1914-1918. It's great to see such a stylish book with its strong text and beautiful art.

It is also interesting that society has skilfully managed to marginalise and accept World War One as a one-off, 'bad' war. Subsequent wars have escaped such critical examination, not least through 'embedding' (controlling) and avoiding critical reporting of the conflicts. We are encouraged, brainwashed even, to believe in the dangerous myth of the 'just' war. So there have been no World War Two or Iraq War equivalents of *Charley's War*. Instead, we get 'War is Hell' stories that may claim to be anti-war but are actually not. These are sometimes seen as being influenced by *Charley* and I make a point of repudiating the connection for an important reason. I'm told US soldiers watched the 'War is Hell'-style movies, such as *Full Metal Jacket* and *Apocalypse Now*, to psyche themselves up just before going into combat

ABOVE: Joe Colquhoun's full-colour artwork from the *Battle* annual of 1985.

in Iraq*. I doubt those same US soldiers also watched *All Quiet On the Western Front,* which was one of the role models for *Charley.*

But, at the deepest level, *Charley's War* is a class war, a war against the poor, which I exemplified at every opportunity. It's estimated that in World War One, American corporations made $16 billion from the conflict. Their normal profits leapt by 200, 300, even 900 per cent! And these profits were shared between just 21,000 billionaires and millionaires. To put that number in perspective, 60,000 British soldiers were killed or wounded on the first day of the Battle of the Somme. Unfortunately, billionaires don't tend to turn up in the trenches, so I could never find a way to dramatise such facts directly. But this is what Charley and his mates were really fighting and dying for. Not nationalism and outmoded power blocs, gallant little Belgium, assassins in Sarajevo or crazy Kaisers. All these are simply the incitements and incidents, the surface level camouflage designed to obscure the truth and endorsed by historians who toe the establishment line. Charley and his mates were actually fighting to make someone else rich.

Michael Moore's *Fahrenheit 9/11*, now a commercially successful mainstream film, makes it very clear that a war against the poor to make the rich richer is the basis of modern wars. He describes the profiteering and how poor Americans are used as modern day cannon fodder, whilst no Congressmen's sons are fighting in Iraq. So nothing has actually changed since 1918, but we're not mature enough in mainstream comics to risk publishing an equivalent of this drama documentary. And so *Charley's War* remains a one-off, an anachronism from a pre-fantasy era.

And yet, somehow, the muse will always find a way to shed new light on war, even in these escapist times. Earlier this year, my French artist Frank Tacito suggested the following scenario for our mainstream French comic book series *Claudia – Vampire Knight.* The series is set in Hell and follows the adventures of the dead who must pay their karmic debts for their crimes in life. Frank suggested we feature an eternal trench war where well-known politicians, wearing yellow uniforms, go endlessly over the top into action. As they charge across no-man's land, they are machine-gunned by their victims for all eternity. These include women and children in Iraq, victims of US and UK 'collateral damage', and the mutant offspring of mothers affected by the use of uranium tipped shells in Iraq and Serbia. I've described in another series, *Savage* (about a modern day fascist invasion of our country), how such shells have caused babies to be born without eyes, limbs, even without heads, or with a single eye, like a Cyclops. Rather like something out of a science fiction movie, actually.

And so the war in the comic trenches continues after all these years. And as it's politicians who start wars, it's surely better that they should be there to fight and die in them, rather than Charley and his mates.

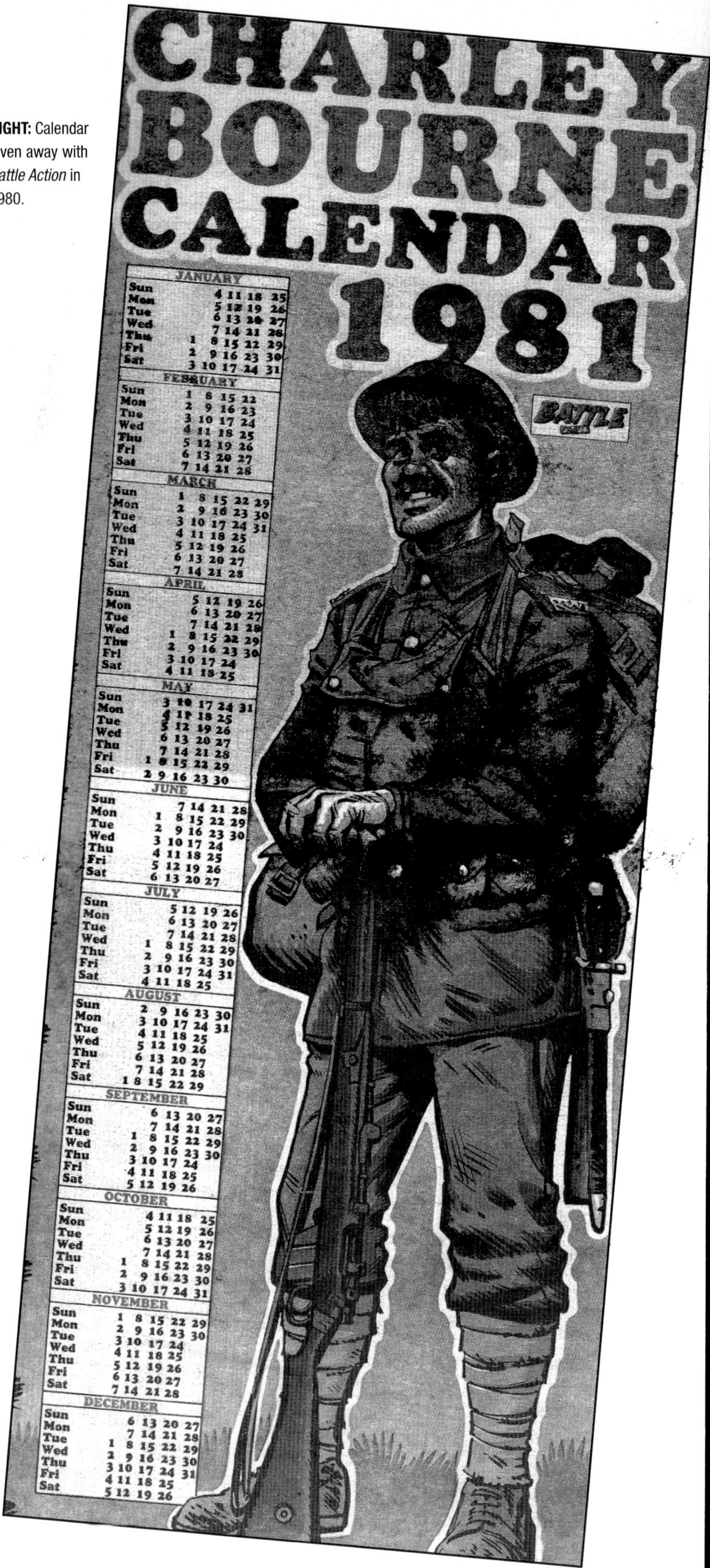
CHARLEY BOURNE CALENDAR 1981
BATTLE
JANUARY
Sun 4 11 18 25
Mon 5 12 19 26
Tue 6 13 20 27
Wed 7 14 21 28
Thu 1 8 15 22 29
Fri 2 9 16 23 30
Sat 3 10 17 24 31
FEBRUARY
Sun 1 8 15 22
Mon 2 9 16 23
Tue 3 10 17 24
Wed 4 11 18 25
Thu 5 12 19 26
Fri 6 13 20 27
Sat 7 14 21 28
MARCH
Sun 1 8 15 22 29
Mon 2 9 16 23 30
Tue 3 10 17 24 31
Wed 4 11 18 25
Thu 5 12 19 26
Fri 6 13 20 27
Sat 7 14 21 28
APRIL
Sun 5 12 19 26
Mon 6 13 20 27
Tue 7 14 21 28
Wed 1 8 15 22 29
Thu 2 9 16 23 30
Fri 3 10 17 24
Sat 4 11 18 25
MAY
Sun 3 10 17 24 31
Mon 4 11 18 25
Tue 5 12 19 26
Wed 6 13 20 27
Thu 7 14 21 28
Fri 1 8 15 22 29
Sat 2 9 16 23 30
JUNE
Sun 7 14 21 28
Mon 1 8 15 22 29
Tue 2 9 16 23 30
Wed 3 10 17 24
Thu 4 11 18 25
Fri 5 12 19 26
Sat 6 13 20 27
JULY
Sun 5 12 19 26
Mon 6 13 20 27
Tue 7 14 21 28
Wed 1 8 15 22 29
Thu 2 9 16 23 30
Fri 3 10 17 24 31
Sat 4 11 18 25
AUGUST
Sun 2 9 16 23 30
Mon 3 10 17 24 31
Tue 4 11 18 25
Wed 5 12 19 26
Thu 6 13 20 27
Fri 7 14 21 28
Sat 1 8 15 22 29
SEPTEMBER
Sun 6 13 20 27
Mon 7 14 21 28
Tue 1 8 15 22 29
Wed 2 9 16 23 30
Thu 3 10 17 24
Fri 4 11 18 25
Sat 5 12 19 26
OCTOBER
Sun 4 11 18 25
Mon 5 12 19 26
Tue 6 13 20 27
Wed 7 14 21 28
Thu 1 8 15 22 29
Fri 2 9 16 23 30
Sat 3 10 17 24 31
NOVEMBER
Sun 1 8 15 22 29
Mon 2 9 16 23 30
Tue 3 10 17 24
Wed 4 11 18 25
Thu 5 12 19 26
Fri 6 13 20 27
Sat 7 14 21 28
DECEMBER
Sun 6 13 20 27
Mon 7 14 21 28
Tue 1 8 15 22 29
Wed 2 9 16 23 30
Thu 3 10 17 24 31
Fri 4 11 18 25
Sat 5 12 19 26

RIGHT: Calendar given away with *Battle Action* in 1980.

*Quoted in *Jarheads: A Soldier's Story of Modern War* by Anthony Swofford.

INTO BATTLE

A Chronology of *Charley's War*

by Neil Emery

Battle Picture Weekly (also known as *Battle Action*), published by IPC, débuted in the UK on 8 March 1975 to counter the successful new comic, *Warlord*, published by IPC's competitors, Thomson. Pat Mills and John Wagner were called in to produce the boys' war comic, and the first stories, whilst good, were somewhat predictable.

However, 29 January 1977 saw the start of one of the comic's more successful sagas, *Johnny Red*, written by Tom Tully, about an ex-RAF pilot who ends up fighting with the Soviet air force. Its artist was Joe Colquhoun, and with his help it quickly became one of the most popular strips in *Battle*, running longer than any other story.

It was Dave Hunt, editor of *Battle*, who in 1979 decided to gamble on the success of *Johnny Red* by taking Joe off the story and starting him on a new project with Pat Mills about the First World War. Joe said years later, "When I was asked to take on a new story after *Johnny Red*, I said to the editor, 'God almighty, how are you going to make any subject matter out of something as static as trench warfare?' And the editor (Dave Hunt) said to me, 'We've got a damn good author – he'll be able to pull it through.' I was sceptical at the time because Pat Mills and his work were unknown to me. But as soon as we started I knew we were on to something. It seemed to catch on."

The story was *Charley's War*, arguably the most important UK comics war story ever. An anti-war story in a pro-war comic, it never glorified or flinched from some of the harshest and most unpalatable aspects of the Great War. Pat Mills observed, "In some ways *Charley's War* was my attempt to reverse the direction of my creation [*Battle*]. I wanted to counteract the danger of war comics helping to recruit cannon fodder for our country's appalling military attacks on other lands, which continue to this day."

The strip was a big risk because, until then, First World War stories had consistently failed in boys' comics. The static nature of the subject made it difficult to hold the interest of readers more familiar with the fast paced adventures of heroes blazing their way across the many theatres of World War Two. If the strip was to be a success it would take an exceptional artist or an exceptional writer. It got both.

The very first episode of *Charley's War* appeared in a four-page wonderfully illustrated and archly written masterpiece on 6 January 1979 – the 200th issue of *Battle*. Dated 'June 2nd 1916', the story opens with the run-up to the British attack on the Somme, a tragedy in which 500,000 British troops perished.

Charley's transformation from idealistic, naïve recruit to hardened, war weary veteran took just ten episodes. His character took final shape in the 17 March 1979 episode

covering the first terrible day of the Somme in which readers saw the senseless deaths of many of the characters whom they had come to know as Charley's friends. The tragedy of the Somme was also a difficult subject for Joe Colquhoun, who said at the time: "You may find it hard to believe, but I find it hard to read them, especially the sequence at the end of the Somme. I was re-reading that in its printed form recently and I was actually close to tears… It's surprising how involved you can get." The episode is as brilliant as it is harrowing, a benchmark in quality that the creators' peers would find hard to equal.

Those early strips are accompanied by poorly spelt, ink-stained letters and postcards sent home by Charley. They say nothing of the horrors of the trenches, focusing instead on more domestic matters, such as his thanks for the scarf his Auntie Mabel sent him, and his own simple impressions of his fellow characters. It is a brilliant narrative device that allows the reader to view another facet of Charley's personality.

The first year saw the introduction of such characters as 'Old Bill' Tozer, Charley's inimitable Platoon Sergeant, Ginger Jones, his deadpan pessimistic best friend, 'Weeper' Watkins, so called because he perpetually cries owing to the effects of poison gas on his eyes, and Captain Snell. Snell

ABOVE: A page of artwork from the much respected and very successful *Johnny Red*, written by Tom Tully and drawn by Joe Colquhoun.

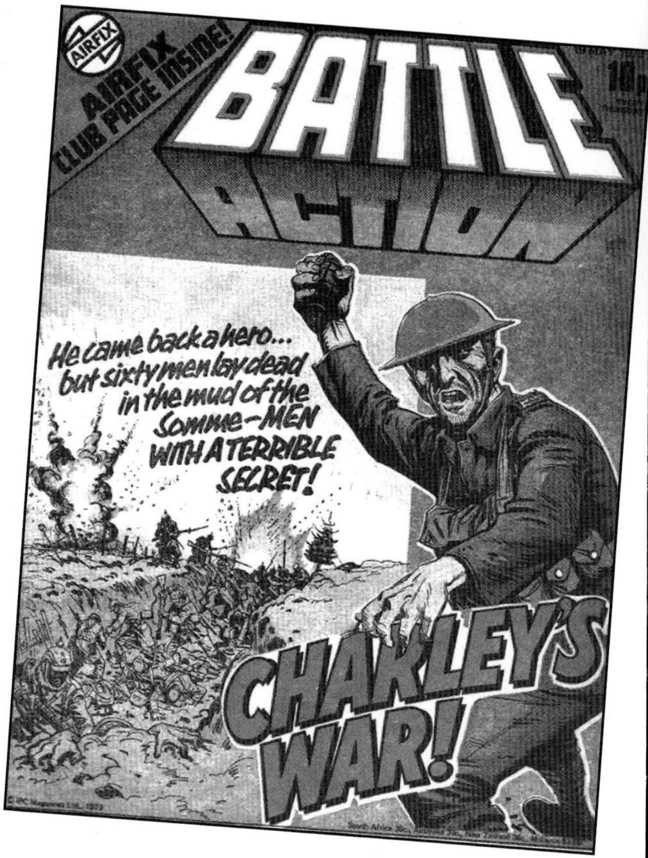
AIRFIX CLUB PAGE INSIDE!
BATTLE
ACTION
He came back a hero... but sixty men lay dead in the mud of the Somme—MEN WITH A TERRIBLE SECRET!
CHARLEY'S WAR!

RIGHT: The *Battle Action* cover for 19 May 1979. Note the Christmas tree in the background.

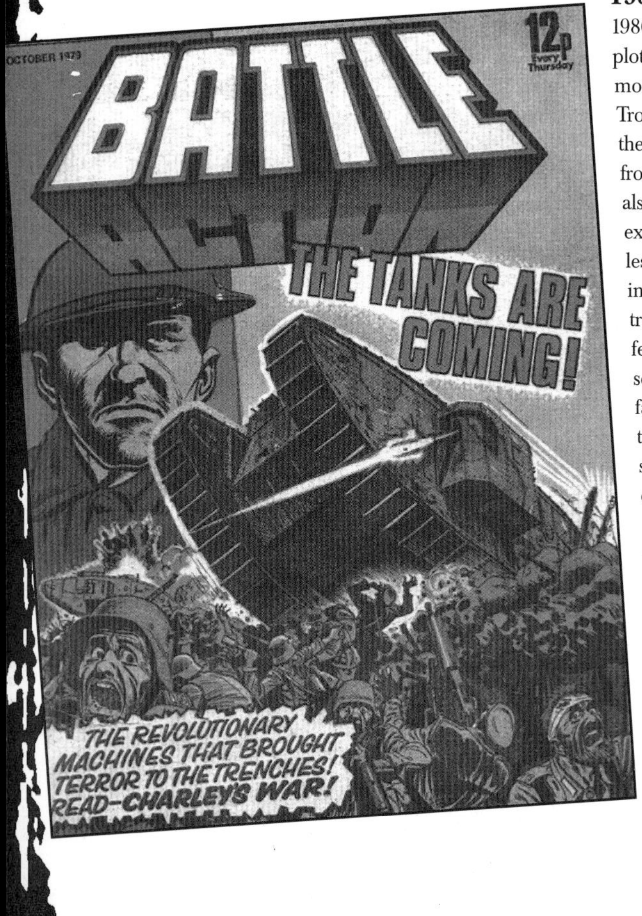
OCTOBER 1979
12p Every Thursday
BATTLE
ACTION
THE TANKS ARE COMING!
THE REVOLUTIONARY MACHINES THAT BROUGHT TERROR TO THE TRENCHES! READ—CHARLEY'S WAR!

BELOW: Cover from the 13 October 1979 *Battle Action*, introducing armoured warfare to *Charley's War*.

embodies the real enemy in the strip – those members of the upper classes who looked on the war as sport, retained servants and dined on hampers from Harrods in comfortable dugouts while their subordinates were exposed to the elements and enemy fire above. Charley's nemesis until the end of the story, Snell is a consistently brilliantly written character.

1979

September 1979 (August 1916 in Charley's world) saw the execution of the platoon's favourite commander, Lieutenant Thomas, who was court-martialled for cowardice after withdrawing his men from a situation that would have seen them needlessly massacred. Thomas' firing squad comes from his own platoon, but Charley and 'Weeper' Watkins refuse to take part. Thomas is shot anyway, and Charley and Watkins are given twenty-eight days of Number One field punishment – basically crucifixion on a gun wheel or fence – a form of discipline used by the British army until the late 1920s.

Shortly after, in the 13 October (September 1916) issue, Ginger was killed by a stray shell, and was subsequently buried by Charley after he had solemnly collected Ginger's remains in a sack. This graphic sudden death killed off the story's second principal supporting character. By killing Ginger, Mills hinted at the tone the script would take in the future: a quick turnover of characters echoing the transient nature of life in the trenches. Characters were introduced, told their own stories and then were taken suddenly in a meaningless death only to be replaced by new 'Tommies'. This difficult writing technique became Mills' signature on the story and adds to the realism of the piece.

1980

1980 saw *Charley's War* begin a plotline that would be one of its most enduring: 'The Judgment Troopers'. Although focusing on these elite German shock troops from the Eastern Front, the plot also tackled such topics as the execution of prisoners, the heartlessness of British doctors (the infamous 'Dr No') and the treachery of the Germans who feigned surrender. It contained some of Joe's best artwork so far, his bold dark inking capturing perfectly the rain-soaked, foreboding desolation of the trenches.

Charley is subsequently wounded and, by 9 August 1980 (Oct 1916), was in hospital with amnesia, allowing Mills and Colquhoun to explore the nature of 'shell shock'. These are brilliantly drawn episodes, full of the horrific swirling nightmares suffered by Charley as he is tormented by Ginger's death. Sergeant Tozer, also wounded, helps Charley eventually rediscover his identity. Both men are then returned to 'Blighty' to recover from their wounds, much to their delight.

Charley's spell of leave is set against the backdrop of the war on the home front, complete with Zeppelin raids and black market dealing. His working class family and background are revealed, set against Colquhoun's wonderfully detailed scenes of Edwardian London.

Set during a Zeppelin raid, the 8 November 1980 episode introduced a character who was to reappear regularly over the next couple of years. Blue, a deserter on the run from the French Foreign Legion, plays a pivotal role in the narrative, establishing the person Charley would have been were it not for the instilled resignation to his fate and sense of duty that he could never shake. The two men become firm friends, sharing a hatred of the lives wasted in France and the apparent insanity gripping the High Command. In flashback, Blue describes to Charley the harshness of the Legion and the harrowing battles he has fought. This approach allows the story to shift its perspective to a new 'hero' and relate events that Charley couldn't possibly have experienced without turning the strip into fantasy – a device that would become Mills' forte throughout *Charley's War*. Blue's narrative formed the basis of *Charley's War* throughout 1980 and into 1981.

1981

1981 saw episodes shift from four pages to a more manageable three. A single episode of *Charley's War* would take Joe five full working days, and more complicated plots up to seven. The strip was his only commitment and therefore his earnings remained modest compared with others who would do two, sometimes three stories a week to boost their income. However, quality and accuracy were always paramount to Joe.

By October 1981 (May-June 1917), Charley and company had joined the 'Clay Kickers' – the navvies and coalminers who had been digging huge mines under the Messines Ridge for the last eighteen months. The trials and terror of working and fighting this poorly known underground war took up most of the year. This long running saga also introduced conscientious objector 'Budgie' Brown in a sub-plot that tells of the shameful treatment of pacifists at the hands of the British Army. Budgie proves himself to be braver in many ways than most by sticking to his ideals in the face of hatred from his peers, a hatred that ultimately leads to his abrupt and untimely death and brings Charley into violent conflict with Captain Snell.

By this time, letters in praise of *Charley's War* were regularly published in *Battle*. Many of them were from veterans of the Great War, acknowledging the strip's excellence after being shown it by grandsons and great-grandsons.

1982

For *Charley's War*, 1982 opened with a stunning colour cover that marked the beginning of the third battle of Ypres. The issue of self-inflicted wounds is touched upon when one of Charley's mates attempts to shoot himself in the foot to escape the battle. Charley's good intentioned efforts to stop him meet with a cruel and ironic twist.

February 1982 (August 1917) saw Charley and his platoon withdrawn from the line and sent to the notorious Etaples training camp, the scene of the British Army's only mutiny in modern times. As many as 100,000 soldiers were housed in the camp at any one time, where they were drilled constantly in the sand dunes of the notorious Bull Ring training area by 'canaries' – non-combatant military police instructors who were hand picked for their harsh methods. The mutiny storyline reintroduces 'Weeper' and Blue, who are part of a gang of deserters who live in the woods outside the town. It also allowed Mills to give greater depth to Charley, who is caught on the horns of a moral dilemma between his natural sympathies with the mutineers and his own sense of duty.

In July 1982, Charley's conscience got the better of him and, sick of the killing, he decided to hand in his rifle and become a stretcher bearer, a non-combatant. Unfortunately, as this plotline began Joe Colquhoun had a heart attack and was off work for three months (sadly, Joe died of a second heart attack in 1987).

He returned to work in October 1982 (October 1917), with Charley working as a stretcher bearer until the end of the year when, in a stroke of genius, Mills delivered a cliffhanger that takes the story into the present time. After Charley rescues a Flying Corps observer, Fred, at Passaendale, a shell burst catches the two men. The reader is then transported to 1982, where we join Fred as an old man visiting the same spot and wondering if Charley survived. The lifelong effects of the war on its survivors are shown as Fred vividly recalls the war seventy years later from the inside of a tour bus.

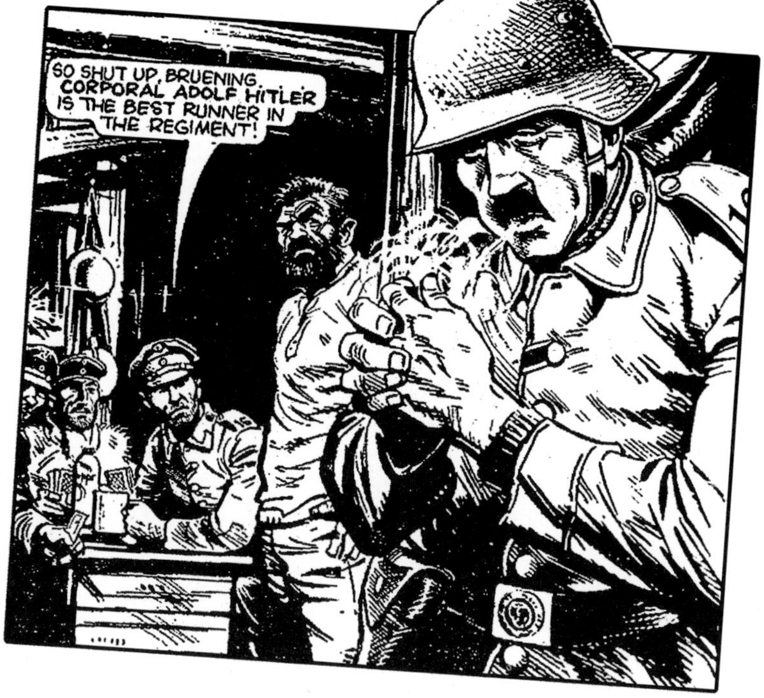
SO SHUT UP, BRUENING. CORPORAL ADOLF HITLER IS THE BEST RUNNER IN THE REGIMENT!

ABOVE: Adolf Hitler joins *Charley's War*.

BELOW: The cover from the 30 May 1981 edition of *Battle Action*. Joe used the classic photo seen below as the basis for his illustration.

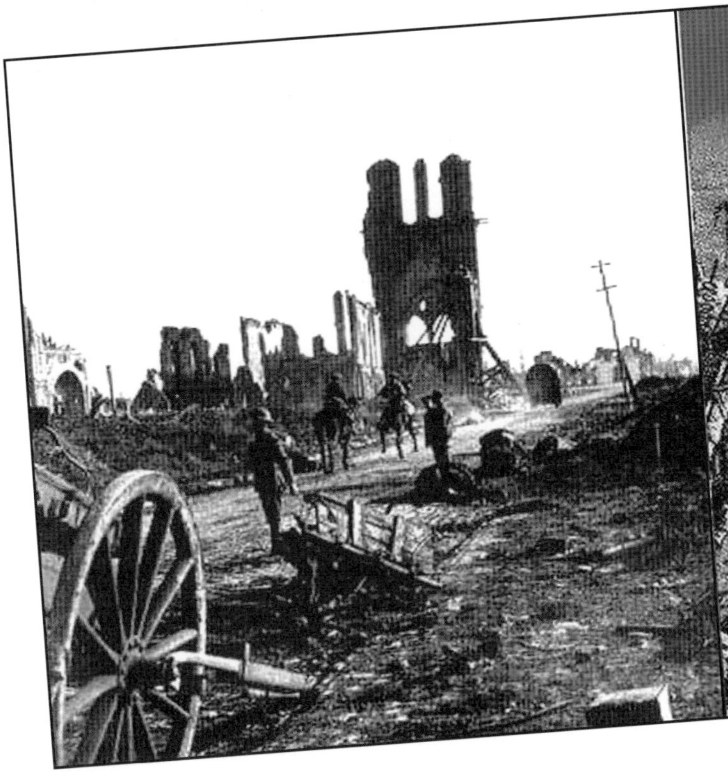

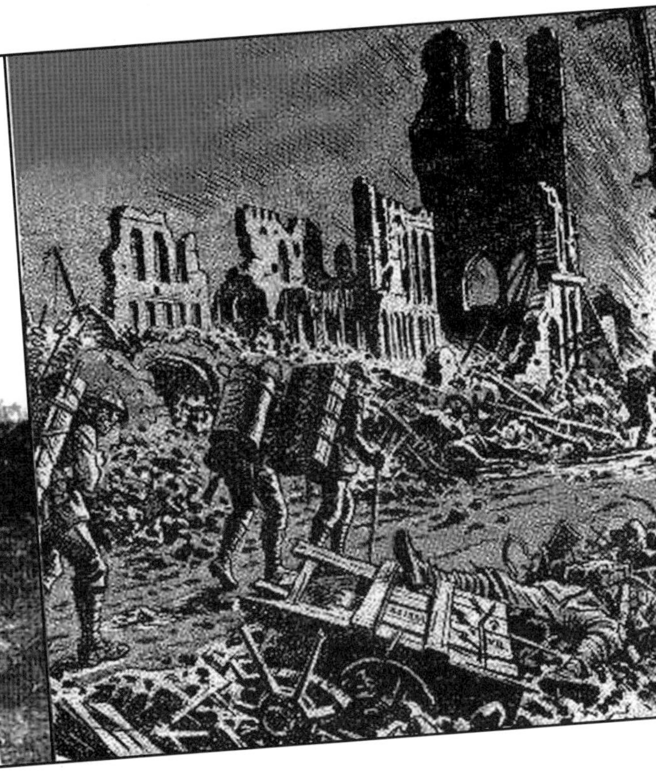

CHARLEY'S WAR
NORTHERN FRANCE... MAY 29th, 1940. ONLY FIFTEEN THOUSAND ALLIED TROOPS HAD BEEN EVACUATED FROM THE BLAZING PORT OF DUNKIRK WHEN THE GERMAN AIRFORCE LAUNCHED ITS MOST DESTRUCTIVE ATTACK. AT FOUR O'CLOCK IN THE AFTERNOON, WAVE AFTER WAVE OF BOMBERS SWEPT IN OVER THE BREAK-WATER WALL KNOWN AS THE EAST MOLE...
FOUR SHIPS HIT, INCLUDING A DESTROYER!
THAT STUKA'S JUST NAILED ANOTHER ONE! DIRECT HIT!
A PACKED STEAMER BURST INTO FLAMES AND DRIFTED TOWARDS THE BEACH...
Writer
Artist
Letterer
OF THE SIX HUNDRED MEN SHE HAD TAKEN ABOARD, ONLY A HANDFUL SURVIVED...
ON THE BEACH ITSELF, TROOPS WERE FIRING RIFLES AND HAND-GUNS IN HELPLESS FURY...
A LUCKY HIT, THAT'S ALL I WANT! A LUCKY HIT!
YOU NEED MORE THAN THAT TO DOWN A DIVE-BOMBER, MATE, YOU NEED A BLOOMING MIRACLE!

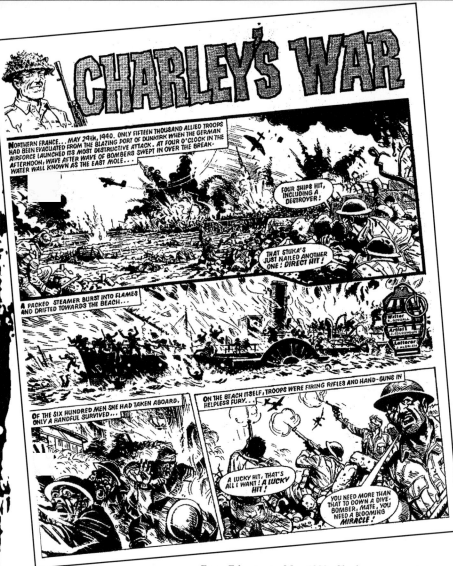

From February to May 1983, Charley, now a sniper after being sacked from the Medical Corps, again took a back seat this strip to the early life of Adolf Hitler, whose-battalion finds itself in trenches opposite Charley's.

1983

The rest of '83 was a wild ride for Charley. He married a nurse called Kate, was court-martialled for cowardice after accidentally shooting himself through the foot, and his brother Wilf, a pilot, was killed over London attacking the first long-range bombers – the German Gotha.

1984

1984 began with Mills exploring the war at sea from the perspective of Charley's cousin, Jack. Jack tells the story of the first Battle of the Falklands where he is serving aboard *HMS Kent* and takes part in the sinking of the *Nuremburg.* Mills had wanted to broaden this story of the war at sea but, as he says, "The readers didn't like it. The editor specifically rang me – the only time ever – to tell me to steer back to the trenches. I was disappointed because I had been hoping to do the Battle of Jutland, an astonishing and hideous event that really needs to be chronicled, and the Falklands had been the warm-up." So, Charley, now a Lance Corporal, returned to the front just in time for the German Spring Offensive of March 1918.

June 1984 introduced the Americans and the story of the African-American soldiers, which led to one of the few occasions when the strip was censored (*see Pat's Commentary for Episode 28*).

Then, on 15th September 1984, the First World War ended for *Charley's War* readers, but not before an eleventh hour showdown with the insane Captain Snell. He sends Charley to participate in the little known invasion of Russia in 1919 by, amongst others, Britain. The rest of 1984 followed this ill-fated campaign.

1985

On 26 January 1985, Pat Mills wrote his last ever script for *Charley's War* following a disagreement over his research budget. He says, "My enduring memory and the true ending of *Charley's War* is in 1933, where Charley is on the dole and he's thinking, 'Tomorrow is another day and things can only get better.' He walks off into the grimy sunset of London's East End as a newspaper announces, 'Adolf Hitler made Chancellor of Germany'. That, to me, sums up Charley and the betrayal of his great, uncomplaining but tragic generation."

Scott Goodall took up scripting chores and the story continued into the Second World War. Charley, now middle aged, is looking for his son Len, who joined up against his father's wishes and is somewhere in France. The last ten months of the story continued into 1986 and saw Charley thrown into the chaos of the British Army's 1940 defeat during Hitler's invasion of France. However, by now the story had sadly lost its edge and although Joe Colquhoun's superlative artwork continued to impress, it could not change the fact that the best days of *Charley's War* were behind it. The series ended in October as Charley was reunited with Len on a ship leaving Dunkirk, and concluded that his fighting days were now over. It was a rushed and somewhat lacklustre ending for such a classic story. A year later, Joe Colquhoun was dead.

Towards the end of *Charley's War*, in a very rare interview, Joe said of his *Magnum Opus*: "Finally, and this is only my personal opinion… *Charley's War* illustrates a period that was already dying then, when words like Honour, Duty and Patriotism actually meant something… I think most decent kids reading this epoch will have a sneaking, almost atavistic feeling that in this present rather sick and selfish world, with violence and amorality seeming to pay dividends, they perhaps are missing out on something. It's a little bit pretentious, but just think about it." ✛

23rd August 1980
BATTLE
14
ACTION
EVERY THURSDAY
CHARLEY'S WAR
©IPC Magazines Ltd., 1980

ABOVE: The escape from Dunkirk as drawn by Joe in the 9 August 1986 edition of *Battle.* Even after six years on the strip, his attention to detail is beyond doubt.

RIGHT: The U-Boat menace – just one of the many facets of the First World War portrayed in *Charley's War.*

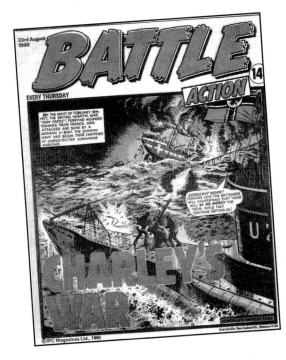

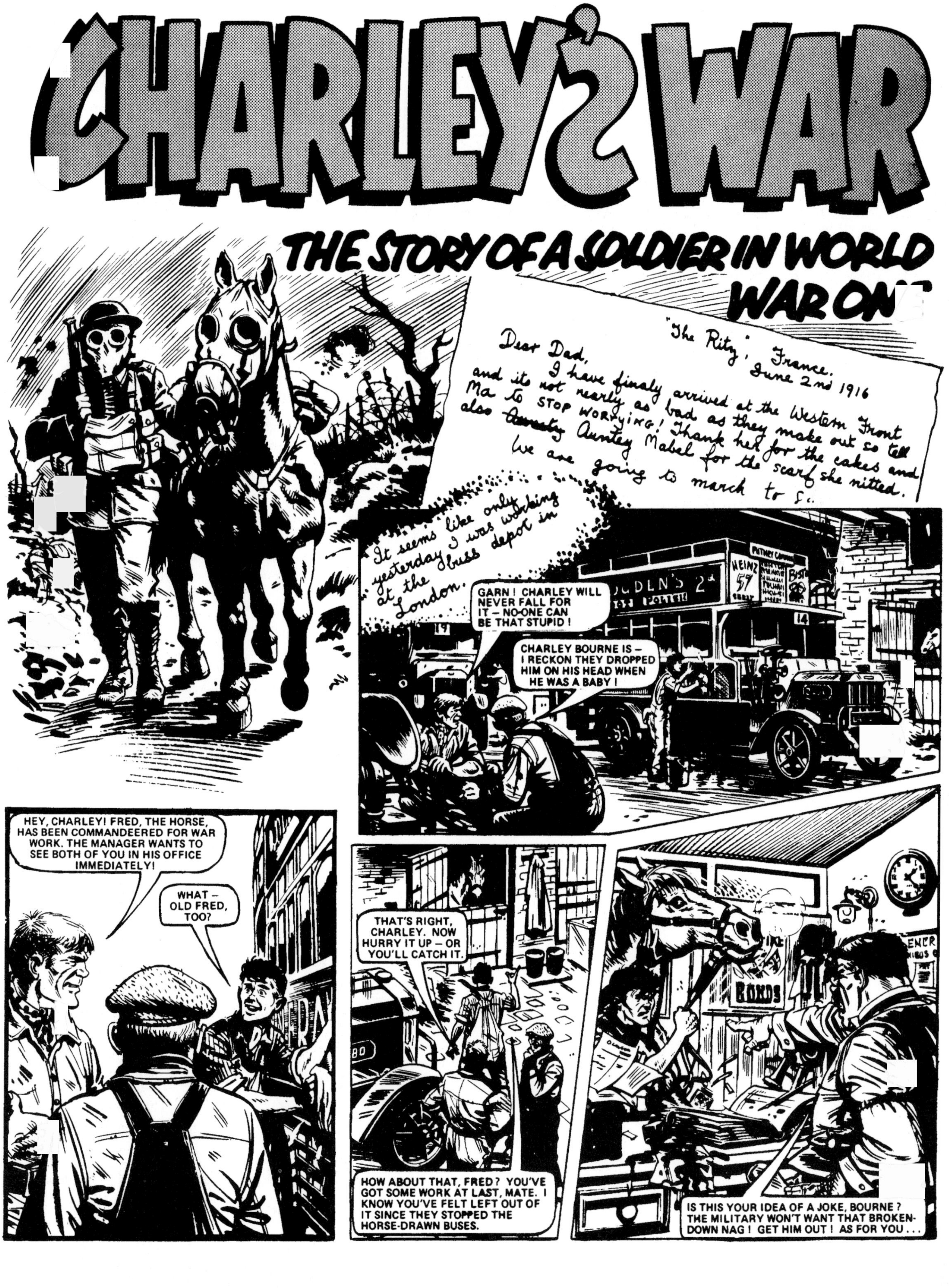
CHARLEY'S WAR
THE STORY OF A SOLDIER IN WORLD WAR ON
"The Ritz", France. June 2nd 1916
Dear Dad, I have finaly arrived at the Western Front and its not nearly as bad as they make out so tell Ma to STOP WORRYING! Thank her for the cakes and also Auntey Mabel for the scarf she nitted. We are going to march to
It seems like only yesterday I was working at the buss depot in London.
GARN! CHARLEY WILL NEVER FALL FOR IT — NO-ONE CAN BE THAT STUPID!
CHARLEY BOURNE IS — I RECKON THEY DROPPED HIM ON HIS HEAD WHEN HE WAS A BABY!
HEY, CHARLEY! FRED, THE HORSE, HAS BEEN COMMANDEERED FOR WAR WORK. THE MANAGER WANTS TO SEE BOTH OF YOU IN HIS OFFICE IMMEDIATELY!
WHAT — OLD FRED, TOO?
THAT'S RIGHT, CHARLEY. NOW HURRY IT UP — OR YOU'LL CATCH IT.
HOW ABOUT THAT, FRED? YOU'VE GOT SOME WORK AT LAST, MATE. I KNOW YOU'VE FELT LEFT OUT OF IT SINCE THEY STOPPED THE HORSE-DRAWN BUSES.
IS THIS YOUR IDEA OF A JOKE, BOURNE? THE MILITARY WON'T WANT THAT BROKEN-DOWN NAG! GET HIM OUT! AS FOR YOU...

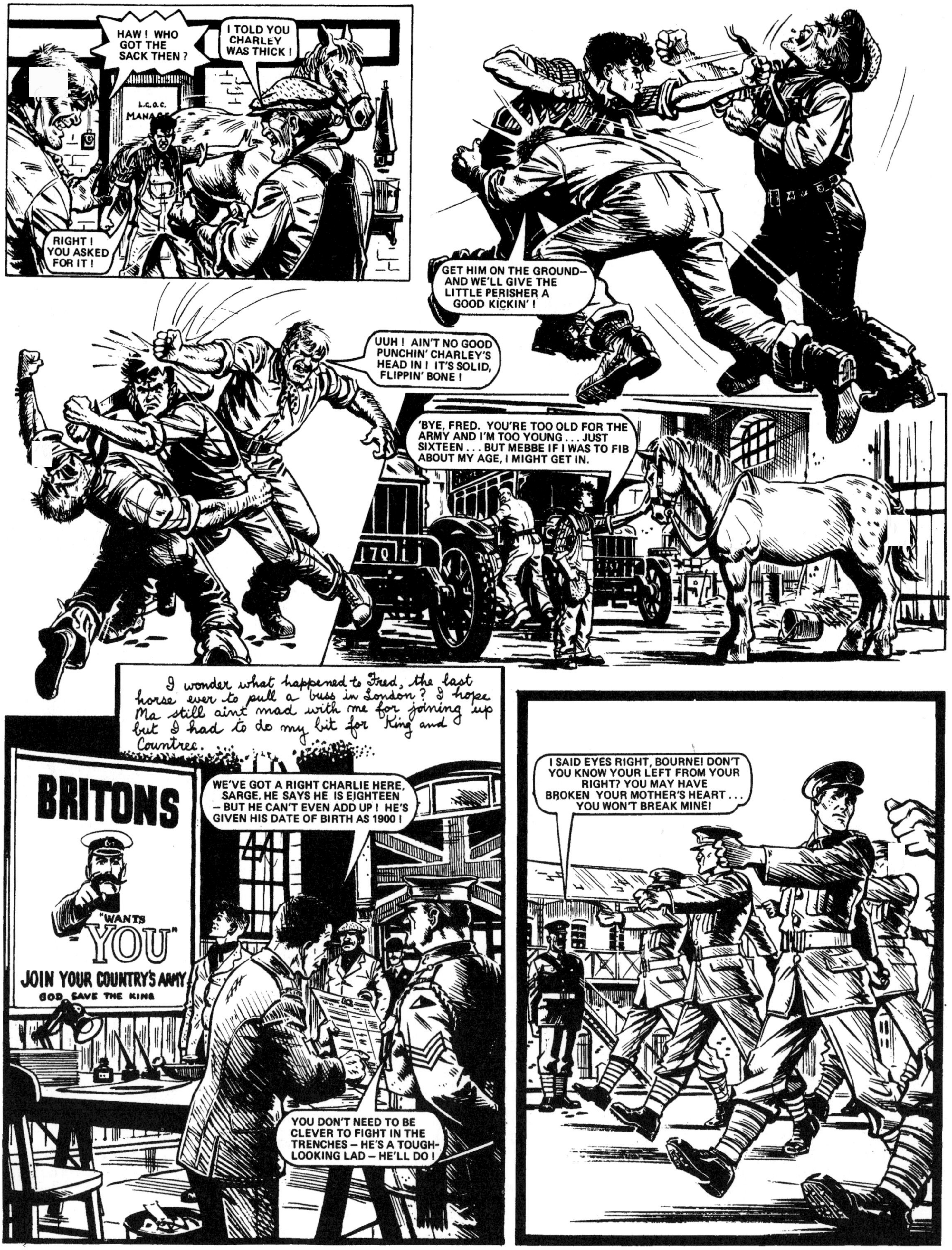
HAW! WHO GOT THE SACK THEN?
I TOLD YOU CHARLEY WAS THICK!
L.G.O.C. MANAG
RIGHT! YOU ASKED FOR IT!
GET HIM ON THE GROUND— AND WE'LL GIVE THE LITTLE PERISHER A GOOD KICKIN'!
UUH! AIN'T NO GOOD PUNCHIN' CHARLEY'S HEAD IN! IT'S SOLID, FLIPPIN' BONE!
'BYE, FRED. YOU'RE TOO OLD FOR THE ARMY AND I'M TOO YOUNG . . . JUST SIXTEEN . . . BUT MEBBE IF I WAS TO FIB ABOUT MY AGE, I MIGHT GET IN.
I wonder what happened to Fred, the last horse ever to pull a buss in London? I hope Ma still aint mad with me for joining up but I had to do my bit for King and Countree.
BRITONS
"WANTS YOU"
JOIN YOUR COUNTRY'S ARMY
GOD SAVE THE KING
WE'VE GOT A RIGHT CHARLIE HERE, SARGE, HE SAYS HE IS EIGHTEEN – BUT HE CAN'T EVEN ADD UP! HE'S GIVEN HIS DATE OF BIRTH AS 1900!
YOU DON'T NEED TO BE CLEVER TO FIGHT IN THE TRENCHES – HE'S A TOUGH-LOOKING LAD – HE'LL DO!
I SAID EYES RIGHT, BOURNE! DON'T YOU KNOW YOUR LEFT FROM YOUR RIGHT? YOU MAY HAVE BROKEN YOUR MOTHER'S HEART . . . YOU WON'T BREAK MINE!

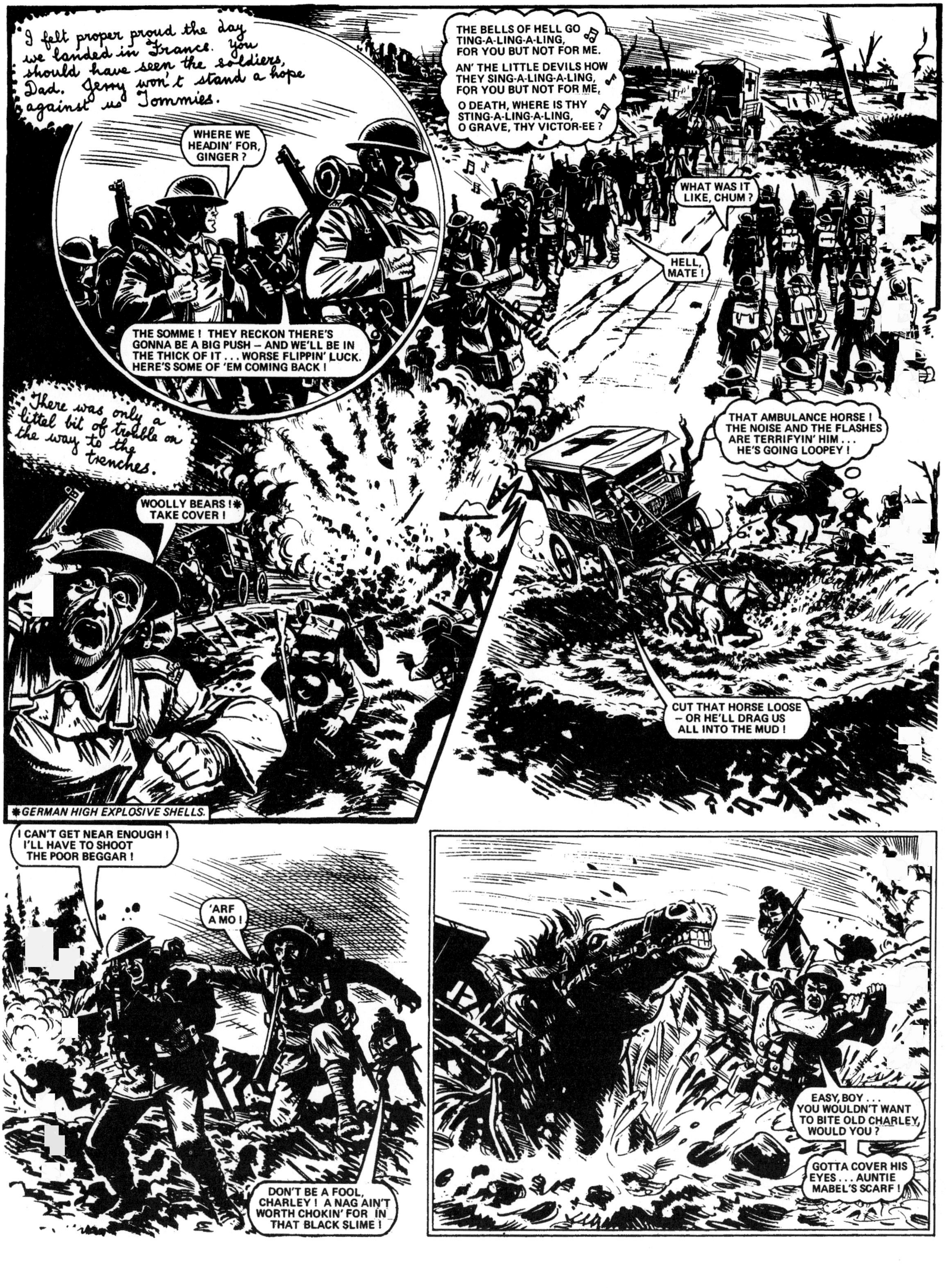
I felt proper proud the day we landed in France. You should have seen the soldiers, Dad. Jerry won't stand a hope against us Tommies.
WHERE WE HEADIN' FOR, GINGER ?
THE SOMME ! THEY RECKON THERE'S GONNA BE A BIG PUSH – AND WE'LL BE IN THE THICK OF IT . . . WORSE FLIPPIN' LUCK. HERE'S SOME OF 'EM COMING BACK !
THE BELLS OF HELL GO TING-A-LING-A-LING, FOR YOU BUT NOT FOR ME.
AN' THE LITTLE DEVILS HOW THEY SING-A-LING-A-LING, FOR YOU BUT NOT FOR ME,
O DEATH, WHERE IS THY STING-A-LING-A-LING, O GRAVE, THY VICTOR-EE ?
WHAT WAS IT LIKE, CHUM ?
HELL, MATE !
There was only a littel bit of trouble on the way to the trenches.
WOOLLY BEARS !* TAKE COVER !
THAT AMBULANCE HORSE ! THE NOISE AND THE FLASHES ARE TERRIFYIN' HIM . . . HE'S GOING LOOPEY !
CUT THAT HORSE LOOSE – OR HE'LL DRAG US ALL INTO THE MUD !
*GERMAN HIGH EXPLOSIVE SHELLS.
I CAN'T GET NEAR ENOUGH ! I'LL HAVE TO SHOOT THE POOR BEGGAR !
'ARF A MO !
DON'T BE A FOOL, CHARLEY ! A NAG AIN'T WORTH CHOKIN' FOR IN THAT BLACK SLIME !
EASY, BOY . . . YOU WOULDN'T WANT TO BITE OLD CHARLEY, WOULD YOU ?
GOTTA COVER HIS EYES . . . AUNTIE MABEL'S SCARF !

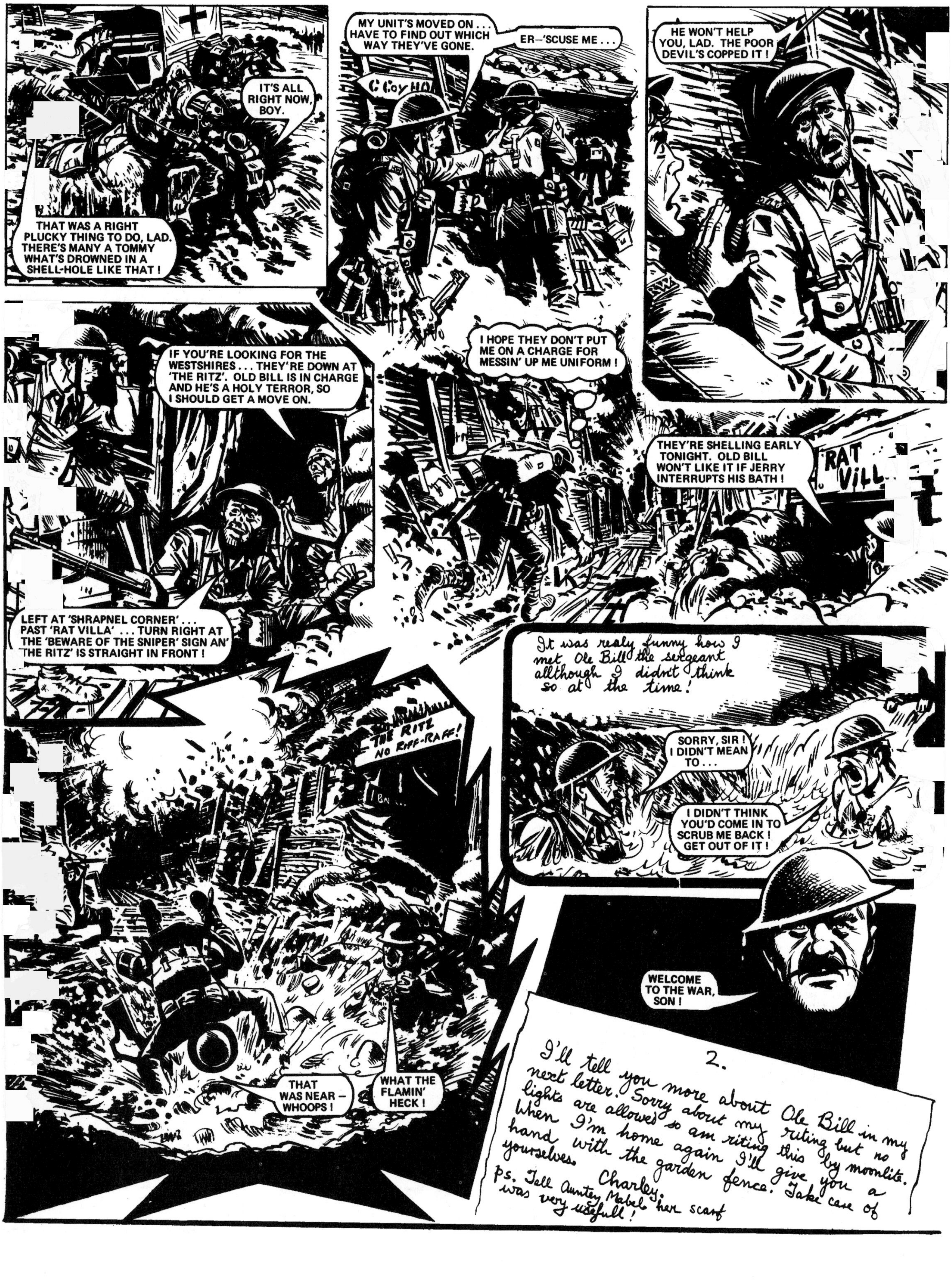
IT'S ALL RIGHT NOW, BOY.
THAT WAS A RIGHT PLUCKY THING TO DO, LAD. THERE'S MANY A TOMMY WHAT'S DROWNED IN A SHELL-HOLE LIKE THAT!
MY UNIT'S MOVED ON... HAVE TO FIND OUT WHICH WAY THEY'VE GONE.
C Coy HQ
ER—'SCUSE ME...
HE WON'T HELP YOU, LAD. THE POOR DEVIL'S COPPED IT!
IF YOU'RE LOOKING FOR THE WESTSHIRES... THEY'RE DOWN AT 'THE RITZ'. OLD BILL IS IN CHARGE AND HE'S A HOLY TERROR, SO I SHOULD GET A MOVE ON.
LEFT AT 'SHRAPNEL CORNER'... PAST 'RAT VILLA'... TURN RIGHT AT THE 'BEWARE OF THE SNIPER' SIGN AN' 'THE RITZ' IS STRAIGHT IN FRONT!
I HOPE THEY DON'T PUT ME ON A CHARGE FOR MESSIN' UP ME UNIFORM!
THEY'RE SHELLING EARLY TONIGHT. OLD BILL WON'T LIKE IT IF JERRY INTERRUPTS HIS BATH!
RAT VILL
THE RITZ NO RIFF-RAFF!
THAT WAS NEAR — WHOOPS!
WHAT THE FLAMIN' HECK!
It was realy funny how I met Ole Bill the sergeant allthough I didn't think so at the time!
SORRY, SIR! I DIDN'T MEAN TO...
I DIDN'T THINK YOU'D COME IN TO SCRUB ME BACK! GET OUT OF IT!
WELCOME TO THE WAR, SON!
2.
I'll tell you more about Ole Bill in my next letter. Sorry about my riting but no lights are allowed so am riting this by moonlite. When I'm home again I'll give you a hand with the garden fence. Take care of yourselves.
Charley.
Ps. Tell Auntey Mabel her scarf was very usefull!

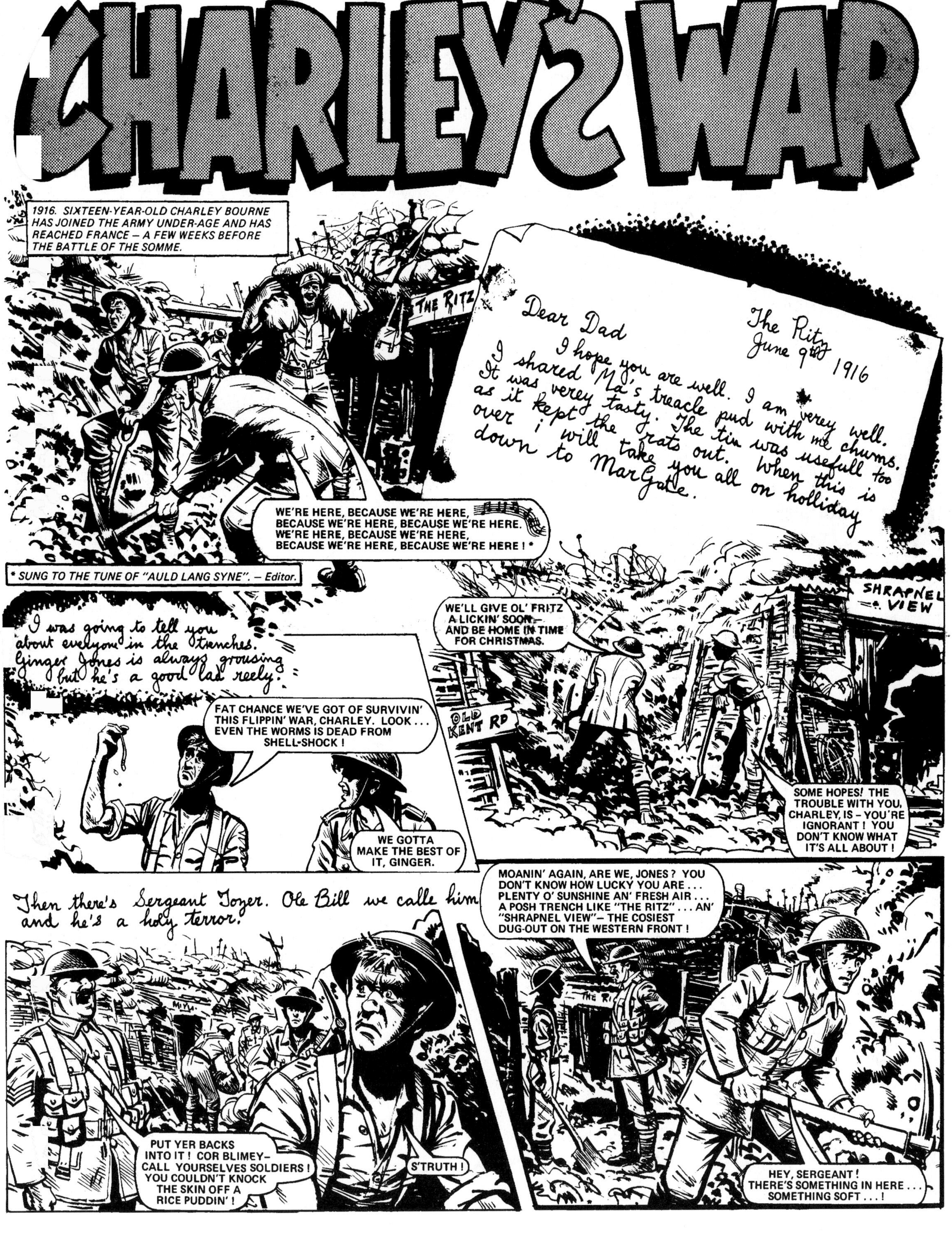
CHARLEY'S WAR
1916. SIXTEEN-YEAR-OLD CHARLEY BOURNE HAS JOINED THE ARMY UNDER-AGE AND HAS REACHED FRANCE – A FEW WEEKS BEFORE THE BATTLE OF THE SOMME.
THE RITZ
Dear Dad The Ritz June 9th 1916
I hope you are well. I am verey well. I shared Ma's treacle pud with me chums. It was verey tasty. The tin was usefull too as it kept the rats out. When this is over i will take you all on holliday down to MarGate.
WE'RE HERE, BECAUSE WE'RE HERE, BECAUSE WE'RE HERE, BECAUSE WE'RE HERE. WE'RE HERE, BECAUSE WE'RE HERE, BECAUSE WE'RE HERE, BECAUSE WE'RE HERE ! *
* SUNG TO THE TUNE OF "AULD LANG SYNE". – Editor.
I was going to tell you about everyone in the trenches. Ginger Jones is always grousing but he's a good lad reely.
FAT CHANCE WE'VE GOT OF SURVIVIN' THIS FLIPPIN' WAR, CHARLEY. LOOK . . . EVEN THE WORMS IS DEAD FROM SHELL-SHOCK !
WE GOTTA MAKE THE BEST OF IT, GINGER.
SHRAPNEL VIEW
OLD KENT RD
WE'LL GIVE OL' FRITZ A LICKIN' SOON – AND BE HOME IN TIME FOR CHRISTMAS.
SOME HOPES! THE TROUBLE WITH YOU, CHARLEY, IS – YOU'RE IGNORANT ! YOU DON'T KNOW WHAT IT'S ALL ABOUT !
Then there's Sergeant Tozer. Ole Bill we calle him and he's a holy terror.
PUT YER BACKS INTO IT ! COR BLIMEY – CALL YOURSELVES SOLDIERS ! YOU COULDN'T KNOCK THE SKIN OFF A RICE PUDDIN' !
S'TRUTH !
MOANIN' AGAIN, ARE WE, JONES ? YOU DON'T KNOW HOW LUCKY YOU ARE . . . PLENTY O' SUNSHINE AN' FRESH AIR . . . A POSH TRENCH LIKE "THE RITZ" . . . AN' "SHRAPNEL VIEW" – THE COSIEST DUG-OUT ON THE WESTERN FRONT !
HEY, SERGEANT ! THERE'S SOMETHING IN HERE . . . SOMETHING SOFT . . . !

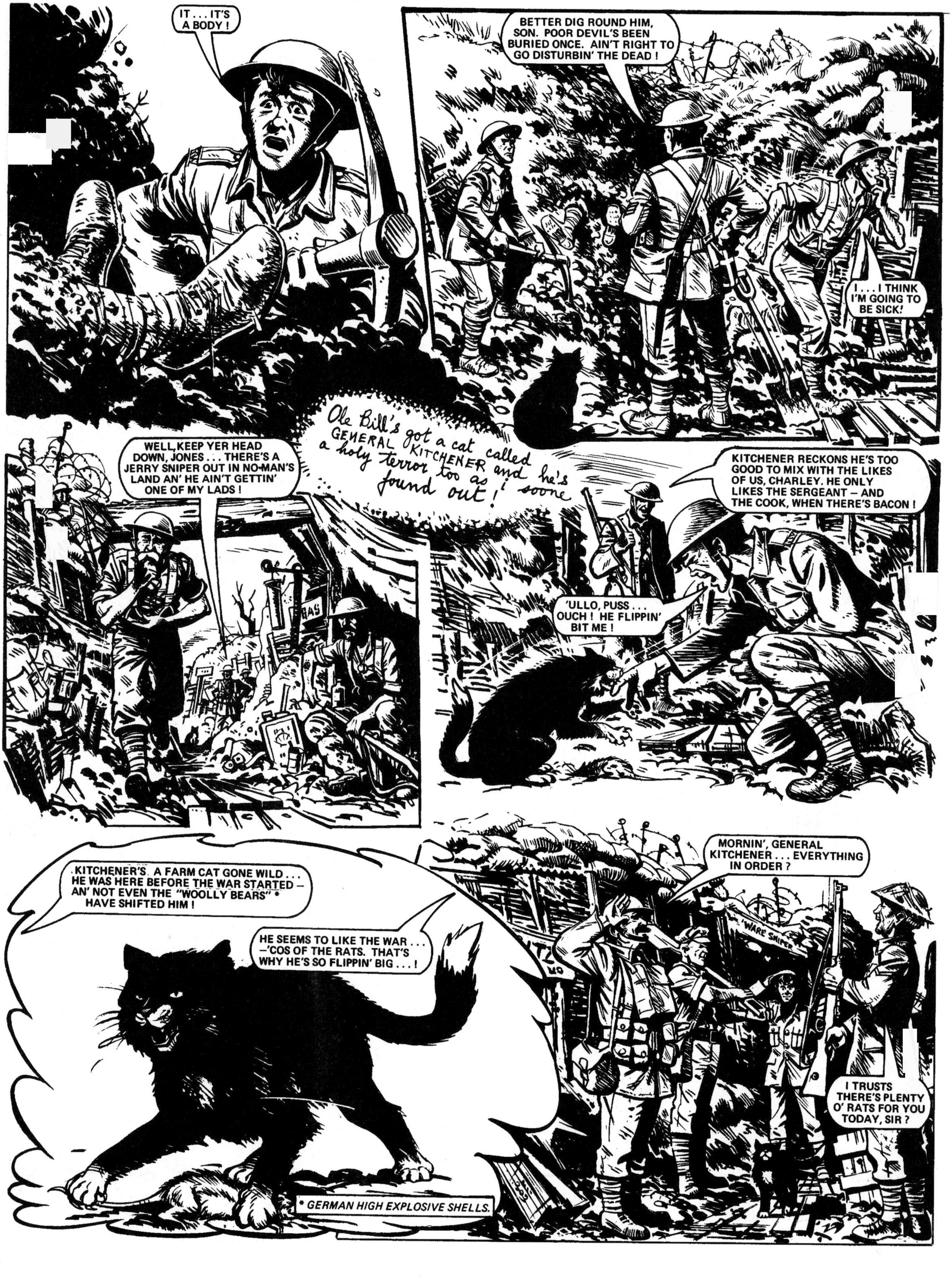

IT . . . IT'S A BODY !
BETTER DIG ROUND HIM, SON. POOR DEVIL'S BEEN BURIED ONCE. AIN'T RIGHT TO GO DISTURBIN' THE DEAD !
I . . . I THINK I'M GOING TO BE SICK!
Ole Bill's got a cat called GENERAL KITCHENER and he's a holy terror too as I soone found out!
WELL, KEEP YER HEAD DOWN, JONES . . . THERE'S A JERRY SNIPER OUT IN NO-MAN'S LAND AN' HE AIN'T GETTIN' ONE OF MY LADS !
GAS
KITCHENER RECKONS HE'S TOO GOOD TO MIX WITH THE LIKES OF US, CHARLEY. HE ONLY LIKES THE SERGEANT – AND THE COOK, WHEN THERE'S BACON !
'ULLO, PUSS . . . OUCH ! HE FLIPPIN' BIT ME !
KITCHENER'S. A FARM CAT GONE WILD . . . HE WAS HERE BEFORE THE WAR STARTED – AN' NOT EVEN THE "WOOLLY BEARS" * HAVE SHIFTED HIM !
HE SEEMS TO LIKE THE WAR . . . –'COS OF THE RATS. THAT'S WHY HE'S SO FLIPPIN' BIG . . . !
* GERMAN HIGH EXPLOSIVE SHELLS.
MORNIN', GENERAL KITCHENER . . . EVERYTHING IN ORDER ?
'WARE SNIPER
I TRUSTS THERE'S PLENTY O' RATS FOR YOU TODAY, SIR ?

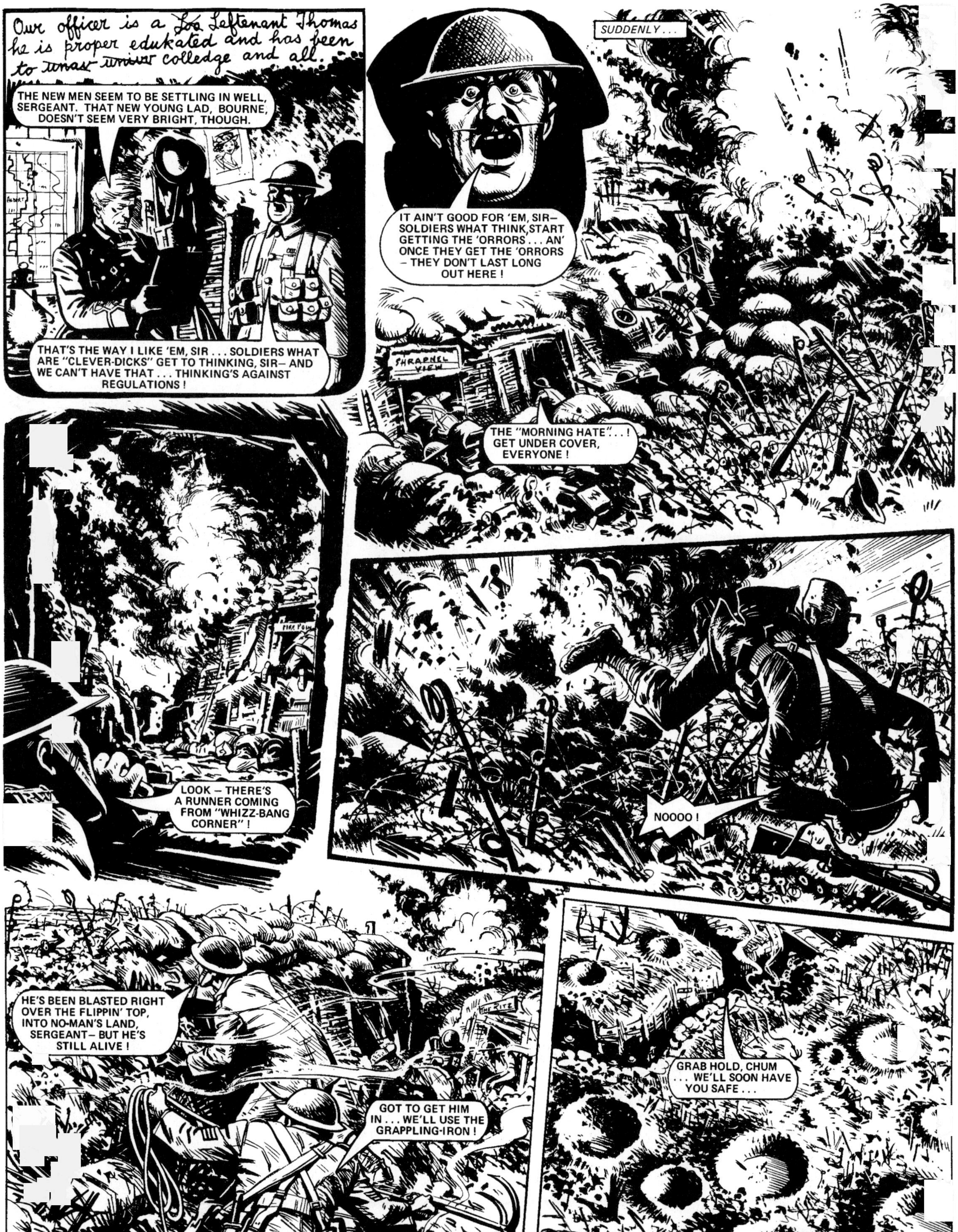
Our officer is a Leftenant Thomas he is proper edukated and has been to colledge and all.
THE NEW MEN SEEM TO BE SETTLING IN WELL, SERGEANT. THAT NEW YOUNG LAD, BOURNE, DOESN'T SEEM VERY BRIGHT, THOUGH.
THAT'S THE WAY I LIKE 'EM, SIR . . . SOLDIERS WHAT ARE "CLEVER-DICKS" GET TO THINKING, SIR– AND WE CAN'T HAVE THAT . . . THINKING'S AGAINST REGULATIONS !
IT AIN'T GOOD FOR 'EM, SIR– SOLDIERS WHAT THINK, START GETTING THE 'ORRORS' . . . AN' ONCE THEY GET THE 'ORRORS – THEY DON'T LAST LONG OUT HERE !
SUDDENLY . . .
SHRAPNEL VIEW
THE "MORNING HATE" . . ! GET UNDER COVER, EVERYONE !
LOOK – THERE'S A RUNNER COMING FROM "WHIZZ-BANG CORNER" !
NOOOO !
HE'S BEEN BLASTED RIGHT OVER THE FLIPPIN' TOP, INTO NO-MAN'S LAND, SERGEANT– BUT HE'S STILL ALIVE !
GOT TO GET HIM IN . . . WE'LL USE THE GRAPPLING-IRON !
THE RITZ
GRAB HOLD, CHUM . . . WE'LL SOON HAVE YOU SAFE . . .

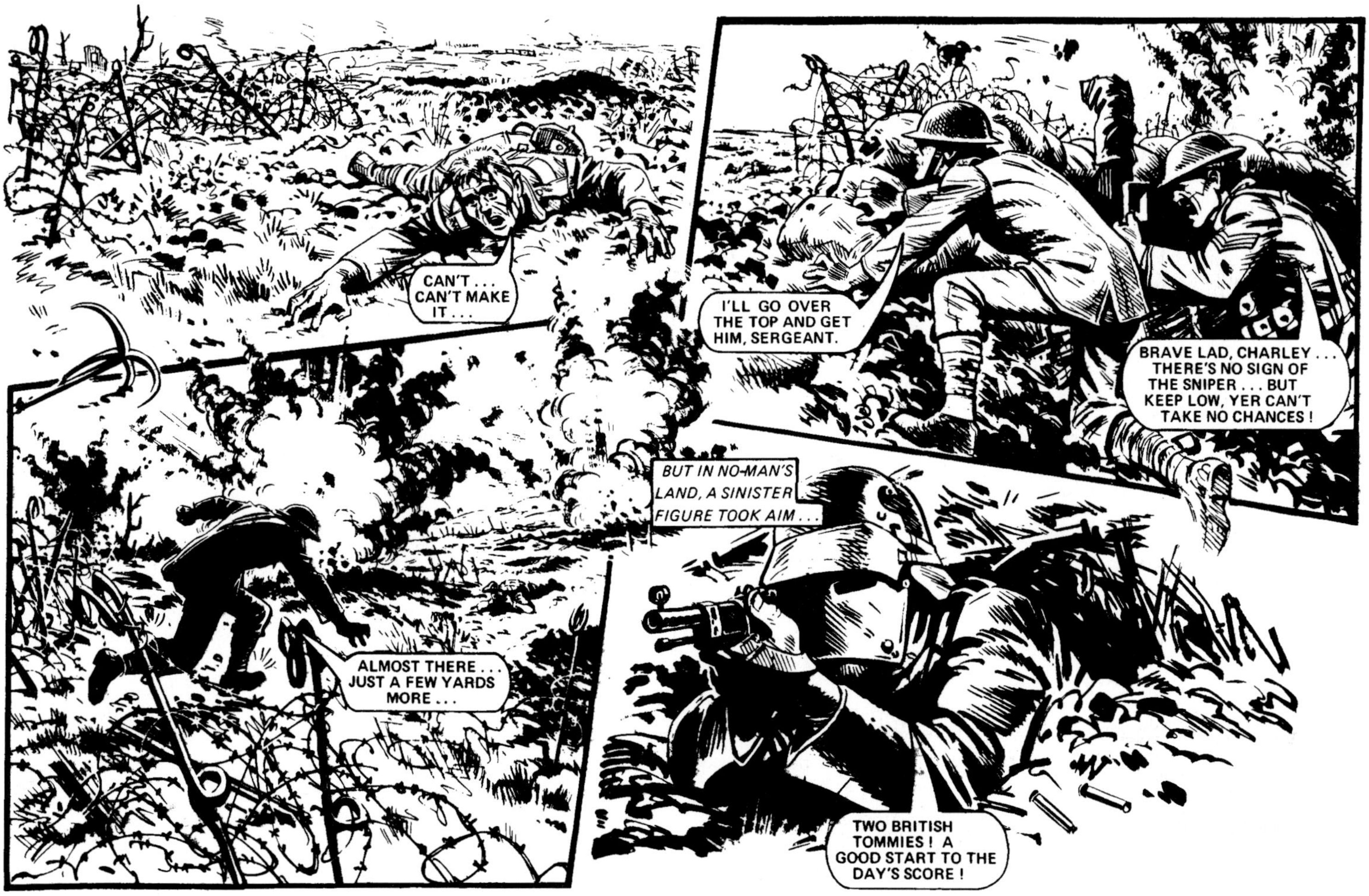
CAN'T . . . CAN'T MAKE IT . . .
I'LL GO OVER THE TOP AND GET HIM, SERGEANT.
BRAVE LAD, CHARLEY . . . THERE'S NO SIGN OF THE SNIPER . . . BUT KEEP LOW, YER CAN'T TAKE NO CHANCES !
ALMOST THERE . . . JUST A FEW YARDS MORE . . .
BUT IN NO-MAN'S LAND, A SINISTER FIGURE TOOK AIM . . .
TWO BRITISH TOMMIES ! A GOOD START TO THE DAY'S SCORE !

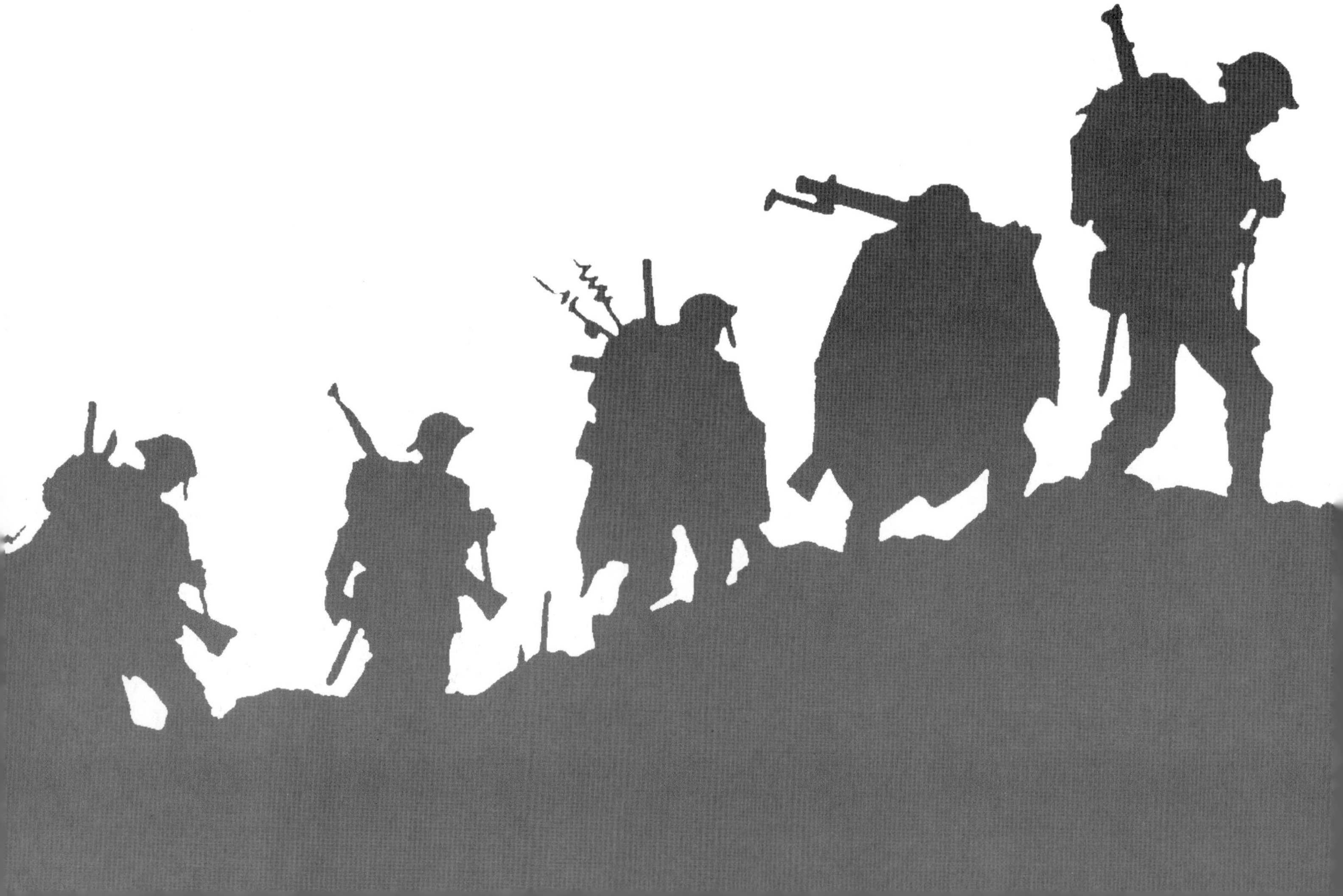

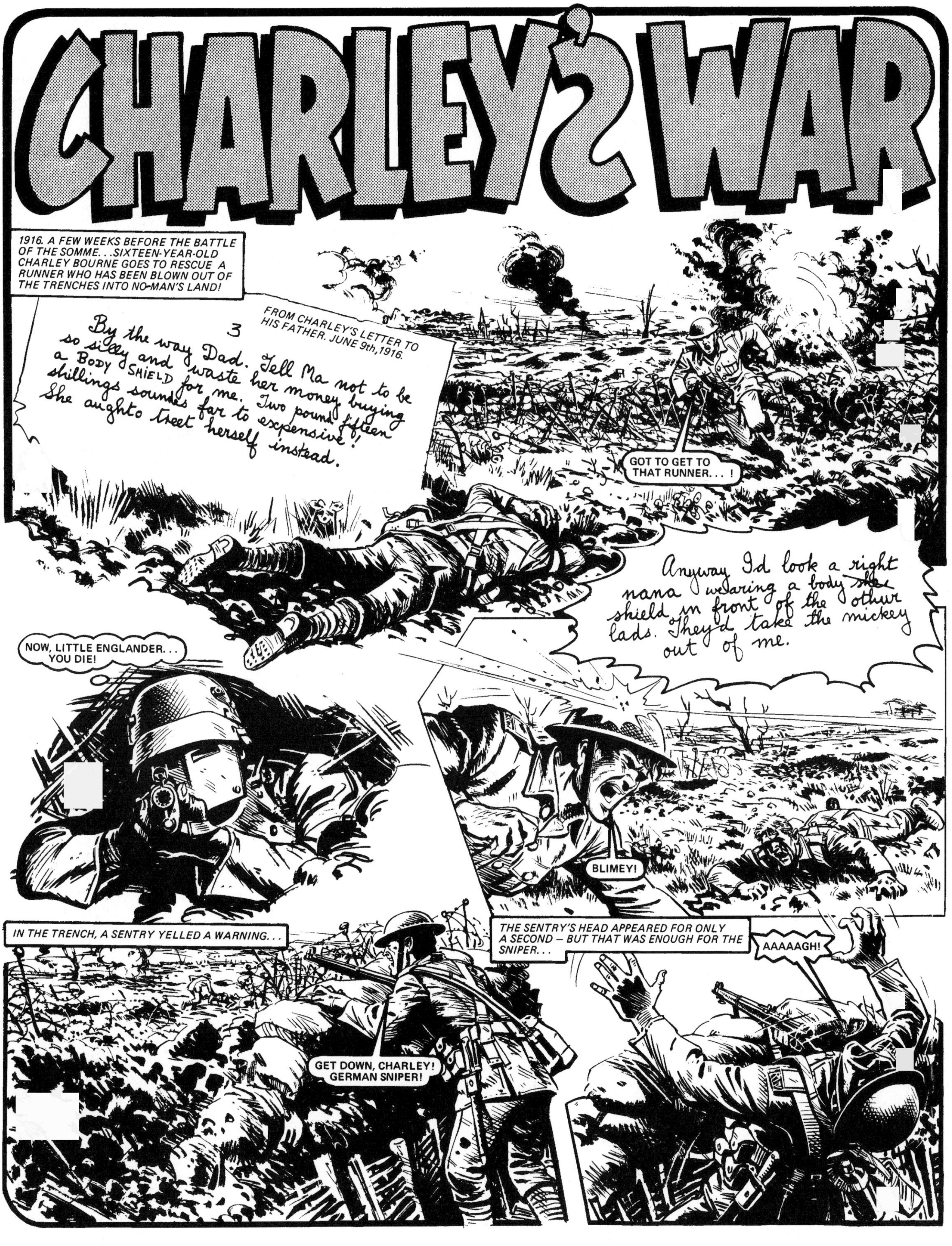
CHARLEY'S WAR
1916. A FEW WEEKS BEFORE THE BATTLE OF THE SOMME. . .SIXTEEN-YEAR-OLD CHARLEY BOURNE GOES TO RESCUE A RUNNER WHO HAS BEEN BLOWN OUT OF THE TRENCHES INTO NO-MAN'S LAND!
FROM CHARLEY'S LETTER TO HIS FATHER. JUNE 9th,1916.
3
By the way Dad. Tell Ma not to be so silly and waste her money buying a BODY SHIELD for me. Two pound fifteen shillings sounds far to expensive! She aughto treet herself instead.
GOT TO GET TO THAT RUNNER. . . !
Anyway I'd look a right nana wearing a body sh shield in front of the other lads. They'd take the mickey out of me.
NOW, LITTLE ENGLANDER. . . YOU DIE!
BLIMEY!
IN THE TRENCH, A SENTRY YELLED A WARNING. . .
GET DOWN, CHARLEY! GERMAN SNIPER!
THE SENTRY'S HEAD APPEARED FOR ONLY A SECOND – BUT THAT WAS ENOUGH FOR THE SNIPER. . .
AAAAAGH!

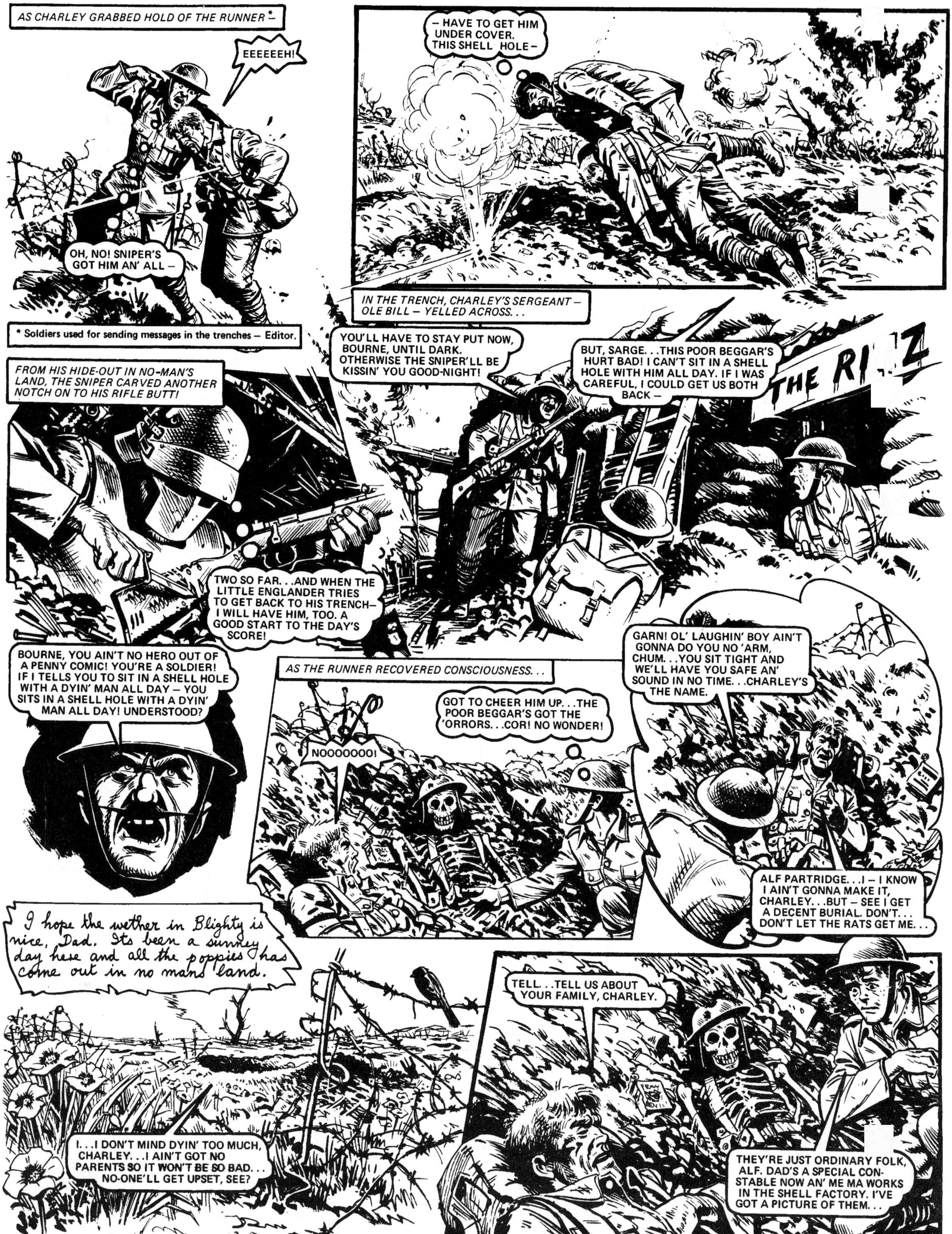

AS CHARLEY GRABBED HOLD OF THE RUNNER*–
EEEEEEH!
OH, NO! SNIPER'S GOT HIM AN' ALL –
* Soldiers used for sending messages in the trenches – Editor.
– HAVE TO GET HIM UNDER COVER. THIS SHELL HOLE –
IN THE TRENCH, CHARLEY'S SERGEANT – OLE BILL – YELLED ACROSS...
FROM HIS HIDE-OUT IN NO-MAN'S LAND, THE SNIPER CARVED ANOTHER NOTCH ON TO HIS RIFLE BUTT!
TWO SO FAR...AND WHEN THE LITTLE ENGLANDER TRIES TO GET BACK TO HIS TRENCH – I WILL HAVE HIM, TOO. A GOOD START TO THE DAY'S SCORE!
YOU'LL HAVE TO STAY PUT NOW, BOURNE, UNTIL DARK. OTHERWISE THE SNIPER'LL BE KISSIN' YOU GOOD-NIGHT!
BUT, SARGE...THIS POOR BEGGAR'S HURT BAD! I CAN'T SIT IN A SHELL HOLE WITH HIM ALL DAY. IF I WAS CAREFUL, I COULD GET US BOTH BACK –
BOURNE, YOU AIN'T NO HERO OUT OF A PENNY COMIC! YOU'RE A SOLDIER! IF I TELLS YOU TO SIT IN A SHELL HOLE WITH A DYIN' MAN ALL DAY – YOU SITS IN A SHELL HOLE WITH A DYIN' MAN ALL DAY! UNDERSTOOD?
AS THE RUNNER RECOVERED CONSCIOUSNESS...
GOT TO CHEER HIM UP...THE POOR BEGGAR'S GOT THE 'ORRORS...COR! NO WONDER!
NOOOOOOO!
GARN! OL' LAUGHIN' BOY AIN'T GONNA DO YOU NO 'ARM, CHUM...YOU SIT TIGHT AND WE'LL HAVE YOU SAFE AN' SOUND IN NO TIME...CHARLEY'S THE NAME.
ALF PARTRIDGE...I – I KNOW I AIN'T GONNA MAKE IT, CHARLEY...BUT – SEE I GET A DECENT BURIAL. DON'T... DON'T LET THE RATS GET ME...
I hope the wether in Blighty is nice, Dad. Its been a sunney day here and all the poppies has come out in no mans land.
I...I DON'T MIND DYIN' TOO MUCH, CHARLEY...I AIN'T GOT NO PARENTS SO IT WON'T BE SO BAD... NO-ONE'LL GET UPSET, SEE?
TELL...TELL US ABOUT YOUR FAMILY, CHARLEY.
THEY'RE JUST ORDINARY FOLK, ALF. DAD'S A SPECIAL CONSTABLE NOW AN' ME MA WORKS IN THE SHELL FACTORY. I'VE GOT A PICTURE OF THEM...

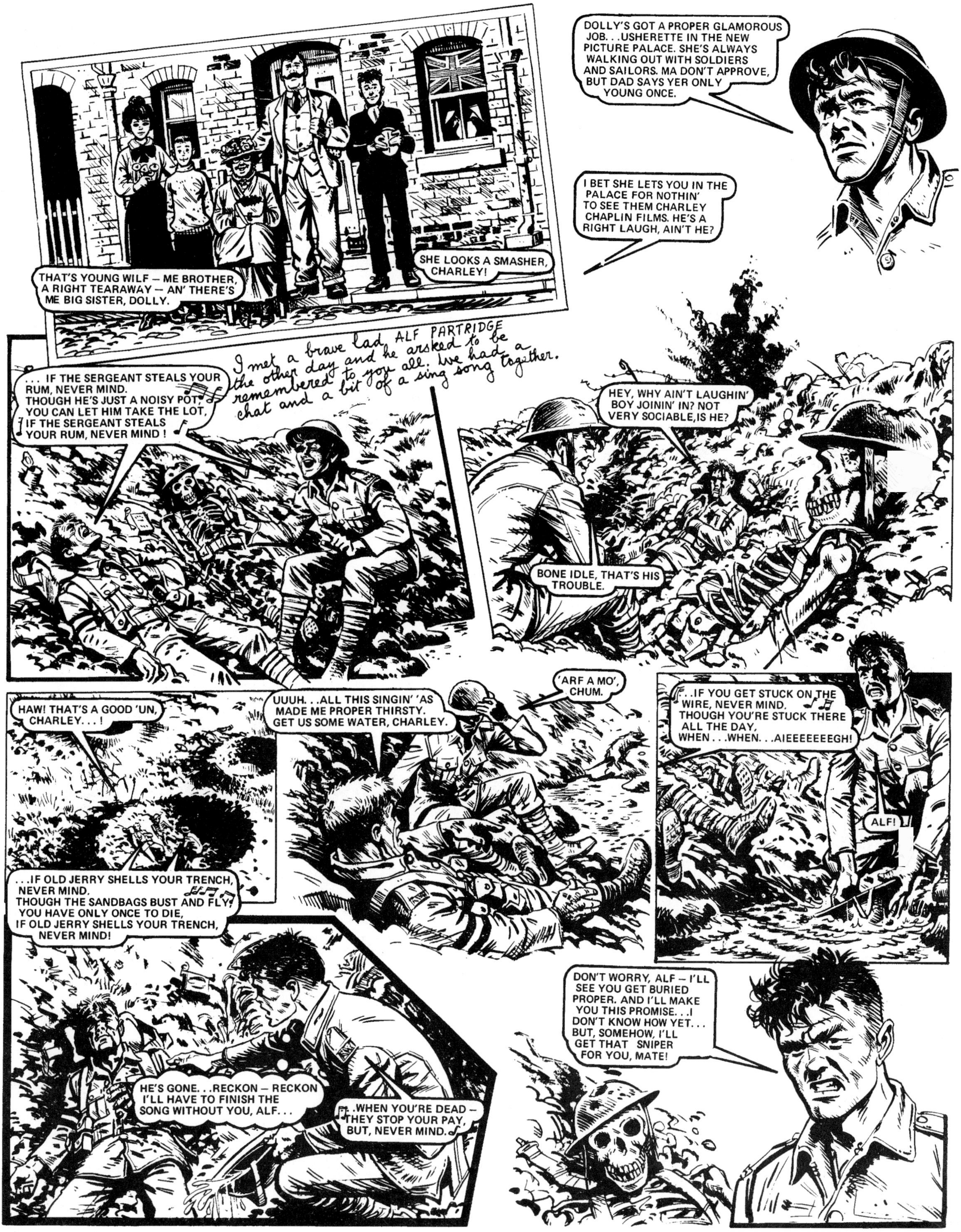
THAT'S YOUNG WILF – ME BROTHER, A RIGHT TEARAWAY – AN' THERE'S ME BIG SISTER, DOLLY.
SHE LOOKS A SMASHER, CHARLEY!
DOLLY'S GOT A PROPER GLAMOROUS JOB. . .USHERETTE IN THE NEW PICTURE PALACE. SHE'S ALWAYS WALKING OUT WITH SOLDIERS AND SAILORS. MA DON'T APPROVE, BUT DAD SAYS YER ONLY YOUNG ONCE.
I BET SHE LETS YOU IN THE PALACE FOR NOTHIN' TO SEE THEM CHARLEY CHAPLIN FILMS. HE'S A RIGHT LAUGH, AIN'T HE?
I met a brave lad ALF PARTRIDGE the other day and he arsked to be remembered to you all. We had a chat and a bit of a sing song together.
. . . IF THE SERGEANT STEALS YOUR RUM, NEVER MIND. THOUGH HE'S JUST A NOISY POT, YOU CAN LET HIM TAKE THE LOT, IF THE SERGEANT STEALS YOUR RUM, NEVER MIND !
HEY, WHY AIN'T LAUGHIN' BOY JOININ' IN? NOT VERY SOCIABLE,IS HE?
BONE IDLE, THAT'S HIS TROUBLE.
HAW! THAT'S A GOOD 'UN, CHARLEY. . . !
. . .IF OLD JERRY SHELLS YOUR TRENCH, NEVER MIND. THOUGH THE SANDBAGS BUST AND FLY, YOU HAVE ONLY ONCE TO DIE, IF OLD JERRY SHELLS YOUR TRENCH, NEVER MIND!
UUUH. . .ALL THIS SINGIN' 'AS MADE ME PROPER THIRSTY. GET US SOME WATER, CHARLEY.
'ARF A MO', CHUM.
. . .IF YOU GET STUCK ON THE WIRE, NEVER MIND. THOUGH YOU'RE STUCK THERE ALL THE DAY, WHEN. . .WHEN. . .AIEEEEEEEGH!
ALF!
HE'S GONE. . .RECKON – RECKON I'LL HAVE TO FINISH THE SONG WITHOUT YOU, ALF. . .
. . .WHEN YOU'RE DEAD – THEY STOP YOUR PAY, BUT, NEVER MIND.
DON'T WORRY, ALF – I'LL SEE YOU GET BURIED PROPER. AND I'LL MAKE YOU THIS PROMISE. . .I DON'T KNOW HOW YET. . . BUT, SOMEHOW, I'LL GET THAT SNIPER FOR YOU, MATE!

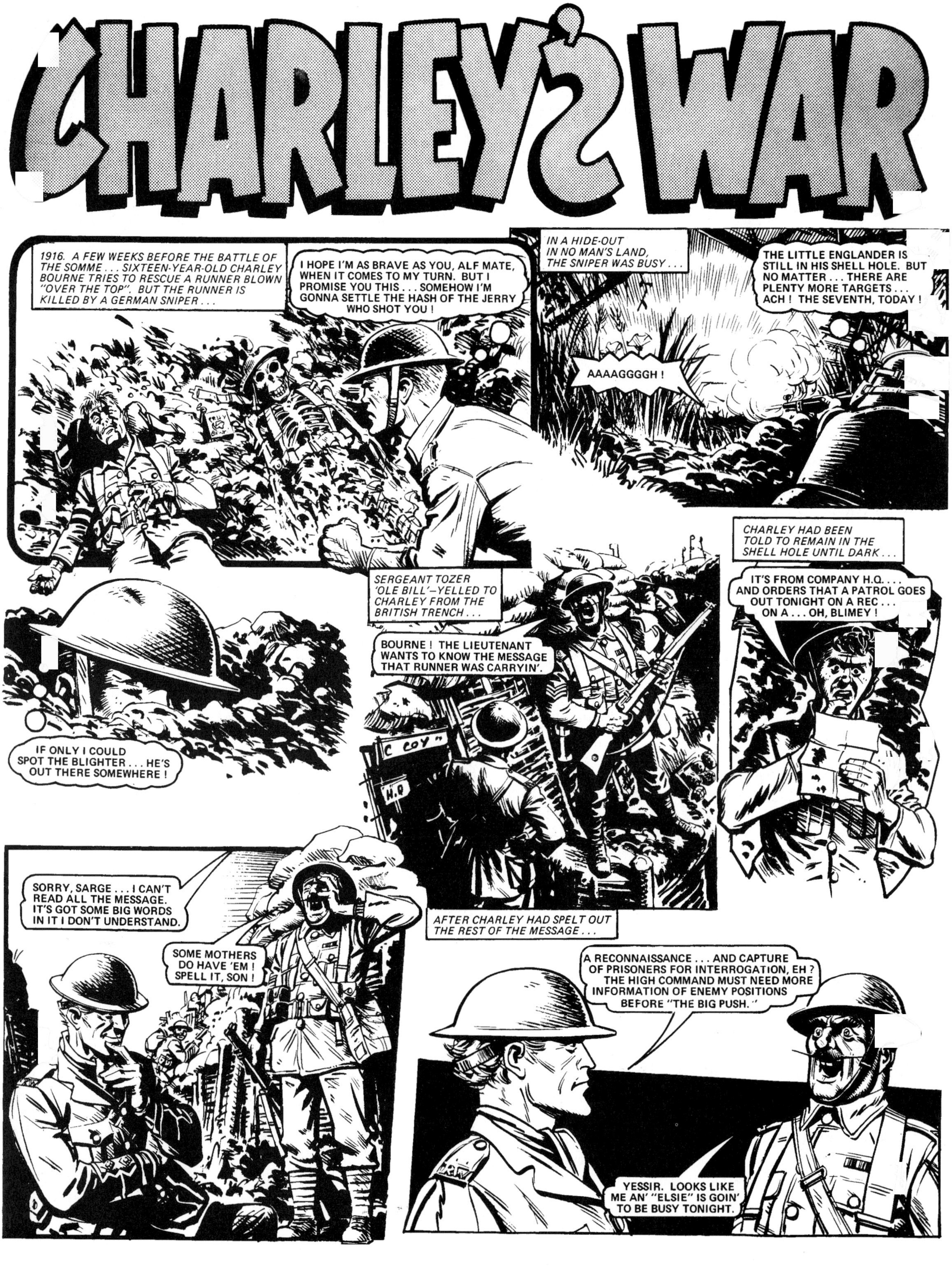

CHARLEY'S WAR
1916. A FEW WEEKS BEFORE THE BATTLE OF THE SOMME . . . SIXTEEN-YEAR-OLD CHARLEY BOURNE TRIES TO RESCUE A RUNNER BLOWN "OVER THE TOP". BUT THE RUNNER IS KILLED BY A GERMAN SNIPER . . .
I HOPE I'M AS BRAVE AS YOU, ALF MATE, WHEN IT COMES TO MY TURN. BUT I PROMISE YOU THIS . . . SOMEHOW I'M GONNA SETTLE THE HASH OF THE JERRY WHO SHOT YOU !
IN A HIDE-OUT IN NO MAN'S LAND, THE SNIPER WAS BUSY . . .
THE LITTLE ENGLANDER IS STILL IN HIS SHELL HOLE. BUT NO MATTER . . . THERE ARE PLENTY MORE TARGETS . . . ACH ! THE SEVENTH, TODAY !
AAAAGGGGH !
IF ONLY I COULD SPOT THE BLIGHTER . . . HE'S OUT THERE SOMEWHERE !
SERGEANT TOZER 'OLE BILL'—YELLED TO CHARLEY FROM THE BRITISH TRENCH . . .
BOURNE ! THE LIEUTENANT WANTS TO KNOW THE MESSAGE THAT RUNNER WAS CARRYIN'.
C COY
H.Q
CHARLEY HAD BEEN TOLD TO REMAIN IN THE SHELL HOLE UNTIL DARK . . .
IT'S FROM COMPANY H.Q. . . . AND ORDERS THAT A PATROL GOES OUT TONIGHT ON A REC . . . ON A . . . OH, BLIMEY !
SORRY, SARGE . . . I CAN'T READ ALL THE MESSAGE. IT'S GOT SOME BIG WORDS IN IT I DON'T UNDERSTAND.
SOME MOTHERS DO HAVE 'EM ! SPELL IT, SON !
AFTER CHARLEY HAD SPELT OUT THE REST OF THE MESSAGE . . .
A RECONNAISSANCE . . . AND CAPTURE OF PRISONERS FOR INTERROGATION, EH ? THE HIGH COMMAND MUST NEED MORE INFORMATION OF ENEMY POSITIONS BEFORE "THE BIG PUSH."
YESSIR. LOOKS LIKE ME AN' "ELSIE" IS GOIN' TO BE BUSY TONIGHT.

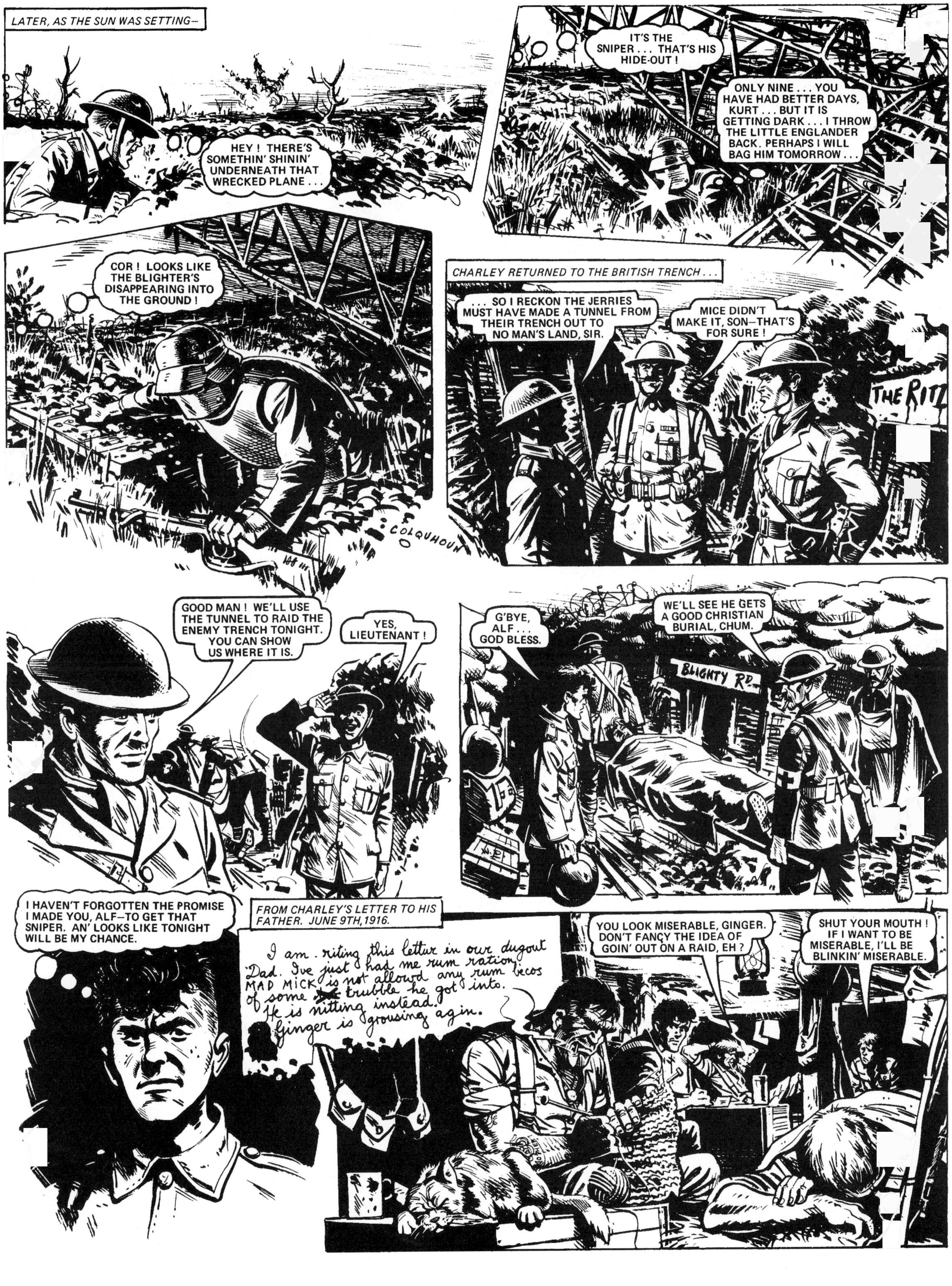
LATER, AS THE SUN WAS SETTING—
HEY ! THERE'S SOMETHIN' SHININ' UNDERNEATH THAT WRECKED PLANE . . .
IT'S THE SNIPER . . . THAT'S HIS HIDE-OUT !
ONLY NINE . . . YOU HAVE HAD BETTER DAYS, KURT . . . BUT IT IS GETTING DARK . . . I THROW THE LITTLE ENGLANDER BACK. PERHAPS I WILL BAG HIM TOMORROW . . .
COR ! LOOKS LIKE THE BLIGHTER'S DISAPPEARING INTO THE GROUND !
COLQUHOUN
CHARLEY RETURNED TO THE BRITISH TRENCH . . .
. . . SO I RECKON THE JERRIES MUST HAVE MADE A TUNNEL FROM THEIR TRENCH OUT TO NO MAN'S LAND, SIR.
MICE DIDN'T MAKE IT, SON—THAT'S FOR SURE !
THE RITZ
GOOD MAN ! WE'LL USE THE TUNNEL TO RAID THE ENEMY TRENCH TONIGHT. YOU CAN SHOW US WHERE IT IS.
YES, LIEUTENANT !
G'BYE, ALF . . . GOD BLESS.
WE'LL SEE HE GETS A GOOD CHRISTIAN BURIAL, CHUM.
BLIGHTY RD.
I HAVEN'T FORGOTTEN THE PROMISE I MADE YOU, ALF—TO GET THAT SNIPER. AN' LOOKS LIKE TONIGHT WILL BE MY CHANCE.
FROM CHARLEY'S LETTER TO HIS FATHER. JUNE 9TH,1916.
I am riting this letter in our dugout Dad. Ive just had me rum ration. MAD MICK is not allowed any rum becos of some trubble he got into. He is nitting instead. Ginger is grousing agin.
YOU LOOK MISERABLE, GINGER. DON'T FANCY THE IDEA OF GOIN' OUT ON A RAID, EH ?
SHUT YOUR MOUTH ! IF I WANT TO BE MISERABLE, I'LL BE BLINKIN' MISERABLE.

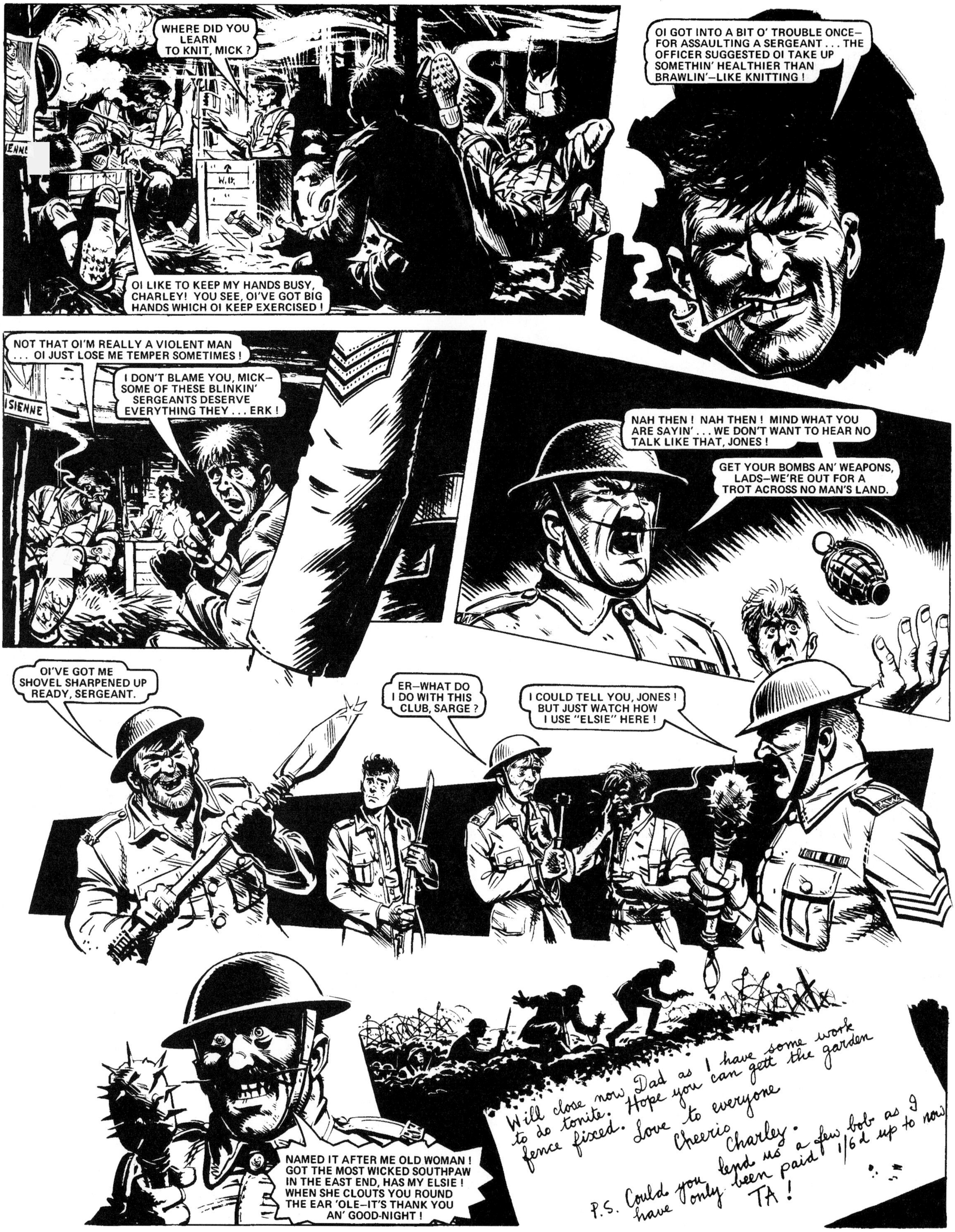

WHERE DID YOU LEARN TO KNIT, MICK ?
OI LIKE TO KEEP MY HANDS BUSY, CHARLEY! YOU SEE, OI'VE GOT BIG HANDS WHICH OI KEEP EXERCISED !
OI GOT INTO A BIT O' TROUBLE ONCE– FOR ASSAULTING A SERGEANT . . . THE OFFICER SUGGESTED OI TAKE UP SOMETHIN' HEALTHIER THAN BRAWLIN'–LIKE KNITTING !
NOT THAT OI'M REALLY A VIOLENT MAN . . . OI JUST LOSE ME TEMPER SOMETIMES !
I DON'T BLAME YOU, MICK– SOME OF THESE BLINKIN' SERGEANTS DESERVE EVERYTHING THEY . . . ERK !
NAH THEN ! NAH THEN ! MIND WHAT YOU ARE SAYIN' . . . WE DON'T WANT TO HEAR NO TALK LIKE THAT, JONES !
GET YOUR BOMBS AN' WEAPONS, LADS–WE'RE OUT FOR A TROT ACROSS NO MAN'S LAND.
OI'VE GOT ME SHOVEL SHARPENED UP READY, SERGEANT.
ER–WHAT DO I DO WITH THIS CLUB, SARGE ?
I COULD TELL YOU, JONES ! BUT JUST WATCH HOW I USE "ELSIE" HERE !
NAMED IT AFTER ME OLD WOMAN ! GOT THE MOST WICKED SOUTHPAW IN THE EAST END, HAS MY ELSIE ! WHEN SHE CLOUTS YOU ROUND THE EAR 'OLE–IT'S THANK YOU AN' GOOD-NIGHT !
Will close now Dad as I have some work to do tonite. Hope you can gett the garden fence fixed. Love to everyone
Cheerio
Charley.
P.S. Could you lend us a few bob as I have only been paid 1/6d up to now
TA !

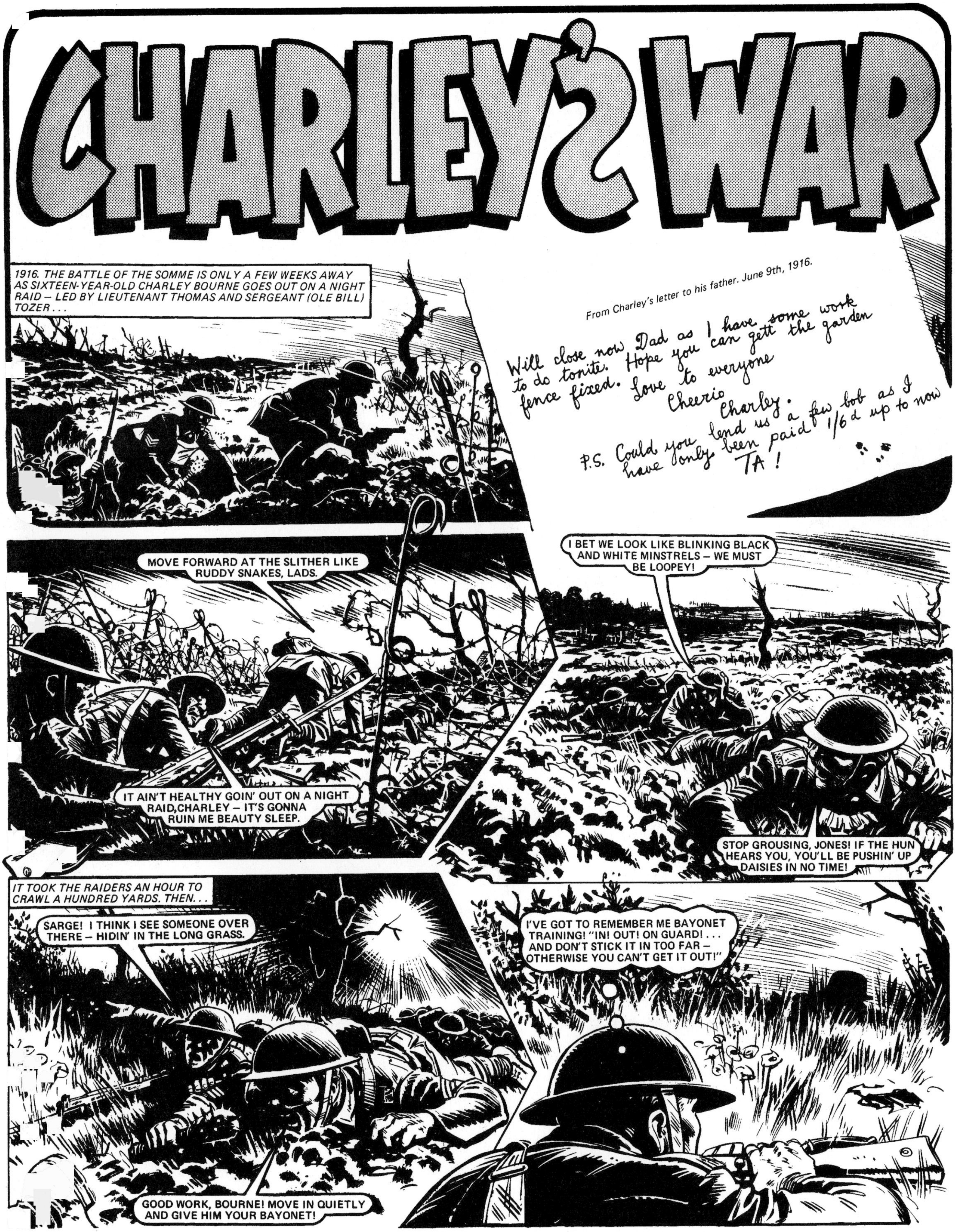
CHARLEY'S WAR
1916. THE BATTLE OF THE SOMME IS ONLY A FEW WEEKS AWAY AS SIXTEEN-YEAR-OLD CHARLEY BOURNE GOES OUT ON A NIGHT RAID – LED BY LIEUTENANT THOMAS AND SERGEANT (OLE BILL) TOZER . . .
From Charley's letter to his father. June 9th, 1916.
Will close now Dad as I have some work to do tonite. Hope you can gett the garden fence fixed. Love to everyone
Cheerio
Charley.
P.S. Could you lend us a few bob as I have only been paid 1/6d up to now
TA!
MOVE FORWARD AT THE SLITHER LIKE RUDDY SNAKES, LADS.
IT AIN'T HEALTHY GOIN' OUT ON A NIGHT RAID,CHARLEY – IT'S GONNA RUIN ME BEAUTY SLEEP.
I BET WE LOOK LIKE BLINKING BLACK AND WHITE MINSTRELS – WE MUST BE LOOPEY!
STOP GROUSING, JONES! IF THE HUN HEARS YOU, YOU'LL BE PUSHIN' UP DAISIES IN NO TIME!
IT TOOK THE RAIDERS AN HOUR TO CRAWL A HUNDRED YARDS. THEN. . .
SARGE! I THINK I SEE SOMEONE OVER THERE – HIDIN' IN THE LONG GRASS.
GOOD WORK, BOURNE! MOVE IN QUIETLY AND GIVE HIM YOUR BAYONET!
I'VE GOT TO REMEMBER ME BAYONET TRAINING! "IN! OUT! ON GUARD! . . . AND DON'T STICK IT IN TOO FAR – OTHERWISE YOU CAN'T GET IT OUT!"

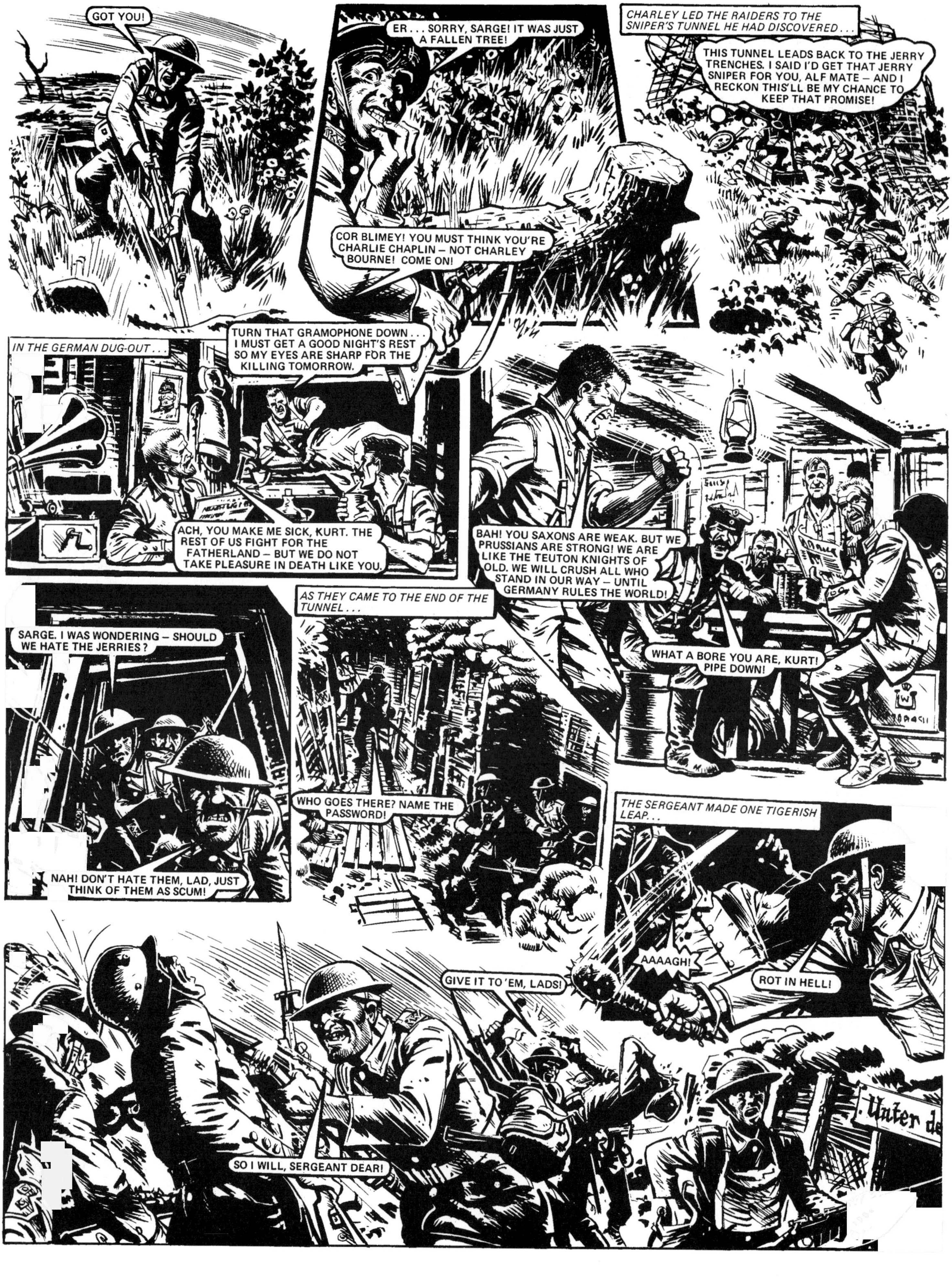
GOT YOU!
ER . . . SORRY, SARGE! IT WAS JUST A FALLEN TREE!
COR BLIMEY! YOU MUST THINK YOU'RE CHARLIE CHAPLIN – NOT CHARLEY BOURNE! COME ON!
CHARLEY LED THE RAIDERS TO THE SNIPER'S TUNNEL HE HAD DISCOVERED . . .
THIS TUNNEL LEADS BACK TO THE JERRY TRENCHES. I SAID I'D GET THAT JERRY SNIPER FOR YOU, ALF MATE – AND I RECKON THIS'LL BE MY CHANCE TO KEEP THAT PROMISE!
IN THE GERMAN DUG-OUT . . .
TURN THAT GRAMOPHONE DOWN . . . I MUST GET A GOOD NIGHT'S REST SO MY EYES ARE SHARP FOR THE KILLING TOMORROW.
ACH, YOU MAKE ME SICK, KURT. THE REST OF US FIGHT FOR THE FATHERLAND – BUT WE DO NOT TAKE PLEASURE IN DEATH LIKE YOU.
BAH! YOU SAXONS ARE WEAK. BUT WE PRUSSIANS ARE STRONG! WE ARE LIKE THE TEUTON KNIGHTS OF OLD. WE WILL CRUSH ALL WHO STAND IN OUR WAY – UNTIL GERMANY RULES THE WORLD!
WHAT A BORE YOU ARE, KURT! PIPE DOWN!
SARGE. I WAS WONDERING – SHOULD WE HATE THE JERRIES?
NAH! DON'T HATE THEM, LAD, JUST THINK OF THEM AS SCUM!
AS THEY CAME TO THE END OF THE TUNNEL . . .
WHO GOES THERE? NAME THE PASSWORD!
THE SERGEANT MADE ONE TIGERISH LEAP . . .
AAAAGH!
ROT IN HELL!
GIVE IT TO 'EM, LADS!
SO I WILL, SERGEANT DEAR!
Unter de

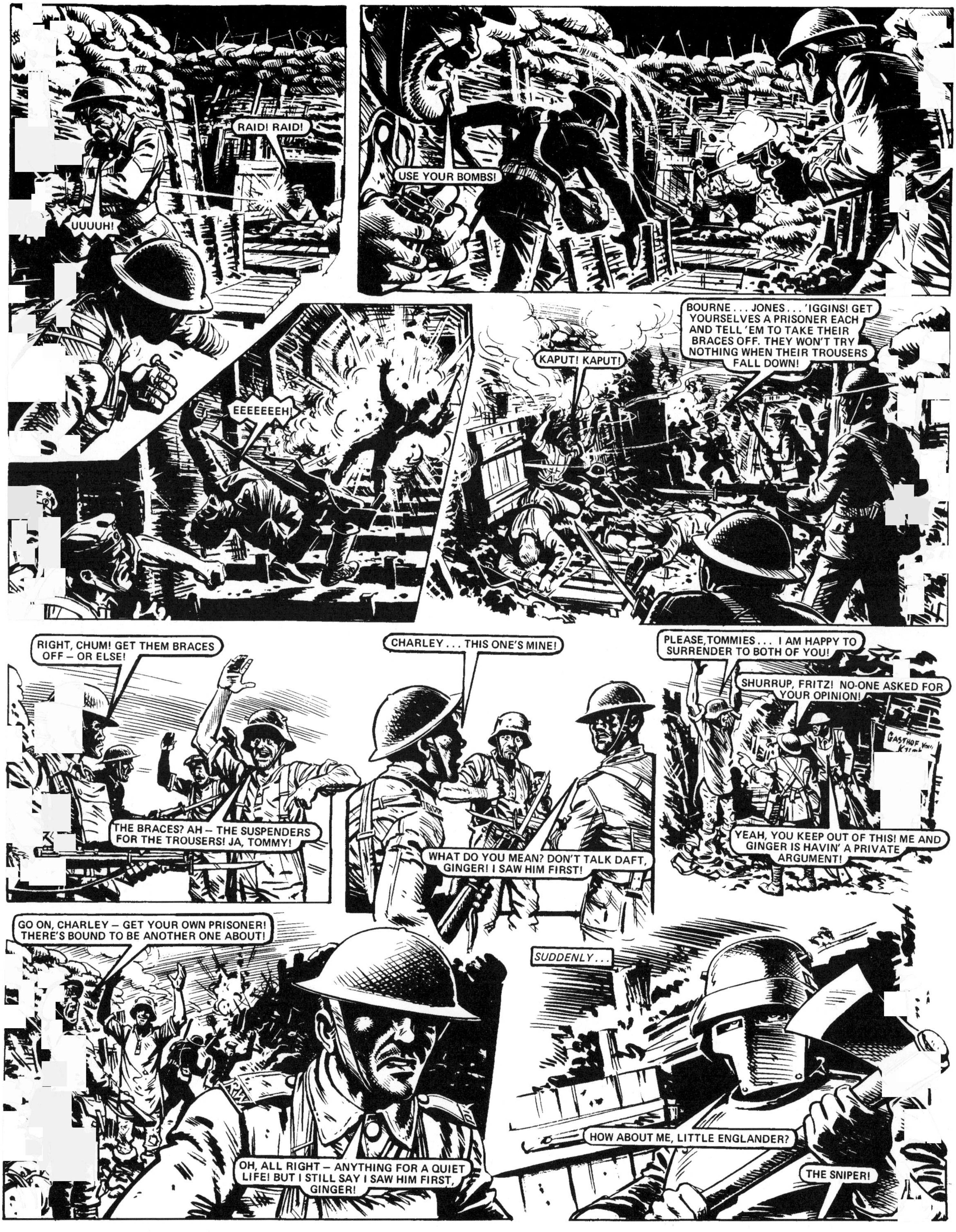
RAID! RAID!
UUUUH!
USE YOUR BOMBS!
EEEEEEEH!
KAPUT! KAPUT!
BOURNE . . . JONES . . . 'IGGINS! GET YOURSELVES A PRISONER EACH AND TELL 'EM TO TAKE THEIR BRACES OFF. THEY WON'T TRY NOTHING WHEN THEIR TROUSERS FALL DOWN!
RIGHT, CHUM! GET THEM BRACES OFF – OR ELSE!
THE BRACES? AH – THE SUSPENDERS FOR THE TROUSERS! JA, TOMMY!
CHARLEY . . . THIS ONE'S MINE!
WHAT DO YOU MEAN? DON'T TALK DAFT, GINGER! I SAW HIM FIRST!
PLEASE, TOMMIES . . . I AM HAPPY TO SURRENDER TO BOTH OF YOU!
SHURRUP, FRITZ! NO-ONE ASKED FOR YOUR OPINION!
YEAH, YOU KEEP OUT OF THIS! ME AND GINGER IS HAVIN' A PRIVATE ARGUMENT!
GO ON, CHARLEY – GET YOUR OWN PRISONER! THERE'S BOUND TO BE ANOTHER ONE ABOUT!
OH, ALL RIGHT – ANYTHING FOR A QUIET LIFE! BUT I STILL SAY I SAW HIM FIRST, GINGER!
SUDDENLY . . .
HOW ABOUT ME, LITTLE ENGLANDER?
THE SNIPER!

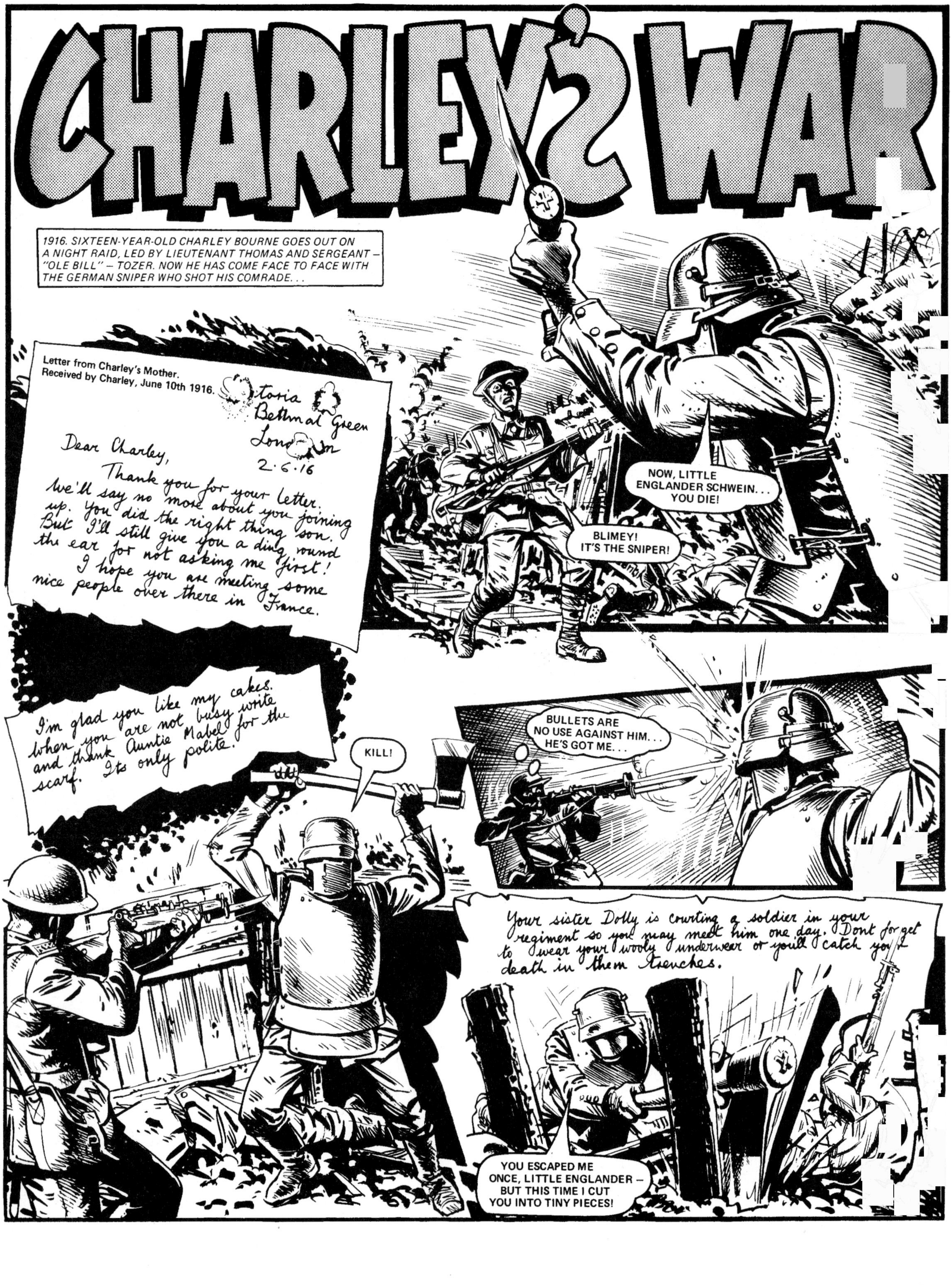
CHARLEY'S WAR
1916. SIXTEEN-YEAR-OLD CHARLEY BOURNE GOES OUT ON A NIGHT RAID, LED BY LIEUTENANT THOMAS AND SERGEANT – "OLE BILL" – TOZER. NOW HE HAS COME FACE TO FACE WITH THE GERMAN SNIPER WHO SHOT HIS COMRADE. . .
Letter from Charley's Mother. Received by Charley, June 10th 1916.
toria
Bethnal Green
Lond n
2.6.16
Dear Charley,
Thank you for your letter. We'll say no more about you joining up. You did the right thing son. But I'll still give you a ding round the ear for not asking me first! I hope you are meeting some nice people over there in France.
NOW, LITTLE ENGLANDER SCHWEIN. . . YOU DIE!
BLIMEY! IT'S THE SNIPER!
I'm glad you like my cakes. When you are not busy write and thank Auntie Mabel for the scarf. Its only polite.
KILL!
BULLETS ARE NO USE AGAINST HIM. . . HE'S GOT ME. . .
Your sister Dolly is courting a soldier in your regiment so you may meet him one day. Dont forget to wear your wooly underwear or you'll catch your death in them trenches.
YOU ESCAPED ME ONCE, LITTLE ENGLANDER – BUT THIS TIME I CUT YOU INTO TINY PIECES!

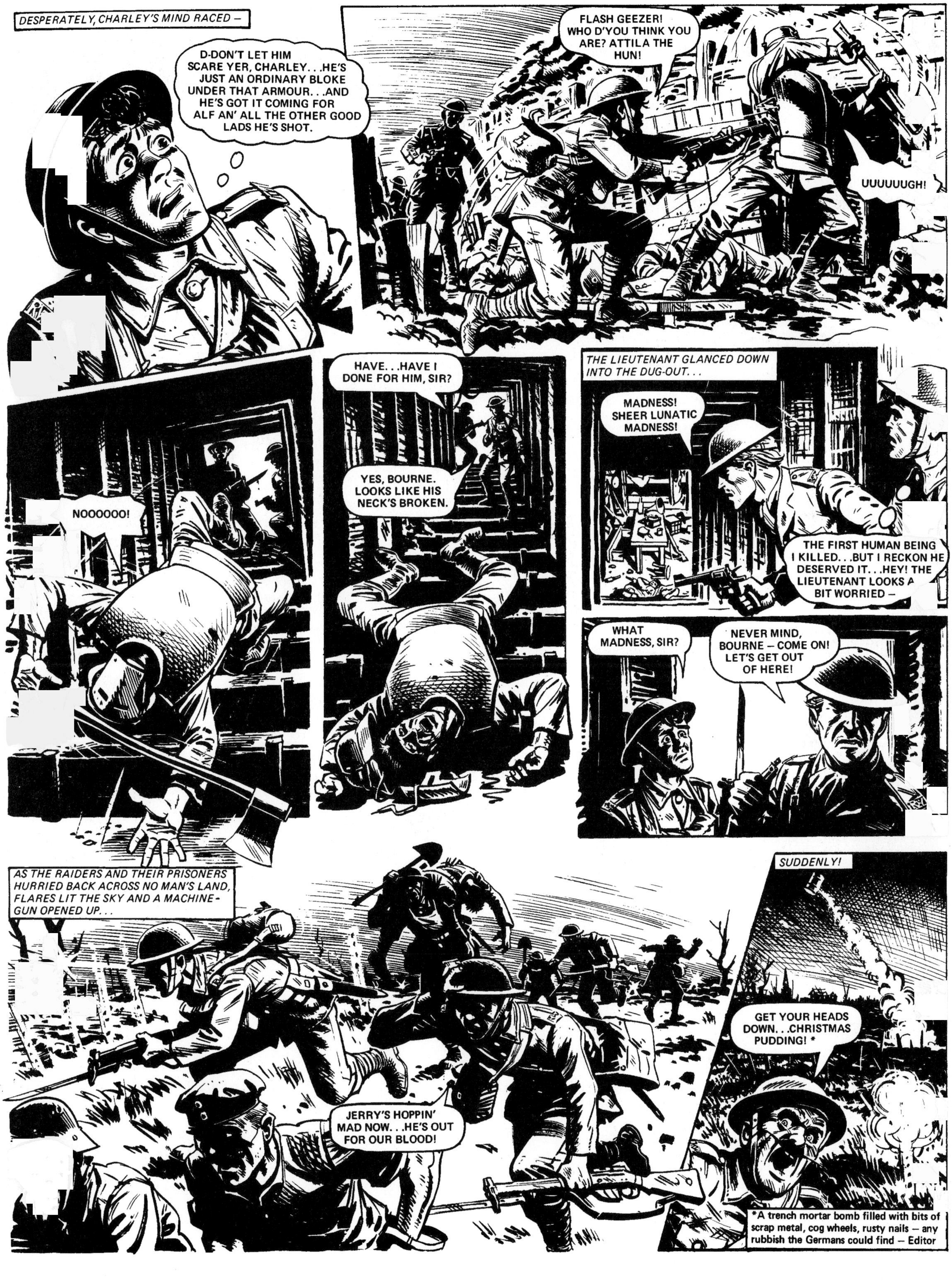

DESPERATELY, CHARLEY'S MIND RACED –
D-DON'T LET HIM SCARE YER, CHARLEY. . .HE'S JUST AN ORDINARY BLOKE UNDER THAT ARMOUR. . .AND HE'S GOT IT COMING FOR ALF AN' ALL THE OTHER GOOD LADS HE'S SHOT.
FLASH GEEZER! WHO D'YOU THINK YOU ARE? ATTILA THE HUN!
UUUUUUGH!
NOOOOOO!
HAVE. . .HAVE I DONE FOR HIM, SIR?
YES, BOURNE. LOOKS LIKE HIS NECK'S BROKEN.
THE LIEUTENANT GLANCED DOWN INTO THE DUG-OUT. . .
MADNESS! SHEER LUNATIC MADNESS!
THE FIRST HUMAN BEING I KILLED. . .BUT I RECKON HE DESERVED IT. . .HEY! THE LIEUTENANT LOOKS A BIT WORRIED –
WHAT MADNESS, SIR?
NEVER MIND, BOURNE – COME ON! LET'S GET OUT OF HERE!
AS THE RAIDERS AND THEIR PRISONERS HURRIED BACK ACROSS NO MAN'S LAND, FLARES LIT THE SKY AND A MACHINE-GUN OPENED UP. . .
JERRY'S HOPPIN' MAD NOW. . .HE'S OUT FOR OUR BLOOD!
SUDDENLY!
GET YOUR HEADS DOWN. . .CHRISTMAS PUDDING! *
*A trench mortar bomb filled with bits of scrap metal, cog wheels, rusty nails – any rubbish the Germans could find – Editor

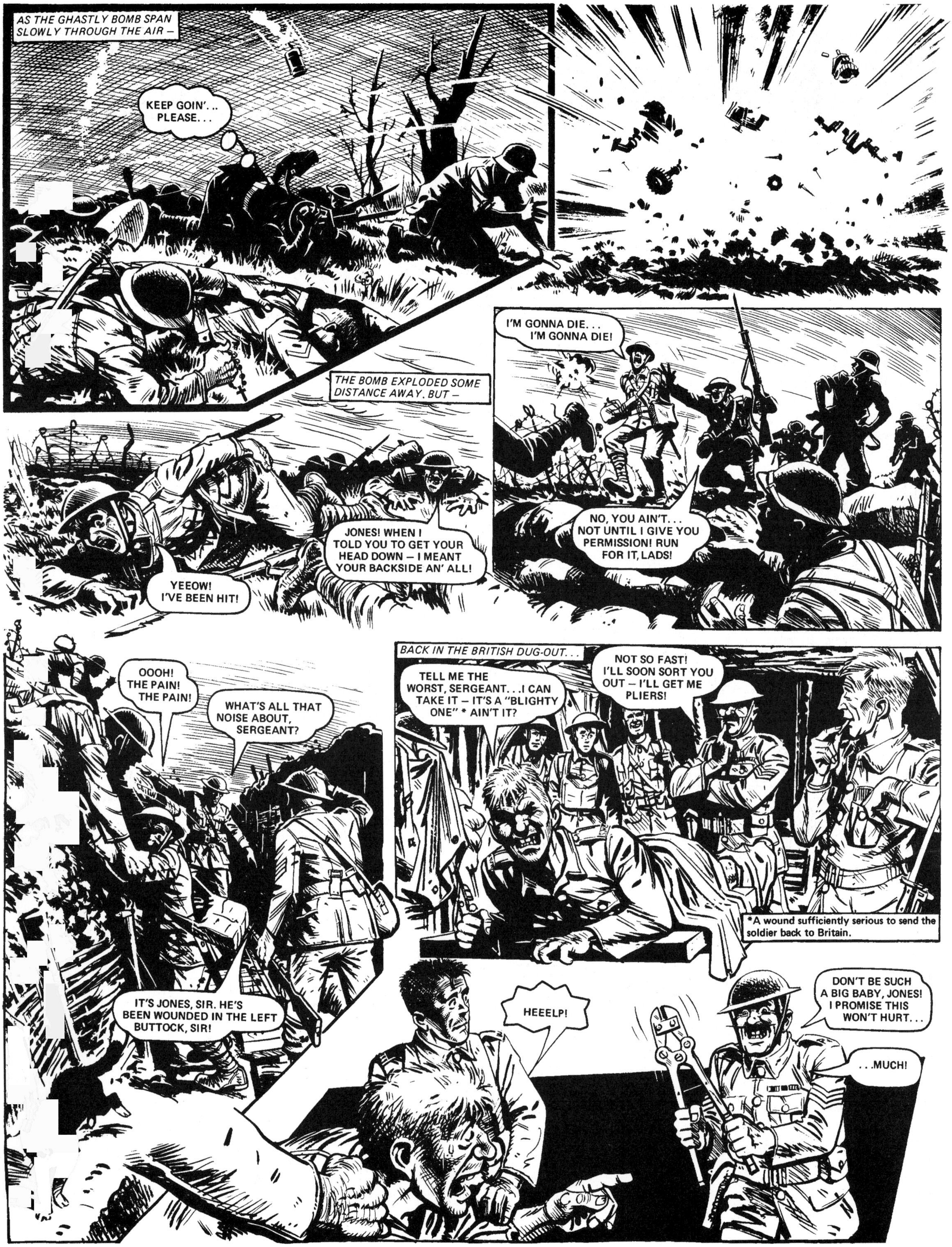
AS THE GHASTLY BOMB SPAN SLOWLY THROUGH THE AIR –
KEEP GOIN'.. PLEASE. . .
THE BOMB EXPLODED SOME DISTANCE AWAY. BUT –
YEEOW! I'VE BEEN HIT!
JONES! WHEN I TOLD YOU TO GET YOUR HEAD DOWN – I MEANT YOUR BACKSIDE AN' ALL!
I'M GONNA DIE. . . I'M GONNA DIE!
NO, YOU AIN'T. . . NOT UNTIL I GIVE YOU PERMISSION! RUN FOR IT, LADS!
OOOH! THE PAIN! THE PAIN!
WHAT'S ALL THAT NOISE ABOUT, SERGEANT?
IT'S JONES, SIR. HE'S BEEN WOUNDED IN THE LEFT BUTTOCK, SIR!
BACK IN THE BRITISH DUG-OUT. . .
TELL ME THE WORST, SERGEANT. . . I CAN TAKE IT – IT'S A "BLIGHTY ONE" * AIN'T IT?
NOT SO FAST! I'LL SOON SORT YOU OUT – I'LL GET ME PLIERS!
*A wound sufficiently serious to send the soldier back to Britain.
HEEELP!
DON'T BE SUCH A BIG BABY, JONES! I PROMISE THIS WON'T HURT. . .
. . .MUCH!

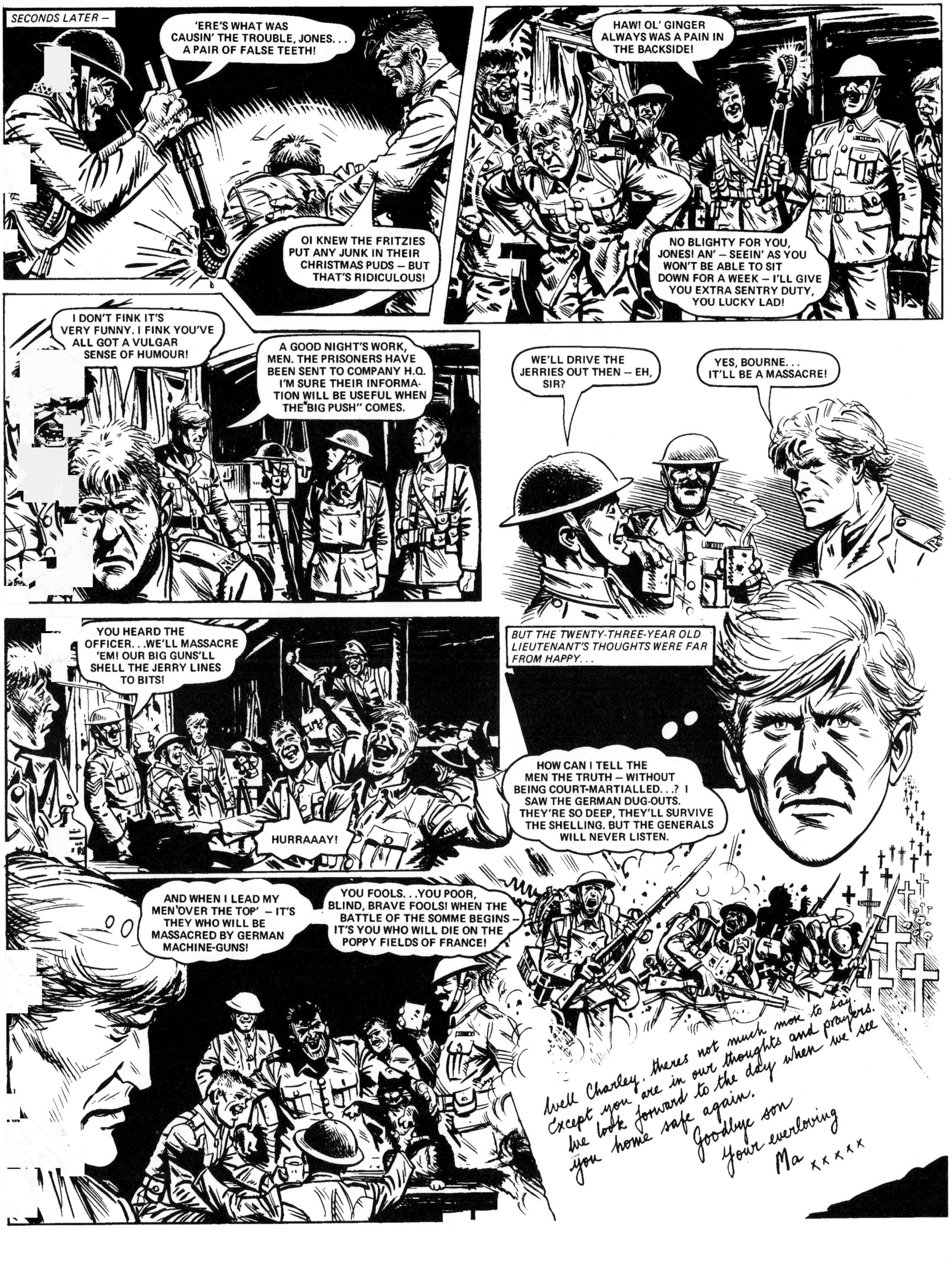
SECONDS LATER –
'ERE'S WHAT WAS CAUSIN' THE TROUBLE, JONES. . . A PAIR OF FALSE TEETH!
OI KNEW THE FRITZIES PUT ANY JUNK IN THEIR CHRISTMAS PUDS – BUT THAT'S RIDICULOUS!
HAW! OL' GINGER ALWAYS WAS A PAIN IN THE BACKSIDE!
NO BLIGHTY FOR YOU, JONES! AN' – SEEIN' AS YOU WON'T BE ABLE TO SIT DOWN FOR A WEEK – I'LL GIVE YOU EXTRA SENTRY DUTY, YOU LUCKY LAD!
I DON'T FINK IT'S VERY FUNNY. I FINK YOU'VE ALL GOT A VULGAR SENSE OF HUMOUR!
A GOOD NIGHT'S WORK, MEN. THE PRISONERS HAVE BEEN SENT TO COMPANY H.Q. I'M SURE THEIR INFORMATION WILL BE USEFUL WHEN THE "BIG PUSH" COMES.
WE'LL DRIVE THE JERRIES OUT THEN – EH, SIR?
YES, BOURNE. . . IT'LL BE A MASSACRE!
YOU HEARD THE OFFICER. . . WE'LL MASSACRE 'EM! OUR BIG GUNS'LL SHELL THE JERRY LINES TO BITS!
HURRAAAY!
BUT THE TWENTY-THREE-YEAR OLD LIEUTENANT'S THOUGHTS WERE FAR FROM HAPPY. . .
HOW CAN I TELL THE MEN THE TRUTH – WITHOUT BEING COURT-MARTIALLED. . .? I SAW THE GERMAN DUG-OUTS. THEY'RE SO DEEP, THEY'LL SURVIVE THE SHELLING. BUT THE GENERALS WILL NEVER LISTEN.
AND WHEN I LEAD MY MEN 'OVER THE TOP' – IT'S THEY WHO WILL BE MASSACRED BY GERMAN MACHINE-GUNS!
YOU FOOLS. . . YOU POOR, BLIND, BRAVE FOOLS! WHEN THE BATTLE OF THE SOMME BEGINS – IT'S YOU WHO WILL DIE ON THE POPPY FIELDS OF FRANCE!
Well Charley, theres not much more to say
Except you are in our thoughts and prayers.
We look forward to the day when we see
you home safe again.
Goodbye son
Your everloving
Ma xxxxx

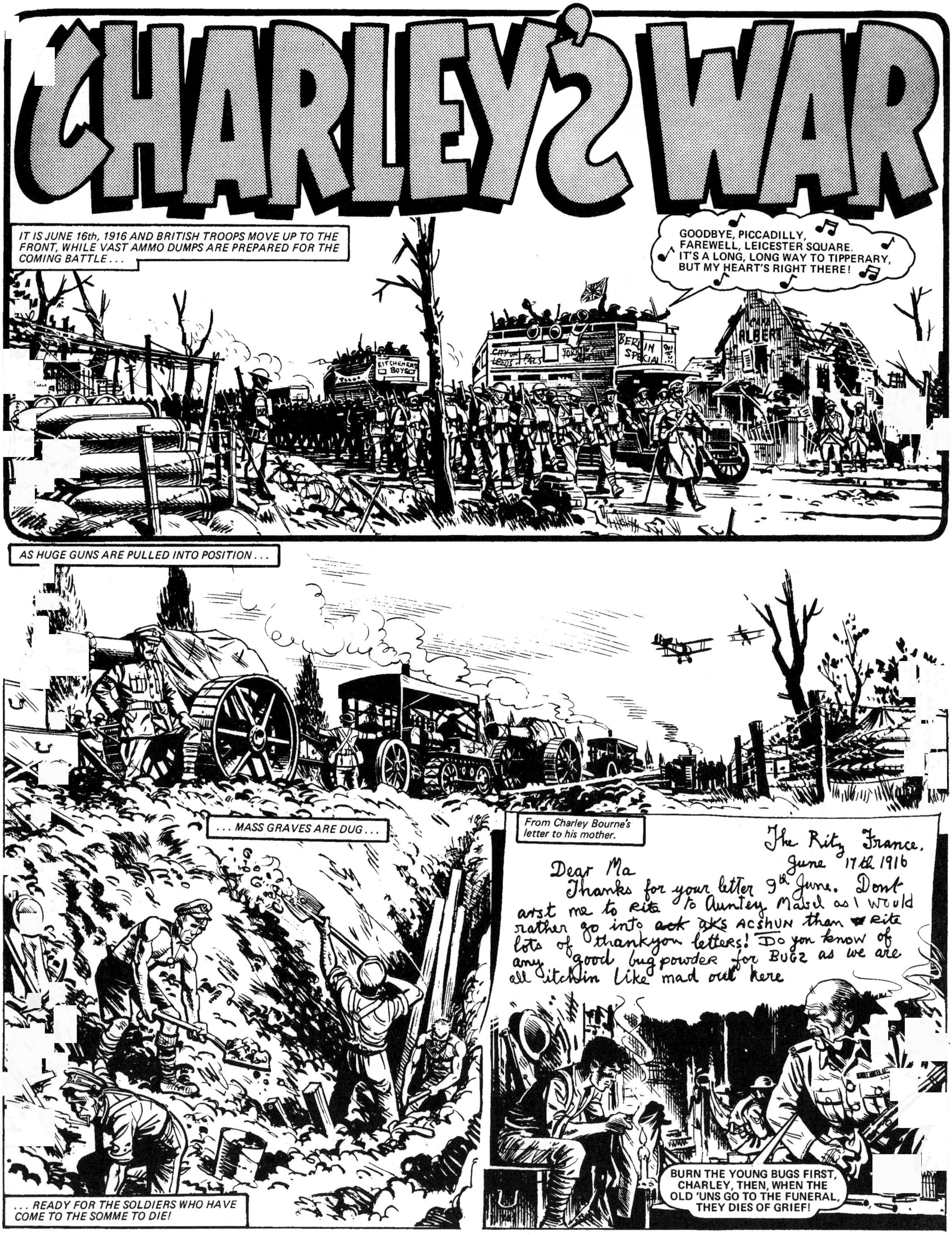
CHARLEY'S WAR
IT IS JUNE 16th, 1916 AND BRITISH TROOPS MOVE UP TO THE FRONT, WHILE VAST AMMO DUMPS ARE PREPARED FOR THE COMING BATTLE . . .
GOODBYE, PICCADILLY, FAREWELL, LEICESTER SQUARE. IT'S A LONG, LONG WAY TO TIPPERARY, BUT MY HEART'S RIGHT THERE!
KITCHENER'S BOYS
BERLIN SPECIAL
ALBERT
AS HUGE GUNS ARE PULLED INTO POSITION . . .
. . . MASS GRAVES ARE DUG . . .
. . . READY FOR THE SOLDIERS WHO HAVE COME TO THE SOMME TO DIE!
From Charley Bourne's letter to his mother.
The Ritz France.
June 17th 1916
Dear Ma
Thanks for your letter 9th June. Dont arst me to rite to Auntey Mabel as I would rather go into ~~ack~~ ~~aks~~ ACSHUN than rite lots of thankyou letters! Do you know of any good bug powder for BUGZ as we are all itchin like mad out here
BURN THE YOUNG BUGS FIRST, CHARLEY, THEN, WHEN THE OLD 'UNS GO TO THE FUNERAL, THEY DIES OF GRIEF!

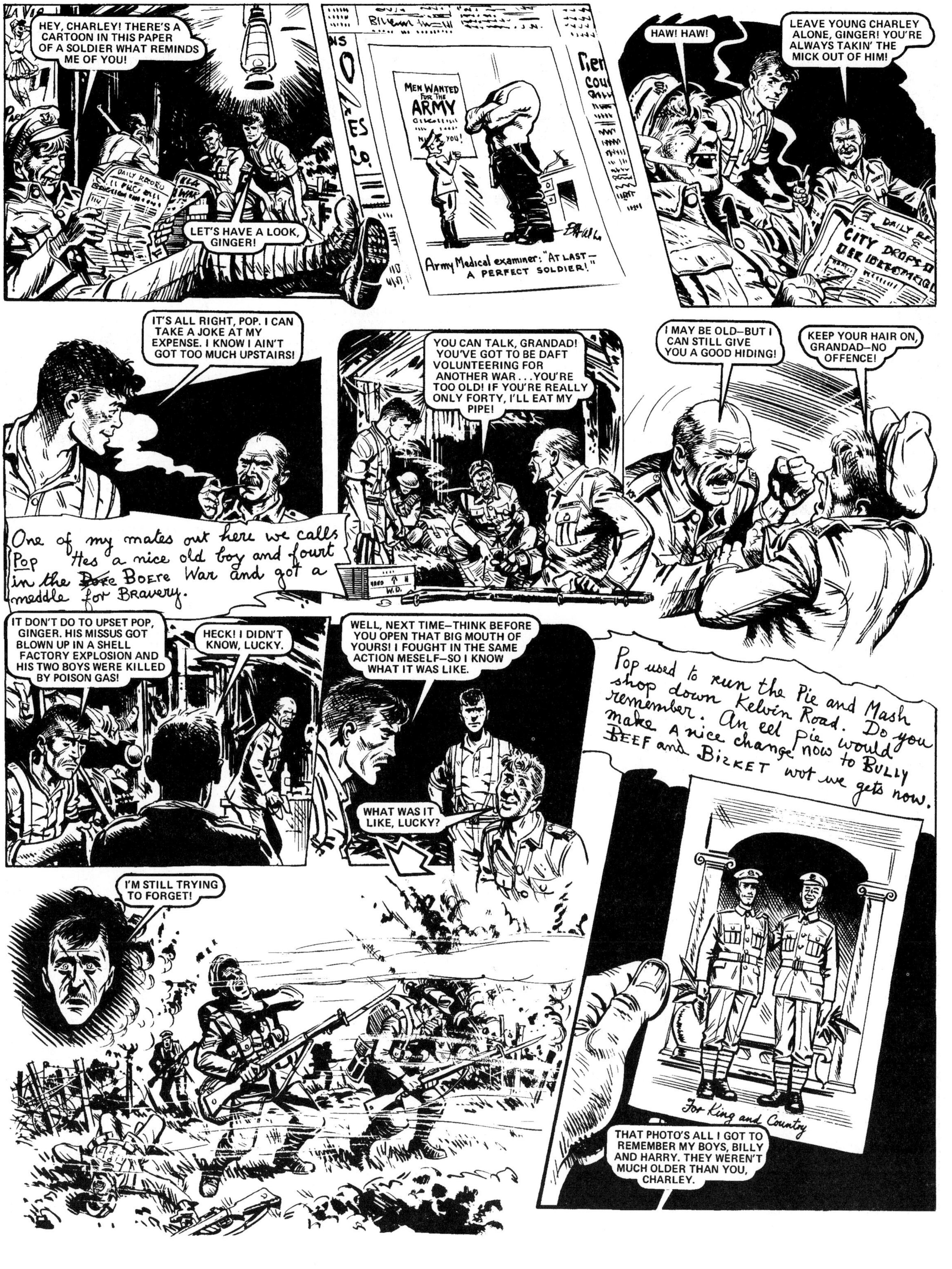
HEY, CHARLEY! THERE'S A CARTOON IN THIS PAPER OF A SOLDIER WHAT REMINDS ME OF YOU!
LET'S HAVE A LOOK, GINGER!
MEN WANTED FOR THE ARMY
Army Medical examiner: "AT LAST — A PERFECT SOLDIER!"
HAW! HAW!
LEAVE YOUNG CHARLEY ALONE, GINGER! YOU'RE ALWAYS TAKIN' THE MICK OUT OF HIM!
IT'S ALL RIGHT, POP. I CAN TAKE A JOKE AT MY EXPENSE. I KNOW I AIN'T GOT TOO MUCH UPSTAIRS!
One of my mates out here we calls Pop Hes a nice old boy and fourt in the ~~Bore~~ Boere War and got a meddle for Bravery.
YOU CAN TALK, GRANDAD! YOU'VE GOT TO BE DAFT VOLUNTEERING FOR ANOTHER WAR . . . YOU'RE TOO OLD! IF YOU'RE REALLY ONLY FORTY, I'LL EAT MY PIPE!
I MAY BE OLD—BUT I CAN STILL GIVE YOU A GOOD HIDING!
KEEP YOUR HAIR ON, GRANDAD—NO OFFENCE!
IT DON'T DO TO UPSET POP, GINGER. HIS MISSUS GOT BLOWN UP IN A SHELL FACTORY EXPLOSION AND HIS TWO BOYS WERE KILLED BY POISON GAS!
HECK! I DIDN'T KNOW, LUCKY.
WELL, NEXT TIME—THINK BEFORE YOU OPEN THAT BIG MOUTH OF YOURS! I FOUGHT IN THE SAME ACTION MESELF—SO I KNOW WHAT IT WAS LIKE.
WHAT WAS IT LIKE, LUCKY?
Pop used to run the Pie and Mash shop down Kelvin Road. Do you remember. An eel Pie would make a nice change now to Bully Beef and Bizket wot we gets now.
I'M STILL TRYING TO FORGET!
For King and Country
THAT PHOTO'S ALL I GOT TO REMEMBER MY BOYS, BILLY AND HARRY. THEY WEREN'T MUCH OLDER THAN YOU, CHARLEY.

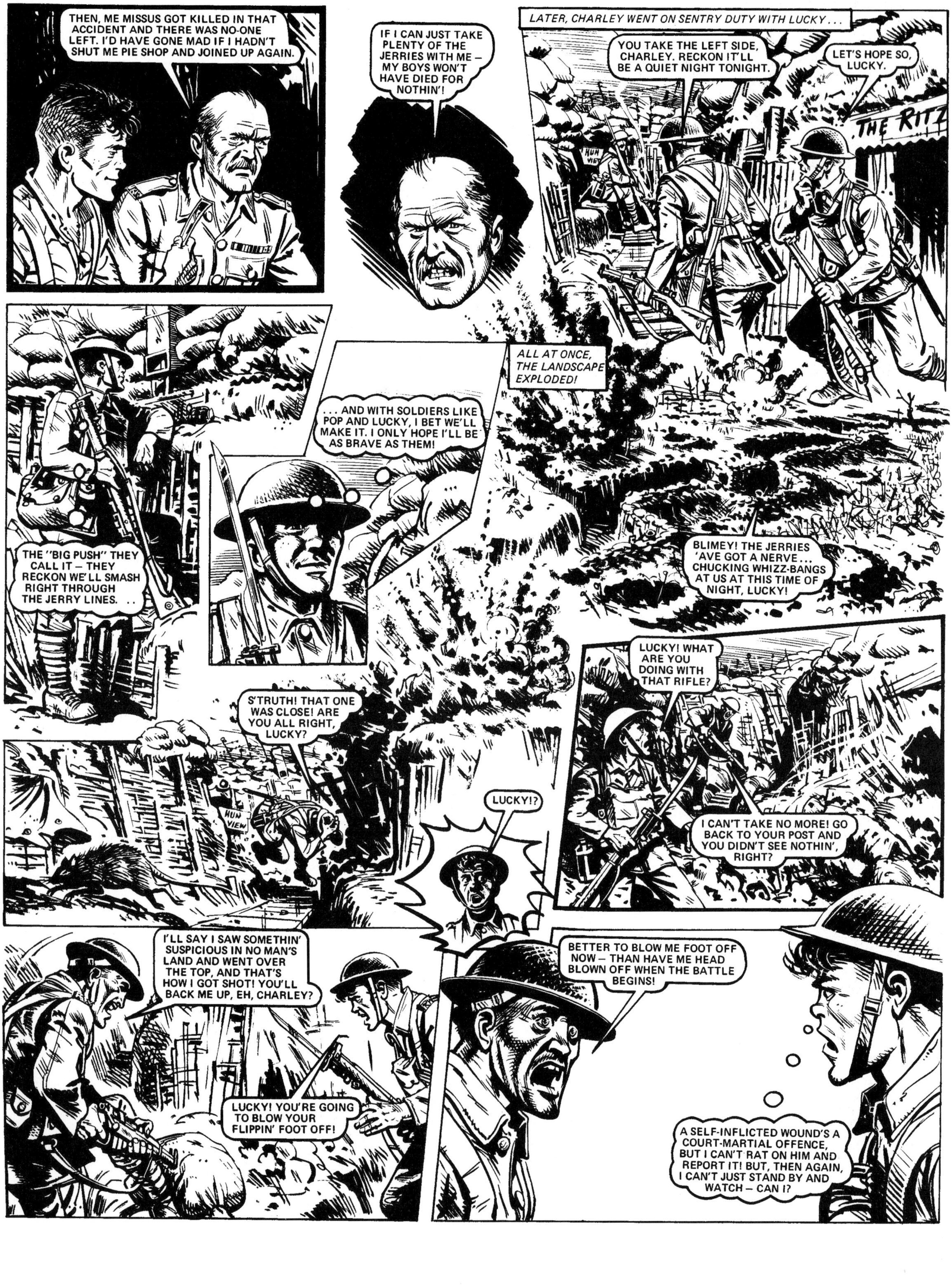
THEN, ME MISSUS GOT KILLED IN THAT ACCIDENT AND THERE WAS NO-ONE LEFT. I'D HAVE GONE MAD IF I HADN'T SHUT ME PIE SHOP AND JOINED UP AGAIN.
IF I CAN JUST TAKE PLENTY OF THE JERRIES WITH ME — MY BOYS WON'T HAVE DIED FOR NOTHIN'!
LATER, CHARLEY WENT ON SENTRY DUTY WITH LUCKY . . .
YOU TAKE THE LEFT SIDE, CHARLEY. RECKON IT'LL BE A QUIET NIGHT TONIGHT.
LET'S HOPE SO, LUCKY.
THE RITZ
THE "BIG PUSH" THEY CALL IT — THEY RECKON WE'LL SMASH RIGHT THROUGH THE JERRY LINES. . .
. . . AND WITH SOLDIERS LIKE POP AND LUCKY, I BET WE'LL MAKE IT. I ONLY HOPE I'LL BE AS BRAVE AS THEM!
ALL AT ONCE, THE LANDSCAPE EXPLODED!
BLIMEY! THE JERRIES 'AVE GOT A NERVE . . . CHUCKING WHIZZ-BANGS AT US AT THIS TIME OF NIGHT, LUCKY!
S'TRUTH! THAT ONE WAS CLOSE! ARE YOU ALL RIGHT, LUCKY?
HUN VIEW
LUCKY!?
LUCKY! WHAT ARE YOU DOING WITH THAT RIFLE?
I CAN'T TAKE NO MORE! GO BACK TO YOUR POST AND YOU DIDN'T SEE NOTHIN', RIGHT?
I'LL SAY I SAW SOMETHIN' SUSPICIOUS IN NO MAN'S LAND AND WENT OVER THE TOP, AND THAT'S HOW I GOT SHOT! YOU'LL BACK ME UP, EH, CHARLEY?
LUCKY! YOU'RE GOING TO BLOW YOUR FLIPPIN' FOOT OFF!
BETTER TO BLOW ME FOOT OFF NOW — THAN HAVE ME HEAD BLOWN OFF WHEN THE BATTLE BEGINS!
A SELF-INFLICTED WOUND'S A COURT-MARTIAL OFFENCE, BUT I CAN'T RAT ON HIM AND REPORT IT! BUT, THEN AGAIN, I CAN'T JUST STAND BY AND WATCH — CAN I?

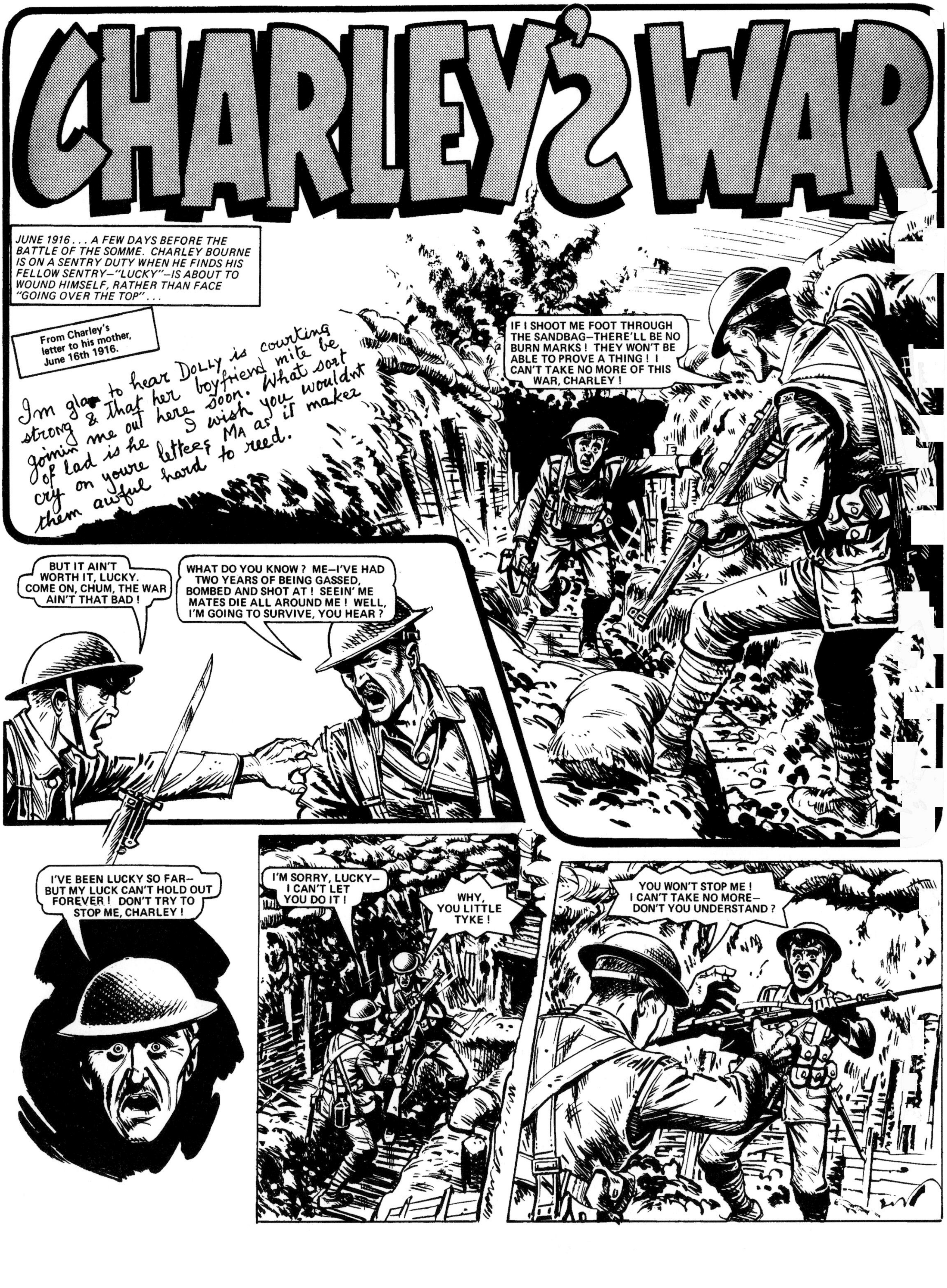
CHARLEY'S WAR
JUNE 1916 . . . A FEW DAYS BEFORE THE BATTLE OF THE SOMME. CHARLEY BOURNE IS ON A SENTRY DUTY WHEN HE FINDS HIS FELLOW SENTRY—"LUCKY"—IS ABOUT TO WOUND HIMSELF, RATHER THAN FACE "GOING OVER THE TOP" . . .
From Charley's letter to his mother, June 16th 1916.
I'm glad to hear Dolly is courting strong & that her boyfriend mite be joinin me out here soon. What sort of lad is he. I wish you wouldnt cry on youre letters Ma as it makes them awful hard to reed.
IF I SHOOT ME FOOT THROUGH THE SANDBAG—THERE'LL BE NO BURN MARKS ! THEY WON'T BE ABLE TO PROVE A THING ! I CAN'T TAKE NO MORE OF THIS WAR, CHARLEY !
BUT IT AIN'T WORTH IT, LUCKY. COME ON, CHUM, THE WAR AIN'T THAT BAD !
WHAT DO YOU KNOW ? ME—I'VE HAD TWO YEARS OF BEING GASSED, BOMBED AND SHOT AT ! SEEIN' ME MATES DIE ALL AROUND ME ! WELL, I'M GOING TO SURVIVE, YOU HEAR ?
I'VE BEEN LUCKY SO FAR—BUT MY LUCK CAN'T HOLD OUT FOREVER ! DON'T TRY TO STOP ME, CHARLEY !
I'M SORRY, LUCKY—I CAN'T LET YOU DO IT !
WHY, YOU LITTLE TYKE !
YOU WON'T STOP ME ! I CAN'T TAKE NO MORE—DON'T YOU UNDERSTAND ?

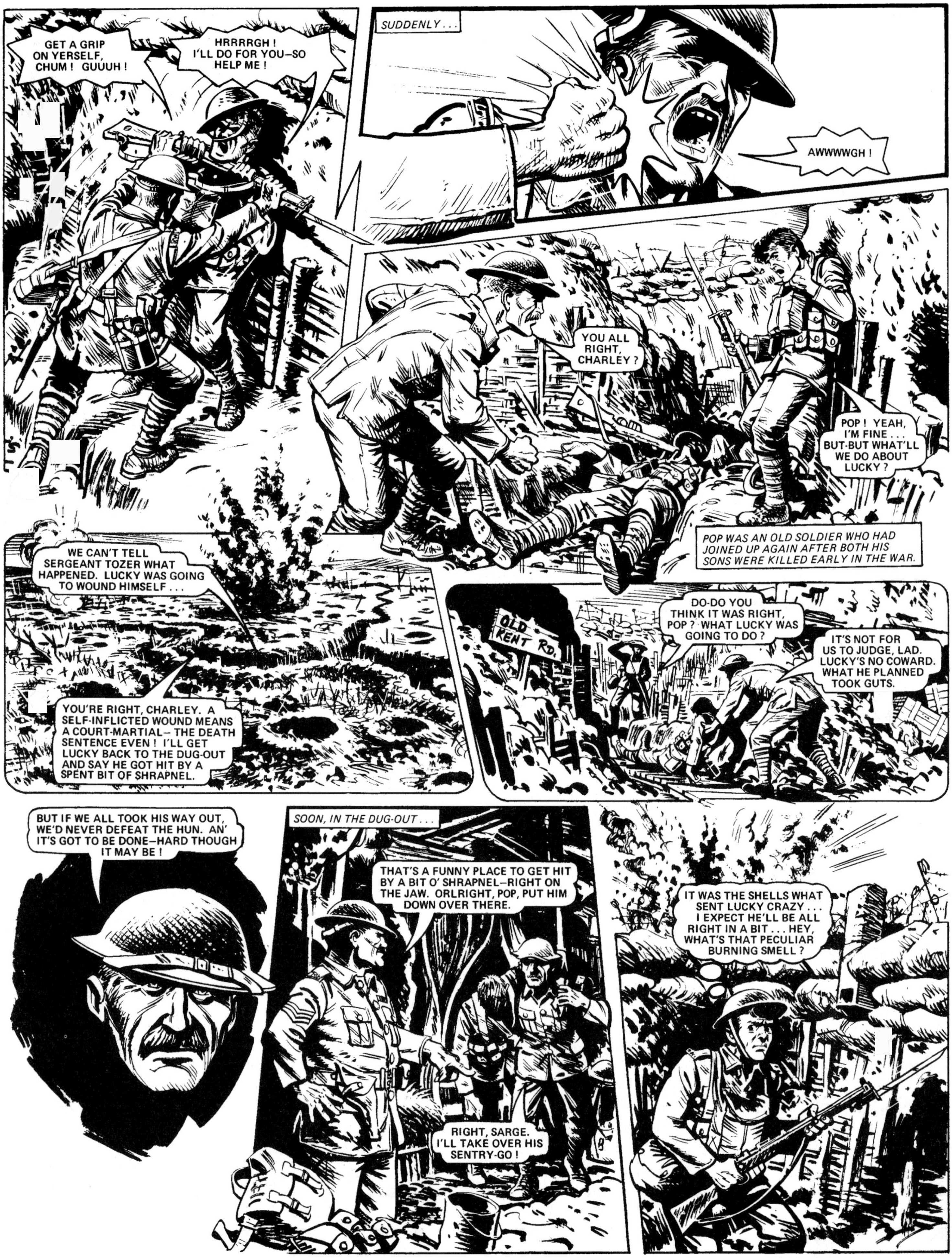
GET A GRIP ON YERSELF, CHUM! GUUUH!
HRRRRGH! I'LL DO FOR YOU—SO HELP ME!
SUDDENLY...
AWWWWGH!
YOU ALL RIGHT, CHARLEY?
POP! YEAH, I'M FINE... BUT-BUT WHAT'LL WE DO ABOUT LUCKY?
POP WAS AN OLD SOLDIER WHO HAD JOINED UP AGAIN AFTER BOTH HIS SONS WERE KILLED EARLY IN THE WAR.
WE CAN'T TELL SERGEANT TOZER WHAT HAPPENED. LUCKY WAS GOING TO WOUND HIMSELF...
YOU'RE RIGHT, CHARLEY. A SELF-INFLICTED WOUND MEANS A COURT-MARTIAL— THE DEATH SENTENCE EVEN! I'LL GET LUCKY BACK TO THE DUG-OUT AND SAY HE GOT HIT BY A SPENT BIT OF SHRAPNEL.
OLD KENT RD.
DO-DO YOU THINK IT WAS RIGHT, POP? WHAT LUCKY WAS GOING TO DO?
IT'S NOT FOR US TO JUDGE, LAD. LUCKY'S NO COWARD. WHAT HE PLANNED TOOK GUTS.
BUT IF WE ALL TOOK HIS WAY OUT, WE'D NEVER DEFEAT THE HUN. AN' IT'S GOT TO BE DONE—HARD THOUGH IT MAY BE!
SOON, IN THE DUG-OUT...
THAT'S A FUNNY PLACE TO GET HIT BY A BIT O' SHRAPNEL—RIGHT ON THE JAW. ORLRIGHT, POP, PUT HIM DOWN OVER THERE.
RIGHT, SARGE. I'LL TAKE OVER HIS SENTRY-GO!
IT WAS THE SHELLS WHAT SENT LUCKY CRAZY... I EXPECT HE'LL BE ALL RIGHT IN A BIT... HEY, WHAT'S THAT PECULIAR BURNING SMELL?

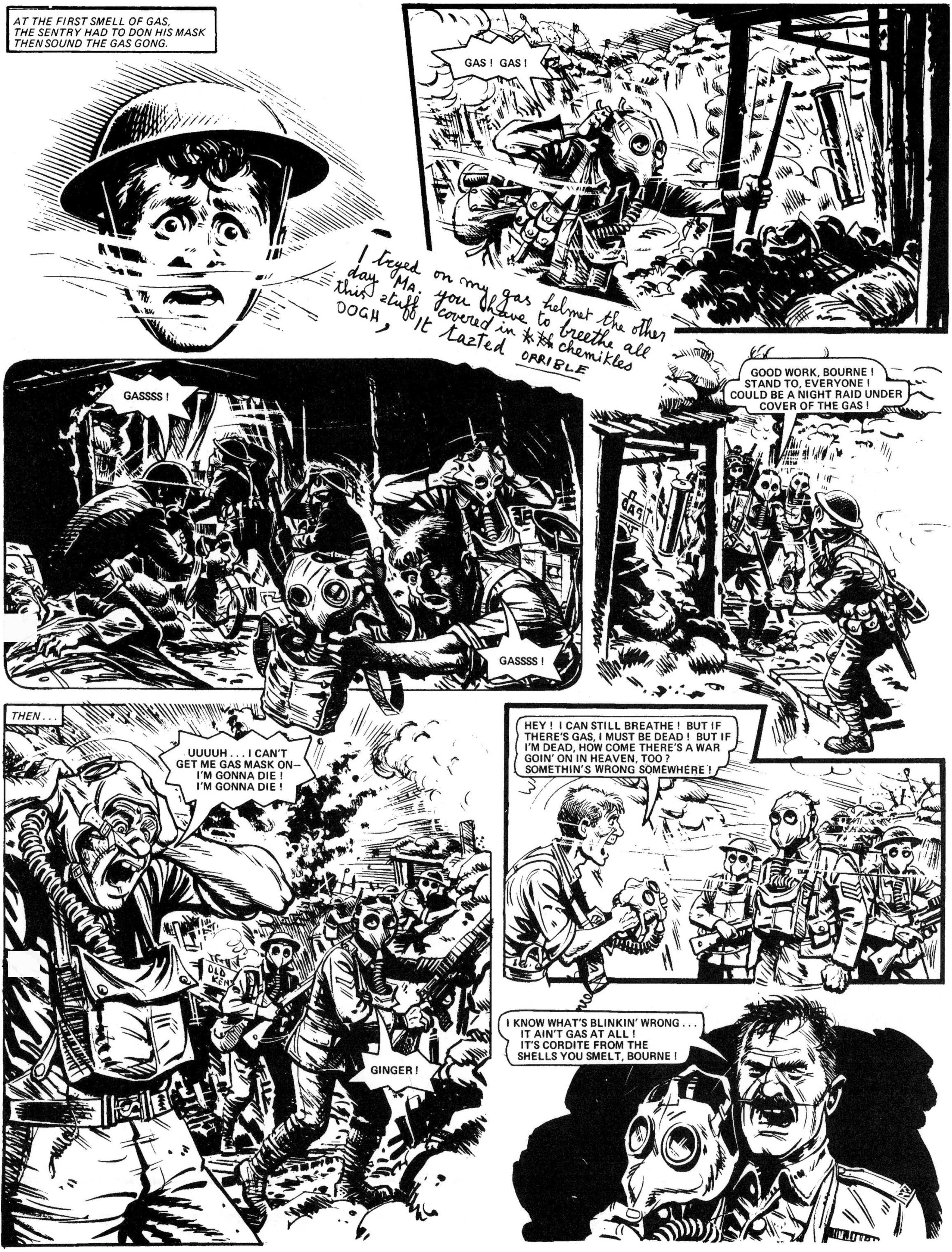
AT THE FIRST SMELL OF GAS, THE SENTRY HAD TO DON HIS MASK THEN SOUND THE GAS GONG.
GAS ! GAS !
I tryed on my gas helmet the other day MA, you have to breethe all this stuff covered in ** chemikles OOGH, It tazted ORRIBLE
GASSSS !
GASSSS !
GOOD WORK, BOURNE ! STAND TO, EVERYONE ! COULD BE A NIGHT RAID UNDER COVER OF THE GAS !
THEN . . .
UUUUH . . . I CAN'T GET ME GAS MASK ON– I'M GONNA DIE ! I'M GONNA DIE !
GINGER !
HEY ! I CAN STILL BREATHE ! BUT IF THERE'S GAS, I MUST BE DEAD ! BUT IF I'M DEAD, HOW COME THERE'S A WAR GOIN' ON IN HEAVEN, TOO ? SOMETHIN'S WRONG SOMEWHERE !
I KNOW WHAT'S BLINKIN' WRONG . . . IT AIN'T GAS AT ALL ! IT'S CORDITE FROM THE SHELLS YOU SMELT, BOURNE !

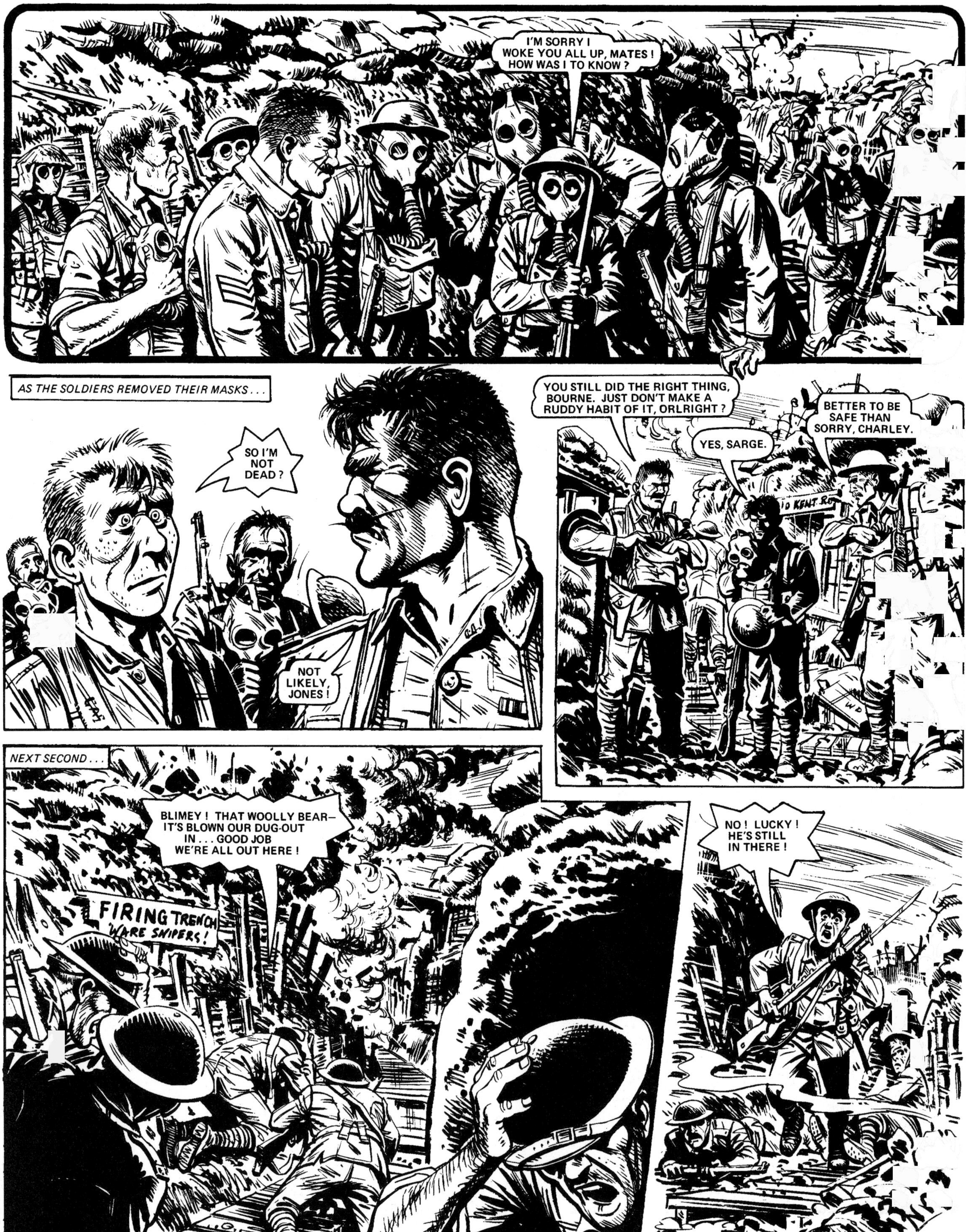
I'M SORRY I WOKE YOU ALL UP, MATES! HOW WAS I TO KNOW?
AS THE SOLDIERS REMOVED THEIR MASKS...
SO I'M NOT DEAD?
NOT LIKELY, JONES!
YOU STILL DID THE RIGHT THING, BOURNE. JUST DON'T MAKE A RUDDY HABIT OF IT, ORLRIGHT?
YES, SARGE.
BETTER TO BE SAFE THAN SORRY, CHARLEY.
NEXT SECOND...
BLIMEY! THAT WOOLLY BEAR— IT'S BLOWN OUR DUG-OUT IN... GOOD JOB WE'RE ALL OUT HERE!
FIRING TRENCH
'WARE SNIPERS!
NO! LUCKY! HE'S STILL IN THERE!

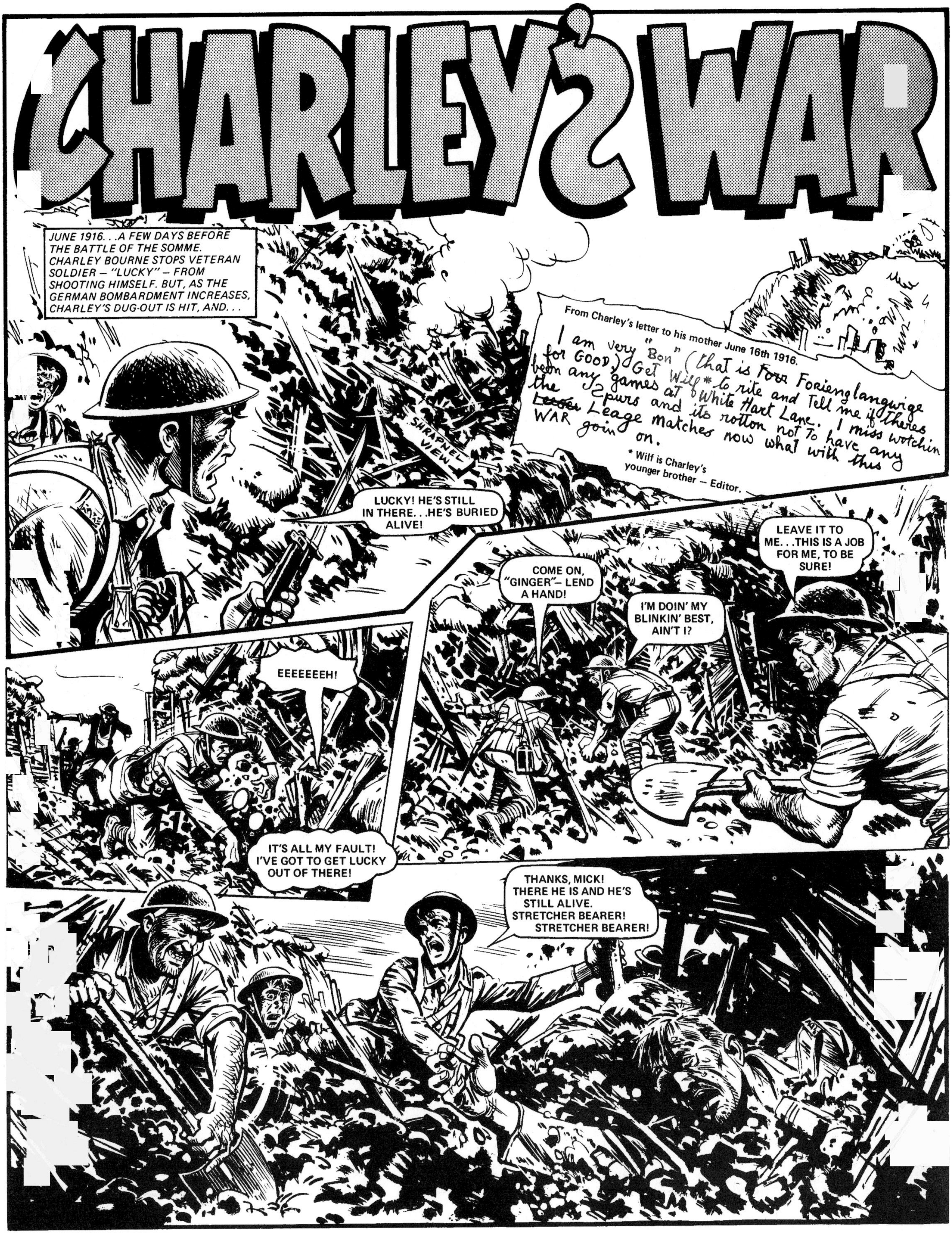
CHARLEY'S WAR
JUNE 1916. . .A FEW DAYS BEFORE THE BATTLE OF THE SOMME. CHARLEY BOURNE STOPS VETERAN SOLDIER – "LUCKY" – FROM SHOOTING HIMSELF. BUT, AS THE GERMAN BOMBARDMENT INCREASES, CHARLEY'S DUG-OUT IS HIT, AND. . .
From Charley's letter to his mother June 16th 1916.
I am very "Bon" (that is Forr Forienglangwige for GOOD) Get Wilf* to rite and Tell me if theres been any games at White Hart Lane. I miss watchin the Spurs and its rotton not to have any Leage matches now what with this WAR goin on.
* Wilf is Charley's younger brother – Editor.
SHRAPNEL VIEW
LUCKY! HE'S STILL IN THERE. . .HE'S BURIED ALIVE!
COME ON, "GINGER"– LEND A HAND!
I'M DOIN' MY BLINKIN' BEST, AIN'T I?
LEAVE IT TO ME. . .THIS IS A JOB FOR ME, TO BE SURE!
EEEEEEEH!
IT'S ALL MY FAULT! I'VE GOT TO GET LUCKY OUT OF THERE!
THANKS, MICK! THERE HE IS AND HE'S STILL ALIVE. STRETCHER BEARER! STRETCHER BEARER!

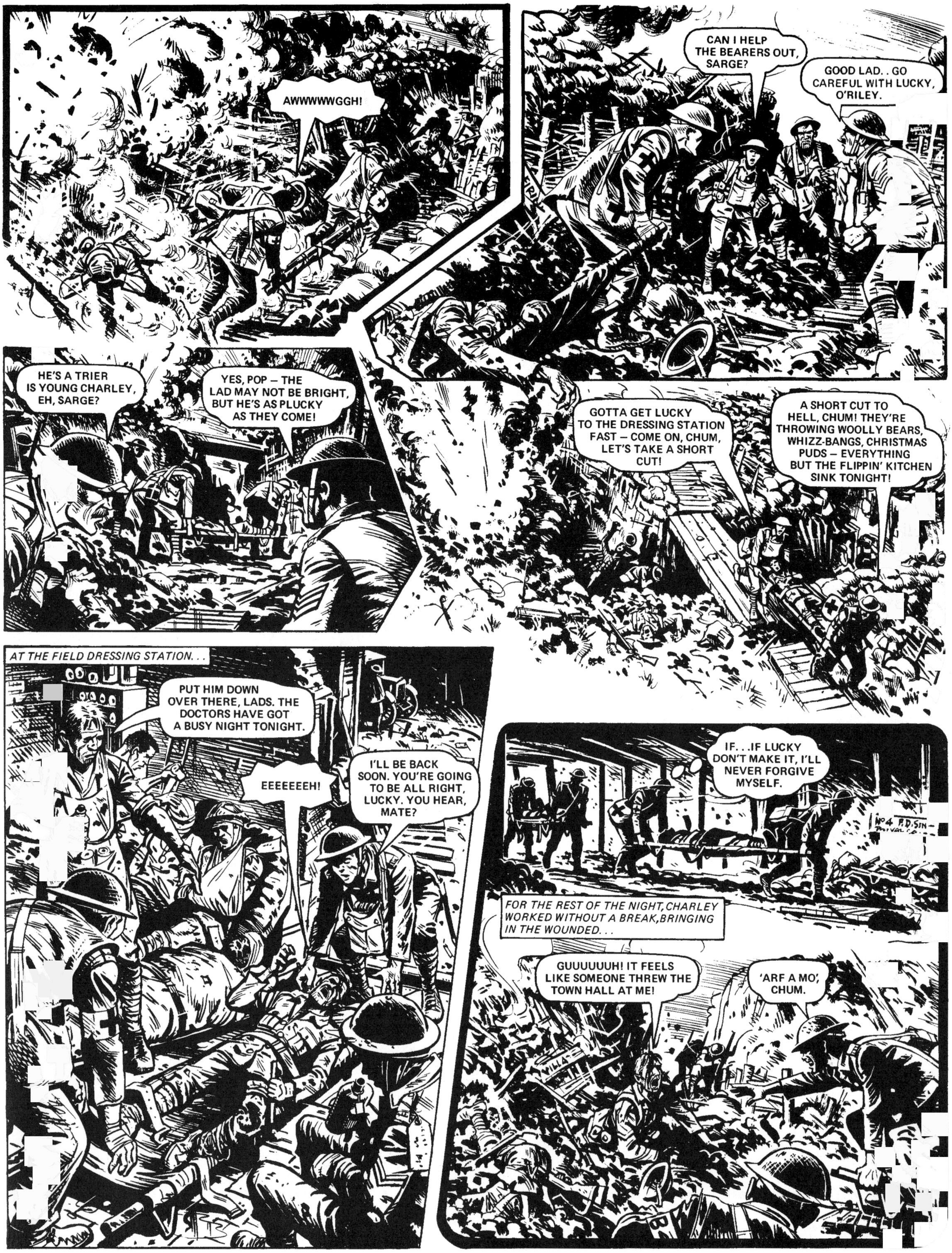
AWWWWWGGH!
CAN I HELP THE BEARERS OUT, SARGE?
GOOD LAD. . GO CAREFUL WITH LUCKY, O'RILEY.
HE'S A TRIER IS YOUNG CHARLEY, EH, SARGE?
YES, POP – THE LAD MAY NOT BE BRIGHT, BUT HE'S AS PLUCKY AS THEY COME!
GOTTA GET LUCKY TO THE DRESSING STATION FAST – COME ON, CHUM, LET'S TAKE A SHORT CUT!
A SHORT CUT TO HELL, CHUM! THEY'RE THROWING WOOLLY BEARS, WHIZZ-BANGS, CHRISTMAS PUDS – EVERYTHING BUT THE FLIPPIN' KITCHEN SINK TONIGHT!
AT THE FIELD DRESSING STATION. . .
PUT HIM DOWN OVER THERE, LADS. THE DOCTORS HAVE GOT A BUSY NIGHT TONIGHT.
EEEEEEEH!
I'LL BE BACK SOON. YOU'RE GOING TO BE ALL RIGHT, LUCKY. YOU HEAR, MATE?
IF. . .IF LUCKY DON'T MAKE IT, I'LL NEVER FORGIVE MYSELF.
FOR THE REST OF THE NIGHT, CHARLEY WORKED WITHOUT A BREAK, BRINGING IN THE WOUNDED. . .
GUUUUUUH! IT FEELS LIKE SOMEONE THREW THE TOWN HALL AT ME!
'ARF A MO', CHUM.

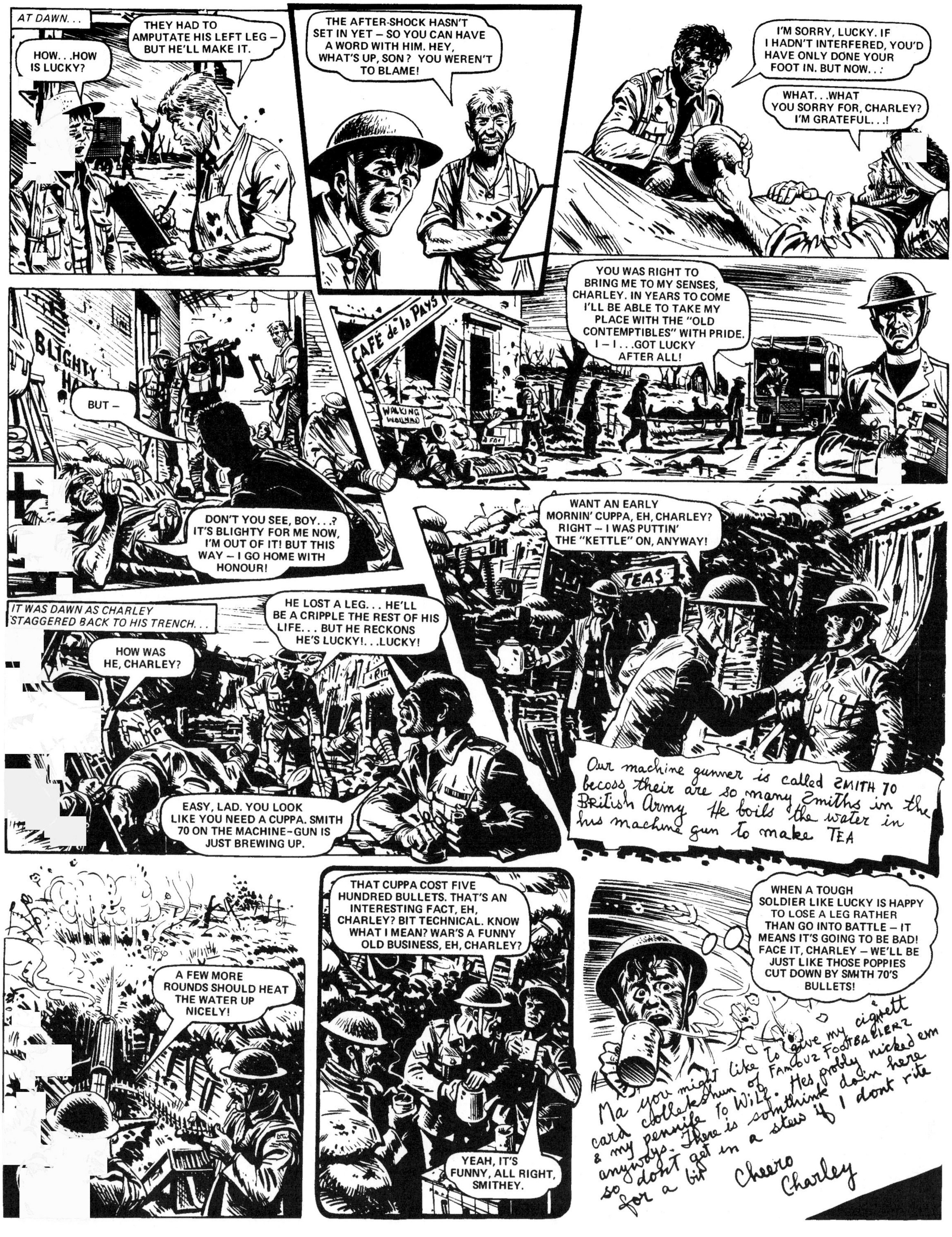
AT DAWN...
HOW...HOW IS LUCKY?
THEY HAD TO AMPUTATE HIS LEFT LEG – BUT HE'LL MAKE IT.
THE AFTER-SHOCK HASN'T SET IN YET – SO YOU CAN HAVE A WORD WITH HIM. HEY, WHAT'S UP, SON? YOU WEREN'T TO BLAME!
I'M SORRY, LUCKY. IF I HADN'T INTERFERED, YOU'D HAVE ONLY DONE YOUR FOOT IN. BUT NOW...:
WHAT...WHAT YOU SORRY FOR, CHARLEY? I'M GRATEFUL...!
BLIGHTY
BUT –
DON'T YOU SEE, BOY...? IT'S BLIGHTY FOR ME NOW, I'M OUT OF IT! BUT THIS WAY – I GO HOME WITH HONOUR!
CAFÉ de la PAYS
WALKING WOUNDED
YOU WAS RIGHT TO BRING ME TO MY SENSES, CHARLEY. IN YEARS TO COME I'LL BE ABLE TO TAKE MY PLACE WITH THE "OLD CONTEMPTIBLES" WITH PRIDE. I – I...GOT LUCKY AFTER ALL!
IT WAS DAWN AS CHARLEY STAGGERED BACK TO HIS TRENCH...
HOW WAS HE, CHARLEY?
HE LOST A LEG... HE'LL BE A CRIPPLE THE REST OF HIS LIFE... BUT HE RECKONS HE'S LUCKY!...LUCKY!
EASY, LAD. YOU LOOK LIKE YOU NEED A CUPPA. SMITH 70 ON THE MACHINE-GUN IS JUST BREWING UP.
WANT AN EARLY MORNIN' CUPPA, EH, CHARLEY? RIGHT – I WAS PUTTIN' THE "KETTLE" ON, ANYWAY!
TEAS
Our machine gunner is called SMITH 70 becoss their are so many Smiths in the British Army He boils the water in his machine gun to make TEA
A FEW MORE ROUNDS SHOULD HEAT THE WATER UP NICELY!
THAT CUPPA COST FIVE HUNDRED BULLETS. THAT'S AN INTERESTING FACT, EH, CHARLEY? BIT TECHNICAL. KNOW WHAT I MEAN? WAR'S A FUNNY OLD BUSINESS, EH, CHARLEY?
YEAH, IT'S FUNNY, ALL RIGHT, SMITHEY.
WHEN A TOUGH SOLDIER LIKE LUCKY IS HAPPY TO LOSE A LEG RATHER THAN GO INTO BATTLE – IT MEANS IT'S GOING TO BE BAD! FACE IT, CHARLEY – WE'LL BE JUST LIKE THOSE POPPIES CUT DOWN BY SMITH 70'S BULLETS!
Ma you might like to give my cigrett card collekshun of FAMOUZ FOOTBALLERZ & my pennife to WILL. Hes probly nicked em anyways. There is somthink doin here so dont get in a stew if I dont rite for a bit
Cheero
Charley

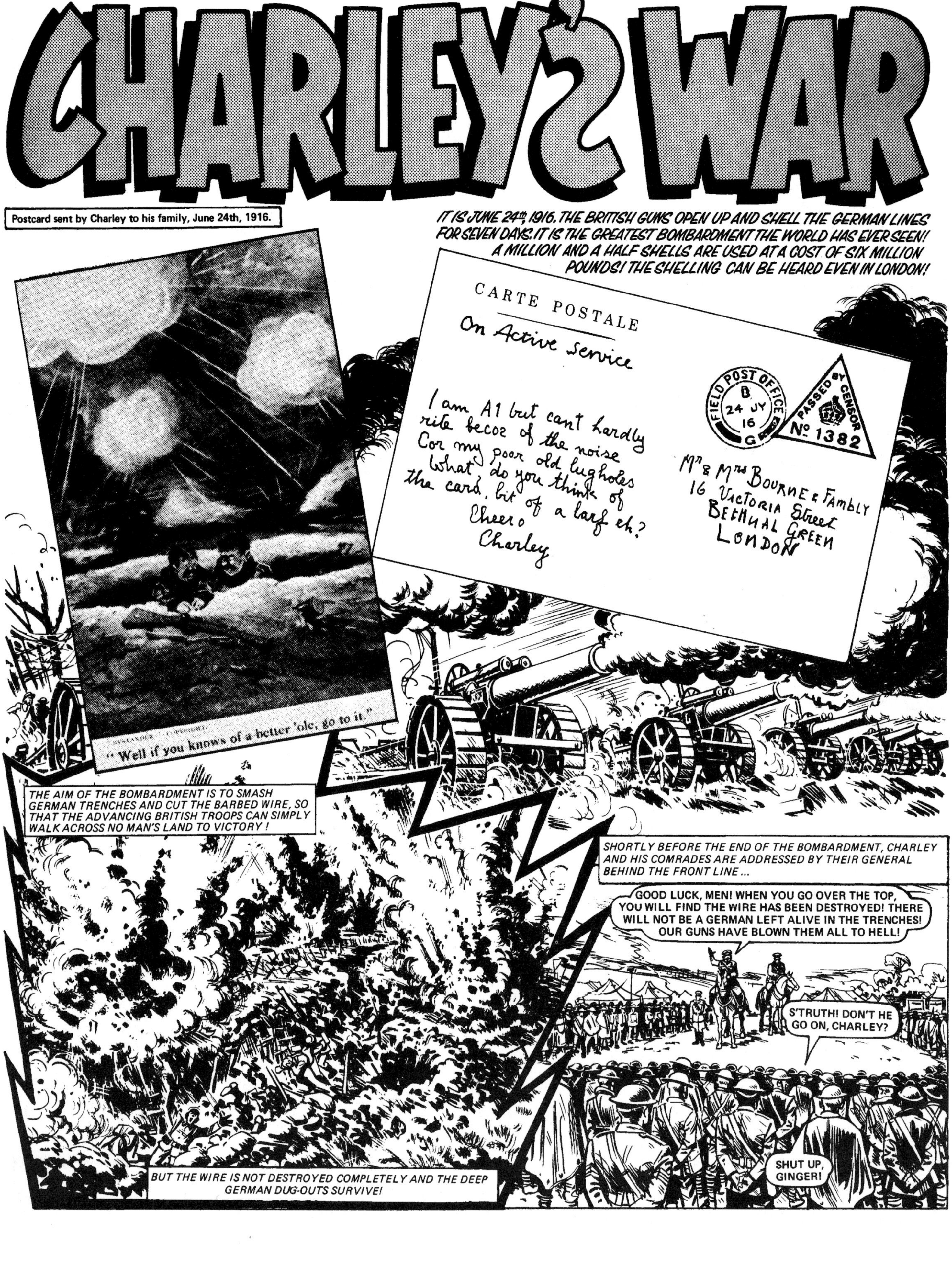
CHARLEY'S WAR
Postcard sent by Charley to his family, June 24th, 1916.
IT IS JUNE 24th 1916. THE BRITISH GUNS OPEN UP AND SHELL THE GERMAN LINES FOR SEVEN DAYS. IT IS THE GREATEST BOMBARDMENT THE WORLD HAS EVER SEEN! A MILLION AND A HALF SHELLS ARE USED AT A COST OF SIX MILLION POUNDS! THE SHELLING CAN BE HEARD EVEN IN LONDON!
" Well if you knows of a better 'ole, go to it."
CARTE POSTALE
On Active service
I am A1 but cant hardly rite becoz of the noise Cor my poor old lugholes What do you think of the card. bit of a larf eh? Cheero Charley
FIELD POST OFFICE B 24 JY 16 G
PASSED BY CENSOR No 1382
Mr & Mrs Bourne & Fambly
16 Victoria Street
Bethnal Green
London
THE AIM OF THE BOMBARDMENT IS TO SMASH GERMAN TRENCHES AND CUT THE BARBED WIRE, SO THAT THE ADVANCING BRITISH TROOPS CAN SIMPLY WALK ACROSS NO MAN'S LAND TO VICTORY!
BUT THE WIRE IS NOT DESTROYED COMPLETELY AND THE DEEP GERMAN DUG-OUTS SURVIVE!
SHORTLY BEFORE THE END OF THE BOMBARDMENT, CHARLEY AND HIS COMRADES ARE ADDRESSED BY THEIR GENERAL BEHIND THE FRONT LINE...
GOOD LUCK, MEN! WHEN YOU GO OVER THE TOP, YOU WILL FIND THE WIRE HAS BEEN DESTROYED! THERE WILL NOT BE A GERMAN LEFT ALIVE IN THE TRENCHES! OUR GUNS HAVE BLOWN THEM ALL TO HELL!
S'TRUTH! DON'T HE GO ON, CHARLEY?
SHUT UP, GINGER!

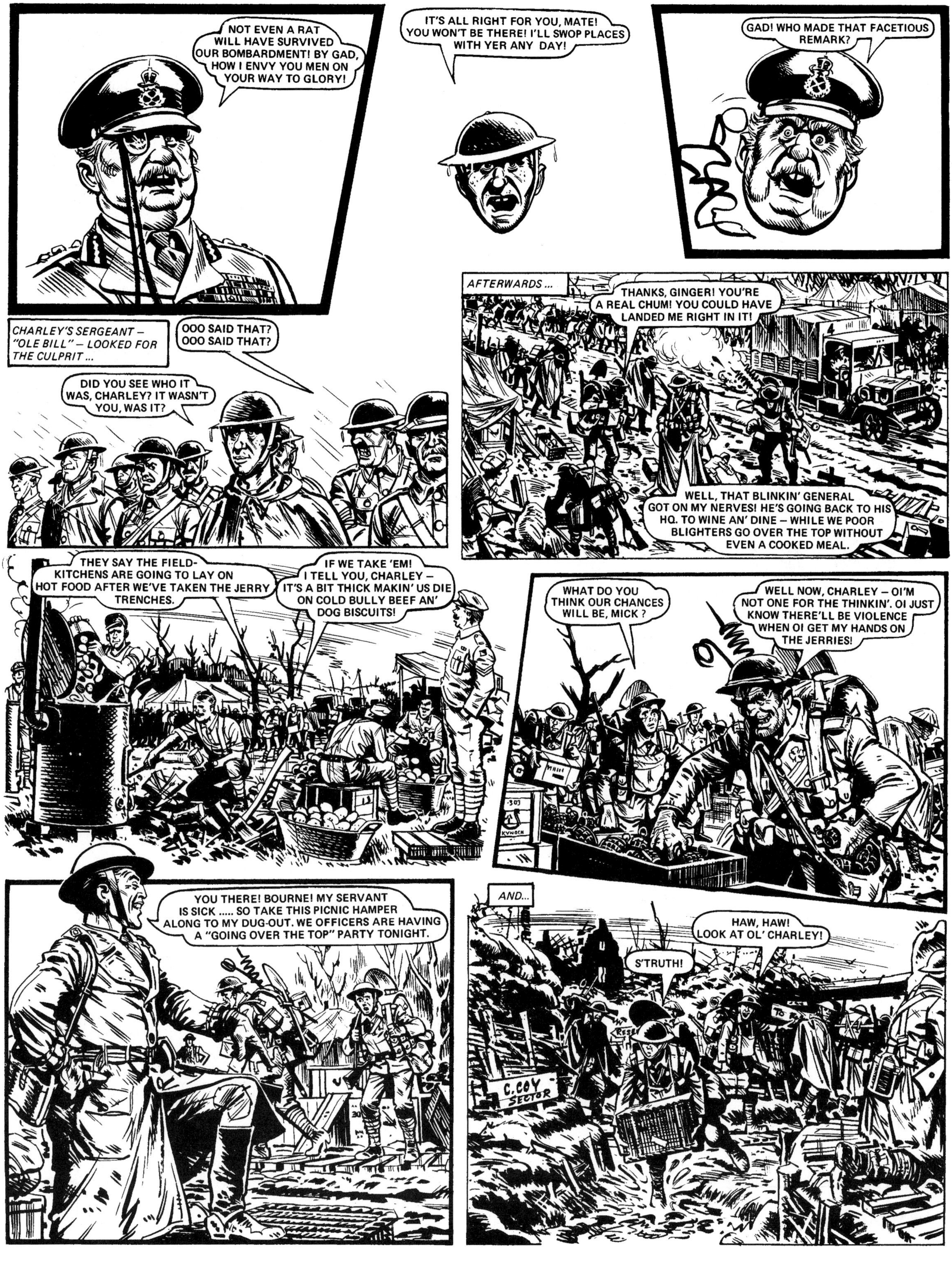
NOT EVEN A RAT WILL HAVE SURVIVED OUR BOMBARDMENT! BY GAD, HOW I ENVY YOU MEN ON YOUR WAY TO GLORY!
IT'S ALL RIGHT FOR YOU, MATE! YOU WON'T BE THERE! I'LL SWOP PLACES WITH YER ANY DAY!
GAD! WHO MADE THAT FACETIOUS REMARK?
CHARLEY'S SERGEANT – "OLE BILL" – LOOKED FOR THE CULPRIT ...
OOO SAID THAT? OOO SAID THAT?
DID YOU SEE WHO IT WAS, CHARLEY? IT WASN'T YOU, WAS IT?
AFTERWARDS ...
THANKS, GINGER! YOU'RE A REAL CHUM! YOU COULD HAVE LANDED ME RIGHT IN IT!
WELL, THAT BLINKIN' GENERAL GOT ON MY NERVES! HE'S GOING BACK TO HIS HQ. TO WINE AN' DINE – WHILE WE POOR BLIGHTERS GO OVER THE TOP WITHOUT EVEN A COOKED MEAL.
THEY SAY THE FIELD-KITCHENS ARE GOING TO LAY ON HOT FOOD AFTER WE'VE TAKEN THE JERRY TRENCHES.
IF WE TAKE 'EM! I TELL YOU, CHARLEY – IT'S A BIT THICK MAKIN' US DIE ON COLD BULLY BEEF AN' DOG BISCUITS!
WHAT DO YOU THINK OUR CHANCES WILL BE, MICK ?
WELL NOW, CHARLEY – OI'M NOT ONE FOR THE THINKIN'. OI JUST KNOW THERE'LL BE VIOLENCE WHEN OI GET MY HANDS ON THE JERRIES!
KYNOCH
YOU THERE! BOURNE! MY SERVANT IS SICK ..... SO TAKE THIS PICNIC HAMPER ALONG TO MY DUG-OUT. WE OFFICERS ARE HAVING A "GOING OVER THE TOP" PARTY TONIGHT.
AND...
HAW, HAW! LOOK AT OL' CHARLEY!
S'TRUTH!
C. COY SECTOR

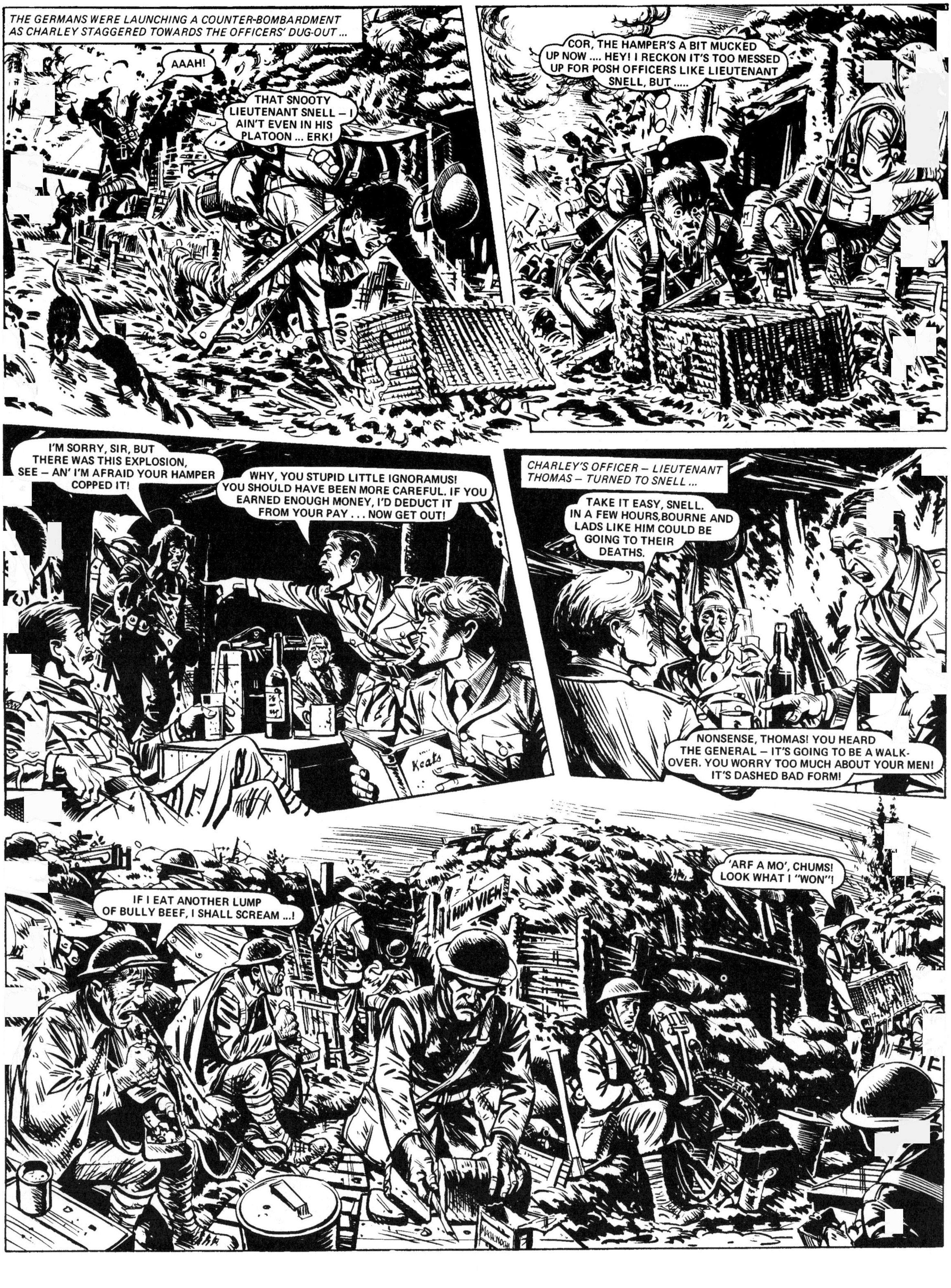
THE GERMANS WERE LAUNCHING A COUNTER-BOMBARDMENT AS CHARLEY STAGGERED TOWARDS THE OFFICERS' DUG-OUT ...
AAAH!
THAT SNOOTY LIEUTENANT SNELL – I AIN'T EVEN IN HIS PLATOON ... ERK!
COR, THE HAMPER'S A BIT MUCKED UP NOW .... HEY! I RECKON IT'S TOO MESSED UP FOR POSH OFFICERS LIKE LIEUTENANT SNELL, BUT .....
I'M SORRY, SIR, BUT THERE WAS THIS EXPLOSION, SEE – AN' I'M AFRAID YOUR HAMPER COPPED IT!
WHY, YOU STUPID LITTLE IGNORAMUS! YOU SHOULD HAVE BEEN MORE CAREFUL. IF YOU EARNED ENOUGH MONEY, I'D DEDUCT IT FROM YOUR PAY . . . NOW GET OUT!
Keats
CHARLEY'S OFFICER – LIEUTENANT THOMAS – TURNED TO SNELL ...
TAKE IT EASY, SNELL. IN A FEW HOURS,BOURNE AND LADS LIKE HIM COULD BE GOING TO THEIR DEATHS.
NONSENSE, THOMAS! YOU HEARD THE GENERAL – IT'S GOING TO BE A WALK-OVER. YOU WORRY TOO MUCH ABOUT YOUR MEN! IT'S DASHED BAD FORM!
IF I EAT ANOTHER LUMP OF BULLY BEEF, I SHALL SCREAM ...!
HUN VIEW
'ARF A MO', CHUMS! LOOK WHAT I "WON"!

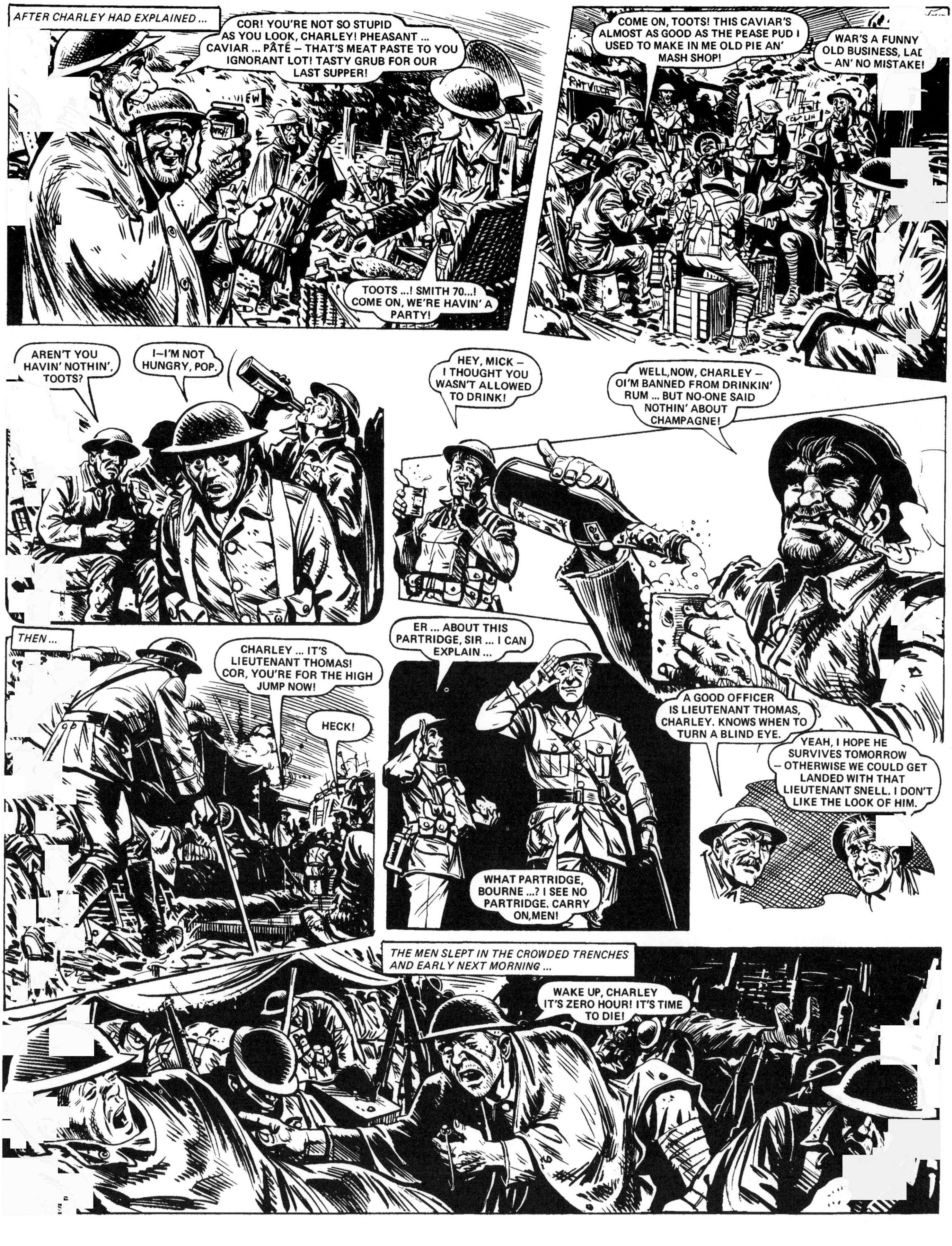
AFTER CHARLEY HAD EXPLAINED ...
COR! YOU'RE NOT SO STUPID AS YOU LOOK, CHARLEY! PHEASANT ... CAVIAR ... PÂTÉ – THAT'S MEAT PASTE TO YOU IGNORANT LOT! TASTY GRUB FOR OUR LAST SUPPER!
TOOTS ...! SMITH 70...! COME ON, WE'RE HAVIN' A PARTY!
COME ON, TOOTS! THIS CAVIAR'S ALMOST AS GOOD AS THE PEASE PUD I USED TO MAKE IN ME OLD PIE AN' MASH SHOP!
WAR'S A FUNNY OLD BUSINESS, LAD – AN' NO MISTAKE!
AREN'T YOU HAVIN' NOTHIN', TOOTS?
I–I'M NOT HUNGRY, POP.
HEY, MICK – I THOUGHT YOU WASN'T ALLOWED TO DRINK!
WELL,NOW, CHARLEY – OI'M BANNED FROM DRINKIN' RUM ... BUT NO-ONE SAID NOTHIN' ABOUT CHAMPAGNE!
THEN ...
CHARLEY ... IT'S LIEUTENANT THOMAS! COR, YOU'RE FOR THE HIGH JUMP NOW!
HECK!
ER ... ABOUT THIS PARTRIDGE, SIR ... I CAN EXPLAIN ...
WHAT PARTRIDGE, BOURNE ...? I SEE NO PARTRIDGE. CARRY ON,MEN!
A GOOD OFFICER IS LIEUTENANT THOMAS, CHARLEY. KNOWS WHEN TO TURN A BLIND EYE.
YEAH, I HOPE HE SURVIVES TOMORROW – OTHERWISE WE COULD GET LANDED WITH THAT LIEUTENANT SNELL. I DON'T LIKE THE LOOK OF HIM.
THE MEN SLEPT IN THE CROWDED TRENCHES AND EARLY NEXT MORNING ...
WAKE UP, CHARLEY IT'S ZERO HOUR! IT'S TIME TO DIE!

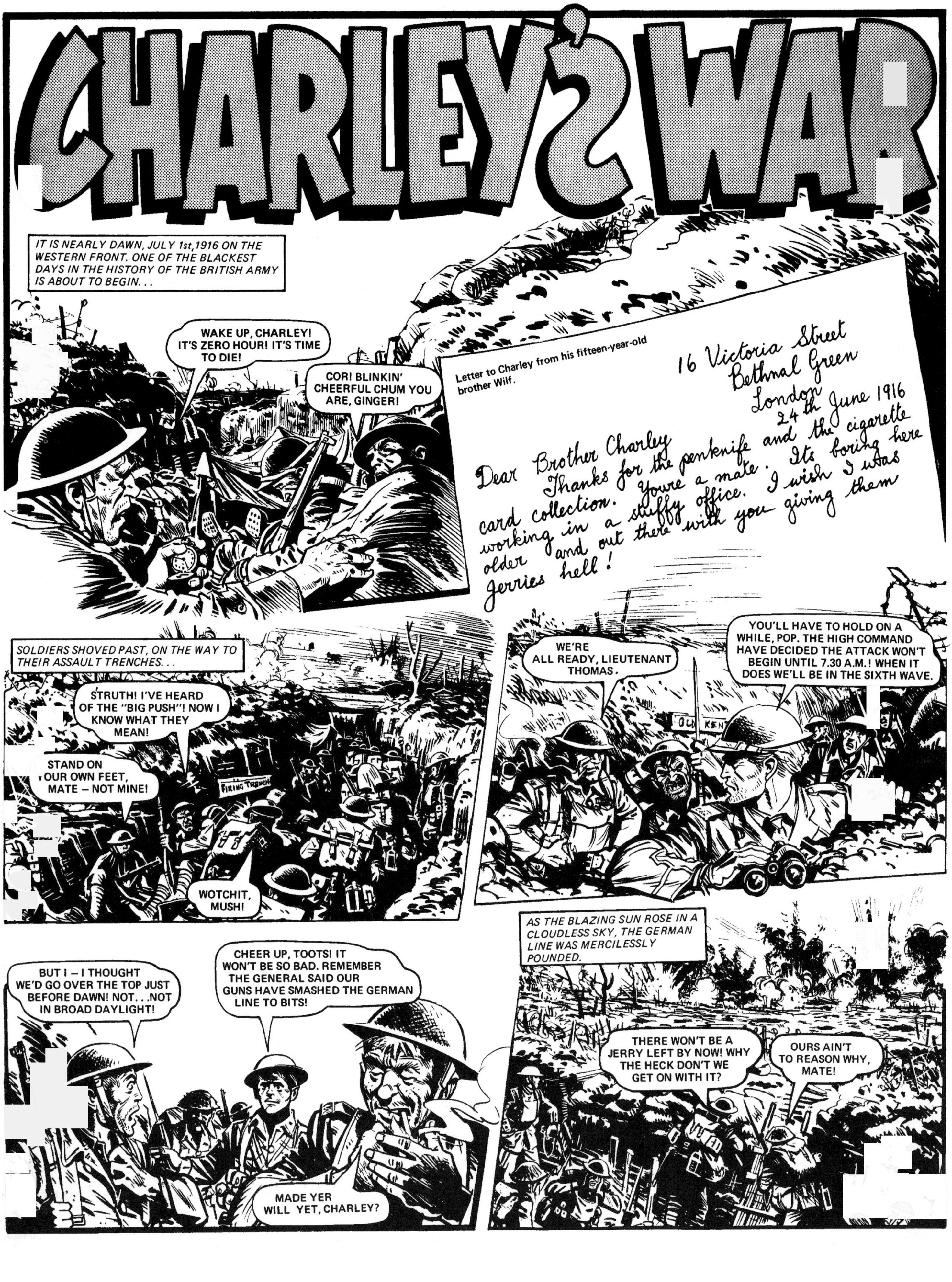
CHARLEY'S WAR
IT IS NEARLY DAWN, JULY 1st,1916 ON THE WESTERN FRONT. ONE OF THE BLACKEST DAYS IN THE HISTORY OF THE BRITISH ARMY IS ABOUT TO BEGIN. . .
WAKE UP, CHARLEY! IT'S ZERO HOUR! IT'S TIME TO DIE!
COR! BLINKIN' CHEERFUL CHUM YOU ARE, GINGER!
Letter to Charley from his fifteen-year-old brother Wilf.
16 Victoria Street
Bethnal Green
London
24 th June 1916
Dear Brother Charley
Thanks for the penknife and the cigarette card collection. Youre a mate. Its boring here working in a stuffy office. I wish I was older and out there with you giving them Jerries hell!
SOLDIERS SHOVED PAST, ON THE WAY TO THEIR ASSAULT TRENCHES. . .
STRUTH! I'VE HEARD OF THE "BIG PUSH"! NOW I KNOW WHAT THEY MEAN!
STAND ON YOUR OWN FEET, MATE – NOT MINE!
FIRING TRENCH
WOTCHIT, MUSH!
WE'RE ALL READY, LIEUTENANT THOMAS.
YOU'LL HAVE TO HOLD ON A WHILE, POP. THE HIGH COMMAND HAVE DECIDED THE ATTACK WON'T BEGIN UNTIL 7.30 A.M.! WHEN IT DOES WE'LL BE IN THE SIXTH WAVE.
BUT I – I THOUGHT WE'D GO OVER THE TOP JUST BEFORE DAWN! NOT. . .NOT IN BROAD DAYLIGHT!
CHEER UP, TOOTS! IT WON'T BE SO BAD. REMEMBER THE GENERAL SAID OUR GUNS HAVE SMASHED THE GERMAN LINE TO BITS!
MADE YER WILL YET, CHARLEY?
AS THE BLAZING SUN ROSE IN A CLOUDLESS SKY, THE GERMAN LINE WAS MERCILESSLY POUNDED.
THERE WON'T BE A JERRY LEFT BY NOW! WHY THE HECK DON'T WE GET ON WITH IT?
OURS AIN'T TO REASON WHY, MATE!

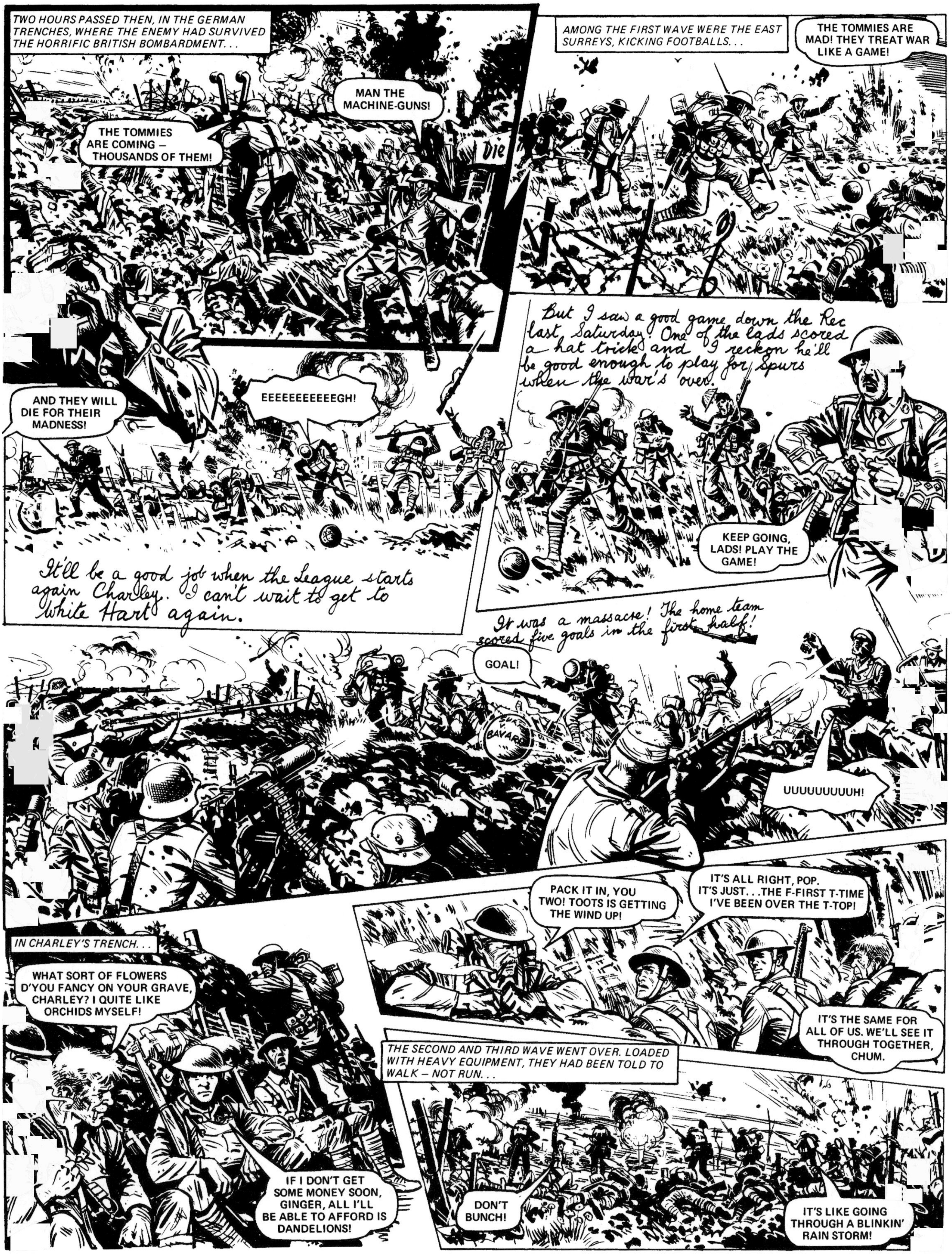

TWO HOURS PASSED THEN, IN THE GERMAN TRENCHES, WHERE THE ENEMY HAD SURVIVED THE HORRIFIC BRITISH BOMBARDMENT...
THE TOMMIES ARE COMING – THOUSANDS OF THEM!
MAN THE MACHINE-GUNS!
AMONG THE FIRST WAVE WERE THE EAST SURREYS, KICKING FOOTBALLS...
THE TOMMIES ARE MAD! THEY TREAT WAR LIKE A GAME!
AND THEY WILL DIE FOR THEIR MADNESS!
EEEEEEEEEEEGH!
It'll be a good job when the League starts again Charley. I can't wait to get to White Hart again.
But I saw a good game down the Rec last Saturday. One of the lads scored a hat trick and I reckon he'll be good enough to play for Spurs when the War's over.
KEEP GOING, LADS! PLAY THE GAME!
It was a massacre! The home team scored five goals in the first half!
GOAL!
UUUUUUUUUH!
IN CHARLEY'S TRENCH...
WHAT SORT OF FLOWERS D'YOU FANCY ON YOUR GRAVE, CHARLEY? I QUITE LIKE ORCHIDS MYSELF!
IF I DON'T GET SOME MONEY SOON, GINGER, ALL I'LL BE ABLE TO AFFORD IS DANDELIONS!
PACK IT IN, YOU TWO! TOOTS IS GETTING THE WIND UP!
IT'S ALL RIGHT, POP. IT'S JUST...THE F-FIRST T-TIME I'VE BEEN OVER THE T-TOP!
IT'S THE SAME FOR ALL OF US. WE'LL SEE IT THROUGH TOGETHER, CHUM.
THE SECOND AND THIRD WAVE WENT OVER. LOADED WITH HEAVY EQUIPMENT, THEY HAD BEEN TOLD TO WALK – NOT RUN...
DON'T BUNCH!
IT'S LIKE GOING THROUGH A BLINKIN' RAIN STORM!

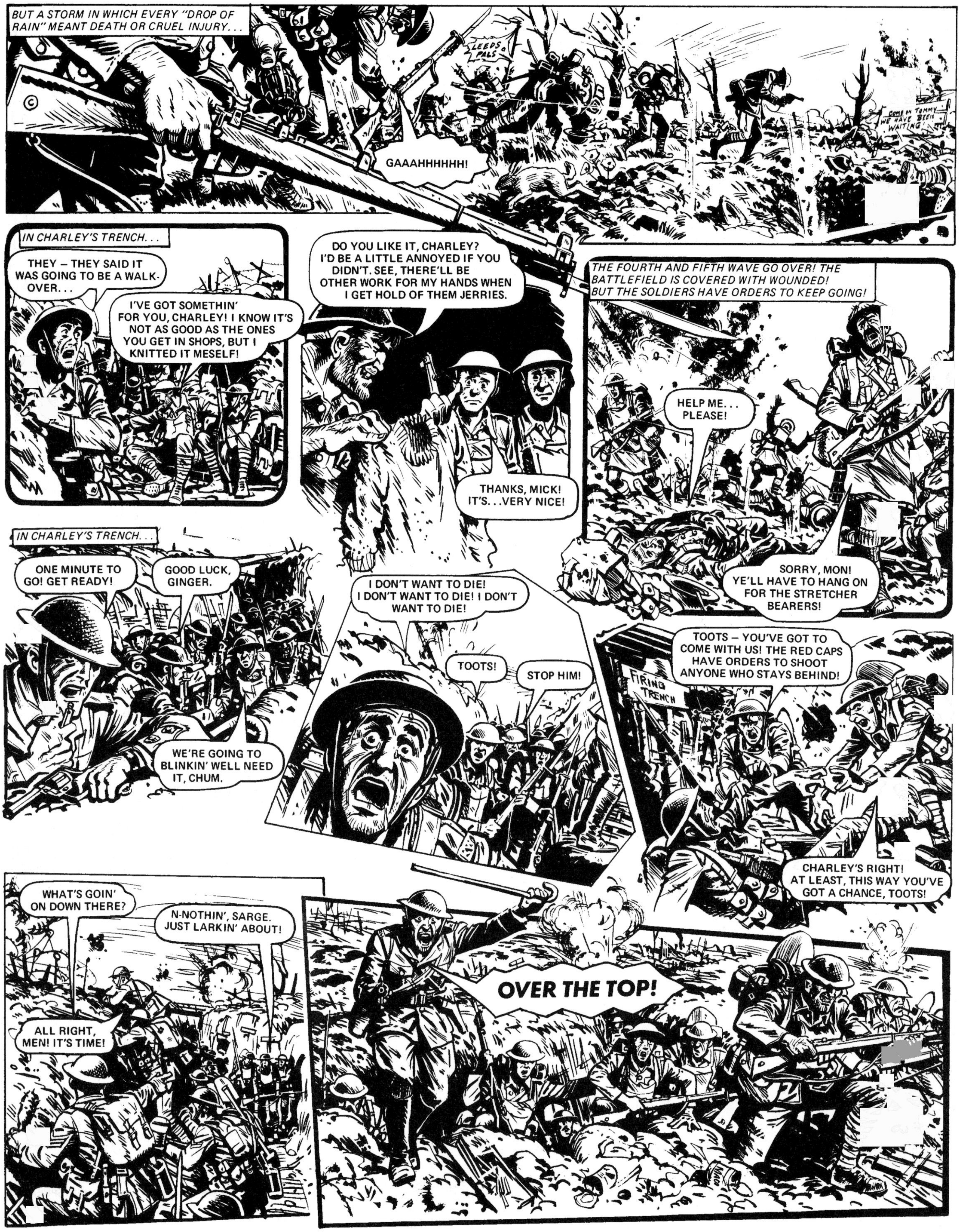

BUT A STORM IN WHICH EVERY "DROP OF RAIN" MEANT DEATH OR CRUEL INJURY...
LEEDS PALS
COME ON TOMMY WE HAVE BEEN WAITING
GAAAHHHHHH!
IN CHARLEY'S TRENCH...
THEY – THEY SAID IT WAS GOING TO BE A WALK-OVER...
I'VE GOT SOMETHIN' FOR YOU, CHARLEY! I KNOW IT'S NOT AS GOOD AS THE ONES YOU GET IN SHOPS, BUT I KNITTED IT MESELF!
DO YOU LIKE IT, CHARLEY? I'D BE A LITTLE ANNOYED IF YOU DIDN'T. SEE, THERE'LL BE OTHER WORK FOR MY HANDS WHEN I GET HOLD OF THEM JERRIES.
THANKS, MICK! IT'S...VERY NICE!
THE FOURTH AND FIFTH WAVE GO OVER! THE BATTLEFIELD IS COVERED WITH WOUNDED! BUT THE SOLDIERS HAVE ORDERS TO KEEP GOING!
HELP ME... PLEASE!
SORRY, MON! YE'LL HAVE TO HANG ON FOR THE STRETCHER BEARERS!
IN CHARLEY'S TRENCH...
ONE MINUTE TO GO! GET READY!
GOOD LUCK, GINGER.
WE'RE GOING TO BLINKIN' WELL NEED IT, CHUM.
I DON'T WANT TO DIE! I DON'T WANT TO DIE! I DON'T WANT TO DIE!
TOOTS!
STOP HIM!
FIRING TRENCH
TOOTS – YOU'VE GOT TO COME WITH US! THE RED CAPS HAVE ORDERS TO SHOOT ANYONE WHO STAYS BEHIND!
CHARLEY'S RIGHT! AT LEAST, THIS WAY YOU'VE GOT A CHANCE, TOOTS!
WHAT'S GOIN' ON DOWN THERE?
N-NOTHIN', SARGE. JUST LARKIN' ABOUT!
ALL RIGHT, MEN! IT'S TIME!
OVER THE TOP!

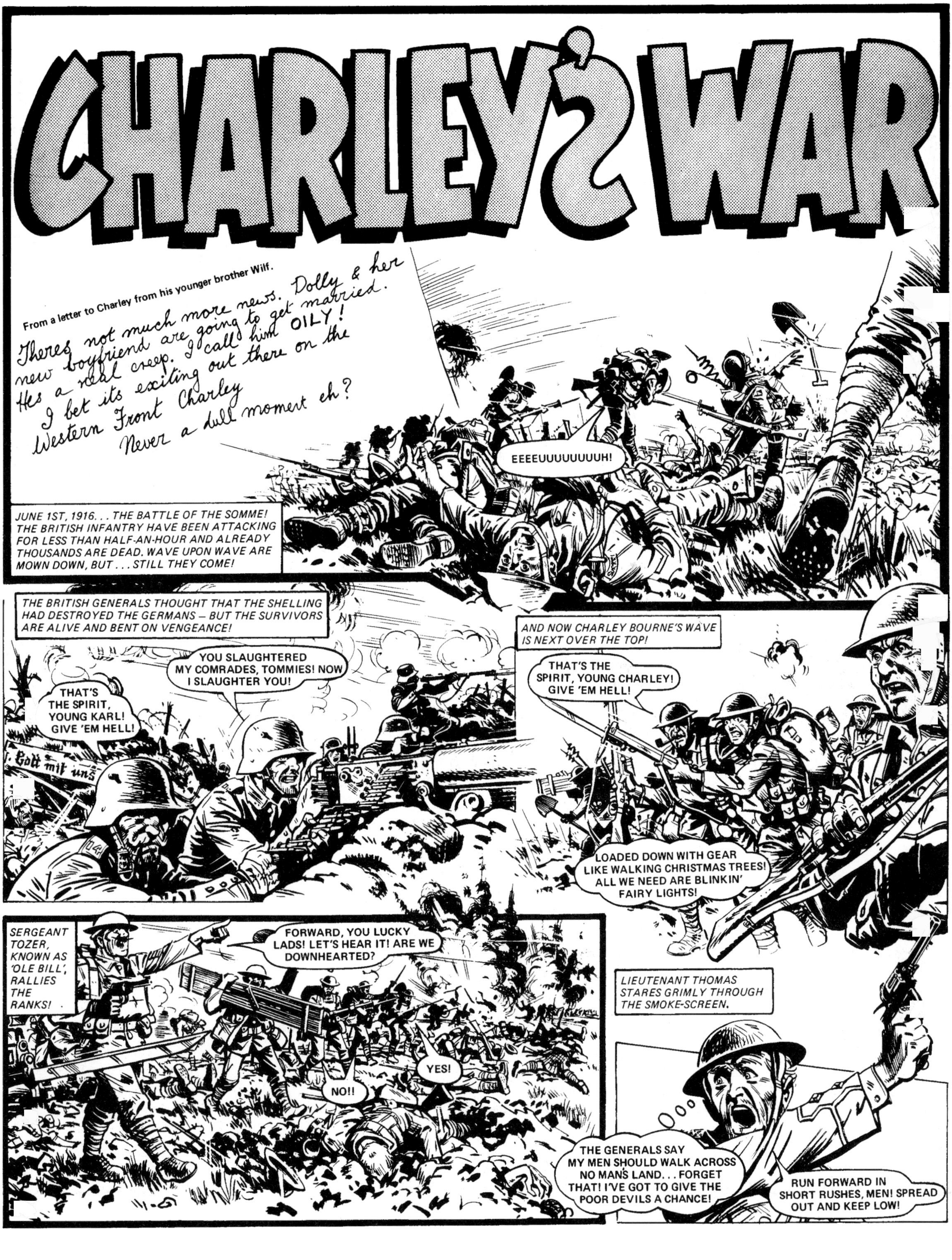
CHARLEY'S WAR
From a letter to Charley from his younger brother Wilf.
Theres not much more news. Dolly & her new boyfriend are going to get married. Hes a real creep. I call him OILY! I bet its exciting out there on the Western Front Charley Never a dull moment eh?
EEEEUUUUUUUUH!
JUNE 1ST, 1916... THE BATTLE OF THE SOMME! THE BRITISH INFANTRY HAVE BEEN ATTACKING FOR LESS THAN HALF-AN-HOUR AND ALREADY THOUSANDS ARE DEAD. WAVE UPON WAVE ARE MOWN DOWN, BUT... STILL THEY COME!
THE BRITISH GENERALS THOUGHT THAT THE SHELLING HAD DESTROYED THE GERMANS – BUT THE SURVIVORS ARE ALIVE AND BENT ON VENGEANCE!
YOU SLAUGHTERED MY COMRADES, TOMMIES! NOW I SLAUGHTER YOU!
THAT'S THE SPIRIT, YOUNG KARL! GIVE 'EM HELL!
Gott mit uns
AND NOW CHARLEY BOURNE'S WAVE IS NEXT OVER THE TOP!
THAT'S THE SPIRIT, YOUNG CHARLEY! GIVE 'EM HELL!
LOADED DOWN WITH GEAR LIKE WALKING CHRISTMAS TREES! ALL WE NEED ARE BLINKIN' FAIRY LIGHTS!
SERGEANT TOZER, KNOWN AS 'OLE BILL', RALLIES THE RANKS!
FORWARD, YOU LUCKY LADS! LET'S HEAR IT! ARE WE DOWNHEARTED?
YES!
NO!!
LIEUTENANT THOMAS STARES GRIMLY THROUGH THE SMOKE-SCREEN.
THE GENERALS SAY MY MEN SHOULD WALK ACROSS NO MAN'S LAND... FORGET THAT! I'VE GOT TO GIVE THE POOR DEVILS A CHANCE!
RUN FORWARD IN SHORT RUSHES, MEN! SPREAD OUT AND KEEP LOW!

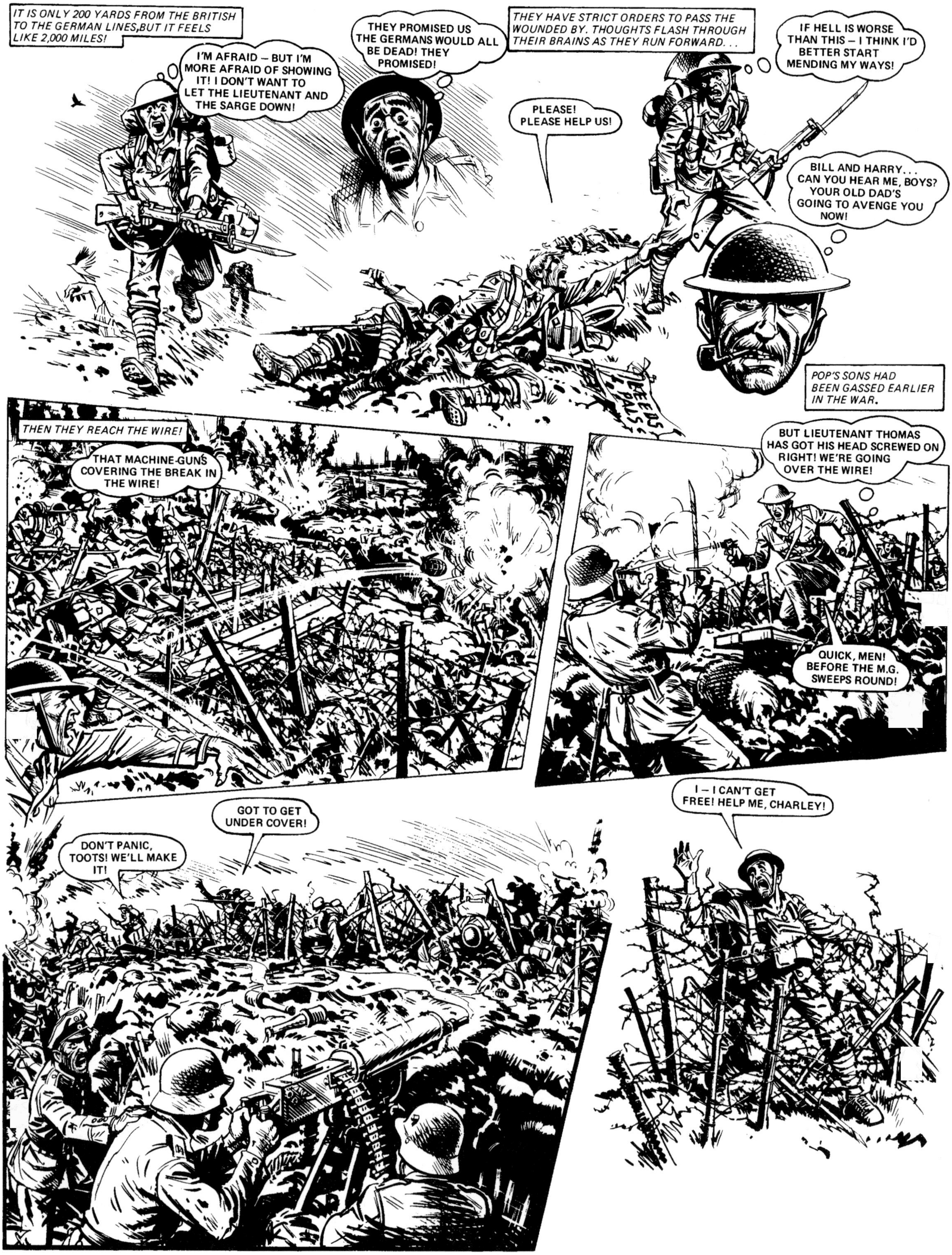

IT IS ONLY 200 YARDS FROM THE BRITISH TO THE GERMAN LINES,BUT IT FEELS LIKE 2,000 MILES!
I'M AFRAID – BUT I'M MORE AFRAID OF SHOWING IT! I DON'T WANT TO LET THE LIEUTENANT AND THE SARGE DOWN!
THEY PROMISED US THE GERMANS WOULD ALL BE DEAD! THEY PROMISED!
THEY HAVE STRICT ORDERS TO PASS THE WOUNDED BY. THOUGHTS FLASH THROUGH THEIR BRAINS AS THEY RUN FORWARD...
PLEASE! PLEASE HELP US!
IF HELL IS WORSE THAN THIS – I THINK I'D BETTER START MENDING MY WAYS!
BILL AND HARRY... CAN YOU HEAR ME, BOYS? YOUR OLD DAD'S GOING TO AVENGE YOU NOW!
POP'S SONS HAD BEEN GASSED EARLIER IN THE WAR.
THEN THEY REACH THE WIRE!
THAT MACHINE-GUN'S COVERING THE BREAK IN THE WIRE!
BUT LIEUTENANT THOMAS HAS GOT HIS HEAD SCREWED ON RIGHT! WE'RE GOING OVER THE WIRE!
QUICK, MEN! BEFORE THE M.G. SWEEPS ROUND!
DON'T PANIC, TOOTS! WE'LL MAKE IT!
GOT TO GET UNDER COVER!
I – I CAN'T GET FREE! HELP ME, CHARLEY!

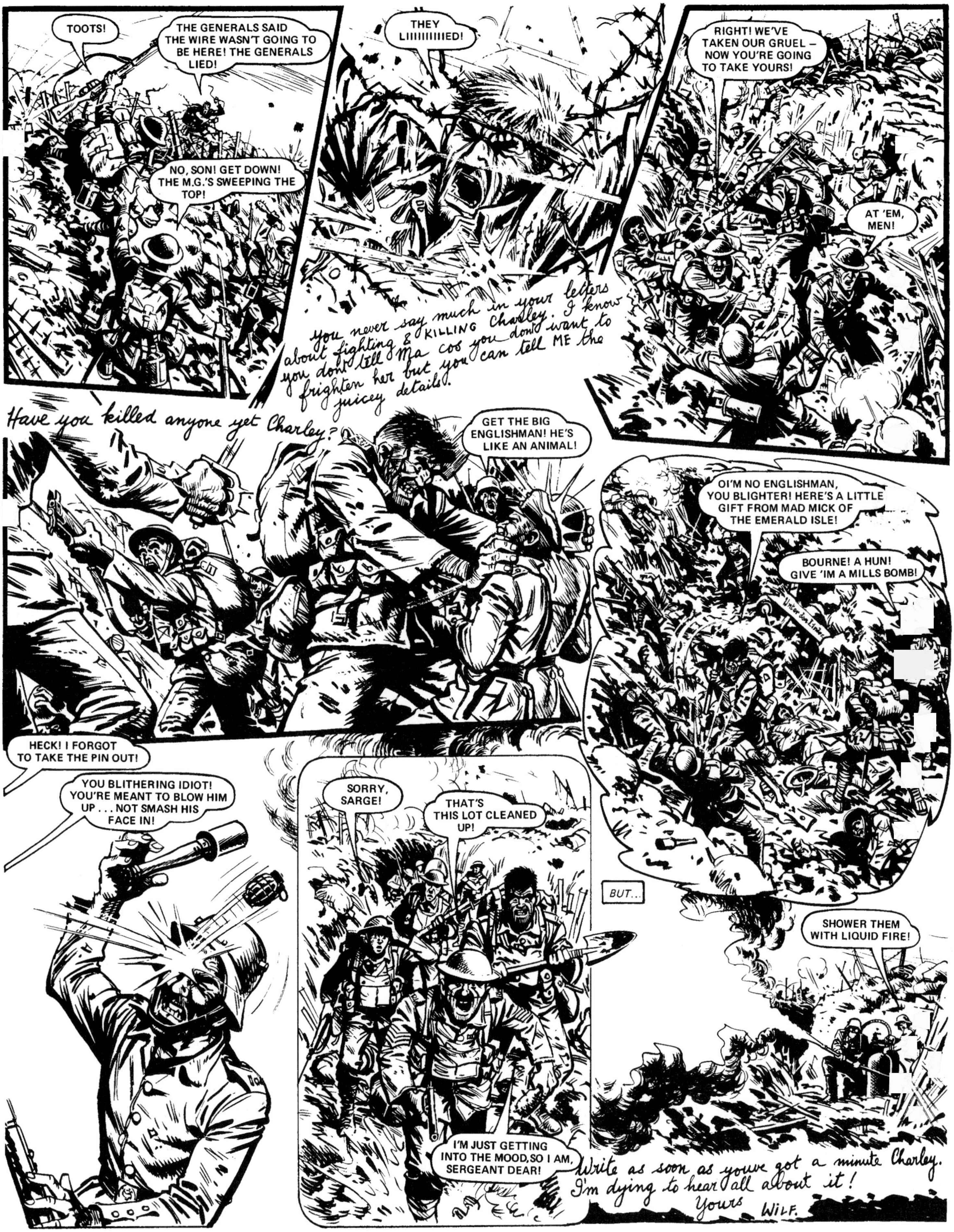

TOOTS!
THE GENERALS SAID THE WIRE WASN'T GOING TO BE HERE! THE GENERALS LIED!
NO, SON! GET DOWN! THE M.G.'S SWEEPING THE TOP!
THEY LIIIIIIIIIIED!
RIGHT! WE'VE TAKEN OUR GRUEL – NOW YOU'RE GOING TO TAKE YOURS!
AT 'EM, MEN!
You never say much in your letters about fighting & KILLING Charley. I know you don't tell Ma cos you don't want to frighten her but you can tell ME the juicey details.
Have you killed anyone yet Charley?
GET THE BIG ENGLISHMAN! HE'S LIKE AN ANIMAL!
OI'M NO ENGLISHMAN, YOU BLIGHTER! HERE'S A LITTLE GIFT FROM MAD MICK OF THE EMERALD ISLE!
BOURNE! A HUN! GIVE 'IM A MILLS BOMB!
HECK! I FORGOT TO TAKE THE PIN OUT!
YOU BLITHERING IDIOT! YOU'RE MEANT TO BLOW HIM UP . . . NOT SMASH HIS FACE IN!
SORRY, SARGE!
THAT'S THIS LOT CLEANED UP!
I'M JUST GETTING INTO THE MOOD, SO I AM, SERGEANT DEAR!
BUT...
SHOWER THEM WITH LIQUID FIRE!
Write as soon as youve got a minute Charley. I'm dying to hear all about it! Yours WILF.

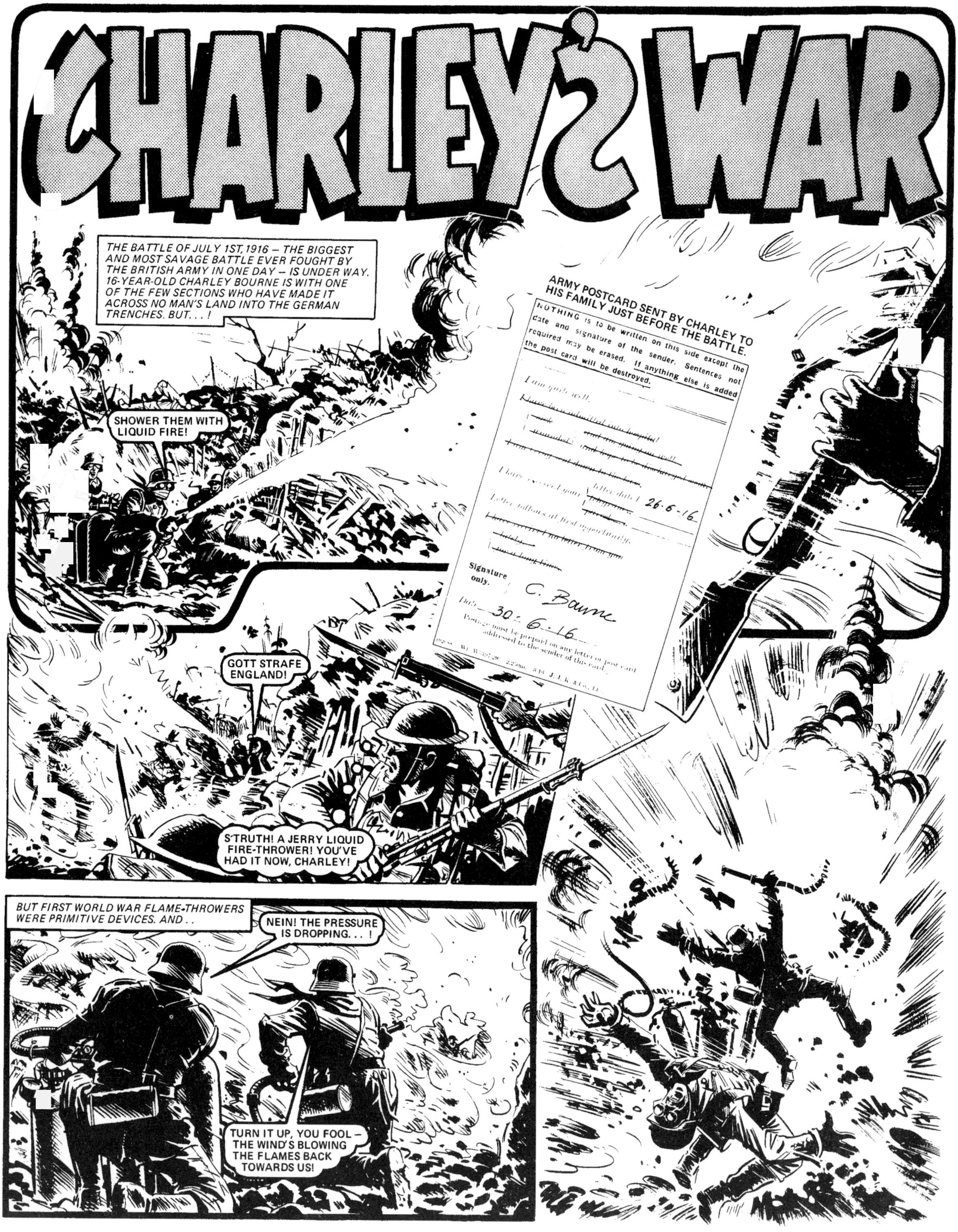
CHARLEY'S WAR
THE BATTLE OF JULY 1ST, 1916 – THE BIGGEST AND MOST SAVAGE BATTLE EVER FOUGHT BY THE BRITISH ARMY IN ONE DAY – IS UNDER WAY. 16-YEAR-OLD CHARLEY BOURNE IS WITH ONE OF THE FEW SECTIONS WHO HAVE MADE IT ACROSS NO MAN'S LAND INTO THE GERMAN TRENCHES. BUT. . . !
ARMY POSTCARD SENT BY CHARLEY TO HIS FAMILY JUST BEFORE THE BATTLE.
NOTHING is to be written on this side except the date and signature of the sender. Sentences not required may be erased. If anything else is added the post card will be destroyed.
I am quite well.
I have received your letter dated 26.6.16
Letter follows at first opportunity.
Signature only. C. Baune
Date 30 – 6 – 16
Postage must be prepaid on any letter or post card addressed to the sender of this card.
SHOWER THEM WITH LIQUID FIRE!
GOTT STRAFE ENGLAND!
S'TRUTH! A JERRY LIQUID FIRE-THROWER! YOU'VE HAD IT NOW, CHARLEY!
BUT FIRST WORLD WAR FLAME-THROWERS WERE PRIMITIVE DEVICES. AND . .
NEIN! THE PRESSURE IS DROPPING. . . !
TURN IT UP, YOU FOOL – THE WIND'S BLOWING THE FLAMES BACK TOWARDS US!

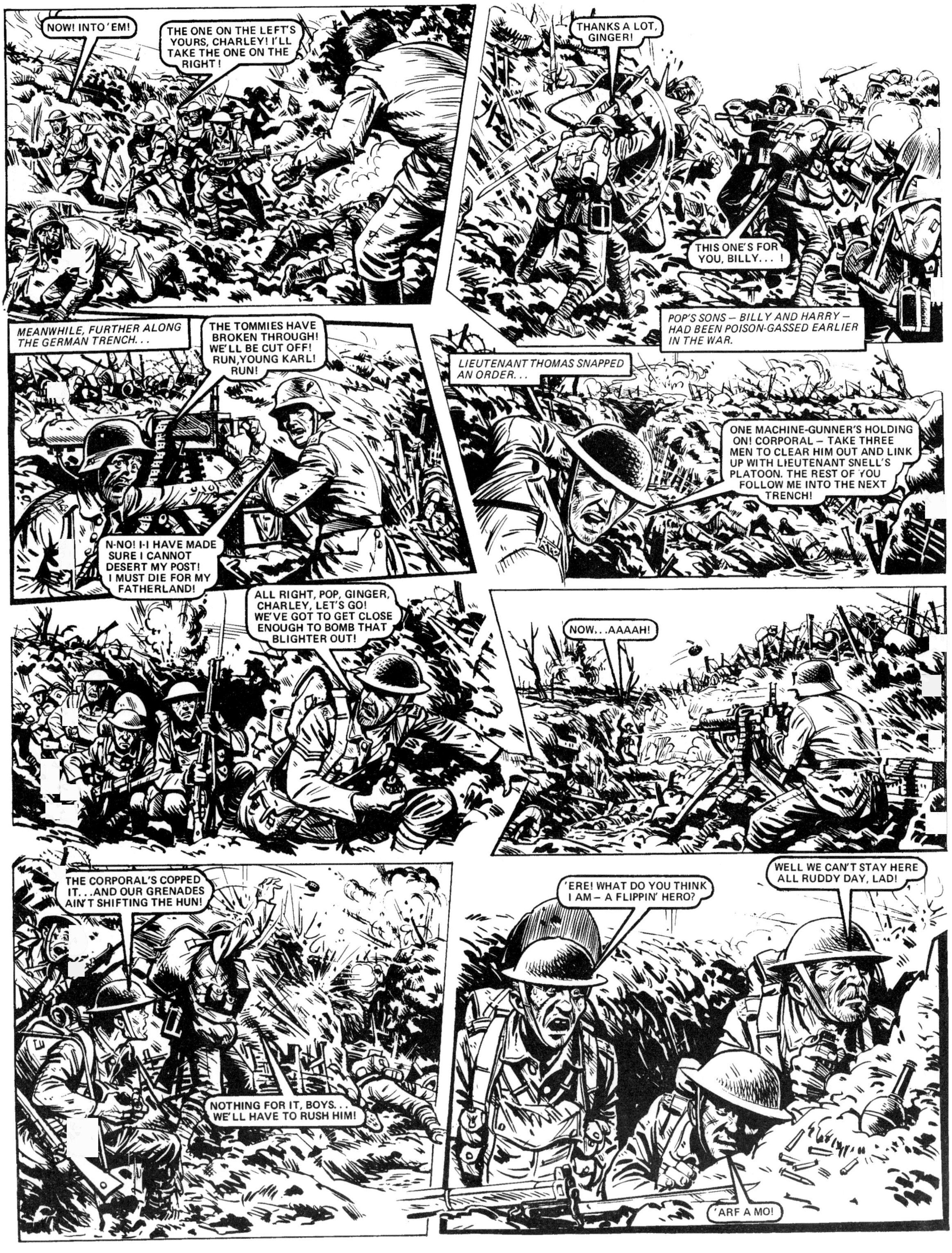
NOW! INTO 'EM!
THE ONE ON THE LEFT'S YOURS, CHARLEY! I'LL TAKE THE ONE ON THE RIGHT!
THANKS A LOT, GINGER!
THIS ONE'S FOR YOU, BILLY... !
POP'S SONS – BILLY AND HARRY – HAD BEEN POISON-GASSED EARLIER IN THE WAR.
MEANWHILE, FURTHER ALONG THE GERMAN TRENCH...
THE TOMMIES HAVE BROKEN THROUGH! WE'LL BE CUT OFF! RUN, YOUNG KARL! RUN!
N-NO! I-I HAVE MADE SURE I CANNOT DESERT MY POST! I MUST DIE FOR MY FATHERLAND!
LIEUTENANT THOMAS SNAPPED AN ORDER...
ONE MACHINE-GUNNER'S HOLDING ON! CORPORAL – TAKE THREE MEN TO CLEAR HIM OUT AND LINK UP WITH LIEUTENANT SNELL'S PLATOON. THE REST OF YOU FOLLOW ME INTO THE NEXT TRENCH!
ALL RIGHT, POP, GINGER, CHARLEY, LET'S GO! WE'VE GOT TO GET CLOSE ENOUGH TO BOMB THAT BLIGHTER OUT!
NOW...AAAAH!
THE CORPORAL'S COPPED IT...AND OUR GRENADES AIN'T SHIFTING THE HUN!
NOTHING FOR IT, BOYS... WE'LL HAVE TO RUSH HIM!
'ERE! WHAT DO YOU THINK I AM – A FLIPPIN' HERO?
WELL WE CAN'T STAY HERE ALL RUDDY DAY, LAD!
'ARF A MO!

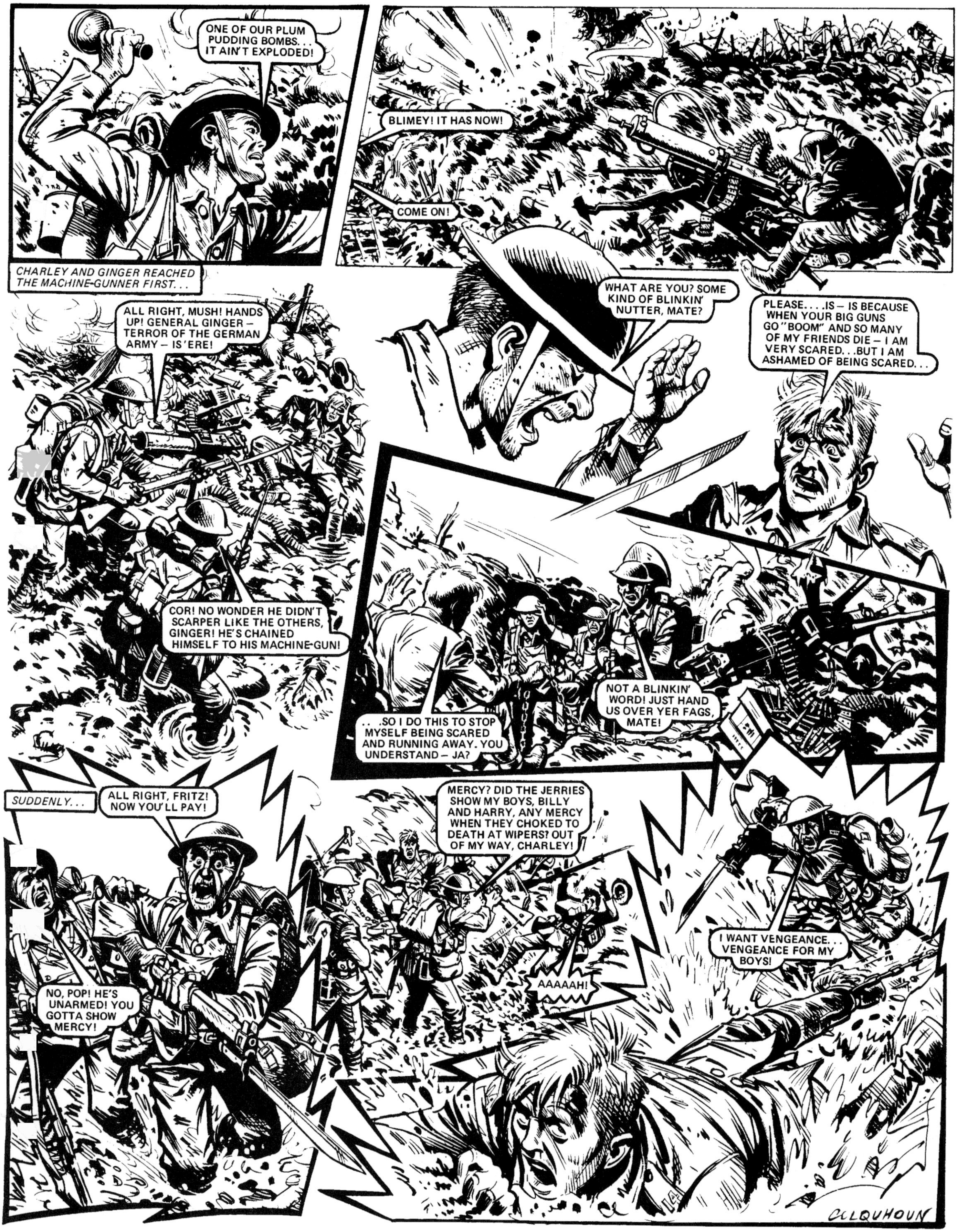
ONE OF OUR PLUM PUDDING BOMBS... IT AIN'T EXPLODED!
BLIMEY! IT HAS NOW!
COME ON!
CHARLEY AND GINGER REACHED THE MACHINE-GUNNER FIRST...
ALL RIGHT, MUSH! HANDS UP! GENERAL GINGER – TERROR OF THE GERMAN ARMY – IS 'ERE!
COR! NO WONDER HE DIDN'T SCARPER LIKE THE OTHERS, GINGER! HE'S CHAINED HIMSELF TO HIS MACHINE-GUN!
WHAT ARE YOU? SOME KIND OF BLINKIN' NUTTER, MATE?
PLEASE.... IS – IS BECAUSE WHEN YOUR BIG GUNS GO "BOOM" AND SO MANY OF MY FRIENDS DIE – I AM VERY SCARED... BUT I AM ASHAMED OF BEING SCARED...
...SO I DO THIS TO STOP MYSELF BEING SCARED AND RUNNING AWAY. YOU UNDERSTAND – JA?
NOT A BLINKIN' WORD! JUST HAND US OVER YER FAGS, MATE!
SUDDENLY...
ALL RIGHT, FRITZ! NOW YOU'LL PAY!
NO, POP! HE'S UNARMED! YOU GOTTA SHOW MERCY!
MERCY? DID THE JERRIES SHOW MY BOYS, BILLY AND HARRY, ANY MERCY WHEN THEY CHOKED TO DEATH AT WIPERS? OUT OF MY WAY, CHARLEY!
AAAAAH!
I WANT VENGEANCE... VENGEANCE FOR MY BOYS!
COLQUHOUN

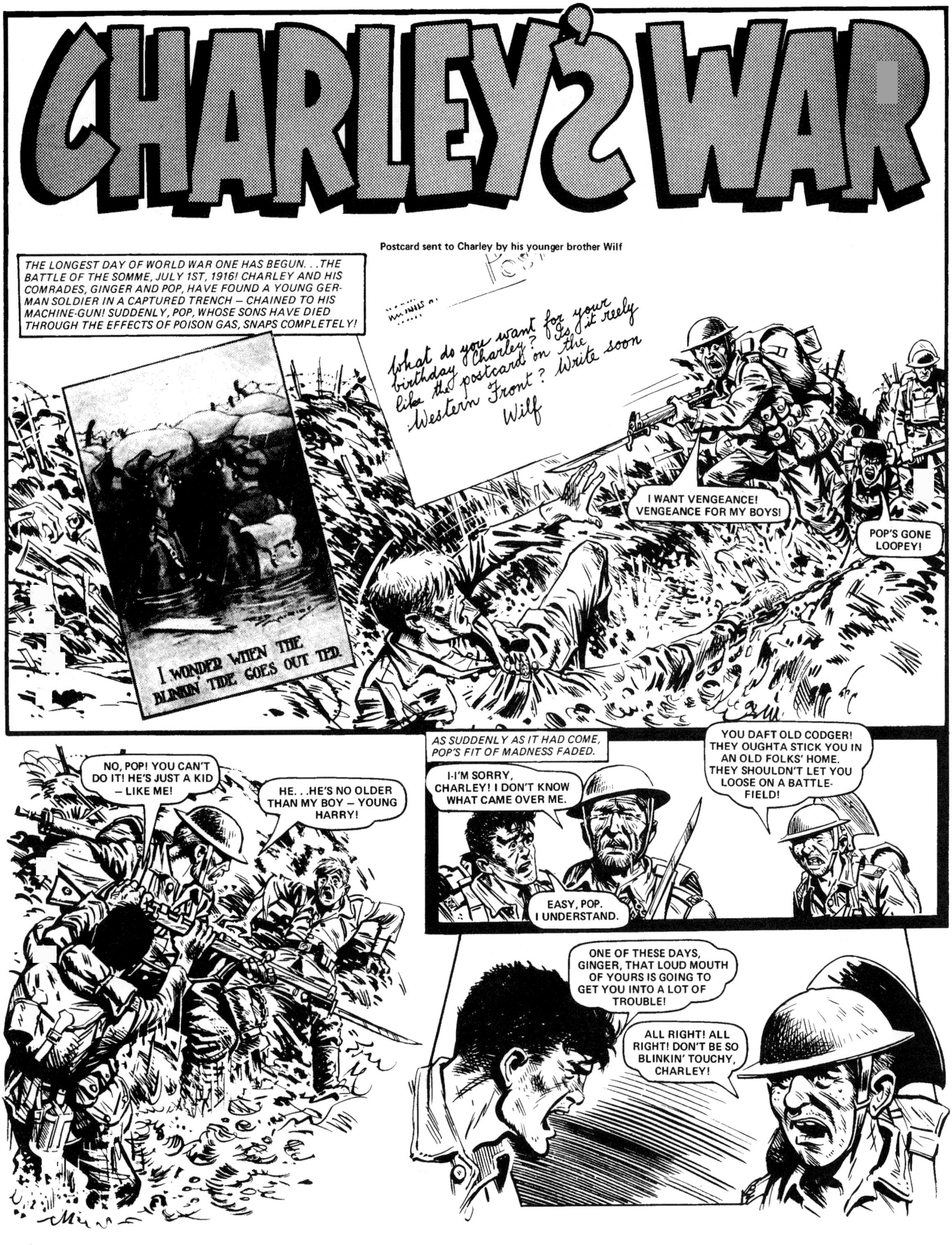
CHARLEY'S WAR
Postcard sent to Charley by his younger brother Wilf
THE LONGEST DAY OF WORLD WAR ONE HAS BEGUN. . .THE BATTLE OF THE SOMME, JULY 1ST, 1916! CHARLEY AND HIS COMRADES, GINGER AND POP, HAVE FOUND A YOUNG GERMAN SOLDIER IN A CAPTURED TRENCH – CHAINED TO HIS MACHINE-GUN! SUDDENLY, POP, WHOSE SONS HAVE DIED THROUGH THE EFFECTS OF POISON GAS, SNAPS COMPLETELY!
What do you want for your birthday Charley? Is it reely like the postcard on the Western Front? Write soon Wilf
I WONDER WHEN THE BLINKIN' TIDE GOES OUT TED.
I WANT VENGEANCE! VENGEANCE FOR MY BOYS!
POP'S GONE LOOPEY!
NO, POP! YOU CAN'T DO IT! HE'S JUST A KID – LIKE ME!
HE. . .HE'S NO OLDER THAN MY BOY – YOUNG HARRY!
AS SUDDENLY AS IT HAD COME, POP'S FIT OF MADNESS FADED.
I-I'M SORRY, CHARLEY! I DON'T KNOW WHAT CAME OVER ME.
EASY, POP. I UNDERSTAND.
YOU DAFT OLD CODGER! THEY OUGHTA STICK YOU IN AN OLD FOLKS' HOME. THEY SHOULDN'T LET YOU LOOSE ON A BATTLE-FIELD!
ONE OF THESE DAYS, GINGER, THAT LOUD MOUTH OF YOURS IS GOING TO GET YOU INTO A LOT OF TROUBLE!
ALL RIGHT! ALL RIGHT! DON'T BE SO BLINKIN' TOUCHY, CHARLEY!

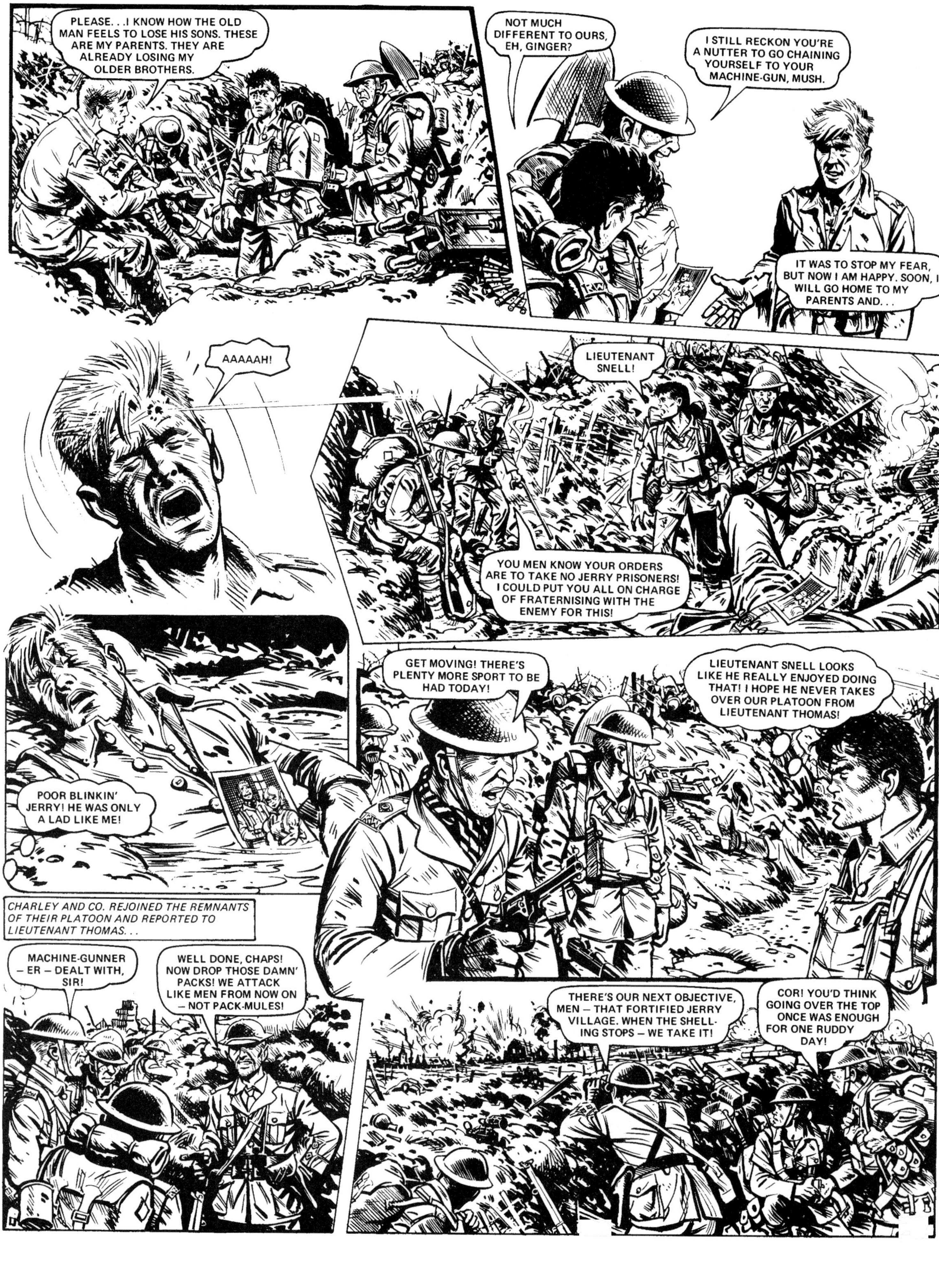

PLEASE. . .I KNOW HOW THE OLD MAN FEELS TO LOSE HIS SONS. THESE ARE MY PARENTS. THEY ARE ALREADY LOSING MY OLDER BROTHERS.
NOT MUCH DIFFERENT TO OURS, EH, GINGER?
I STILL RECKON YOU'RE A NUTTER TO GO CHAINING YOURSELF TO YOUR MACHINE-GUN, MUSH.
IT WAS TO STOP MY FEAR, BUT NOW I AM HAPPY. SOON, I WILL GO HOME TO MY PARENTS AND. . .
AAAAAH!
LIEUTENANT SNELL!
YOU MEN KNOW YOUR ORDERS ARE TO TAKE NO JERRY PRISONERS! I COULD PUT YOU ALL ON CHARGE OF FRATERNISING WITH THE ENEMY FOR THIS!
POOR BLINKIN' JERRY! HE WAS ONLY A LAD LIKE ME!
GET MOVING! THERE'S PLENTY MORE SPORT TO BE HAD TODAY!
LIEUTENANT SNELL LOOKS LIKE HE REALLY ENJOYED DOING THAT! I HOPE HE NEVER TAKES OVER OUR PLATOON FROM LIEUTENANT THOMAS!
CHARLEY AND CO. REJOINED THE REMNANTS OF THEIR PLATOON AND REPORTED TO LIEUTENANT THOMAS. . .
MACHINE-GUNNER – ER – DEALT WITH, SIR!
WELL DONE, CHAPS! NOW DROP THOSE DAMN' PACKS! WE ATTACK LIKE MEN FROM NOW ON – NOT PACK-MULES!
THERE'S OUR NEXT OBJECTIVE, MEN – THAT FORTIFIED JERRY VILLAGE. WHEN THE SHELL-ING STOPS – WE TAKE IT!
COR! YOU'D THINK GOING OVER THE TOP ONCE WAS ENOUGH FOR ONE RUDDY DAY!

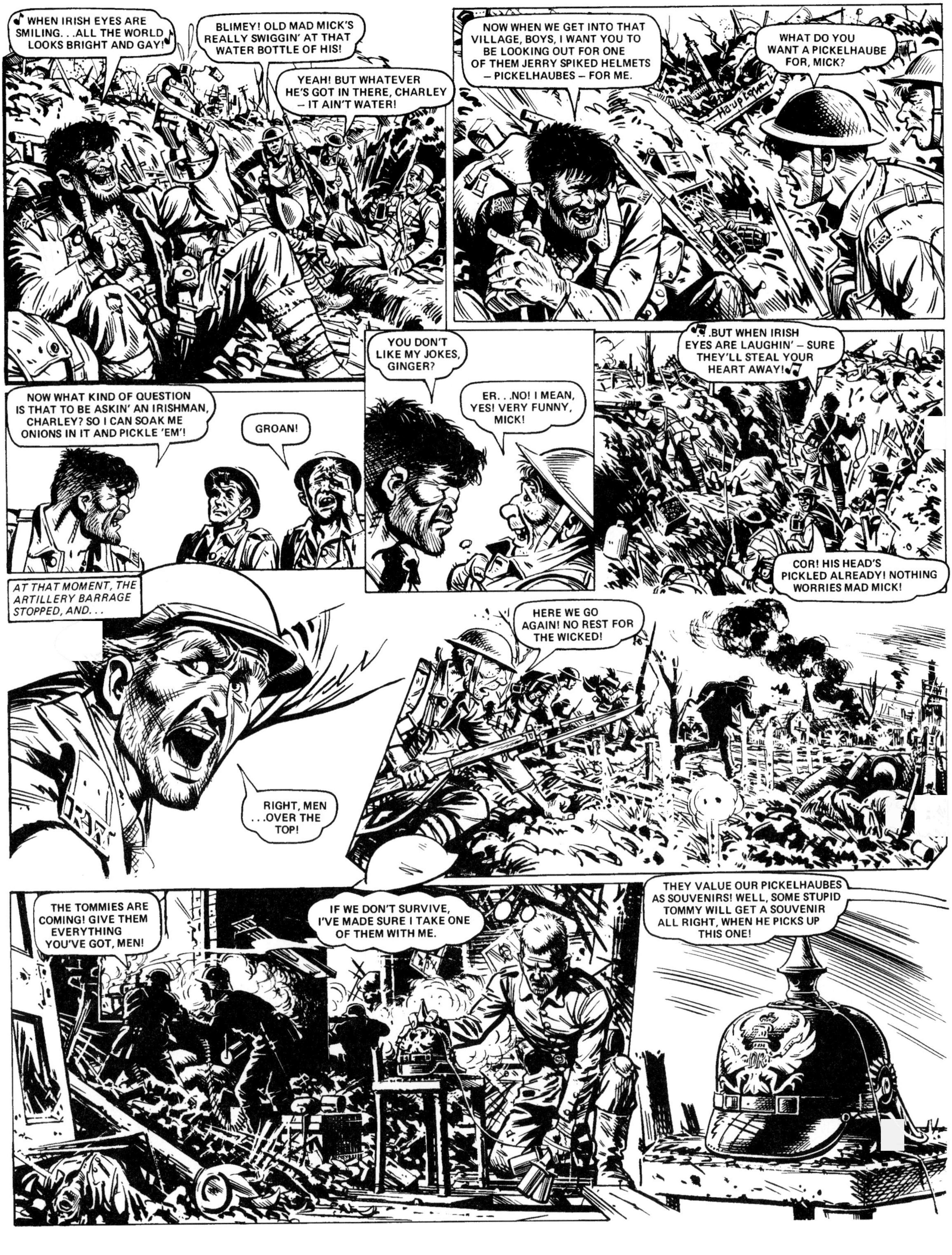
WHEN IRISH EYES ARE SMILING. . .ALL THE WORLD LOOKS BRIGHT AND GAY!
BLIMEY! OLD MAD MICK'S REALLY SWIGGIN' AT THAT WATER BOTTLE OF HIS!
YEAH! BUT WHATEVER HE'S GOT IN THERE, CHARLEY – IT AIN'T WATER!
NOW WHEN WE GET INTO THAT VILLAGE, BOYS, I WANT YOU TO BE LOOKING OUT FOR ONE OF THEM JERRY SPIKED HELMETS – PICKELHAUBES – FOR ME.
WHAT DO YOU WANT A PICKELHAUBE FOR, MICK?
NOW WHAT KIND OF QUESTION IS THAT TO BE ASKIN' AN IRISHMAN, CHARLEY? SO I CAN SOAK ME ONIONS IN IT AND PICKLE 'EM'!
GROAN!
YOU DON'T LIKE MY JOKES, GINGER?
ER. . .NO! I MEAN, YES! VERY FUNNY, MICK!
. .BUT WHEN IRISH EYES ARE LAUGHIN' – SURE THEY'LL STEAL YOUR HEART AWAY!
COR! HIS HEAD'S PICKLED ALREADY! NOTHING WORRIES MAD MICK!
AT THAT MOMENT, THE ARTILLERY BARRAGE STOPPED, AND. . .
RIGHT, MEN . . .OVER THE TOP!
HERE WE GO AGAIN! NO REST FOR THE WICKED!
THE TOMMIES ARE COMING! GIVE THEM EVERYTHING YOU'VE GOT, MEN!
IF WE DON'T SURVIVE, I'VE MADE SURE I TAKE ONE OF THEM WITH ME.
THEY VALUE OUR PICKELHAUBES AS SOUVENIRS! WELL, SOME STUPID TOMMY WILL GET A SOUVENIR ALL RIGHT, WHEN HE PICKS UP THIS ONE!

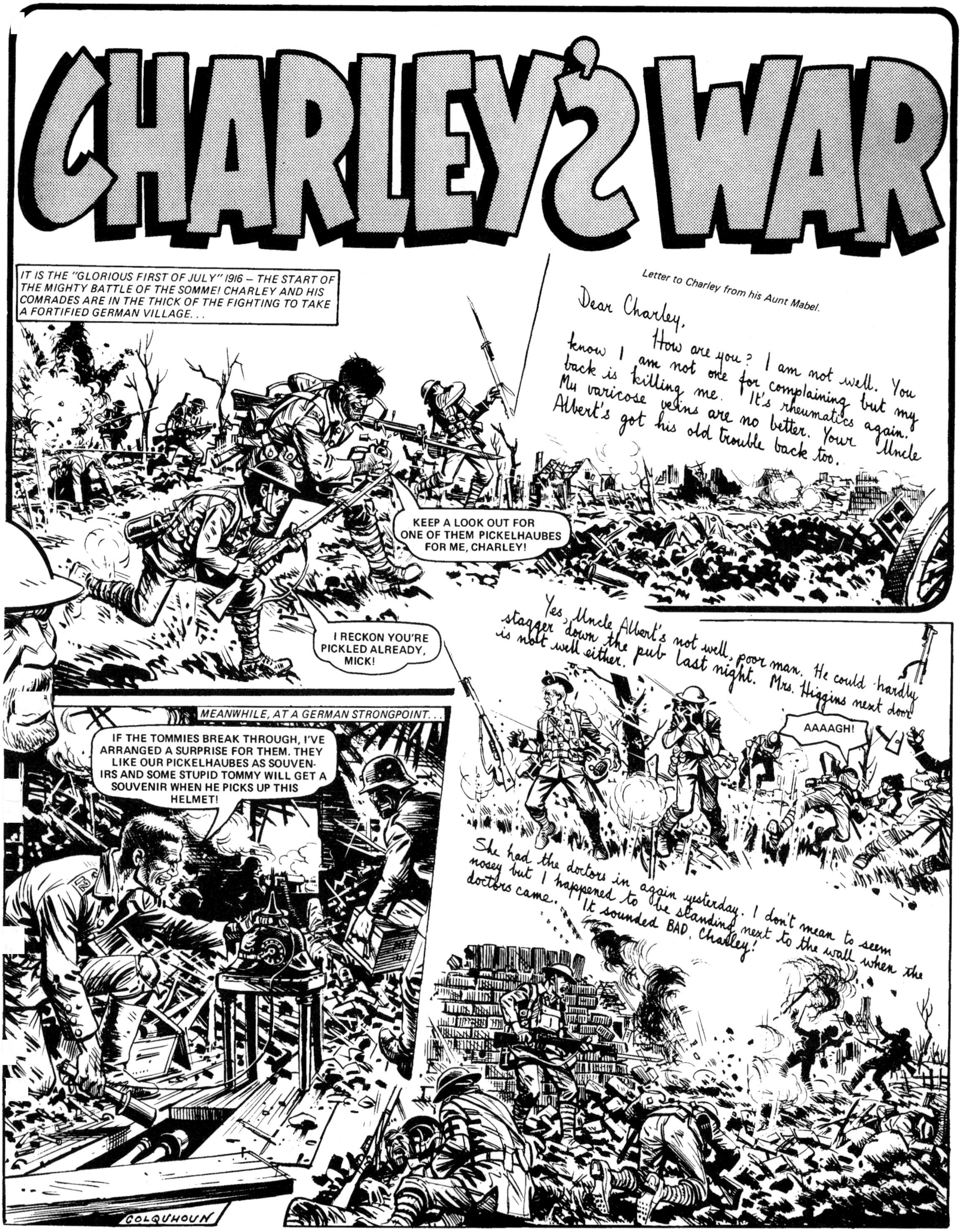
CHARLEY'S WAR
IT IS THE "GLORIOUS FIRST OF JULY" 1916 – THE START OF THE MIGHTY BATTLE OF THE SOMME! CHARLEY AND HIS COMRADES ARE IN THE THICK OF THE FIGHTING TO TAKE A FORTIFIED GERMAN VILLAGE. . .
Letter to Charley from his Aunt Mabel.
Dear Charley,
How are you? I am not well. You know I am not one for complaining but my back is killing me. It's rheumatics again. My varicose veins are no better. Your Uncle Albert's got his old trouble back too.
KEEP A LOOK OUT FOR ONE OF THEM PICKELHAUBES FOR ME, CHARLEY!
I RECKON YOU'RE PICKLED ALREADY, MICK!
Yes, Uncle Albert's not well, poor man. He could hardly stagger down the pub last night. Mrs. Higgins next door is not well either.
AAAAGH!
MEANWHILE, AT A GERMAN STRONGPOINT. . .
IF THE TOMMIES BREAK THROUGH, I'VE ARRANGED A SURPRISE FOR THEM. THEY LIKE OUR PICKELHAUBES AS SOUVENIRS AND SOME STUPID TOMMY WILL GET A SOUVENIR WHEN HE PICKS UP THIS HELMET!
She had the doctors in again yesterday. I don't mean to seem nosey but I happened to be standing next to the wall when the doctors came. It sounded BAD, Charley!
COLQUHOUN

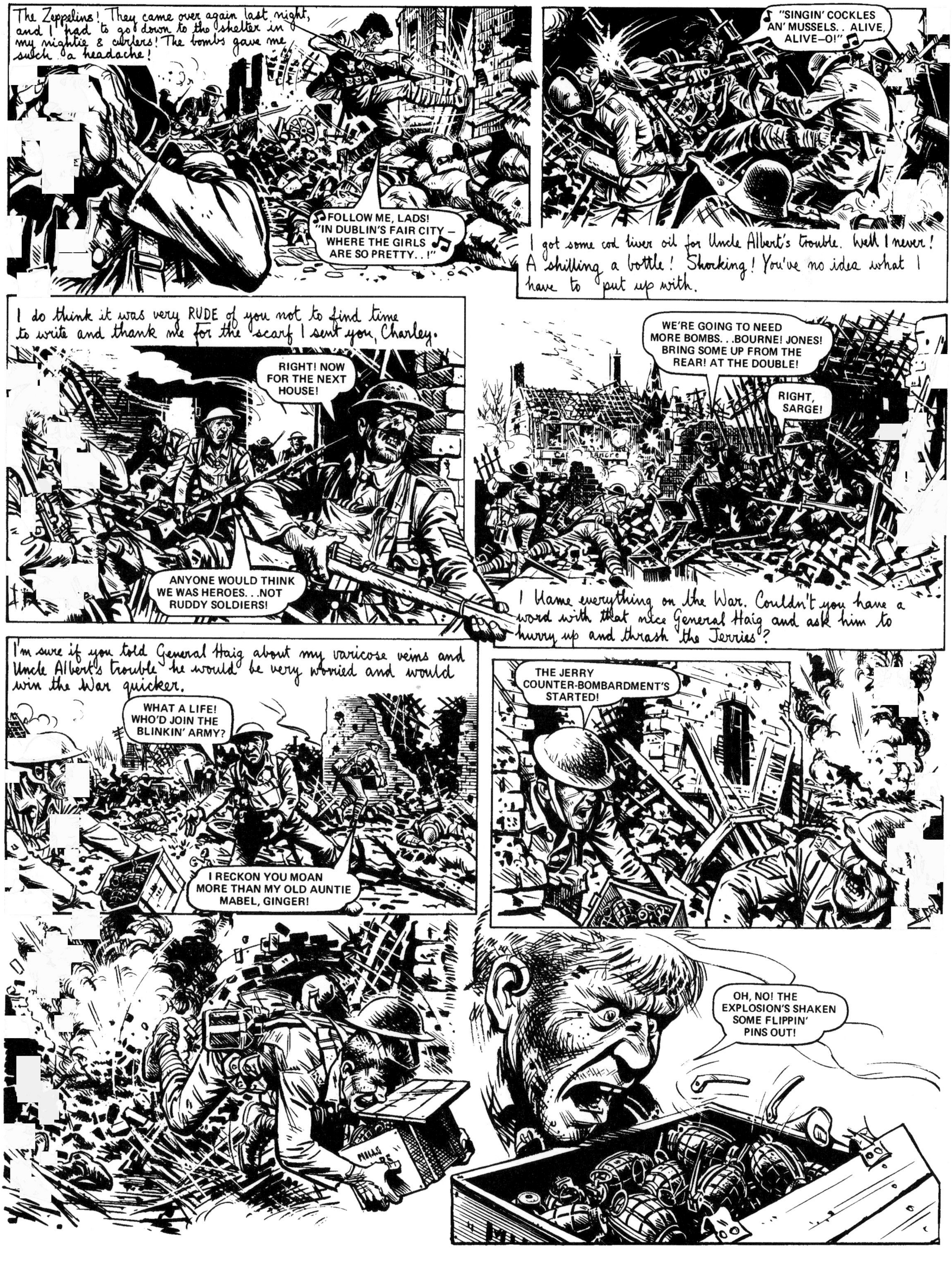

The Zeppelins! They came over again last night, and I had to go down to the shelter in my nightie & curlers! The bombs gave me such a headache!
FOLLOW ME, LADS! "IN DUBLIN'S FAIR CITY – WHERE THE GIRLS ARE SO PRETTY..!"
"SINGIN' COCKLES AN' MUSSELS.. ALIVE, ALIVE-O!"
I got some cod liver oil for Uncle Albert's trouble. Well I never! A shilling a bottle! Shocking! You've no idea what I have to put up with.
I do think it was very RUDE of you not to find time to write and thank me for the scarf I sent you, Charley.
RIGHT! NOW FOR THE NEXT HOUSE!
ANYONE WOULD THINK WE WAS HEROES...NOT RUDDY SOLDIERS!
WE'RE GOING TO NEED MORE BOMBS...BOURNE! JONES! BRING SOME UP FROM THE REAR! AT THE DOUBLE!
RIGHT, SARGE!
I blame everything on the War. Couldn't you have a word with that nice General Haig and ask him to hurry up and thrash the Jerries?
I'm sure if you told General Haig about my varicose veins and Uncle Albert's trouble he would be very worried and would win the War quicker.
WHAT A LIFE! WHO'D JOIN THE BLINKIN' ARMY?
I RECKON YOU MOAN MORE THAN MY OLD AUNTIE MABEL, GINGER!
THE JERRY COUNTER-BOMBARDMENT'S STARTED!
OH, NO! THE EXPLOSION'S SHAKEN SOME FLIPPIN' PINS OUT!

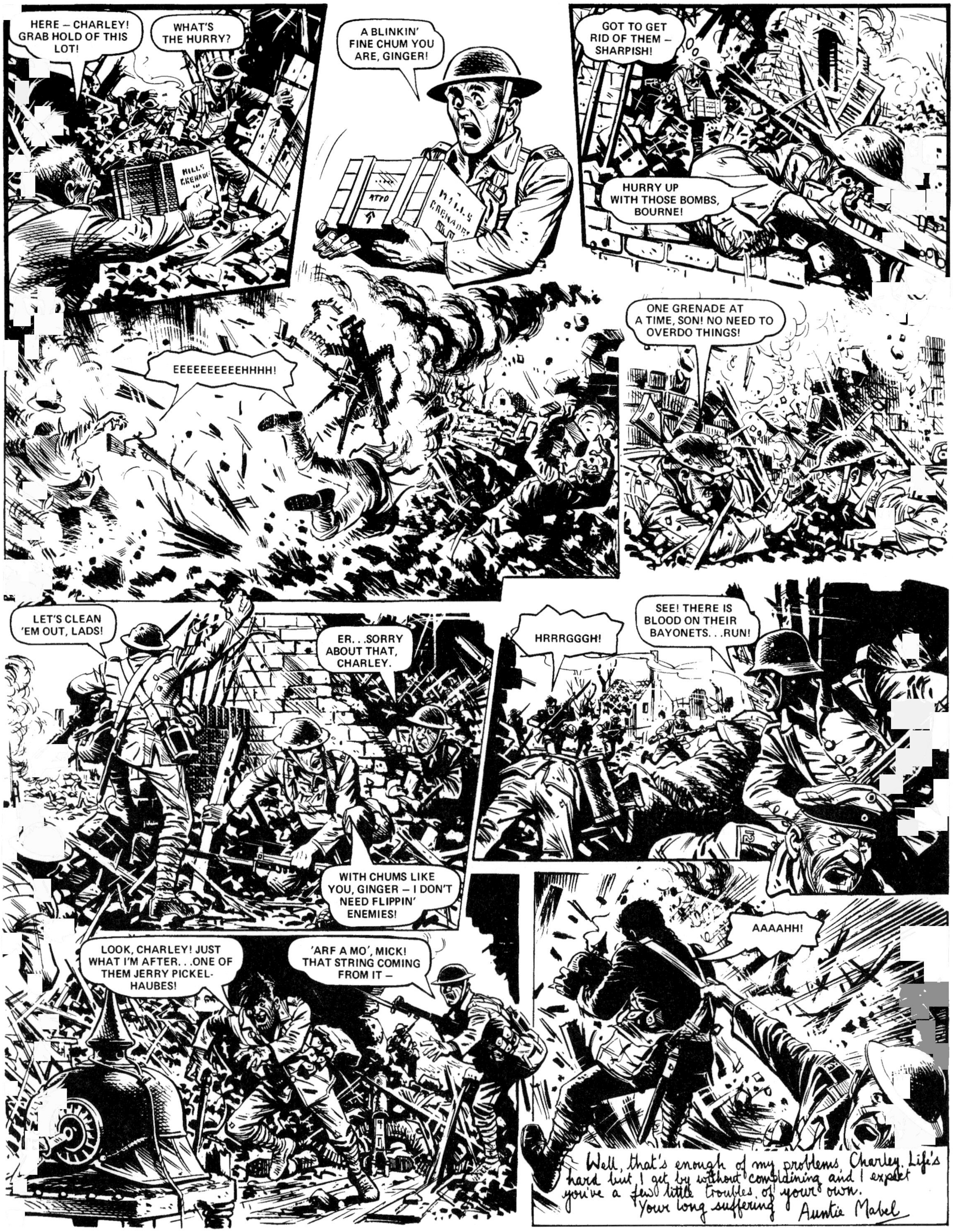

HERE – CHARLEY! GRAB HOLD OF THIS LOT!
WHAT'S THE HURRY?
A BLINKIN' FINE CHUM YOU ARE, GINGER!
GOT TO GET RID OF THEM – SHARPISH!
HURRY UP WITH THOSE BOMBS, BOURNE!
EEEEEEEEEEHHHH!
ONE GRENADE AT A TIME, SON! NO NEED TO OVERDO THINGS!
LET'S CLEAN 'EM OUT, LADS!
ER. . .SORRY ABOUT THAT, CHARLEY.
WITH CHUMS LIKE YOU, GINGER – I DON'T NEED FLIPPIN' ENEMIES!
HRRRGGGH!
SEE! THERE IS BLOOD ON THEIR BAYONETS. . .RUN!
LOOK, CHARLEY! JUST WHAT I'M AFTER. . .ONE OF THEM JERRY PICKEL-HAUBES!
'ARF A MO', MICK! THAT STRING COMING FROM IT –
AAAAHH!
Well, that's enough of my problems Charley. Life's hard but I get by without complaining and I expect you've a few little troubles of your own.
Your long suffering Auntie Mabel

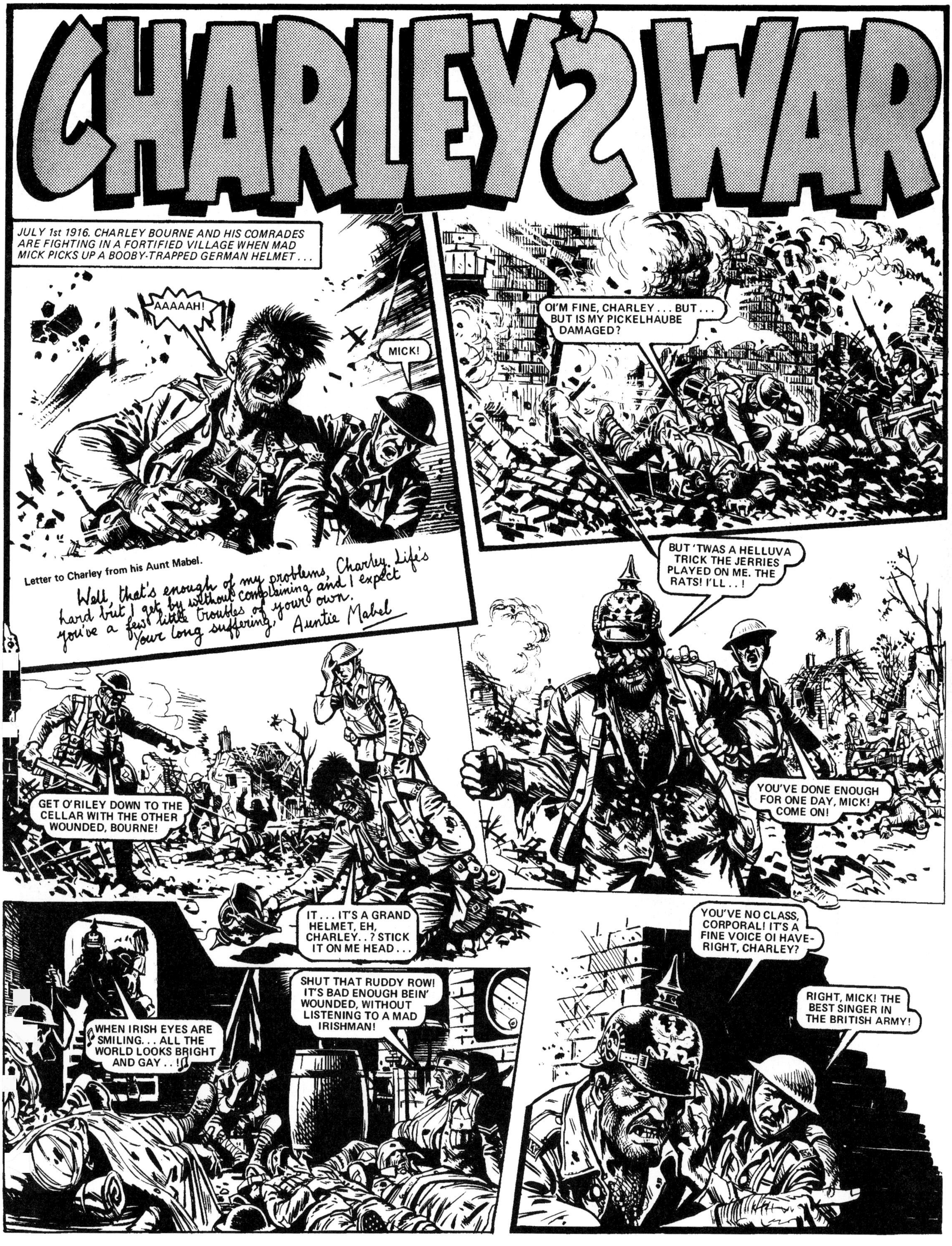

CHARLEY'S WAR
JULY 1st 1916. CHARLEY BOURNE AND HIS COMRADES ARE FIGHTING IN A FORTIFIED VILLAGE WHEN MAD MICK PICKS UP A BOOBY-TRAPPED GERMAN HELMET . . .
AAAAAH!
MICK!
OI'M FINE, CHARLEY . . . BUT . . . BUT IS MY PICKELHAUBE DAMAGED?
Letter to Charley from his Aunt Mabel.
Well, that's enough of my problems, Charley. Life's hard but I get by without complaining and I expect you've a few little troubles of your own.
Your long suffering, Auntie Mabel
BUT 'TWAS A HELLUVA TRICK THE JERRIES PLAYED ON ME. THE RATS! I'LL . . !
YOU'VE DONE ENOUGH FOR ONE DAY, MICK! COME ON!
GET O'RILEY DOWN TO THE CELLAR WITH THE OTHER WOUNDED, BOURNE!
IT . . . IT'S A GRAND HELMET, EH, CHARLEY . . ? STICK IT ON ME HEAD . . .
WHEN IRISH EYES ARE SMILING. . . ALL THE WORLD LOOKS BRIGHT AND GAY . . !
SHUT THAT RUDDY ROW! IT'S BAD ENOUGH BEIN' WOUNDED, WITHOUT LISTENING TO A MAD IRISHMAN!
YOU'VE NO CLASS, CORPORAL! IT'S A FINE VOICE OI HAVE- RIGHT, CHARLEY?
RIGHT, MICK! THE BEST SINGER IN THE BRITISH ARMY!

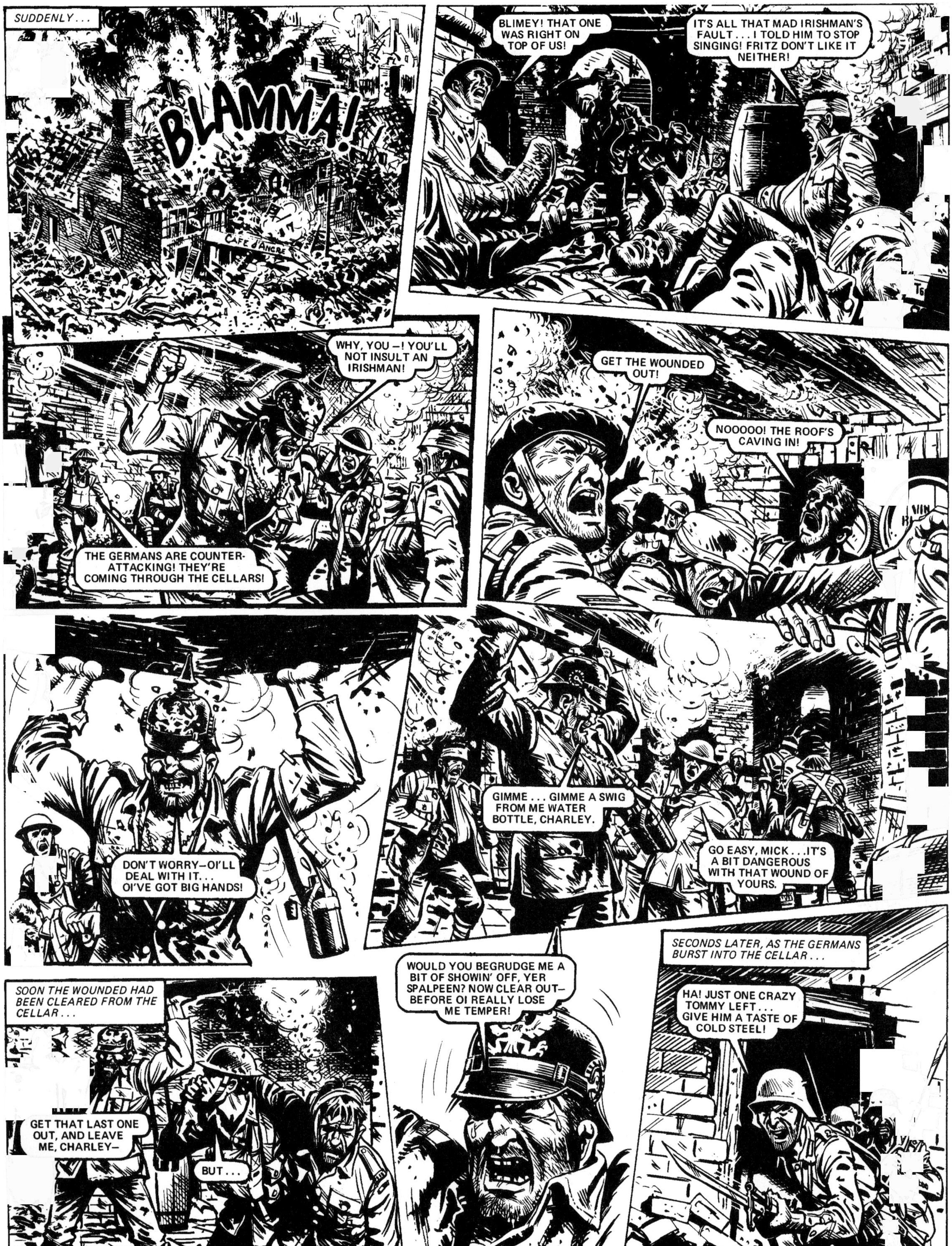
SUDDENLY . . .
BLAMMA!
CAFE D'ANCRE
BLIMEY! THAT ONE WAS RIGHT ON TOP OF US!
IT'S ALL THAT MAD IRISHMAN'S FAULT . . . I TOLD HIM TO STOP SINGING! FRITZ DON'T LIKE IT NEITHER!
WHY, YOU –! YOU'LL NOT INSULT AN IRISHMAN!
THE GERMANS ARE COUNTER-ATTACKING! THEY'RE COMING THROUGH THE CELLARS!
GET THE WOUNDED OUT!
NOOOOO! THE ROOF'S CAVING IN!
DON'T WORRY–OI'LL DEAL WITH IT. . . OI'VE GOT BIG HANDS!
GIMME . . . GIMME A SWIG FROM ME WATER BOTTLE, CHARLEY.
GO EASY, MICK . . . IT'S A BIT DANGEROUS WITH THAT WOUND OF YOURS.
SOON THE WOUNDED HAD BEEN CLEARED FROM THE CELLAR . . .
GET THAT LAST ONE OUT, AND LEAVE ME, CHARLEY–
BUT . . .
WOULD YOU BEGRUDGE ME A BIT OF SHOWIN' OFF, YER SPALPEEN? NOW CLEAR OUT–BEFORE OI REALLY LOSE ME TEMPER!
SECONDS LATER, AS THE GERMANS BURST INTO THE CELLAR . . .
HA! JUST ONE CRAZY TOMMY LEFT . . . GIVE HIM A TASTE OF COLD STEEL!

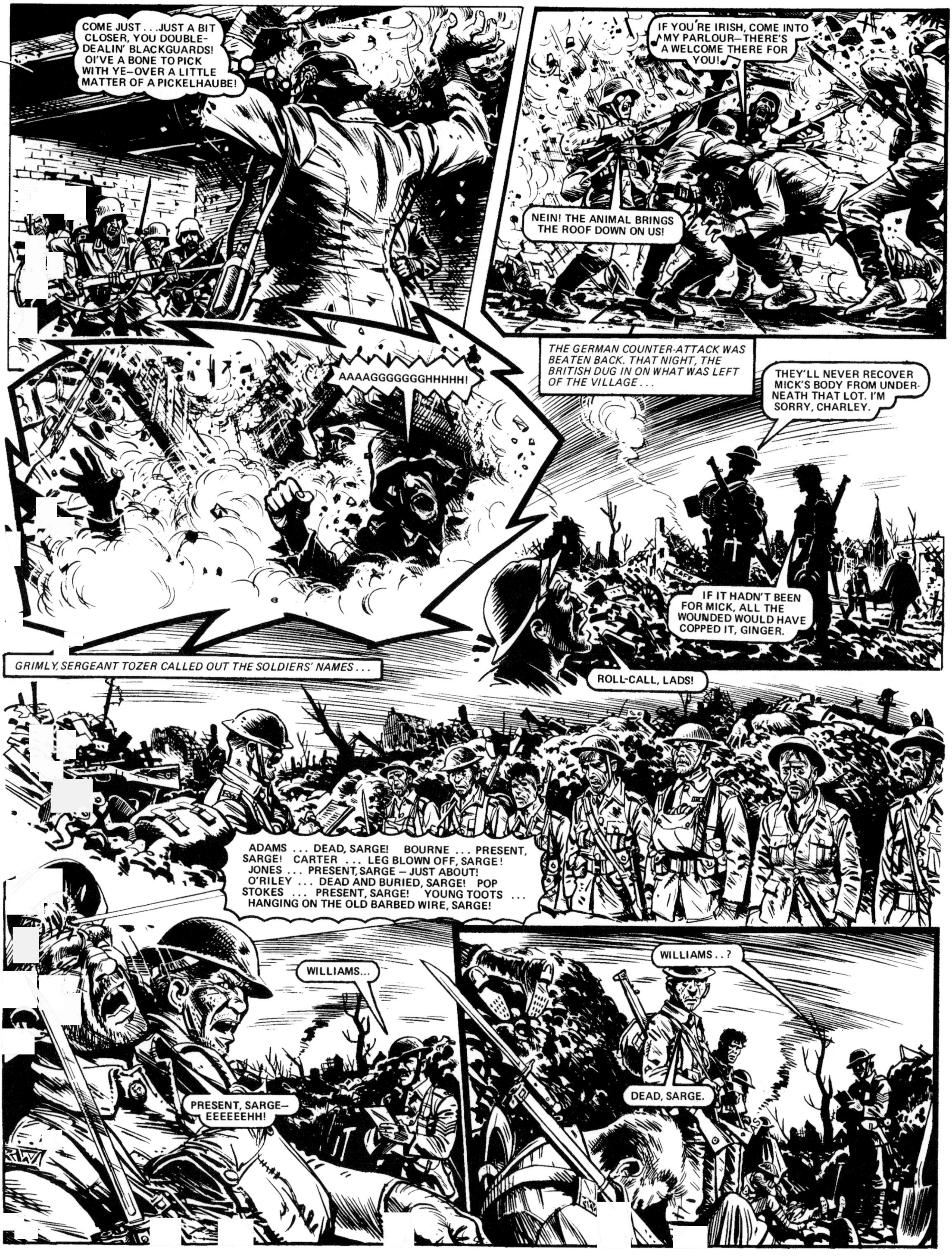

COME JUST . . . JUST A BIT CLOSER, YOU DOUBLE-DEALIN' BLACKGUARDS! OI'VE A BONE TO PICK WITH YE—OVER A LITTLE MATTER OF A PICKELHAUBE!
IF YOU'RE IRISH, COME INTO MY PARLOUR—THERE'S A WELCOME THERE FOR YOU!
NEIN! THE ANIMAL BRINGS THE ROOF DOWN ON US!
AAAAGGGGGGGHHHHH!
THE GERMAN COUNTER-ATTACK WAS BEATEN BACK. THAT NIGHT, THE BRITISH DUG IN ON WHAT WAS LEFT OF THE VILLAGE . . .
THEY'LL NEVER RECOVER MICK'S BODY FROM UNDERNEATH THAT LOT. I'M SORRY, CHARLEY.
IF IT HADN'T BEEN FOR MICK, ALL THE WOUNDED WOULD HAVE COPPED IT, GINGER.
GRIMLY, SERGEANT TOZER CALLED OUT THE SOLDIERS' NAMES . . .
ROLL-CALL, LADS!
ADAMS . . . DEAD, SARGE! BOURNE . . . PRESENT, SARGE! CARTER . . . LEG BLOWN OFF, SARGE! JONES . . . PRESENT, SARGE – JUST ABOUT! O'RILEY . . . DEAD AND BURIED, SARGE! POP STOKES . . . PRESENT, SARGE! YOUNG TOOTS . . . HANGING ON THE OLD BARBED WIRE, SARGE!
WILLIAMS...
PRESENT, SARGE—EEEEEEHH!
WILLIAMS . . ?
DEAD, SARGE.

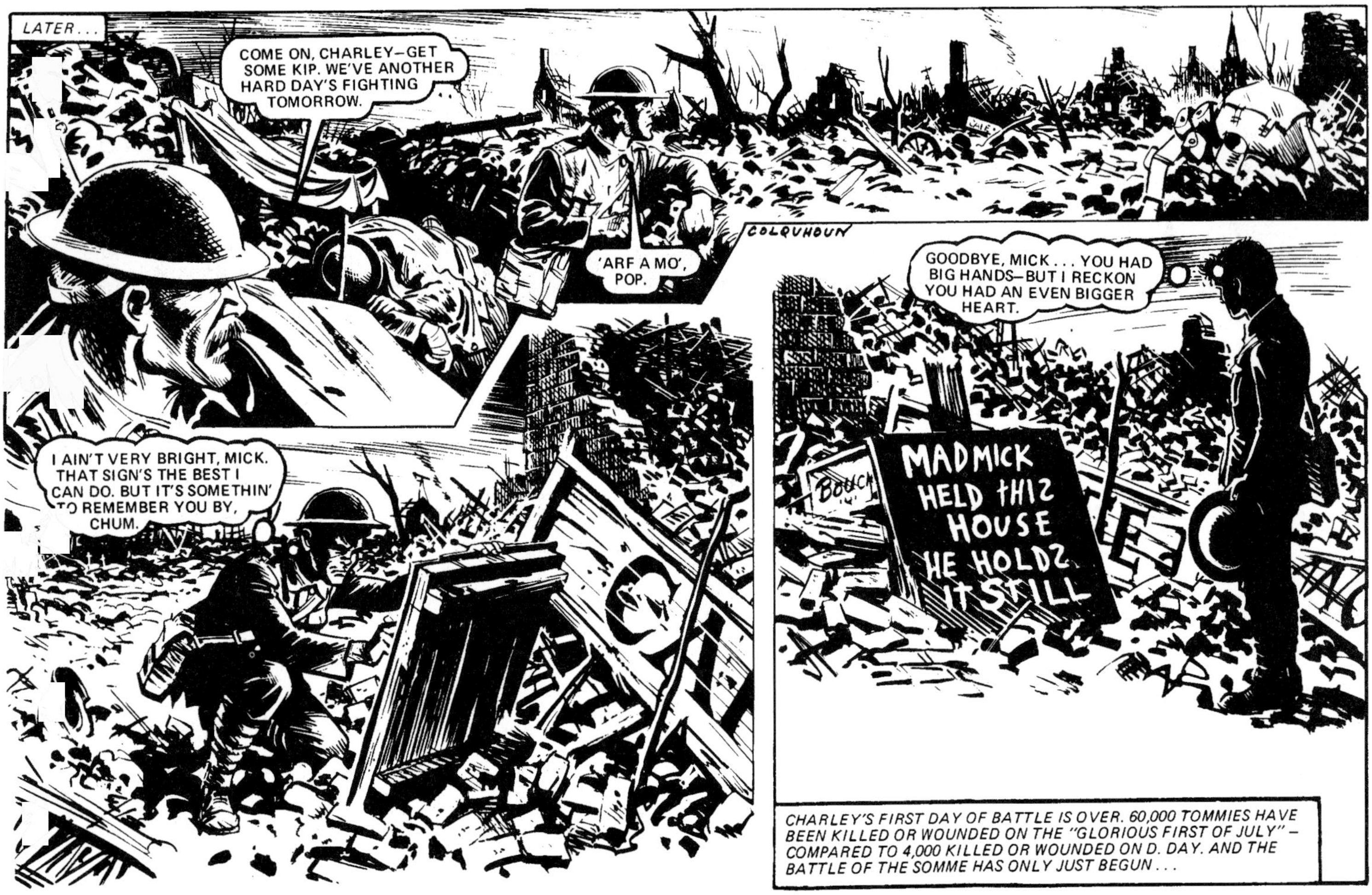
LATER . . .
COME ON, CHARLEY—GET SOME KIP. WE'VE ANOTHER HARD DAY'S FIGHTING TOMORROW.
'ARF A MO', POP.
COLQUHOUN
I AIN'T VERY BRIGHT, MICK. THAT SIGN'S THE BEST I CAN DO. BUT IT'S SOMETHIN' TO REMEMBER YOU BY, CHUM.
GOODBYE, MICK . . . YOU HAD BIG HANDS—BUT I RECKON YOU HAD AN EVEN BIGGER HEART.
MADMICK HELD THIZ HOUSE HE HOLDZ IT STILL
CHARLEY'S FIRST DAY OF BATTLE IS OVER. 60,000 TOMMIES HAVE BEEN KILLED OR WOUNDED ON THE "GLORIOUS FIRST OF JULY" – COMPARED TO 4,000 KILLED OR WOUNDED ON D. DAY. AND THE BATTLE OF THE SOMME HAS ONLY JUST BEGUN . . .

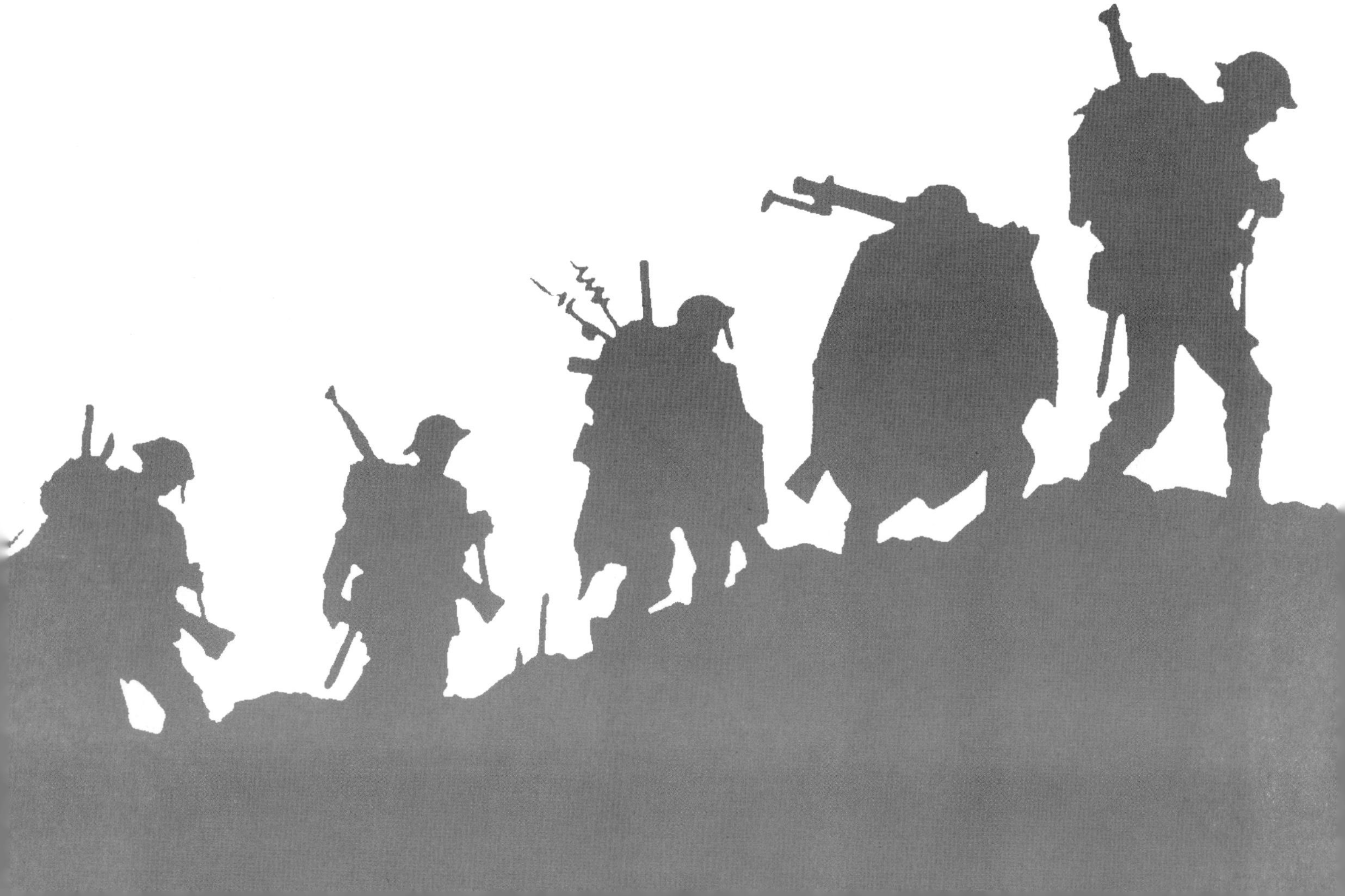

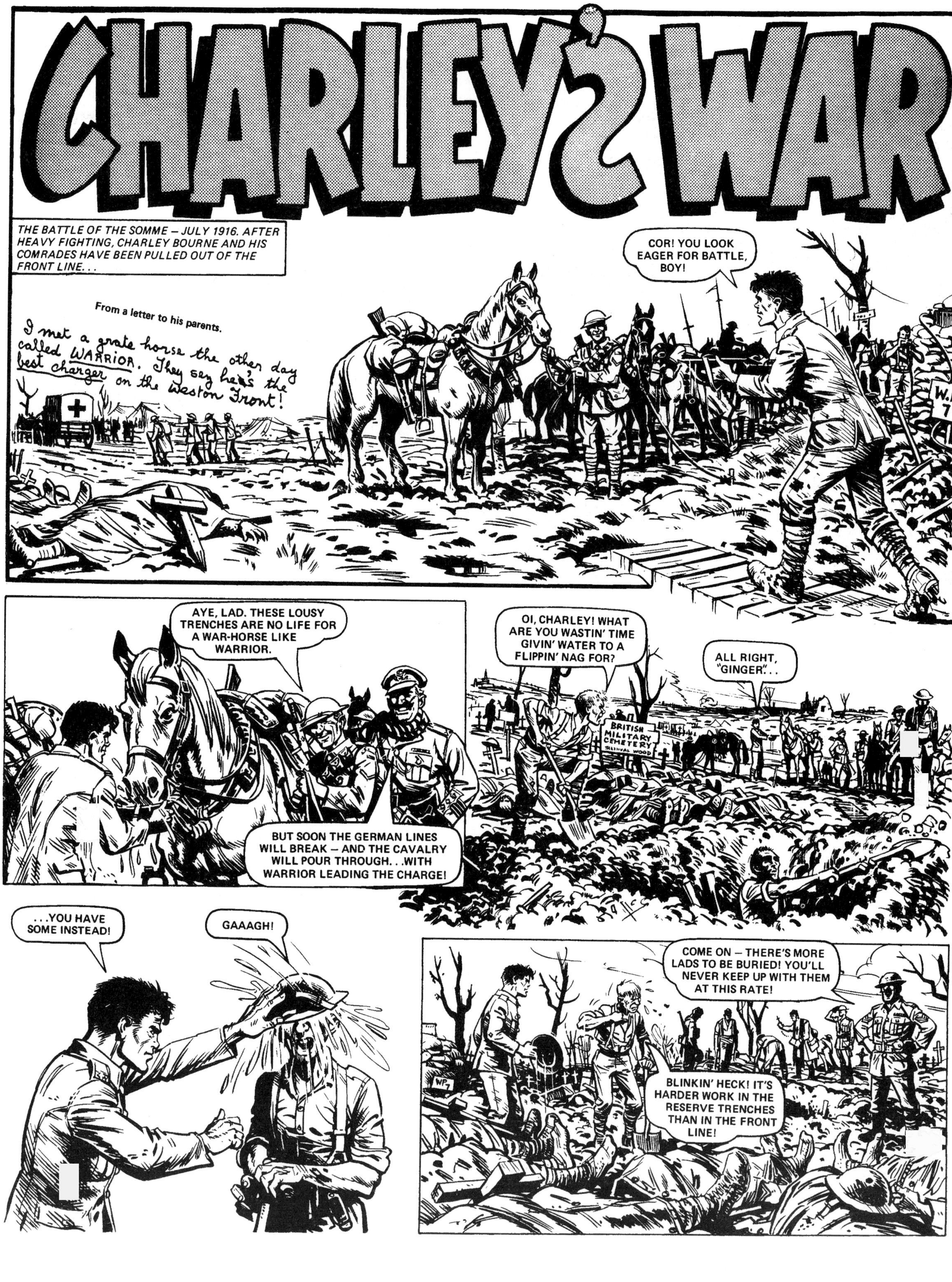
CHARLEY'S WAR
THE BATTLE OF THE SOMME – JULY 1916. AFTER HEAVY FIGHTING, CHARLEY BOURNE AND HIS COMRADES HAVE BEEN PULLED OUT OF THE FRONT LINE...
From a letter to his parents.
I met a grate horse the other day called WARRIOR. They say he's the best charger on the Weston Front!
COR! YOU LOOK EAGER FOR BATTLE, BOY!
AYE, LAD. THESE LOUSY TRENCHES ARE NO LIFE FOR A WAR-HORSE LIKE WARRIOR.
BUT SOON THE GERMAN LINES WILL BREAK – AND THE CAVALRY WILL POUR THROUGH... WITH WARRIOR LEADING THE CHARGE!
OI, CHARLEY! WHAT ARE YOU WASTIN' TIME GIVIN' WATER TO A FLIPPIN' NAG FOR?
ALL RIGHT, "GINGER"...
BRITISH MILITARY CEMETERY
...YOU HAVE SOME INSTEAD!
GAAAGH!
COME ON – THERE'S MORE LADS TO BE BURIED! YOU'LL NEVER KEEP UP WITH THEM AT THIS RATE!
BLINKIN' HECK! IT'S HARDER WORK IN THE RESERVE TRENCHES THAN IN THE FRONT LINE!

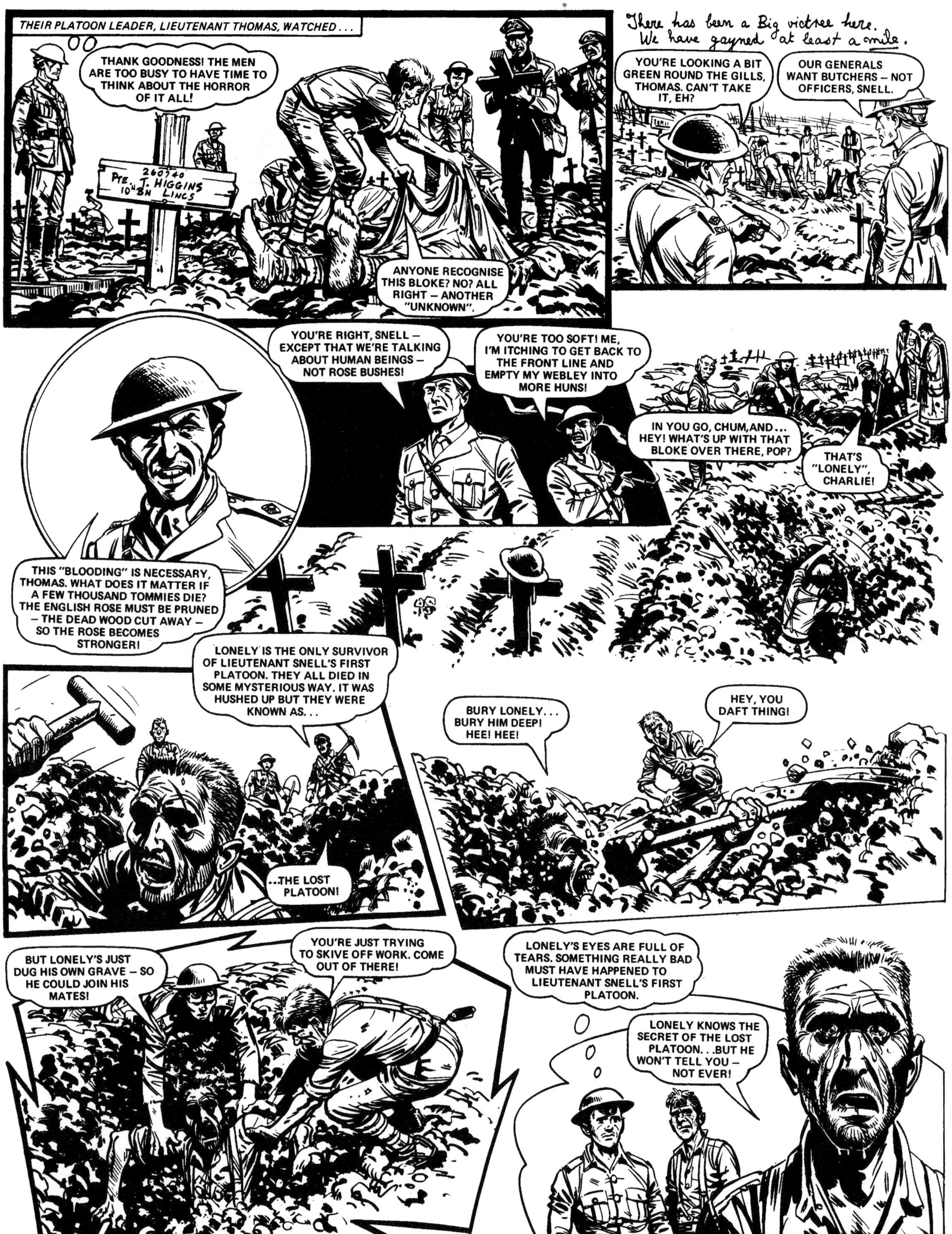

THEIR PLATOON LEADER, LIEUTENANT THOMAS, WATCHED...
THANK GOODNESS! THE MEN ARE TOO BUSY TO HAVE TIME TO THINK ABOUT THE HORROR OF IT ALL!
260740 PTE. J. HIGGINS 10th BN LINCS
ANYONE RECOGNISE THIS BLOKE? NO? ALL RIGHT – ANOTHER "UNKNOWN".
There has been a Big victree here. We have gayned at least a mile.
YOU'RE LOOKING A BIT GREEN ROUND THE GILLS, THOMAS. CAN'T TAKE IT, EH?
OUR GENERALS WANT BUTCHERS – NOT OFFICERS, SNELL.
THIS "BLOODING" IS NECESSARY, THOMAS. WHAT DOES IT MATTER IF A FEW THOUSAND TOMMIES DIE? THE ENGLISH ROSE MUST BE PRUNED – THE DEAD WOOD CUT AWAY – SO THE ROSE BECOMES STRONGER!
YOU'RE RIGHT, SNELL – EXCEPT THAT WE'RE TALKING ABOUT HUMAN BEINGS – NOT ROSE BUSHES!
YOU'RE TOO SOFT! ME, I'M ITCHING TO GET BACK TO THE FRONT LINE AND EMPTY MY WEBLEY INTO MORE HUNS!
IN YOU GO, CHUM, AND... HEY! WHAT'S UP WITH THAT BLOKE OVER THERE, POP?
THAT'S "LONELY", CHARLIE!
LONELY IS THE ONLY SURVIVOR OF LIEUTENANT SNELL'S FIRST PLATOON. THEY ALL DIED IN SOME MYSTERIOUS WAY. IT WAS HUSHED UP BUT THEY WERE KNOWN AS...
...THE LOST PLATOON!
BURY LONELY... BURY HIM DEEP! HEE! HEE!
HEY, YOU DAFT THING!
BUT LONELY'S JUST DUG HIS OWN GRAVE – SO HE COULD JOIN HIS MATES!
YOU'RE JUST TRYING TO SKIVE OFF WORK. COME OUT OF THERE!
LONELY'S EYES ARE FULL OF TEARS. SOMETHING REALLY BAD MUST HAVE HAPPENED TO LIEUTENANT SNELL'S FIRST PLATOON.
LONELY KNOWS THE SECRET OF THE LOST PLATOON...BUT HE WON'T TELL YOU – NOT EVER!

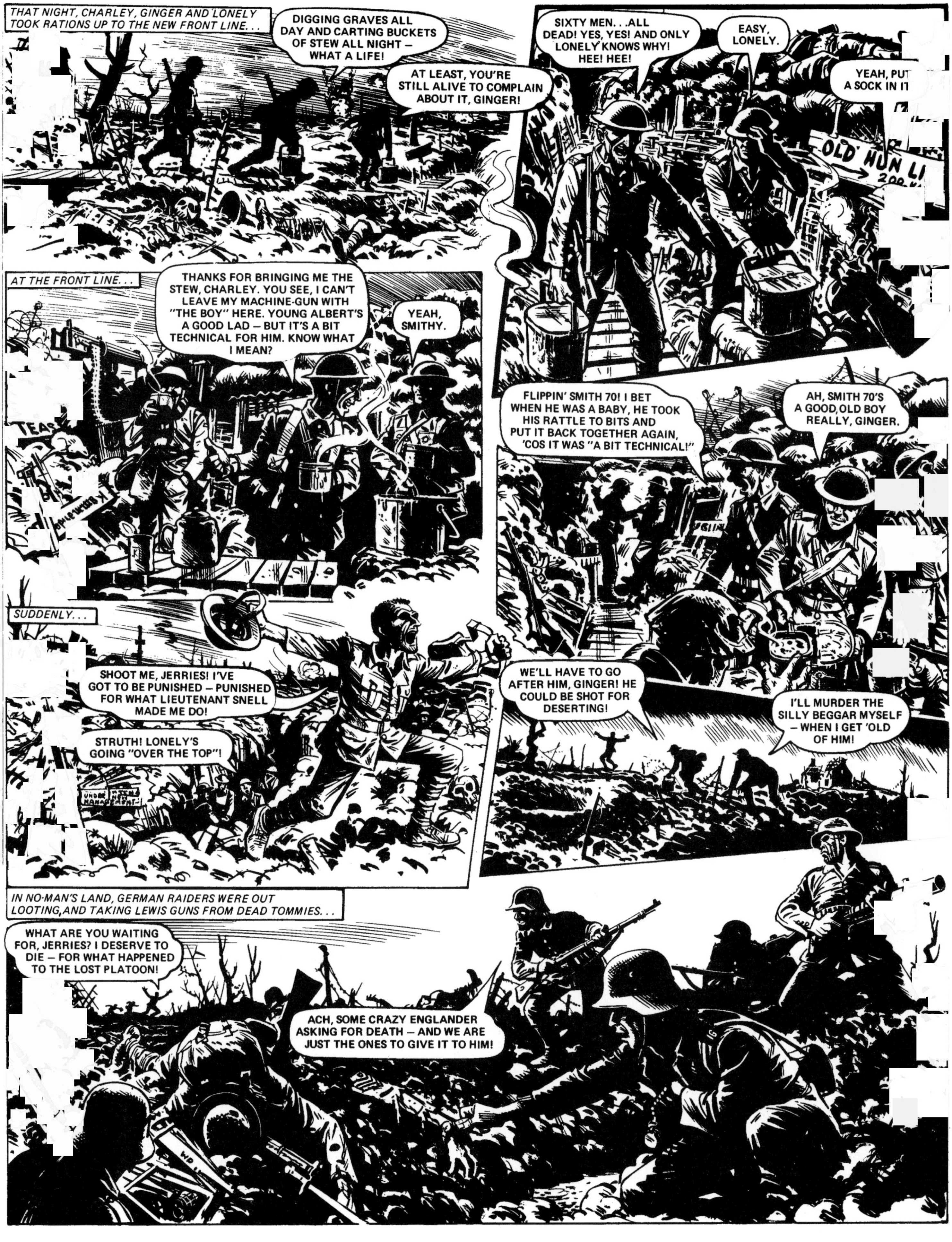

THAT NIGHT, CHARLEY, GINGER AND LONELY TOOK RATIONS UP TO THE NEW FRONT LINE...
DIGGING GRAVES ALL DAY AND CARTING BUCKETS OF STEW ALL NIGHT – WHAT A LIFE!
AT LEAST, YOU'RE STILL ALIVE TO COMPLAIN ABOUT IT, GINGER!
SIXTY MEN...ALL DEAD! YES, YES! AND ONLY LONELY KNOWS WHY! HEE! HEE!
EASY, LONELY.
YEAH, PUT A SOCK IN IT
OLD HUN LI
AT THE FRONT LINE...
THANKS FOR BRINGING ME THE STEW, CHARLEY. YOU SEE, I CAN'T LEAVE MY MACHINE-GUN WITH "THE BOY" HERE. YOUNG ALBERT'S A GOOD LAD – BUT IT'S A BIT TECHNICAL FOR HIM. KNOW WHAT I MEAN?
YEAH, SMITHY.
FLIPPIN' SMITH 70! I BET WHEN HE WAS A BABY, HE TOOK HIS RATTLE TO BITS AND PUT IT BACK TOGETHER AGAIN, 'COS IT WAS "A BIT TECHNICAL!"
AH, SMITH 70'S A GOOD, OLD BOY REALLY, GINGER.
SUDDENLY...
SHOOT ME, JERRIES! I'VE GOT TO BE PUNISHED – PUNISHED FOR WHAT LIEUTENANT SNELL MADE ME DO!
STRUTH! LONELY'S GOING "OVER THE TOP"!
WE'LL HAVE TO GO AFTER HIM, GINGER! HE COULD BE SHOT FOR DESERTING!
I'LL MURDER THE SILLY BEGGAR MYSELF – WHEN I GET 'OLD OF HIM!
IN NO-MAN'S LAND, GERMAN RAIDERS WERE OUT LOOTING, AND TAKING LEWIS GUNS FROM DEAD TOMMIES...
WHAT ARE YOU WAITING FOR, JERRIES? I DESERVE TO DIE – FOR WHAT HAPPENED TO THE LOST PLATOON!
ACH, SOME CRAZY ENGLANDER ASKING FOR DEATH – AND WE ARE JUST THE ONES TO GIVE IT TO HIM!

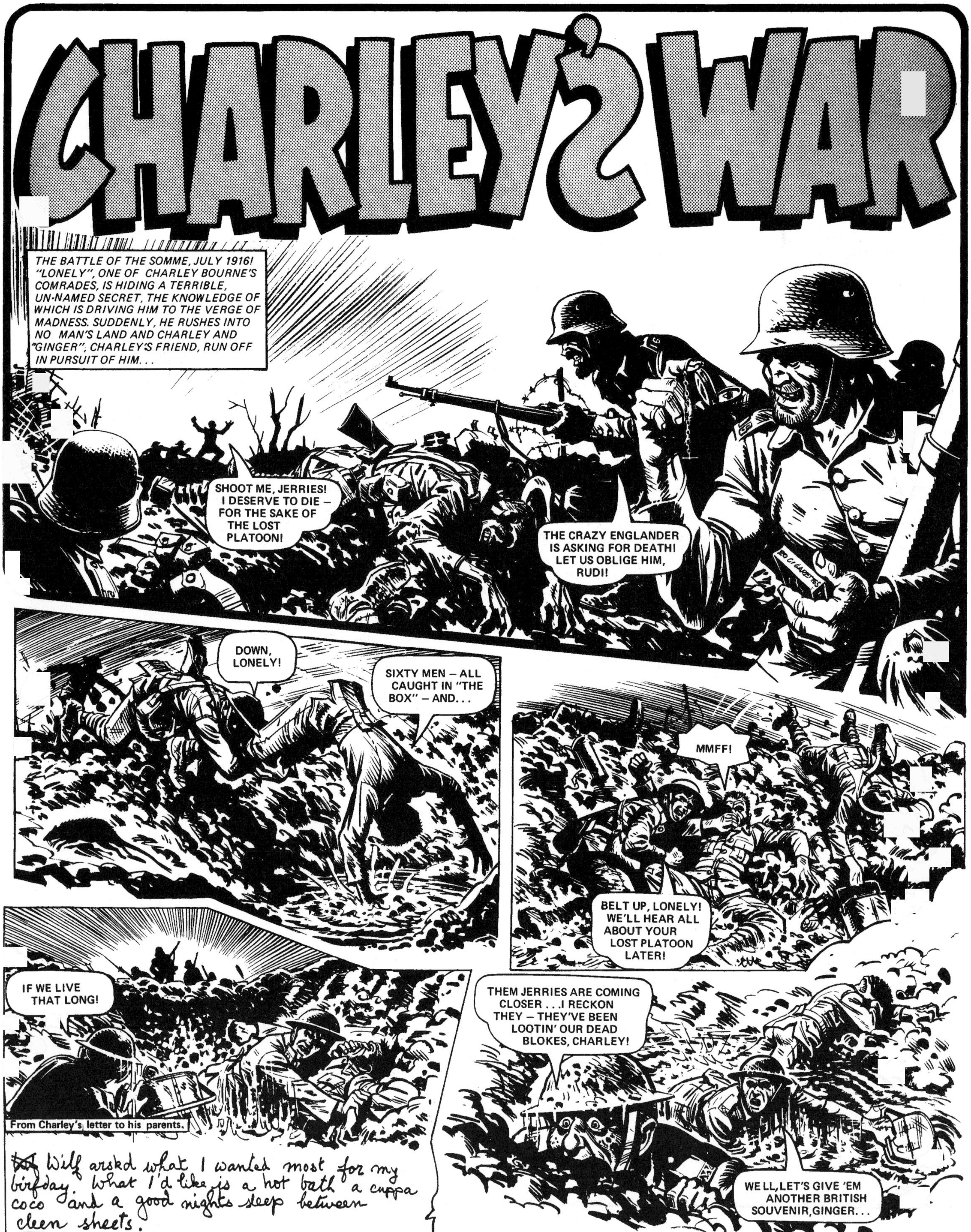
CHARLEY'S WAR
THE BATTLE OF THE SOMME, JULY 1916! "LONELY", ONE OF CHARLEY BOURNE'S COMRADES, IS HIDING A TERRIBLE, UN-NAMED SECRET, THE KNOWLEDGE OF WHICH IS DRIVING HIM TO THE VERGE OF MADNESS. SUDDENLY, HE RUSHES INTO NO MAN'S LAND AND CHARLEY AND "GINGER", CHARLEY'S FRIEND, RUN OFF IN PURSUIT OF HIM...
SHOOT ME, JERRIES! I DESERVE TO DIE – FOR THE SAKE OF THE LOST PLATOON!
THE CRAZY ENGLANDER IS ASKING FOR DEATH! LET US OBLIGE HIM, RUDI!
DOWN, LONELY!
SIXTY MEN – ALL CAUGHT IN "THE BOX" – AND...
MMFF!
BELT UP, LONELY! WE'LL HEAR ALL ABOUT YOUR LOST PLATOON LATER!
IF WE LIVE THAT LONG!
THEM JERRIES ARE COMING CLOSER ... I RECKON THEY – THEY'VE BEEN LOOTIN' OUR DEAD BLOKES, CHARLEY!
WELL, LET'S GIVE 'EM ANOTHER BRITISH SOUVENIR, GINGER...
From Charley's letter to his parents.
Wilf arskd what I wanted most for my birfday. What I'd like is a hot bath a cuppa coco and a good nights sleep between cleen sheets.

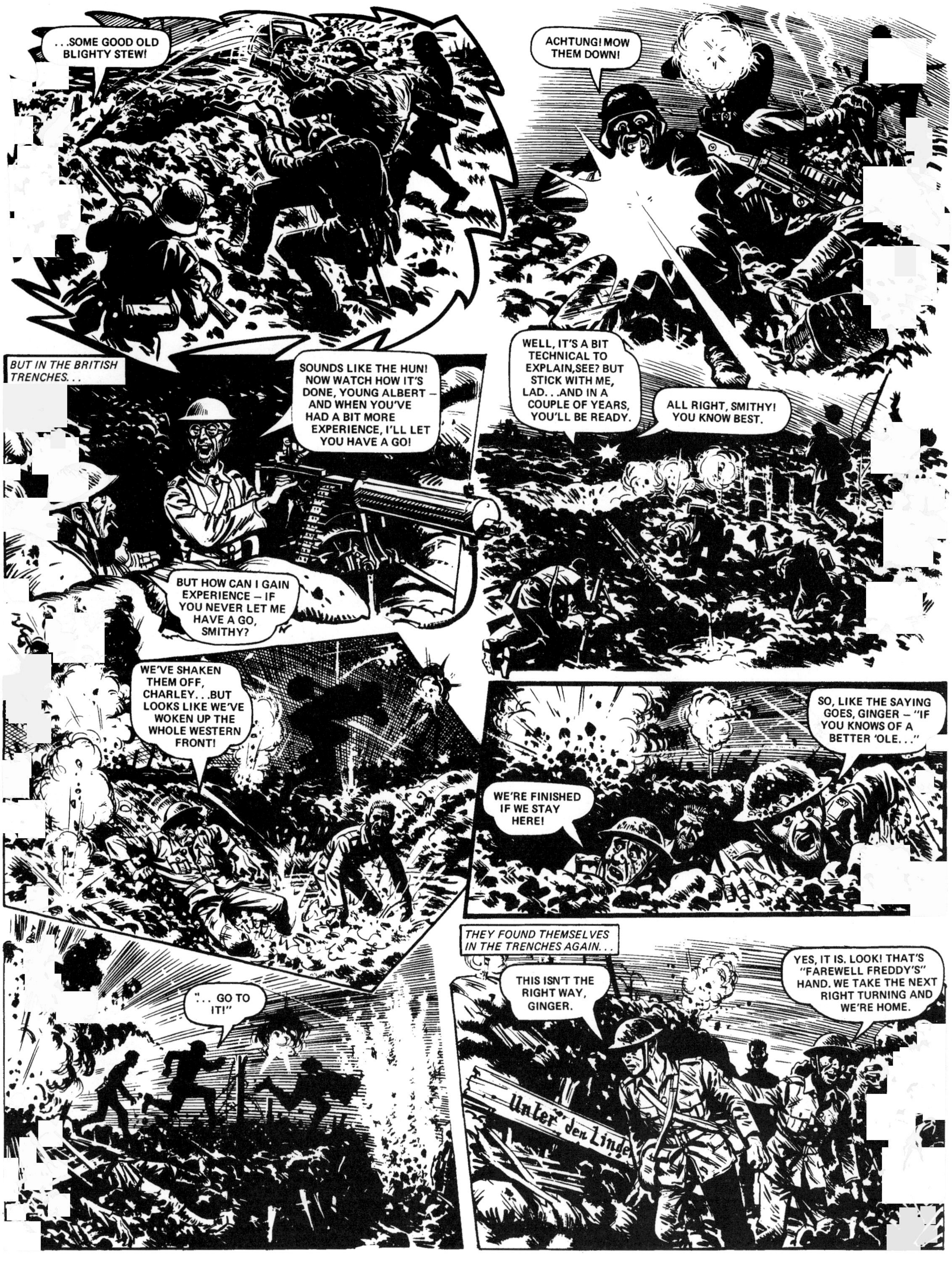

. . .SOME GOOD OLD BLIGHTY STEW!
ACHTUNG! MOW THEM DOWN!
BUT IN THE BRITISH TRENCHES. . .
SOUNDS LIKE THE HUN! NOW WATCH HOW IT'S DONE, YOUNG ALBERT – AND WHEN YOU'VE HAD A BIT MORE EXPERIENCE, I'LL LET YOU HAVE A GO!
BUT HOW CAN I GAIN EXPERIENCE – IF YOU NEVER LET ME HAVE A GO, SMITHY?
WELL, IT'S A BIT TECHNICAL TO EXPLAIN, SEE? BUT STICK WITH ME, LAD. . .AND IN A COUPLE OF YEARS, YOU'LL BE READY.
ALL RIGHT, SMITHY! YOU KNOW BEST.
WE'VE SHAKEN THEM OFF, CHARLEY. . .BUT LOOKS LIKE WE'VE WOKEN UP THE WHOLE WESTERN FRONT!
WE'RE FINISHED IF WE STAY HERE!
SO, LIKE THE SAYING GOES, GINGER – "IF YOU KNOWS OF A BETTER 'OLE. . ."
". . . GO TO IT!"
THEY FOUND THEMSELVES IN THE TRENCHES AGAIN. . .
THIS ISN'T THE RIGHT WAY, GINGER.
YES, IT IS. LOOK! THAT'S "FAREWELL FREDDY'S" HAND. WE TAKE THE NEXT RIGHT TURNING AND WE'RE HOME.
Unter den Linde

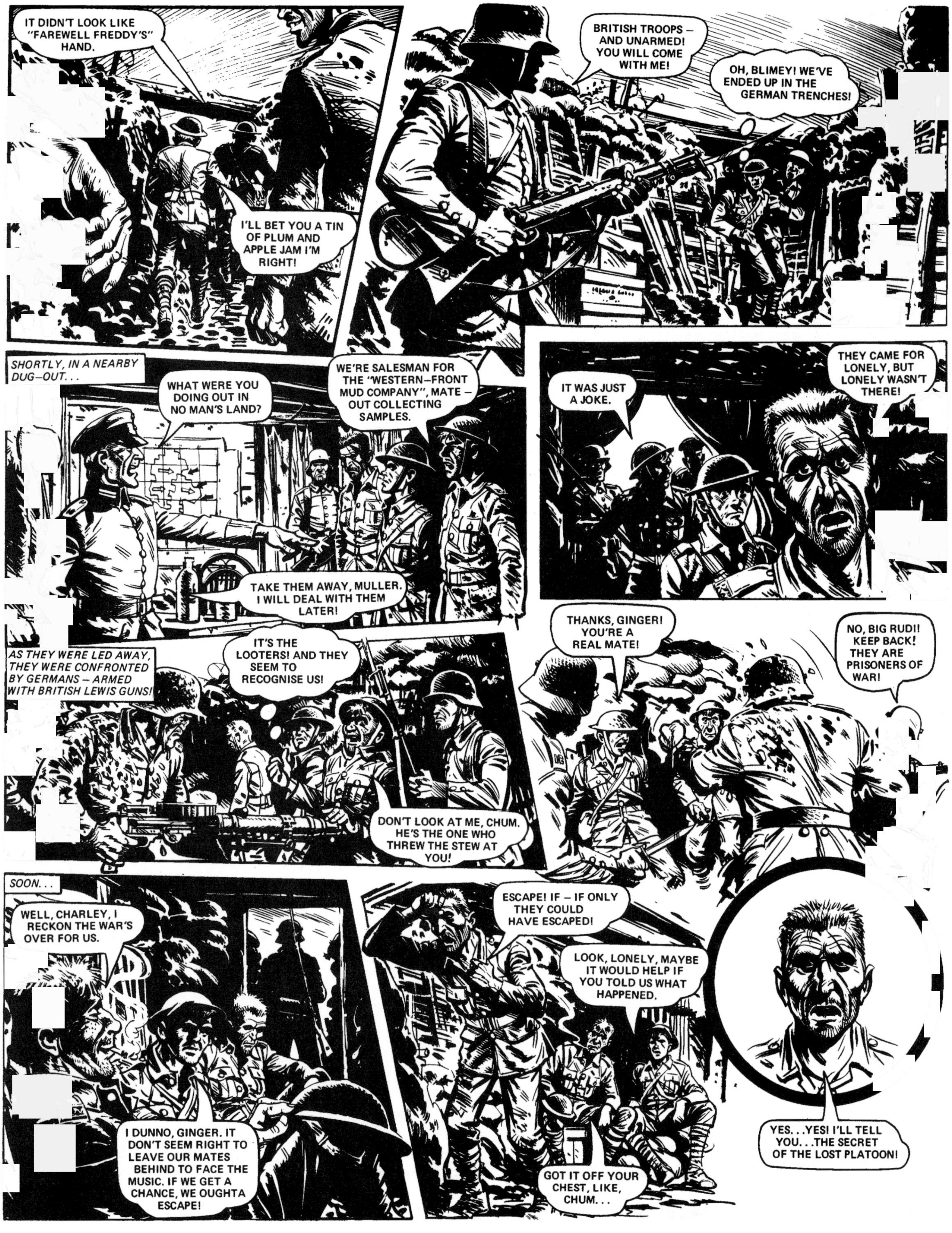
IT DIDN'T LOOK LIKE "FAREWELL FREDDY'S" HAND.
I'LL BET YOU A TIN OF PLUM AND APPLE JAM I'M RIGHT!
BRITISH TROOPS – AND UNARMED! YOU WILL COME WITH ME!
OH, BLIMEY! WE'VE ENDED UP IN THE GERMAN TRENCHES!
SHORTLY, IN A NEARBY DUG-OUT. . .
WHAT WERE YOU DOING OUT IN NO MAN'S LAND?
WE'RE SALESMAN FOR THE "WESTERN-FRONT MUD COMPANY", MATE – OUT COLLECTING SAMPLES.
TAKE THEM AWAY, MULLER. I WILL DEAL WITH THEM LATER!
IT WAS JUST A JOKE.
THEY CAME FOR LONELY, BUT LONELY WASN'T THERE!
AS THEY WERE LED AWAY, THEY WERE CONFRONTED BY GERMANS – ARMED WITH BRITISH LEWIS GUNS!
IT'S THE LOOTERS! AND THEY SEEM TO RECOGNISE US!
DON'T LOOK AT ME, CHUM. HE'S THE ONE WHO THREW THE STEW AT YOU!
THANKS, GINGER! YOU'RE A REAL MATE!
NO, BIG RUDI! KEEP BACK! THEY ARE PRISONERS OF WAR!
SOON. . .
WELL, CHARLEY, I RECKON THE WAR'S OVER FOR US.
I DUNNO, GINGER. IT DON'T SEEM RIGHT TO LEAVE OUR MATES BEHIND TO FACE THE MUSIC. IF WE GET A CHANCE, WE OUGHTA ESCAPE!
ESCAPE! IF – IF ONLY THEY COULD HAVE ESCAPED!
LOOK, LONELY, MAYBE IT WOULD HELP IF YOU TOLD US WHAT HAPPENED.
GOT IT OFF YOUR CHEST, LIKE, CHUM. . .
YES. . .YES! I'LL TELL YOU. . .THE SECRET OF THE LOST PLATOON!

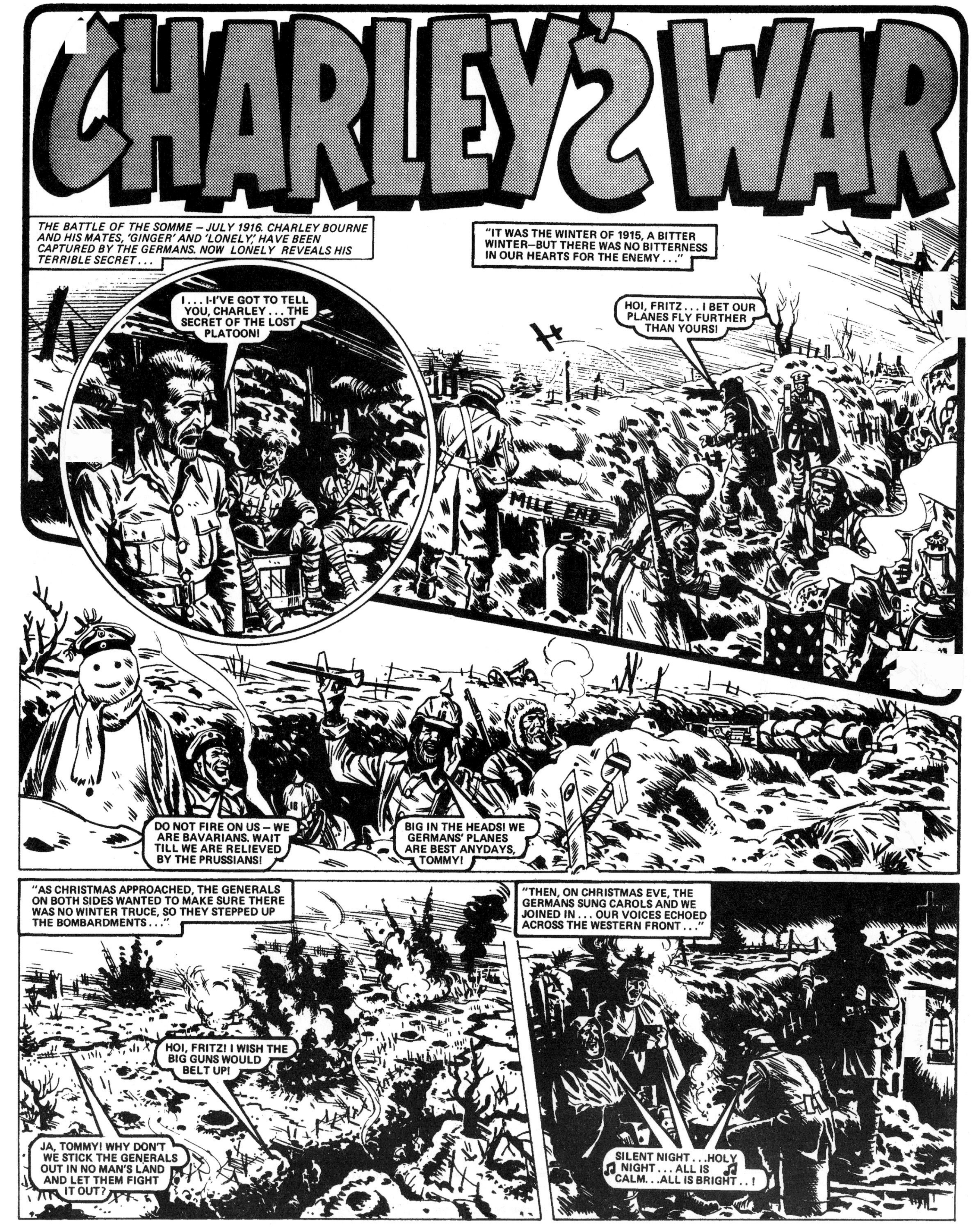
CHARLEY'S WAR
THE BATTLE OF THE SOMME – JULY 1916. CHARLEY BOURNE AND HIS MATES, 'GINGER' AND 'LONELY,' HAVE BEEN CAPTURED BY THE GERMANS. NOW LONELY REVEALS HIS TERRIBLE SECRET . . .
I . . . I-I'VE GOT TO TELL YOU, CHARLEY . . . THE SECRET OF THE LOST PLATOON!
"IT WAS THE WINTER OF 1915, A BITTER WINTER—BUT THERE WAS NO BITTERNESS IN OUR HEARTS FOR THE ENEMY . . ."
HOI, FRITZ . . . I BET OUR PLANES FLY FURTHER THAN YOURS!
MILE END
DO NOT FIRE ON US – WE ARE BAVARIANS. WAIT TILL WE ARE RELIEVED BY THE PRUSSIANS!
BIG IN THE HEADS! WE GERMANS' PLANES ARE BEST ANYDAYS, TOMMY!
"AS CHRISTMAS APPROACHED, THE GENERALS ON BOTH SIDES WANTED TO MAKE SURE THERE WAS NO WINTER TRUCE, SO THEY STEPPED UP THE BOMBARDMENTS . . ."
HOI, FRITZ! I WISH THE BIG GUNS WOULD BELT UP!
JA, TOMMY! WHY DON'T WE STICK THE GENERALS OUT IN NO MAN'S LAND AND LET THEM FIGHT IT OUT?
"THEN, ON CHRISTMAS EVE, THE GERMANS SUNG CAROLS AND WE JOINED IN . . . OUR VOICES ECHOED ACROSS THE WESTERN FRONT . . ."
SILENT NIGHT . . . HOLY NIGHT . . . ALL IS CALM. . . ALL IS BRIGHT . . !

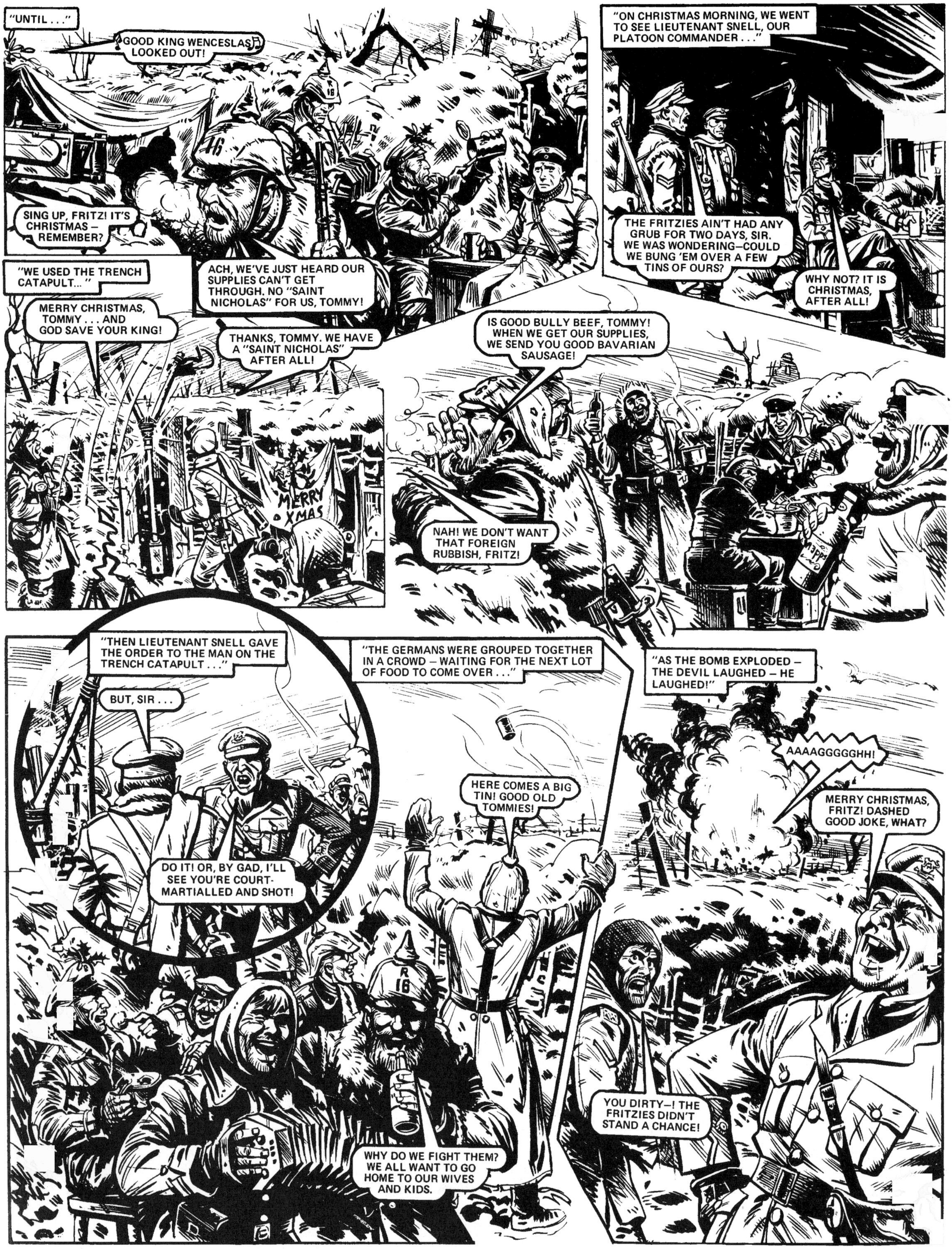

"UNTIL . . ."
GOOD KING WENCESLAS LOOKED OUT!
SING UP, FRITZ! IT'S CHRISTMAS – REMEMBER?
ACH, WE'VE JUST HEARD OUR SUPPLIES CAN'T GET THROUGH. NO "SAINT NICHOLAS" FOR US, TOMMY!
"ON CHRISTMAS MORNING, WE WENT TO SEE LIEUTENANT SNELL, OUR PLATOON COMMANDER . . ."
THE FRITZIES AIN'T HAD ANY GRUB FOR TWO DAYS, SIR. WE WAS WONDERING—COULD WE BUNG 'EM OVER A FEW TINS OF OURS?
WHY NOT? IT IS CHRISTMAS, AFTER ALL!
"WE USED THE TRENCH CATAPULT... "
MERRY CHRISTMAS, TOMMY . . . AND GOD SAVE YOUR KING!
THANKS, TOMMY. WE HAVE A "SAINT NICHOLAS" AFTER ALL!
MERRY XMAS
IS GOOD BULLY BEEF, TOMMY! WHEN WE GET OUR SUPPLIES, WE SEND YOU GOOD BAVARIAN SAUSAGE!
NAH! WE DON'T WANT THAT FOREIGN RUBBISH, FRITZ!
"THEN LIEUTENANT SNELL GAVE THE ORDER TO THE MAN ON THE TRENCH CATAPULT . . ."
BUT, SIR . . .
DO IT! OR, BY GAD, I'LL SEE YOU'RE COURT-MARTIALLED AND SHOT!
"THE GERMANS WERE GROUPED TOGETHER IN A CROWD – WAITING FOR THE NEXT LOT OF FOOD TO COME OVER . . ."
HERE COMES A BIG TIN! GOOD OLD TOMMIES!
WHY DO WE FIGHT THEM? WE ALL WANT TO GO HOME TO OUR WIVES AND KIDS.
"AS THE BOMB EXPLODED – THE DEVIL LAUGHED – HE LAUGHED!"
AAAAGGGGGHH!
MERRY CHRISTMAS, FRITZ! DASHED GOOD JOKE, WHAT?
YOU DIRTY—! THE FRITZIES DIDN'T STAND A CHANCE!

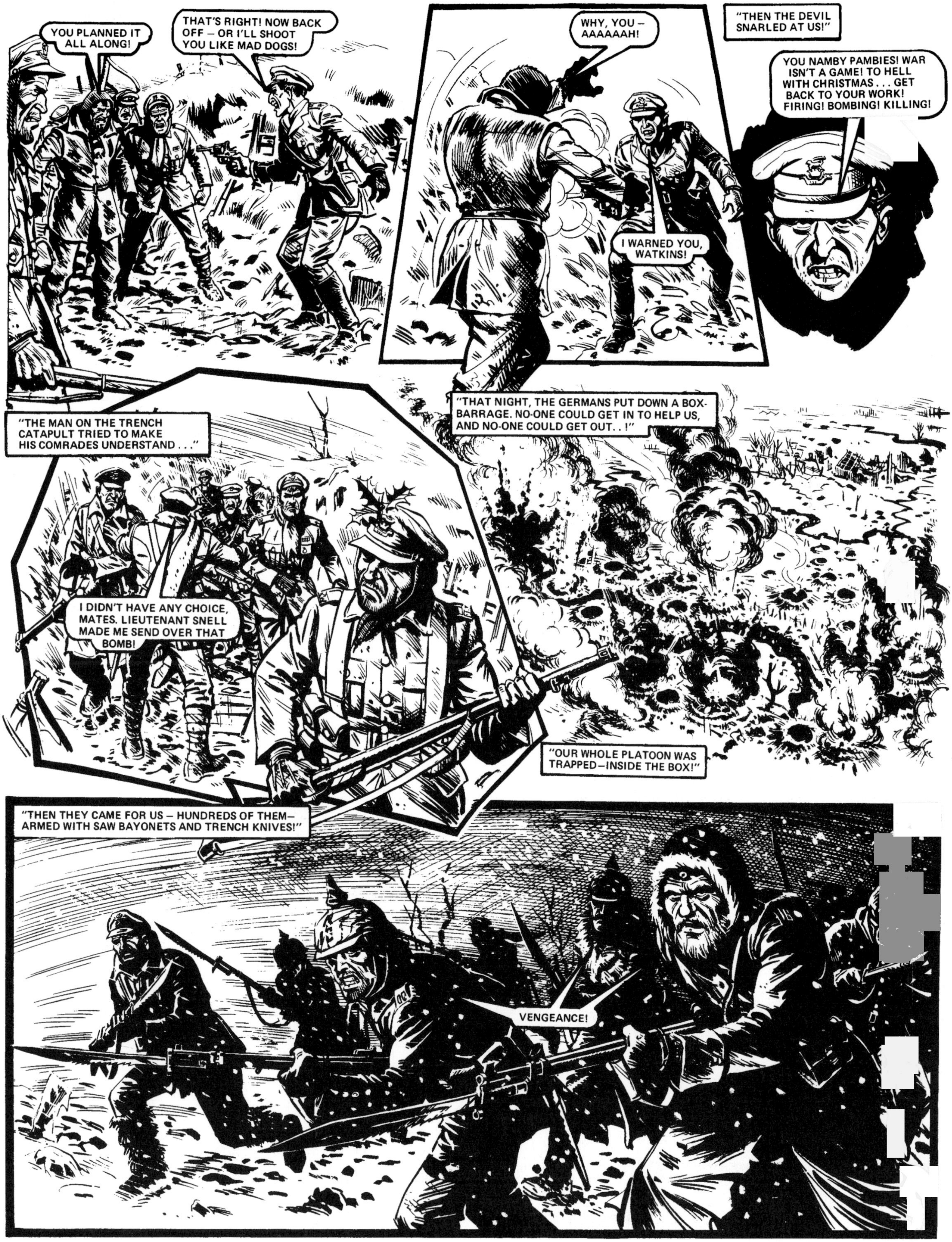
YOU PLANNED IT ALL ALONG!
THAT'S RIGHT! NOW BACK OFF – OR I'LL SHOOT YOU LIKE MAD DOGS!
WHY, YOU – AAAAAAH!
I WARNED YOU, WATKINS!
"THEN THE DEVIL SNARLED AT US!"
YOU NAMBY PAMBIES! WAR ISN'T A GAME! TO HELL WITH CHRISTMAS . . . GET BACK TO YOUR WORK! FIRING! BOMBING! KILLING!
"THE MAN ON THE TRENCH CATAPULT TRIED TO MAKE HIS COMRADES UNDERSTAND . . ."
I DIDN'T HAVE ANY CHOICE, MATES. LIEUTENANT SNELL MADE ME SEND OVER THAT BOMB!
"THAT NIGHT, THE GERMANS PUT DOWN A BOX-BARRAGE. NO-ONE COULD GET IN TO HELP US, AND NO-ONE COULD GET OUT. . !"
"OUR WHOLE PLATOON WAS TRAPPED–INSIDE THE BOX!"
"THEN THEY CAME FOR US – HUNDREDS OF THEM– ARMED WITH SAW BAYONETS AND TRENCH KNIVES!"
VENGEANCE!

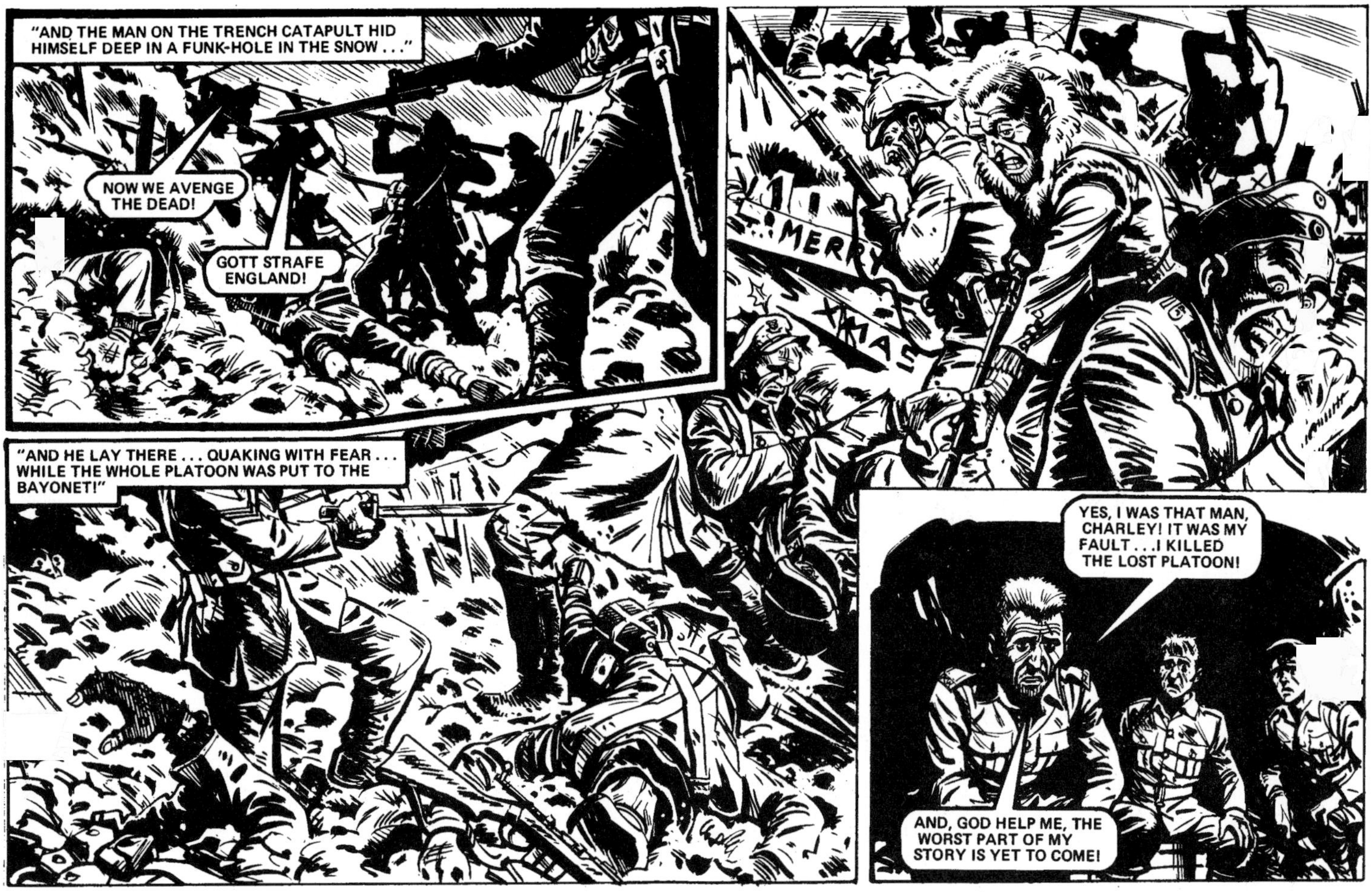
"AND THE MAN ON THE TRENCH CATAPULT HID HIMSELF DEEP IN A FUNK-HOLE IN THE SNOW . . ."
NOW WE AVENGE THE DEAD!
GOTT STRAFE ENGLAND!
MERRY XMAS
"AND HE LAY THERE . . . QUAKING WITH FEAR . . . WHILE THE WHOLE PLATOON WAS PUT TO THE BAYONET!"
YES, I WAS THAT MAN, CHARLEY! IT WAS MY FAULT . . . I KILLED THE LOST PLATOON!
AND, GOD HELP ME, THE WORST PART OF MY STORY IS YET TO COME!

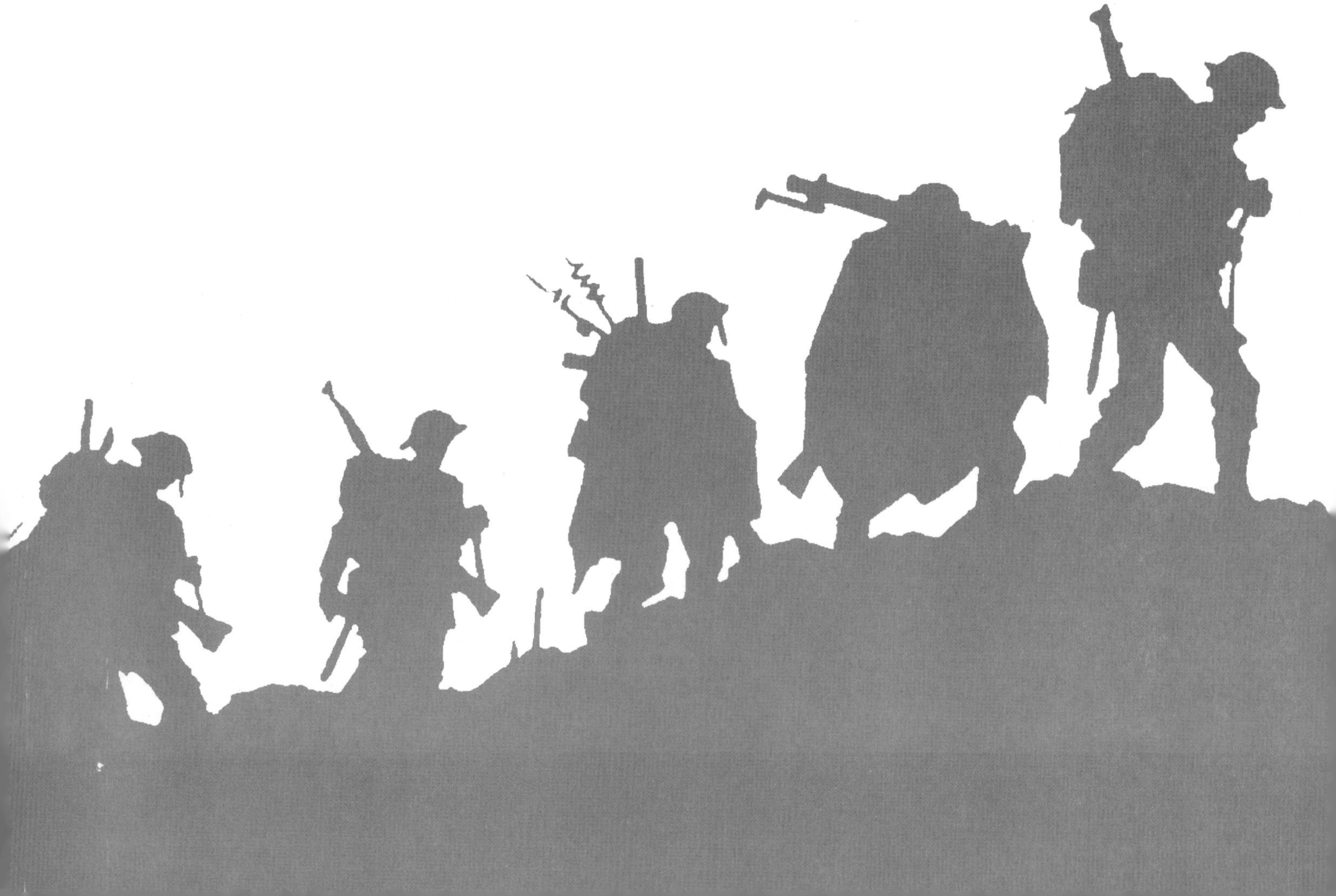

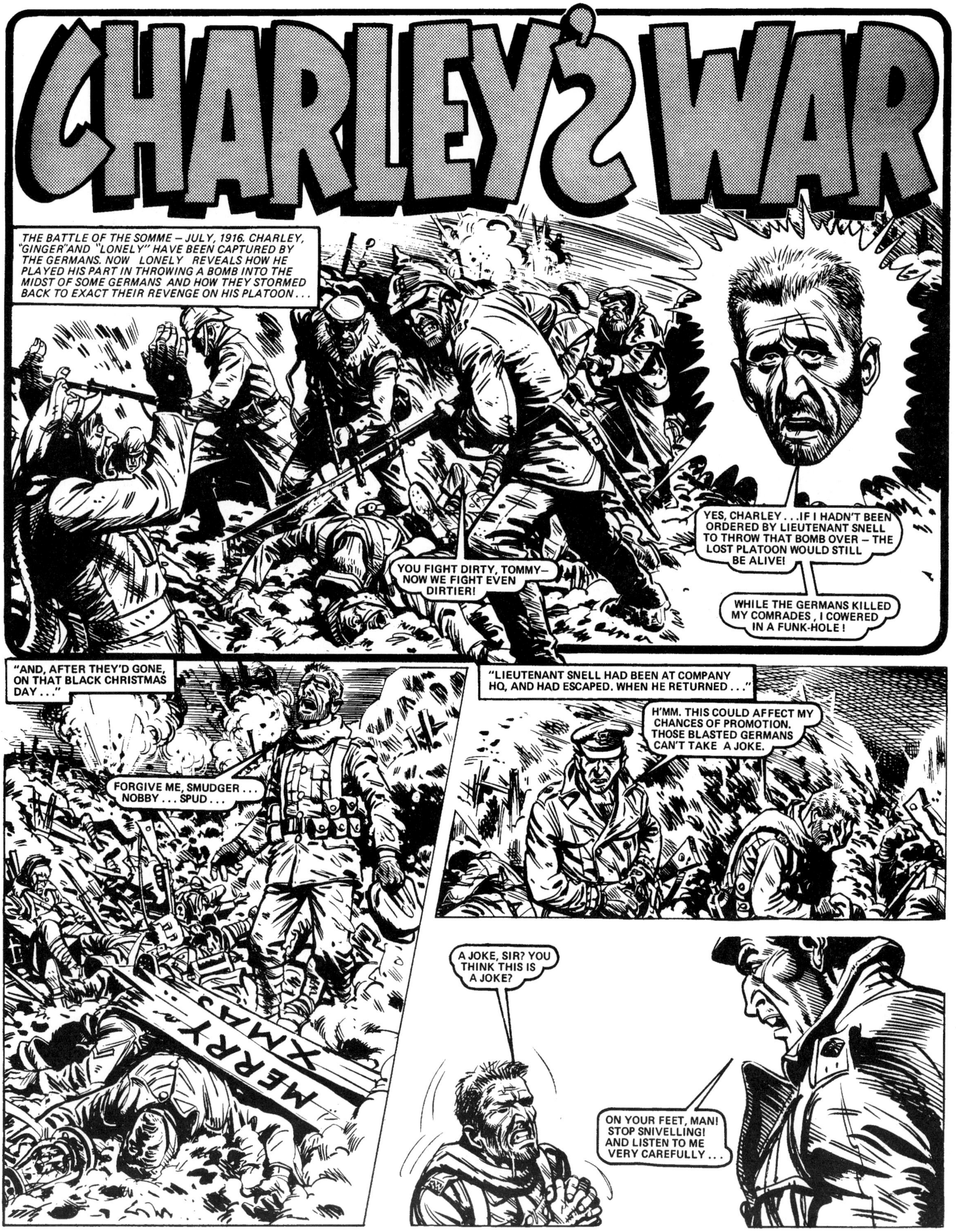
CHARLEY'S WAR
THE BATTLE OF THE SOMME – JULY, 1916. CHARLEY, "GINGER" AND "LONELY" HAVE BEEN CAPTURED BY THE GERMANS. NOW LONELY REVEALS HOW HE PLAYED HIS PART IN THROWING A BOMB INTO THE MIDST OF SOME GERMANS AND HOW THEY STORMED BACK TO EXACT THEIR REVENGE ON HIS PLATOON . . .
YES, CHARLEY . . . IF I HADN'T BEEN ORDERED BY LIEUTENANT SNELL TO THROW THAT BOMB OVER – THE LOST PLATOON WOULD STILL BE ALIVE!
YOU FIGHT DIRTY, TOMMY– NOW WE FIGHT EVEN DIRTIER!
WHILE THE GERMANS KILLED MY COMRADES, I COWERED IN A FUNK-HOLE!
"AND, AFTER THEY'D GONE, ON THAT BLACK CHRISTMAS DAY . . ."
FORGIVE ME, SMUDGER . . . NOBBY . . . SPUD . . .
MERRY XMAS
"LIEUTENANT SNELL HAD BEEN AT COMPANY HQ, AND HAD ESCAPED. WHEN HE RETURNED . . ."
H'MM. THIS COULD AFFECT MY CHANCES OF PROMOTION. THOSE BLASTED GERMANS CAN'T TAKE A JOKE.
A JOKE, SIR? YOU THINK THIS IS A JOKE?
ON YOUR FEET, MAN! STOP SNIVELLING! AND LISTEN TO ME VERY CAREFULLY . . .

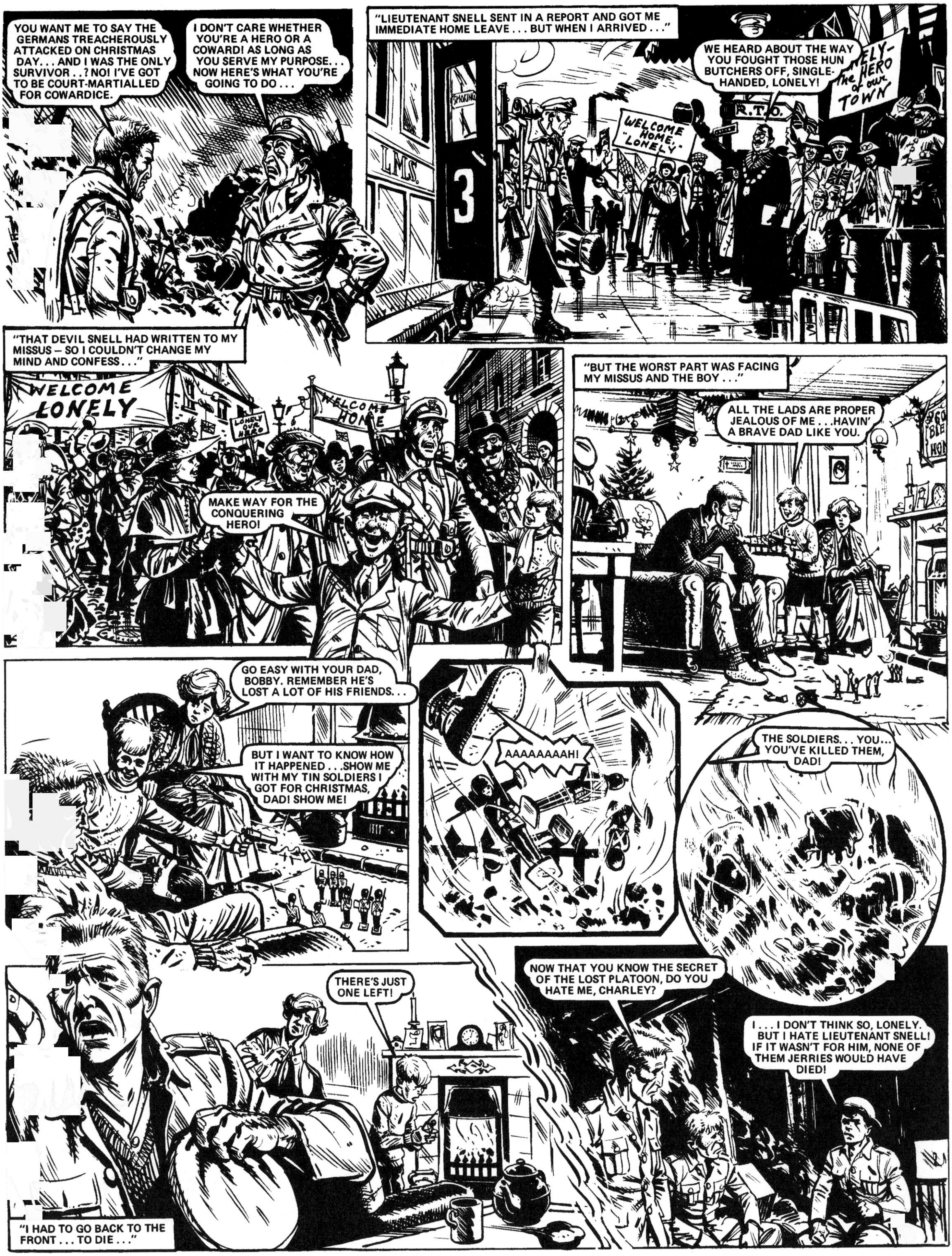
YOU WANT ME TO SAY THE GERMANS TREACHEROUSLY ATTACKED ON CHRISTMAS DAY. . . AND I WAS THE ONLY SURVIVOR . . ? NO! I'VE GOT TO BE COURT-MARTIALLED FOR COWARDICE.
I DON'T CARE WHETHER YOU'RE A HERO OR A COWARD! AS LONG AS YOU SERVE MY PURPOSE. . . NOW HERE'S WHAT YOU'RE GOING TO DO . . .
"LIEUTENANT SNELL SENT IN A REPORT AND GOT ME IMMEDIATE HOME LEAVE . . . BUT WHEN I ARRIVED . . ."
WE HEARD ABOUT THE WAY YOU FOUGHT THOSE HUN BUTCHERS OFF, SINGLE-HANDED, LONELY!
WELCOME HOME, "LONELY"
R.T.O.
L.M.S.
3
"THAT DEVIL SNELL HAD WRITTEN TO MY MISSUS – SO I COULDN'T CHANGE MY MIND AND CONFESS . . ."
WELCOME LONELY
WELCOME HOME
MAKE WAY FOR THE CONQUERING HERO!
"BUT THE WORST PART WAS FACING MY MISSUS AND THE BOY . . ."
ALL THE LADS ARE PROPER JEALOUS OF ME . . .HAVIN' A BRAVE DAD LIKE YOU.
GO EASY WITH YOUR DAD, BOBBY. REMEMBER HE'S LOST A LOT OF HIS FRIENDS. . .
BUT I WANT TO KNOW HOW IT HAPPENED . . .SHOW ME WITH MY TIN SOLDIERS I GOT FOR CHRISTMAS, DAD! SHOW ME!
AAAAAAAAH!
THE SOLDIERS. . . YOU. . . YOU'VE KILLED THEM, DAD!
THERE'S JUST ONE LEFT!
NOW THAT YOU KNOW THE SECRET OF THE LOST PLATOON, DO YOU HATE ME, CHARLEY?
I . . . I DON'T THINK SO, LONELY. BUT I HATE LIEUTENANT SNELL! IF IT WASN'T FOR HIM, NONE OF THEM JERRIES WOULD HAVE DIED!
"I HAD TO GO BACK TO THE FRONT . . . TO DIE . . ."

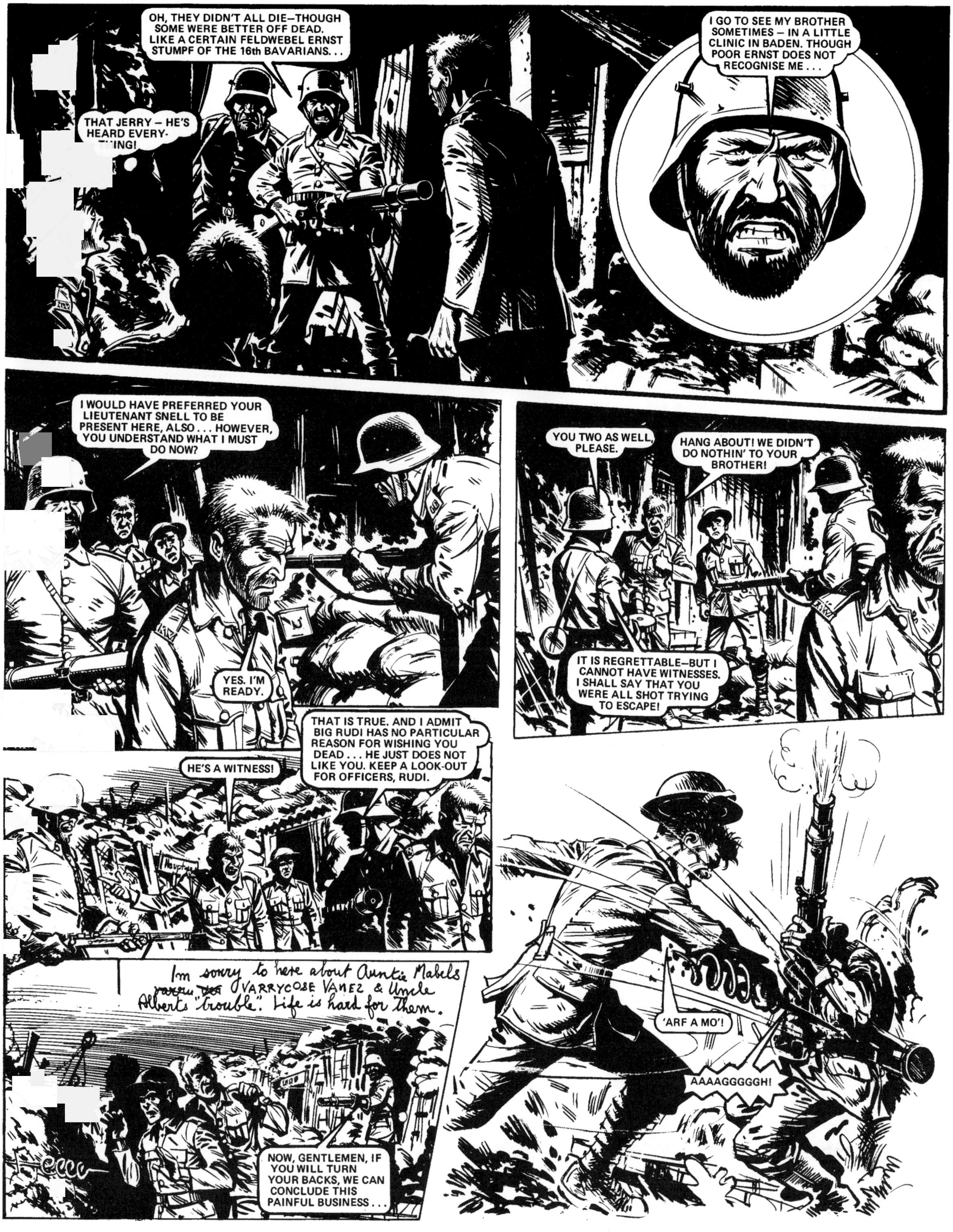

OH, THEY DIDN'T ALL DIE–THOUGH SOME WERE BETTER OFF DEAD. LIKE A CERTAIN FELDWEBEL ERNST STUMPF OF THE 16th BAVARIANS . . .
THAT JERRY – HE'S HEARD EVERY-THING!
I GO TO SEE MY BROTHER SOMETIMES – IN A LITTLE CLINIC IN BADEN. THOUGH POOR ERNST DOES NOT RECOGNISE ME . . .
I WOULD HAVE PREFERRED YOUR LIEUTENANT SNELL TO BE PRESENT HERE, ALSO . . . HOWEVER, YOU UNDERSTAND WHAT I MUST DO NOW?
YES. I'M READY.
YOU TWO AS WELL, PLEASE.
HANG ABOUT! WE DIDN'T DO NOTHIN' TO YOUR BROTHER!
IT IS REGRETTABLE–BUT I CANNOT HAVE WITNESSES. I SHALL SAY THAT YOU WERE ALL SHOT TRYING TO ESCAPE!
HE'S A WITNESS!
THAT IS TRUE. AND I ADMIT BIG RUDI HAS NO PARTICULAR REASON FOR WISHING YOU DEAD . . . HE JUST DOES NOT LIKE YOU. KEEP A LOOK-OUT FOR OFFICERS, RUDI.
I'm sorry to here about Auntie Mabels VARRYCOSE VANEZ & Uncle Alberts "trouble". Life is hard for Them.
NOW, GENTLEMEN, IF YOU WILL TURN YOUR BACKS, WE CAN CONCLUDE THIS PAINFUL BUSINESS . . .
'ARF A MO'!
AAAAGGGGGH!

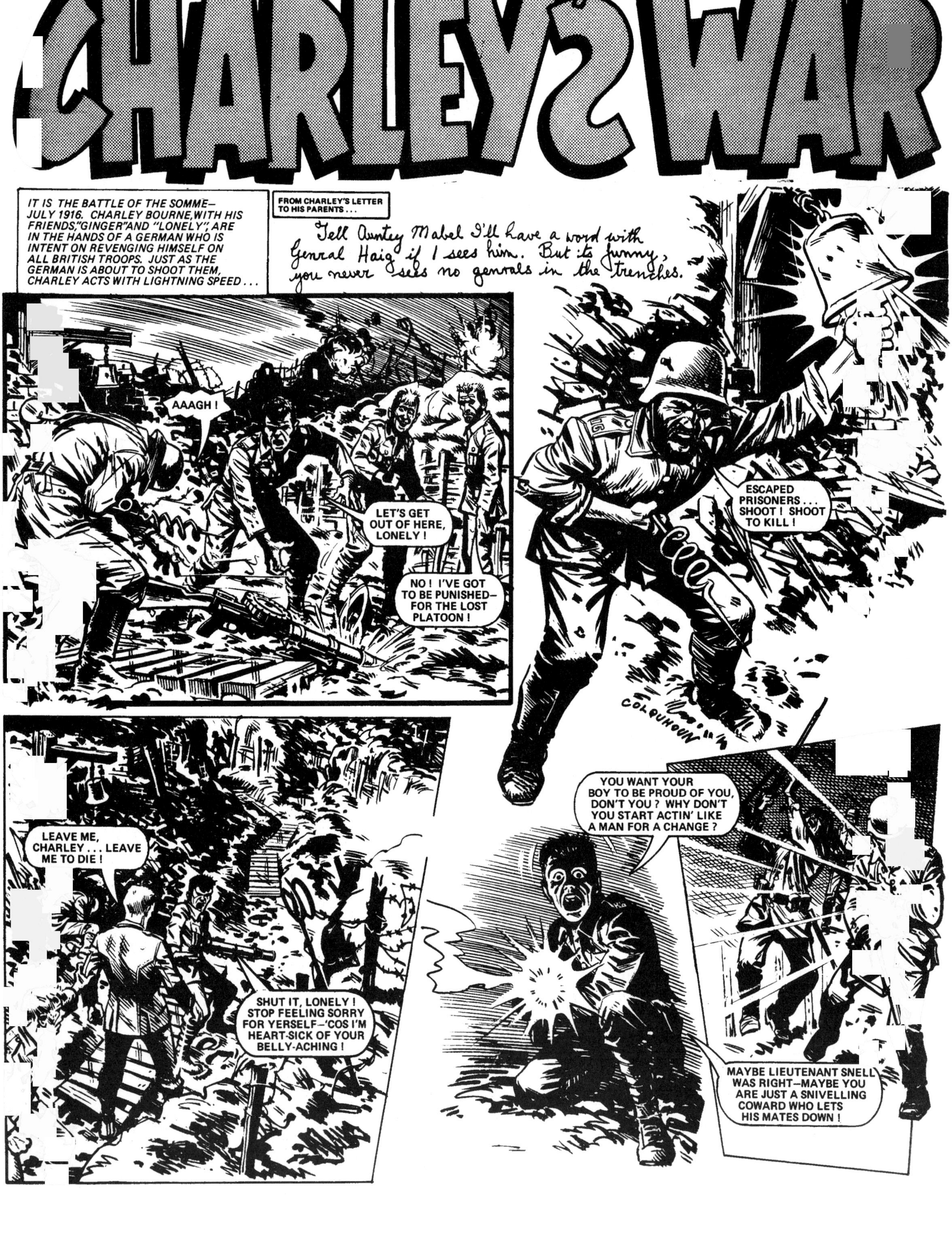
CHARLEY'S WAR
IT IS THE BATTLE OF THE SOMME—JULY 1916. CHARLEY BOURNE, WITH HIS FRIENDS, "GINGER" AND "LONELY", ARE IN THE HANDS OF A GERMAN WHO IS INTENT ON REVENGING HIMSELF ON ALL BRITISH TROOPS. JUST AS THE GERMAN IS ABOUT TO SHOOT THEM, CHARLEY ACTS WITH LIGHTNING SPEED . . .
FROM CHARLEY'S LETTER TO HIS PARENTS . . .
Tell Auntey Mabel I'll have a word with Genral Haig if I sees him. But its funny, you never sees no genrals in the trenches.
AAAGH !
LET'S GET OUT OF HERE, LONELY !
NO ! I'VE GOT TO BE PUNISHED—FOR THE LOST PLATOON !
ESCAPED PRISONERS . . . SHOOT ! SHOOT TO KILL !
COLQUHOUN
LEAVE ME, CHARLEY . . . LEAVE ME TO DIE !
SHUT IT, LONELY ! STOP FEELING SORRY FOR YERSELF—'COS I'M HEART-SICK OF YOUR BELLY-ACHING !
YOU WANT YOUR BOY TO BE PROUD OF YOU, DON'T YOU ? WHY DON'T YOU START ACTIN' LIKE A MAN FOR A CHANGE ?
MAYBE LIEUTENANT SNELL WAS RIGHT—MAYBE YOU ARE JUST A SNIVELLING COWARD WHO LETS HIS MATES DOWN !

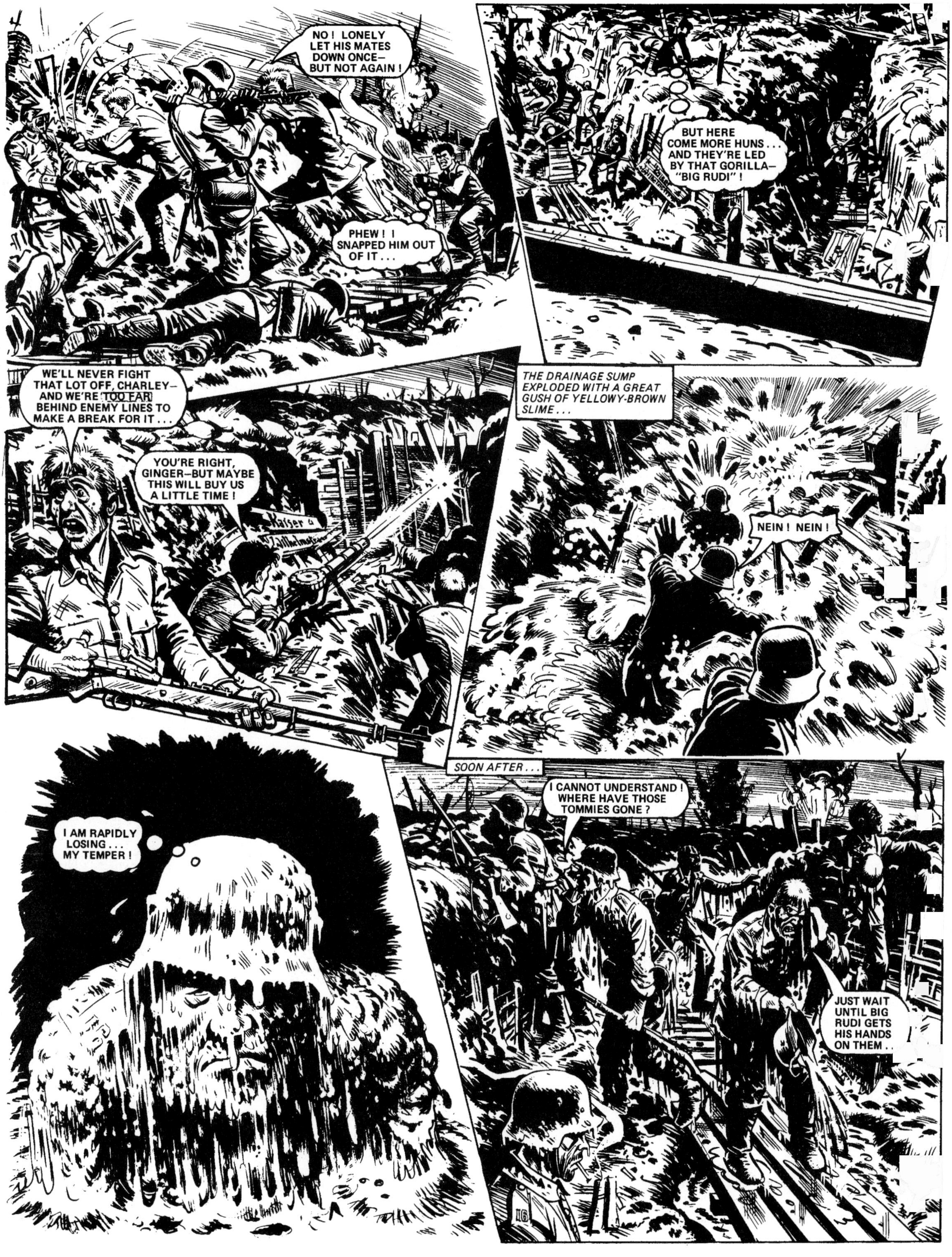
NO! LONELY LET HIS MATES DOWN ONCE– BUT NOT AGAIN!
PHEW! I SNAPPED HIM OUT OF IT . . .
BUT HERE COME MORE HUNS . . . AND THEY'RE LED BY THAT GORILLA– "BIG RUDI"!
WE'LL NEVER FIGHT THAT LOT OFF, CHARLEY– AND WE'RE TOO FAR BEHIND ENEMY LINES TO MAKE A BREAK FOR IT . . .
YOU'RE RIGHT, GINGER–BUT MAYBE THIS WILL BUY US A LITTLE TIME!
Kaiser
THE DRAINAGE SUMP EXPLODED WITH A GREAT GUSH OF YELLOWY-BROWN SLIME . . .
NEIN! NEIN!
I AM RAPIDLY LOSING . . . MY TEMPER!
SOON AFTER . . .
I CANNOT UNDERSTAND! WHERE HAVE THOSE TOMMIES GONE?
JUST WAIT UNTIL BIG RUDI GETS HIS HANDS ON THEM . . .
16

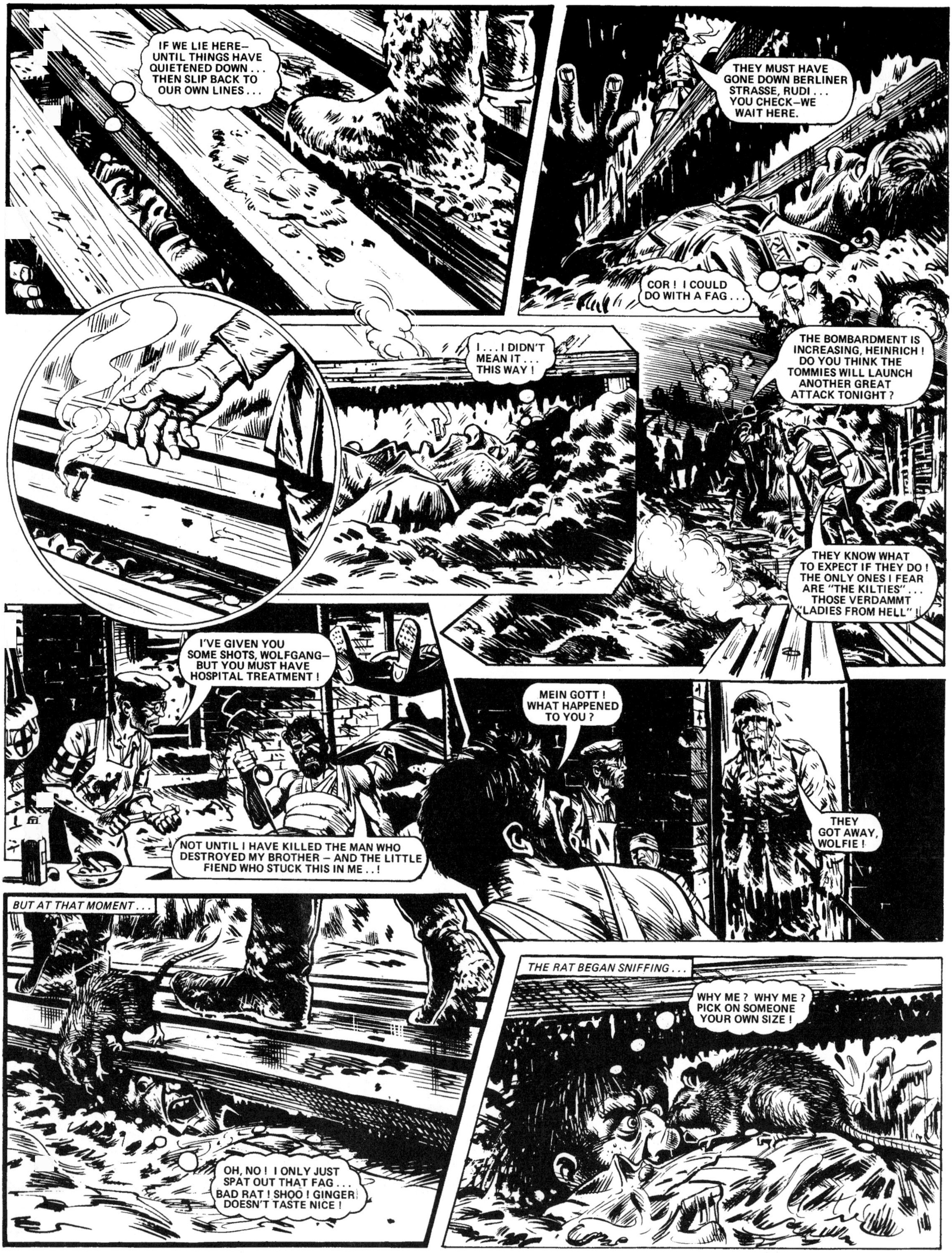

IF WE LIE HERE– UNTIL THINGS HAVE QUIETENED DOWN . . . THEN SLIP BACK TO OUR OWN LINES . . .
THEY MUST HAVE GONE DOWN BERLINER STRASSE, RUDI . . . YOU CHECK–WE WAIT HERE.
COR ! I COULD DO WITH A FAG . . .
I . . . I DIDN'T MEAN IT . . . THIS WAY !
THE BOMBARDMENT IS INCREASING, HEINRICH ! DO YOU THINK THE TOMMIES WILL LAUNCH ANOTHER GREAT ATTACK TONIGHT ?
THEY KNOW WHAT TO EXPECT IF THEY DO ! THE ONLY ONES I FEAR ARE "THE KILTIES" . . . THOSE VERDAMMT "LADIES FROM HELL" !
I'VE GIVEN YOU SOME SHOTS, WOLFGANG– BUT YOU MUST HAVE HOSPITAL TREATMENT !
NOT UNTIL I HAVE KILLED THE MAN WHO DESTROYED MY BROTHER – AND THE LITTLE FIEND WHO STUCK THIS IN ME . . !
MEIN GOTT ! WHAT HAPPENED TO YOU ?
THEY GOT AWAY, WOLFIE !
BUT AT THAT MOMENT . . .
OH, NO ! I ONLY JUST SPAT OUT THAT FAG . . . BAD RAT ! SHOO ! GINGER DOESN'T TASTE NICE !
THE RAT BEGAN SNIFFING . . .
WHY ME ? WHY ME ? PICK ON SOMEONE YOUR OWN SIZE !

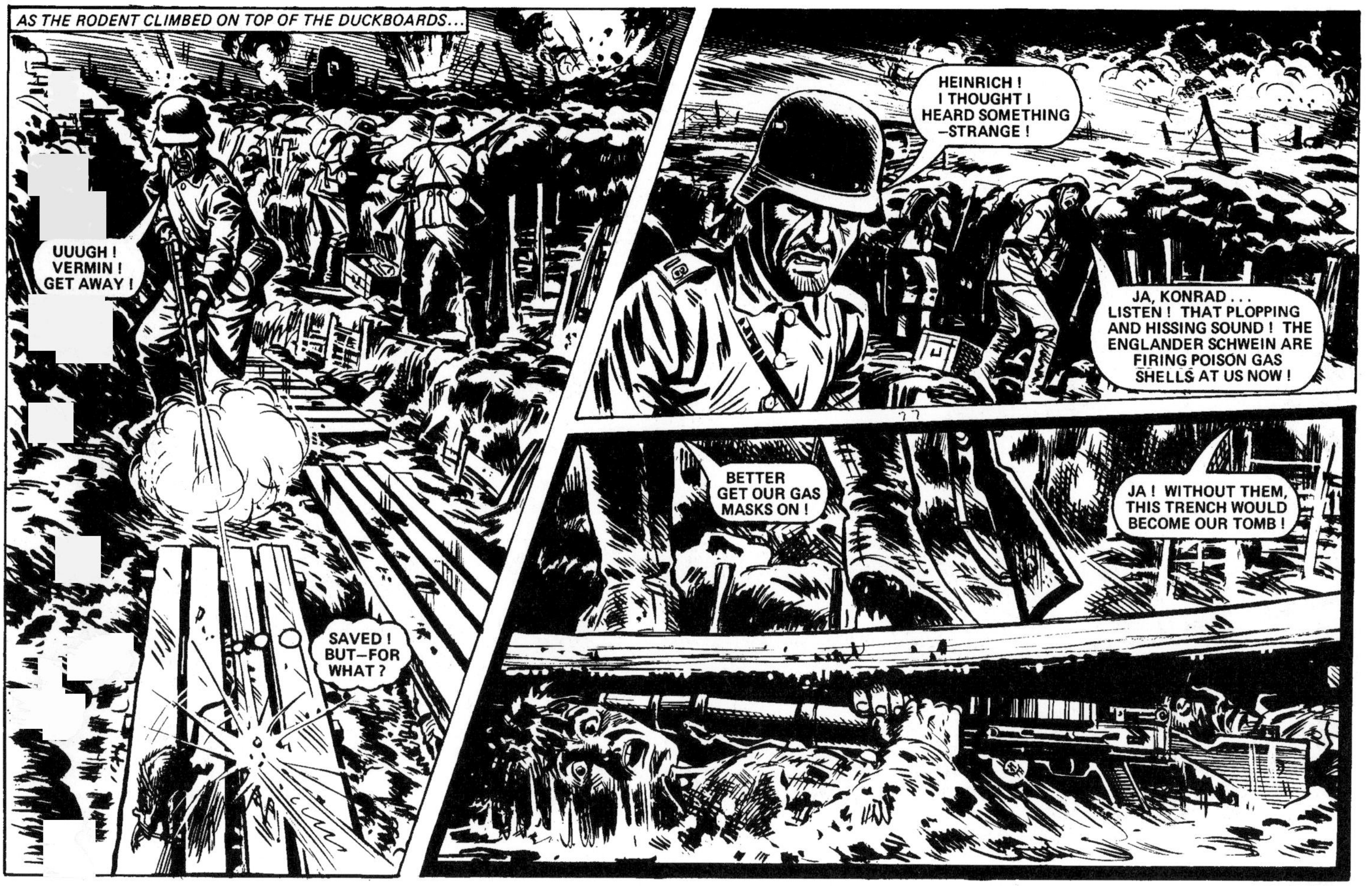
AS THE RODENT CLIMBED ON TOP OF THE DUCKBOARDS...
UUUGH ! VERMIN ! GET AWAY !
SAVED ! BUT—FOR WHAT ?
HEINRICH ! I THOUGHT I HEARD SOMETHING —STRANGE !
JA, KONRAD . . . LISTEN ! THAT PLOPPING AND HISSING SOUND ! THE ENGLANDER SCHWEIN ARE FIRING POISON GAS SHELLS AT US NOW !
BETTER GET OUR GAS MASKS ON !
JA ! WITHOUT THEM, THIS TRENCH WOULD BECOME OUR TOMB !

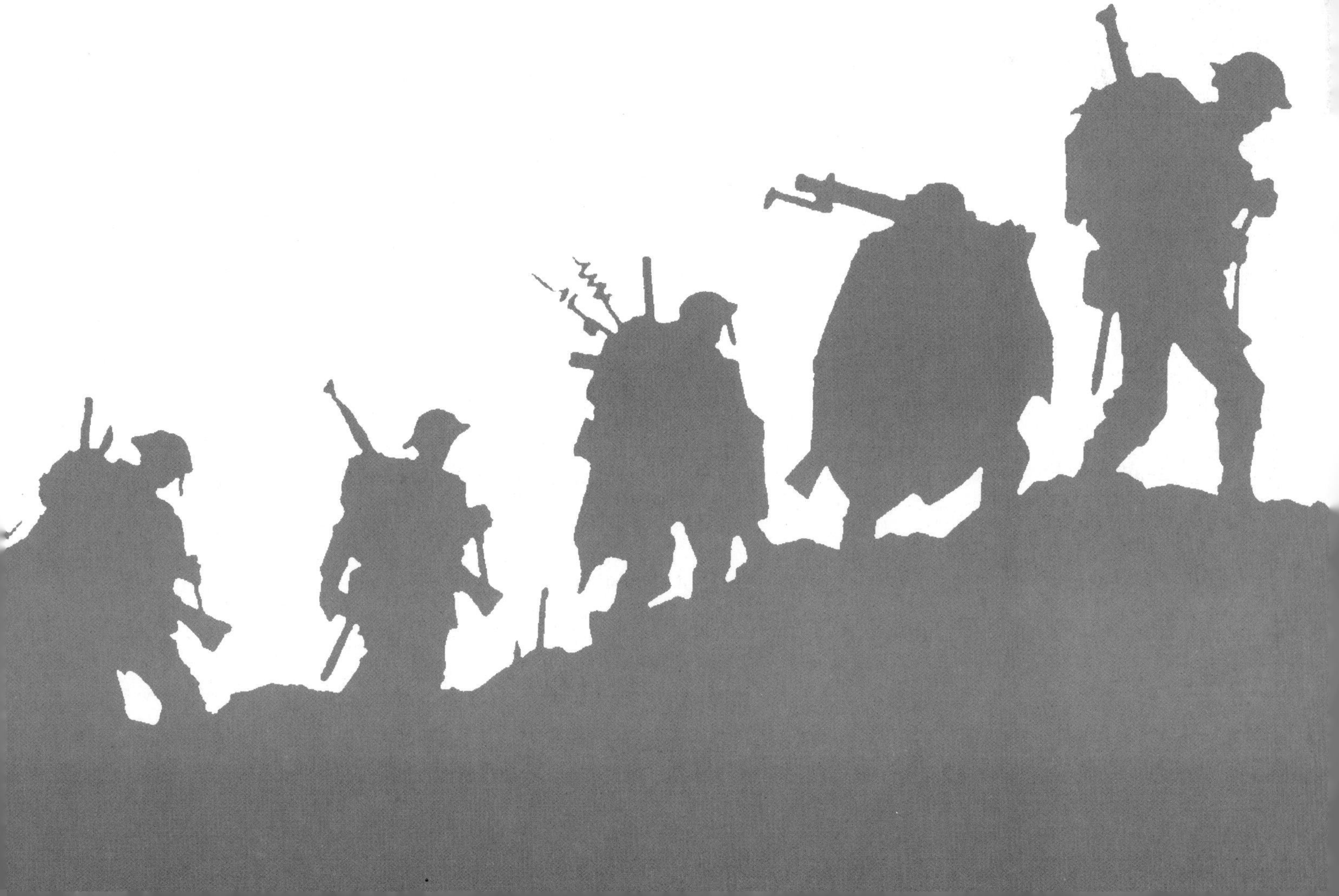

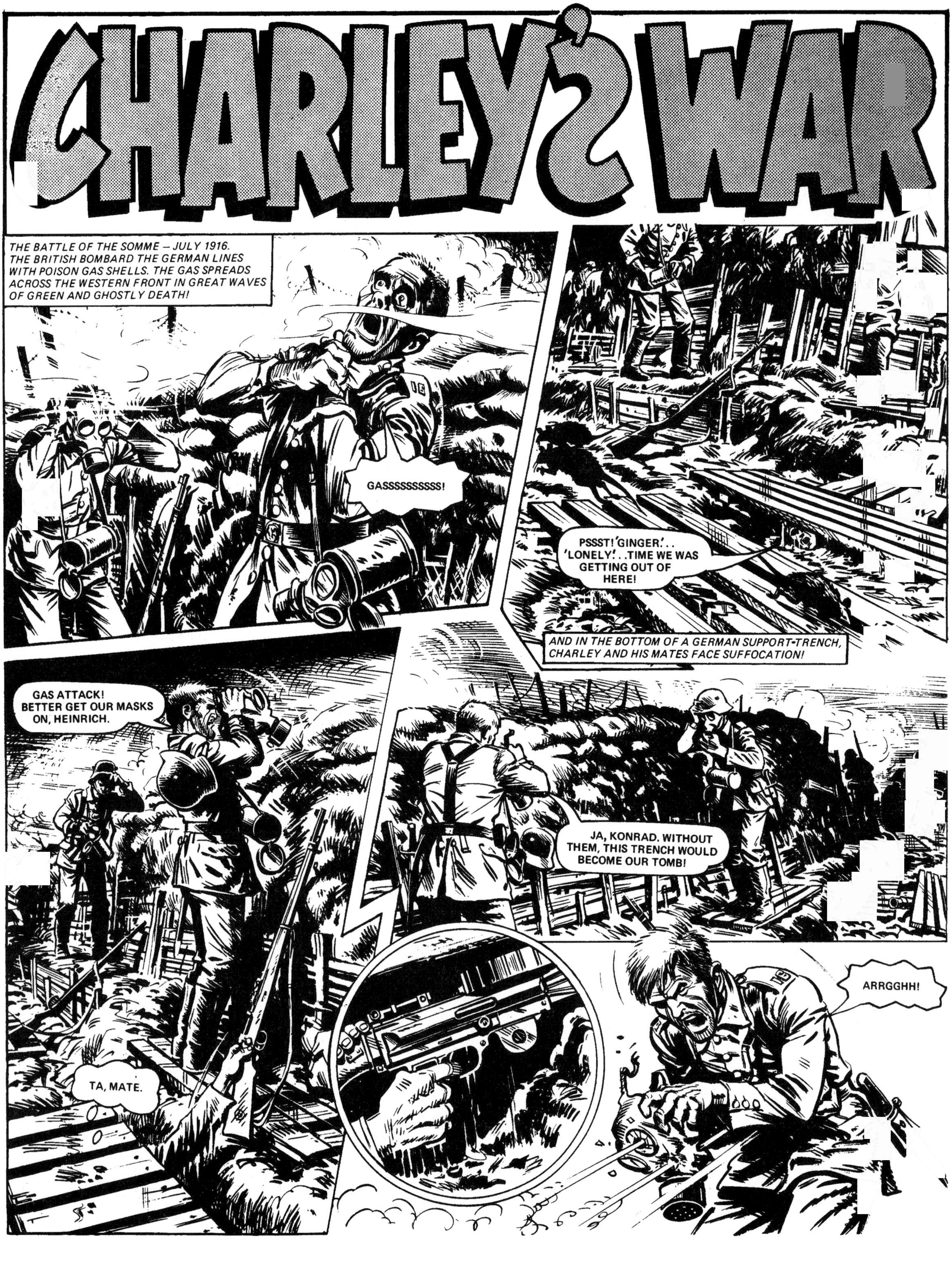
CHARLEY'S WAR
THE BATTLE OF THE SOMME – JULY 1916. THE BRITISH BOMBARD THE GERMAN LINES WITH POISON GAS SHELLS. THE GAS SPREADS ACROSS THE WESTERN FRONT IN GREAT WAVES OF GREEN AND GHOSTLY DEATH!
GASSSSSSSSSS!
PSSST! 'GINGER.' .. 'LONELY.' ..TIME WE WAS GETTING OUT OF HERE!
AND IN THE BOTTOM OF A GERMAN SUPPORT-TRENCH, CHARLEY AND HIS MATES FACE SUFFOCATION!
GAS ATTACK! BETTER GET OUR MASKS ON, HEINRICH.
JA, KONRAD. WITHOUT THEM, THIS TRENCH WOULD BECOME OUR TOMB!
TA, MATE.
ARRGGHH!

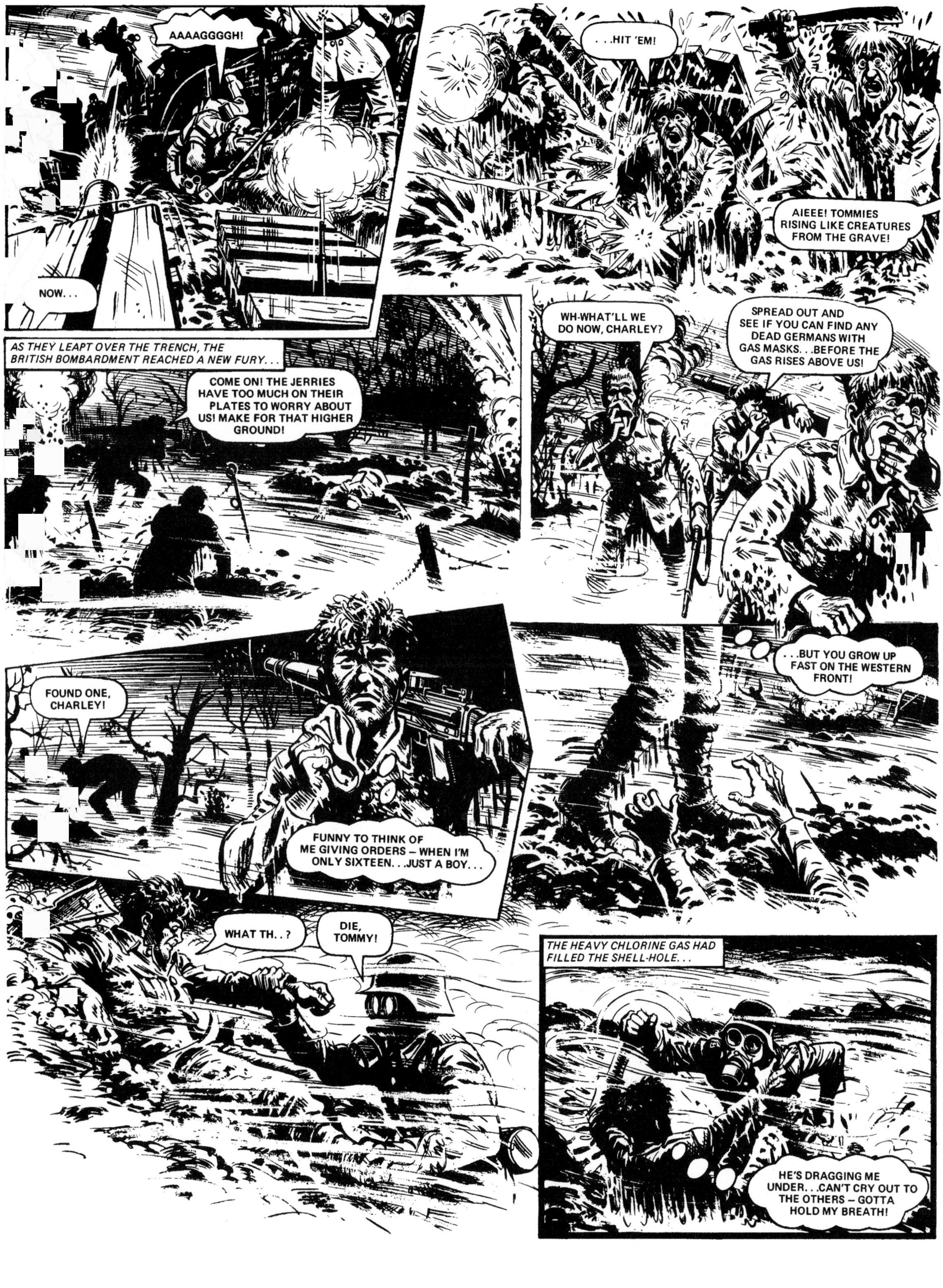
AAAAGGGGH!
NOW...
...HIT 'EM!
AIEEE! TOMMIES RISING LIKE CREATURES FROM THE GRAVE!
AS THEY LEAPT OVER THE TRENCH, THE BRITISH BOMBARDMENT REACHED A NEW FURY...
COME ON! THE JERRIES HAVE TOO MUCH ON THEIR PLATES TO WORRY ABOUT US! MAKE FOR THAT HIGHER GROUND!
WH-WHAT'LL WE DO NOW, CHARLEY?
SPREAD OUT AND SEE IF YOU CAN FIND ANY DEAD GERMANS WITH GAS MASKS...BEFORE THE GAS RISES ABOVE US!
FOUND ONE, CHARLEY!
FUNNY TO THINK OF ME GIVING ORDERS – WHEN I'M ONLY SIXTEEN...JUST A BOY...
...BUT YOU GROW UP FAST ON THE WESTERN FRONT!
WHAT TH..?
DIE, TOMMY!
THE HEAVY CHLORINE GAS HAD FILLED THE SHELL-HOLE...
HE'S DRAGGING ME UNDER...CAN'T CRY OUT TO THE OTHERS – GOTTA HOLD MY BREATH!

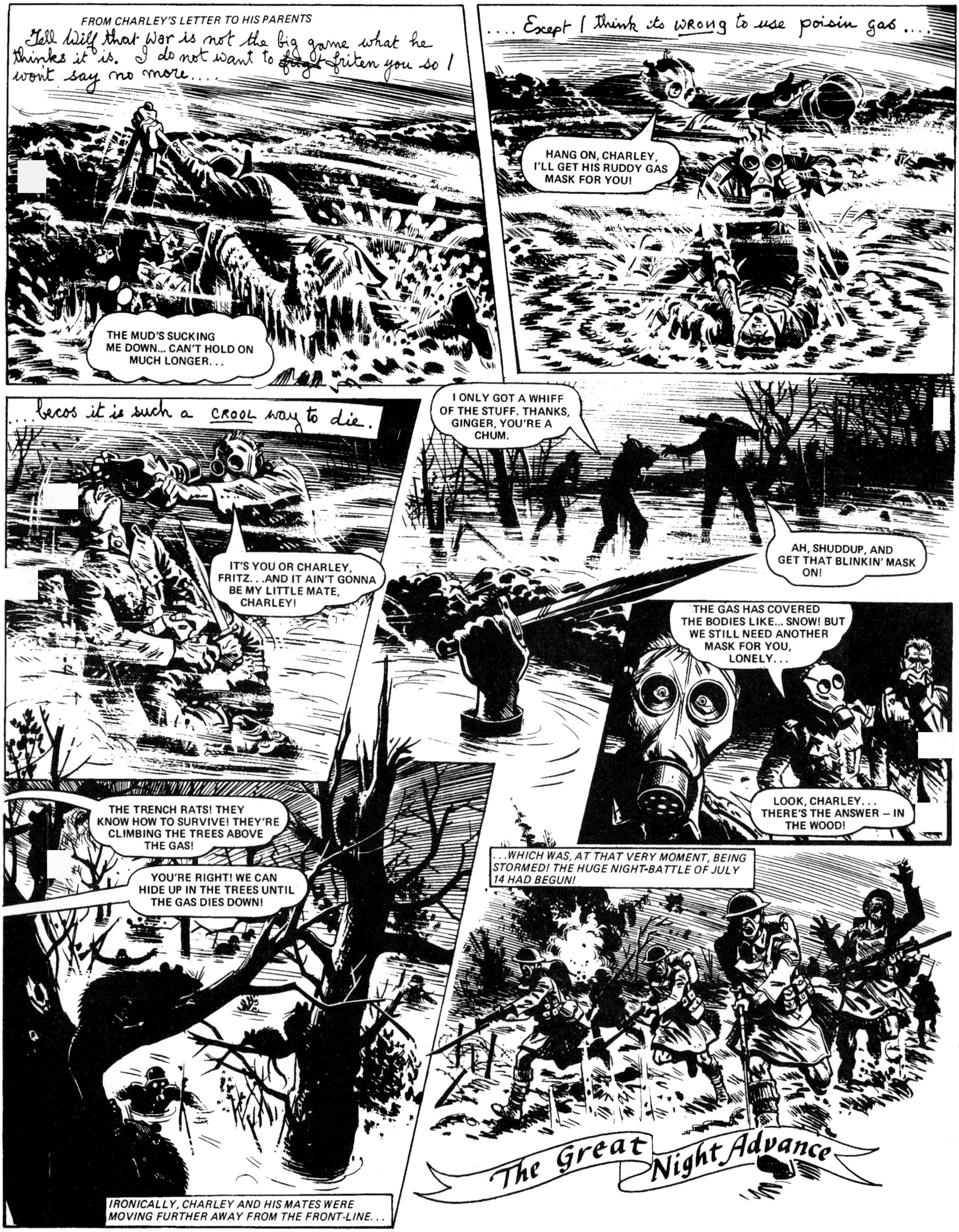

FROM CHARLEY'S LETTER TO HIS PARENTS
Tell Wilf that War is not the big game what he thinks it is. I do not want to frigt friten you so I wont say no more....
THE MUD'S SUCKING ME DOWN... CAN'T HOLD ON MUCH LONGER...
.... Except I think its WRONG to use poisin gas....
HANG ON, CHARLEY, I'LL GET HIS RUDDY GAS MASK FOR YOU!
....becos it is such a CROOL way to die.
IT'S YOU OR CHARLEY, FRITZ...AND IT AIN'T GONNA BE MY LITTLE MATE, CHARLEY!
I ONLY GOT A WHIFF OF THE STUFF. THANKS, GINGER, YOU'RE A CHUM.
AH, SHUDDUP, AND GET THAT BLINKIN' MASK ON!
THE GAS HAS COVERED THE BODIES LIKE... SNOW! BUT WE STILL NEED ANOTHER MASK FOR YOU, LONELY...
LOOK, CHARLEY... THERE'S THE ANSWER – IN THE WOOD!
THE TRENCH RATS! THEY KNOW HOW TO SURVIVE! THEY'RE CLIMBING THE TREES ABOVE THE GAS!
YOU'RE RIGHT! WE CAN HIDE UP IN THE TREES UNTIL THE GAS DIES DOWN!
IRONICALLY, CHARLEY AND HIS MATES WERE MOVING FURTHER AWAY FROM THE FRONT-LINE...
...WHICH WAS, AT THAT VERY MOMENT, BEING STORMED! THE HUGE NIGHT-BATTLE OF JULY 14 HAD BEGUN!
The Great Night Advance

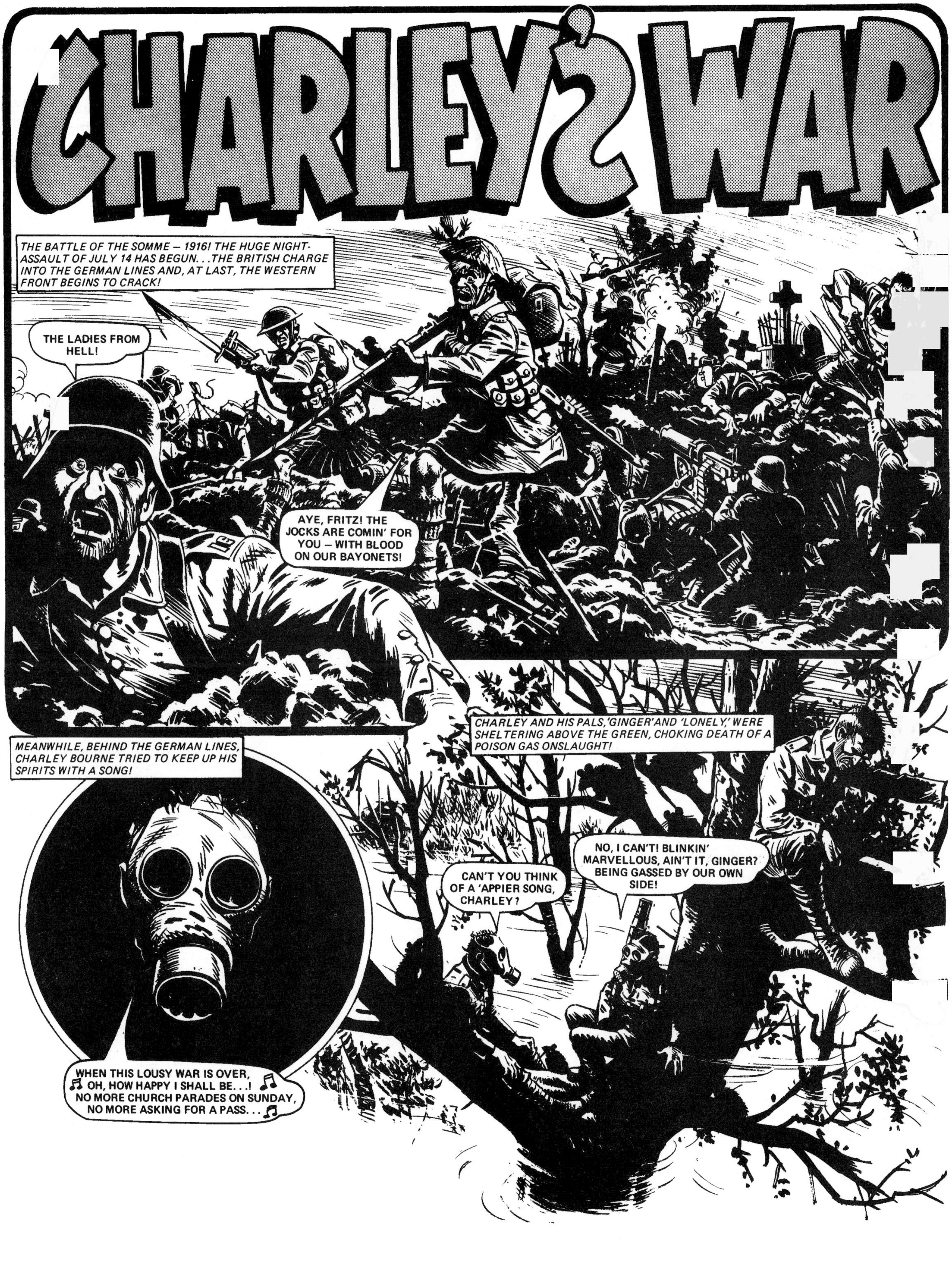
CHARLEY'S WAR
THE BATTLE OF THE SOMME — 1916! THE HUGE NIGHT-ASSAULT OF JULY 14 HAS BEGUN. . .THE BRITISH CHARGE INTO THE GERMAN LINES AND, AT LAST, THE WESTERN FRONT BEGINS TO CRACK!
THE LADIES FROM HELL!
AYE, FRITZ! THE JOCKS ARE COMIN' FOR YOU — WITH BLOOD ON OUR BAYONETS!
MEANWHILE, BEHIND THE GERMAN LINES, CHARLEY BOURNE TRIED TO KEEP UP HIS SPIRITS WITH A SONG!
WHEN THIS LOUSY WAR IS OVER, OH, HOW HAPPY I SHALL BE. . .! NO MORE CHURCH PARADES ON SUNDAY, NO MORE ASKING FOR A PASS. . .
CHARLEY AND HIS PALS, 'GINGER' AND 'LONELY,' WERE SHELTERING ABOVE THE GREEN, CHOKING DEATH OF A POISON GAS ONSLAUGHT!
CAN'T YOU THINK OF A 'APPIER SONG, CHARLEY?
NO, I CAN'T! BLINKIN' MARVELLOUS, AIN'T IT, GINGER? BEING GASSED BY OUR OWN SIDE!

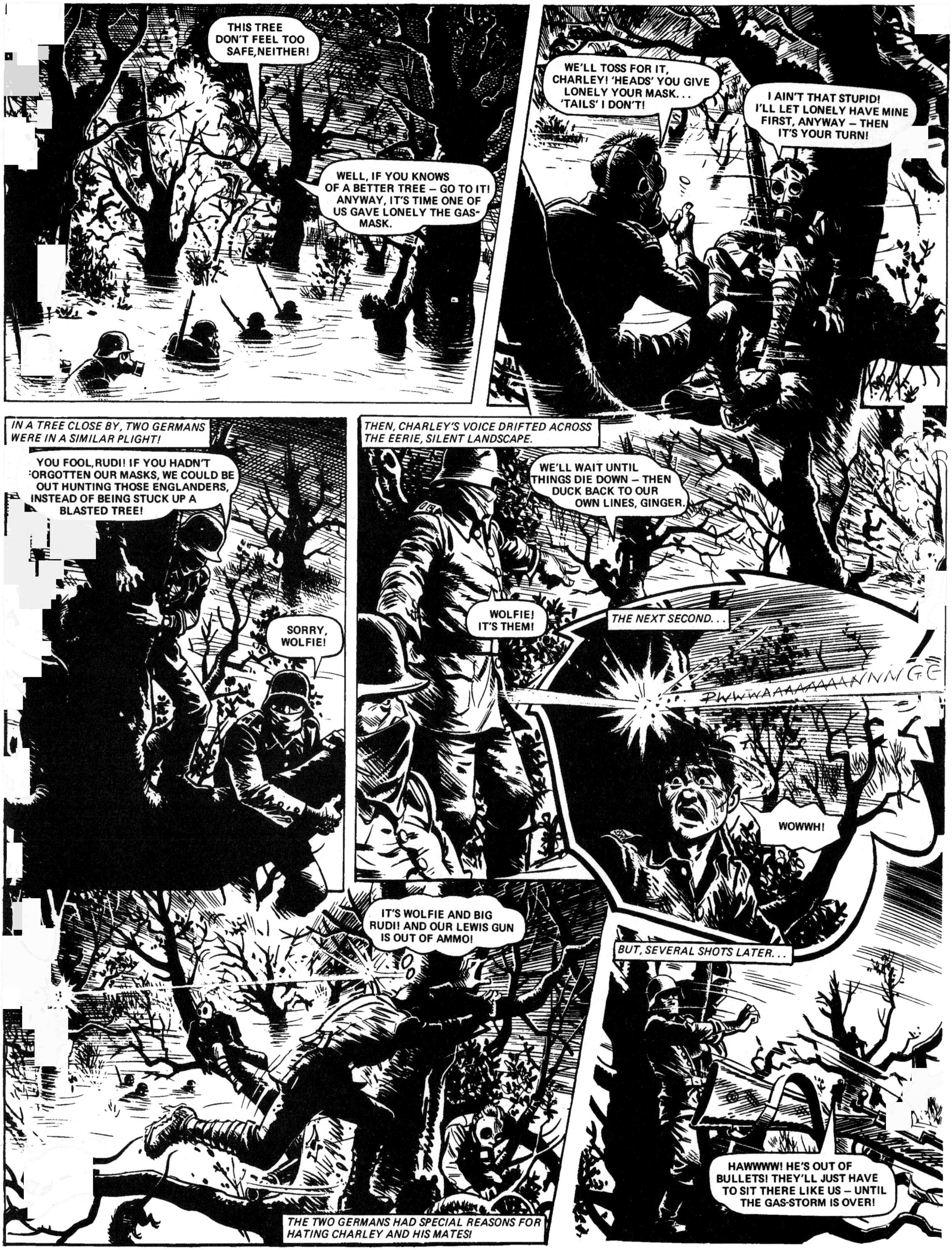
THIS TREE DON'T FEEL TOO SAFE, NEITHER!
WELL, IF YOU KNOWS OF A BETTER TREE – GO TO IT! ANYWAY, IT'S TIME ONE OF US GAVE LONELY THE GAS-MASK.
WE'LL TOSS FOR IT, CHARLEY! 'HEADS' YOU GIVE LONELY YOUR MASK. . . 'TAILS' I DON'T!
I AIN'T THAT STUPID! I'LL LET LONELY HAVE MINE FIRST, ANYWAY – THEN IT'S YOUR TURN!
IN A TREE CLOSE BY, TWO GERMANS WERE IN A SIMILAR PLIGHT!
YOU FOOL, RUDI! IF YOU HADN'T FORGOTTEN OUR MASKS, WE COULD BE OUT HUNTING THOSE ENGLANDERS, INSTEAD OF BEING STUCK UP A BLASTED TREE!
SORRY, WOLFIE!
THEN, CHARLEY'S VOICE DRIFTED ACROSS THE EERIE, SILENT LANDSCAPE.
WE'LL WAIT UNTIL THINGS DIE DOWN – THEN DUCK BACK TO OUR OWN LINES, GINGER.
WOLFIE! IT'S THEM!
THE NEXT SECOND. . .
PWWWAAAAAAAAANNNGG
WOWWH!
IT'S WOLFIE AND BIG RUDI! AND OUR LEWIS GUN IS OUT OF AMMO!
THE TWO GERMANS HAD SPECIAL REASONS FOR HATING CHARLEY AND HIS MATES!
BUT, SEVERAL SHOTS LATER. . .
HAWWWW! HE'S OUT OF BULLETS! THEY'LL JUST HAVE TO SIT THERE LIKE US – UNTIL THE GAS-STORM IS OVER!

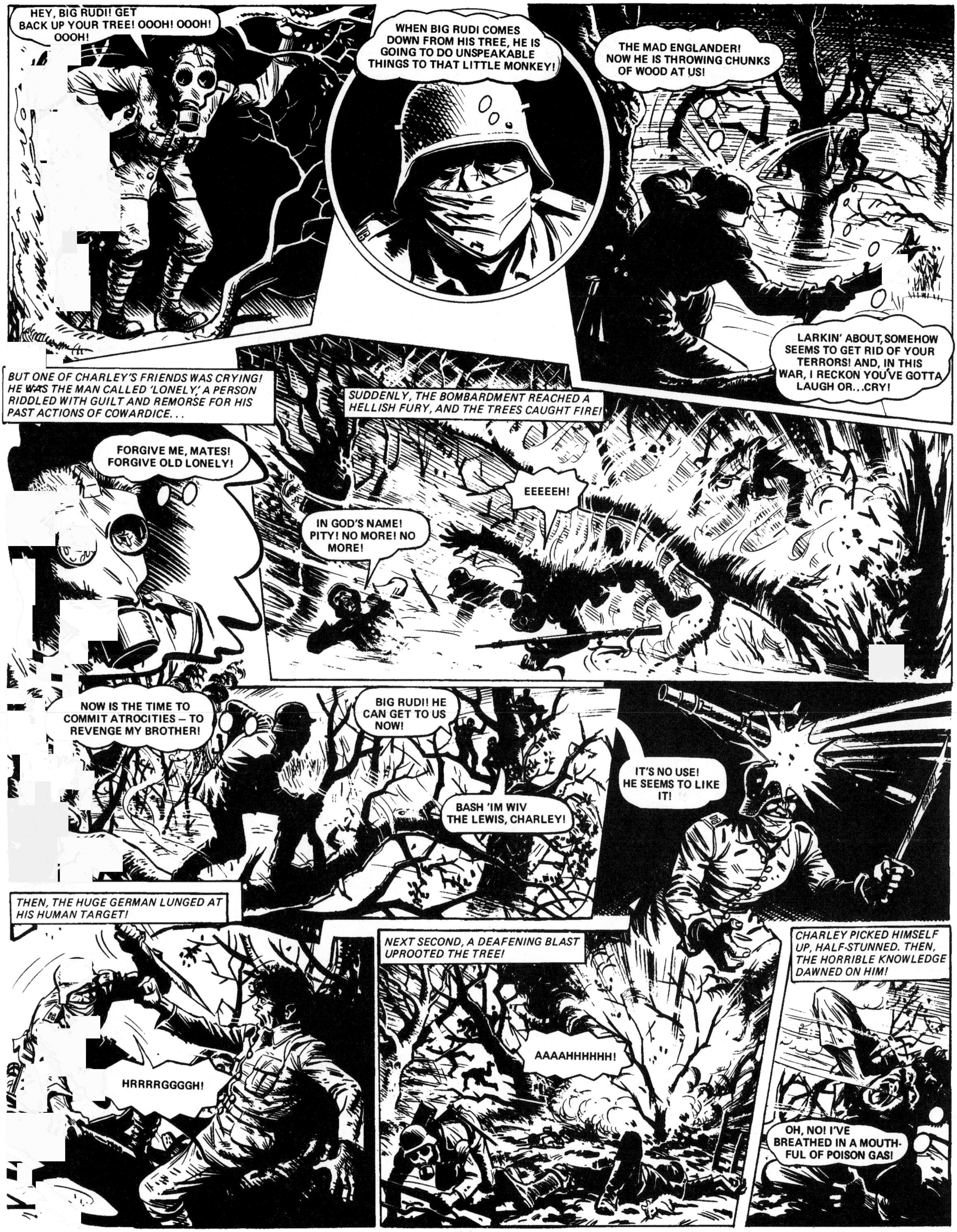
HEY, BIG RUDI! GET BACK UP YOUR TREE! OOOH! OOOH! OOOH!
WHEN BIG RUDI COMES DOWN FROM HIS TREE, HE IS GOING TO DO UNSPEAKABLE THINGS TO THAT LITTLE MONKEY!
THE MAD ENGLANDER! NOW HE IS THROWING CHUNKS OF WOOD AT US!
LARKIN' ABOUT, SOMEHOW SEEMS TO GET RID OF YOUR TERRORS! AND, IN THIS WAR, I RECKON YOU'VE GOTTA LAUGH OR...CRY!
BUT ONE OF CHARLEY'S FRIENDS WAS CRYING! HE WAS THE MAN CALLED 'LONELY,' A PERSON RIDDLED WITH GUILT AND REMORSE FOR HIS PAST ACTIONS OF COWARDICE...
FORGIVE ME, MATES! FORGIVE OLD LONELY!
SUDDENLY, THE BOMBARDMENT REACHED A HELLISH FURY, AND THE TREES CAUGHT FIRE!
EEEEEH!
IN GOD'S NAME! PITY! NO MORE! NO MORE!
NOW IS THE TIME TO COMMIT ATROCITIES — TO REVENGE MY BROTHER!
BIG RUDI! HE CAN GET TO US NOW!
BASH 'IM WIV THE LEWIS, CHARLEY!
IT'S NO USE! HE SEEMS TO LIKE IT!
THEN, THE HUGE GERMAN LUNGED AT HIS HUMAN TARGET!
HRRRRGGGGH!
NEXT SECOND, A DEAFENING BLAST UPROOTED THE TREE!
AAAAHHHHHH!
CHARLEY PICKED HIMSELF UP, HALF-STUNNED. THEN, THE HORRIBLE KNOWLEDGE DAWNED ON HIM!
OH, NO! I'VE BREATHED IN A MOUTHFUL OF POISON GAS!

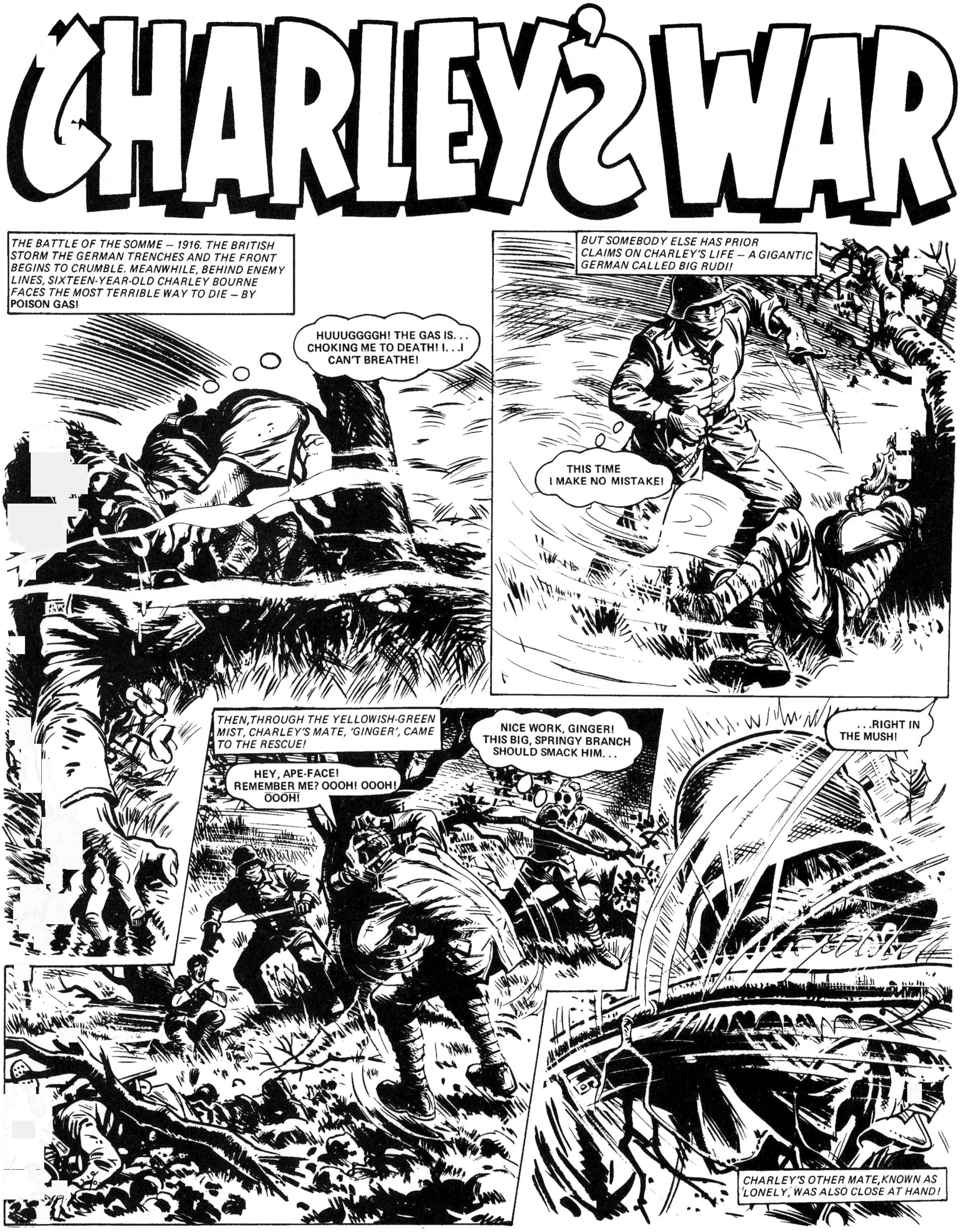
CHARLEY'S WAR
THE BATTLE OF THE SOMME – 1916. THE BRITISH STORM THE GERMAN TRENCHES AND THE FRONT BEGINS TO CRUMBLE. MEANWHILE, BEHIND ENEMY LINES, SIXTEEN-YEAR-OLD CHARLEY BOURNE FACES THE MOST TERRIBLE WAY TO DIE – BY POISON GAS!
HUUUGGGGH! THE GAS IS... CHOKING ME TO DEATH! I...I CAN'T BREATHE!
BUT SOMEBODY ELSE HAS PRIOR CLAIMS ON CHARLEY'S LIFE – A GIGANTIC GERMAN CALLED BIG RUDI!
THIS TIME I MAKE NO MISTAKE!
THEN, THROUGH THE YELLOWISH-GREEN MIST, CHARLEY'S MATE, 'GINGER', CAME TO THE RESCUE!
HEY, APE-FACE! REMEMBER ME? OOOH! OOOH! OOOH!
NICE WORK, GINGER! THIS BIG, SPRINGY BRANCH SHOULD SMACK HIM...
...RIGHT IN THE MUSH!
CHARLEY'S OTHER MATE, KNOWN AS 'LONELY', WAS ALSO CLOSE AT HAND!

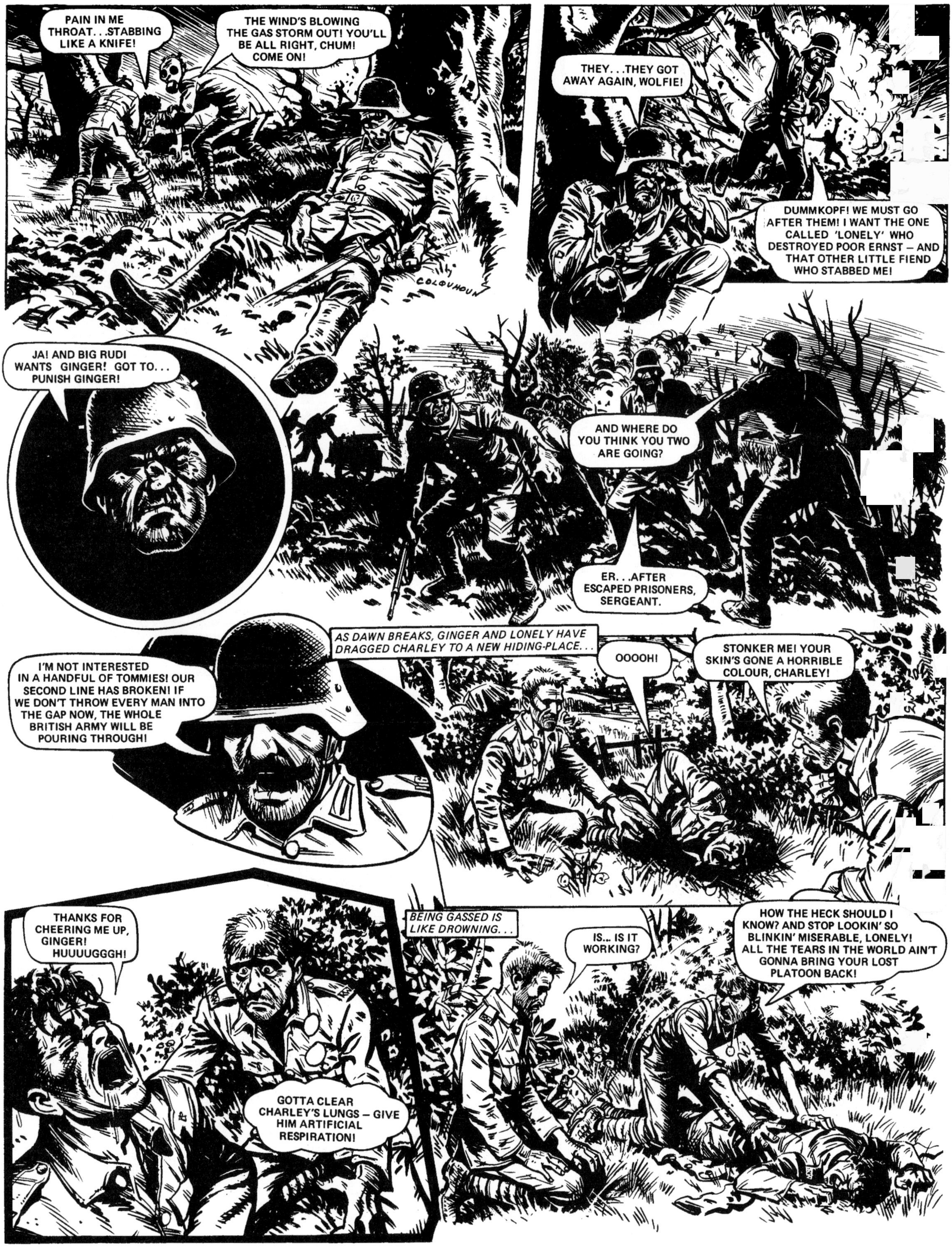
PAIN IN ME THROAT. . .STABBING LIKE A KNIFE!
THE WIND'S BLOWING THE GAS STORM OUT! YOU'LL BE ALL RIGHT, CHUM! COME ON!
COLQUHOUN
THEY. . .THEY GOT AWAY AGAIN, WOLFIE!
DUMMKOPF! WE MUST GO AFTER THEM! I WANT THE ONE CALLED 'LONELY' WHO DESTROYED POOR ERNST – AND THAT OTHER LITTLE FIEND WHO STABBED ME!
JA! AND BIG RUDI WANTS GINGER! GOT TO. . . PUNISH GINGER!
AND WHERE DO YOU THINK YOU TWO ARE GOING?
ER. . .AFTER ESCAPED PRISONERS, SERGEANT.
I'M NOT INTERESTED IN A HANDFUL OF TOMMIES! OUR SECOND LINE HAS BROKEN! IF WE DON'T THROW EVERY MAN INTO THE GAP NOW, THE WHOLE BRITISH ARMY WILL BE POURING THROUGH!
AS DAWN BREAKS, GINGER AND LONELY HAVE DRAGGED CHARLEY TO A NEW HIDING-PLACE. . .
OOOOH!
STONKER ME! YOUR SKIN'S GONE A HORRIBLE COLOUR, CHARLEY!
THANKS FOR CHEERING ME UP, GINGER! HUUUUGGGH!
GOTTA CLEAR CHARLEY'S LUNGS – GIVE HIM ARTIFICIAL RESPIRATION!
BEING GASSED IS LIKE DROWNING. . .
IS... IS IT WORKING?
HOW THE HECK SHOULD I KNOW? AND STOP LOOKIN' SO BLINKIN' MISERABLE, LONELY! ALL THE TEARS IN THE WORLD AIN'T GONNA BRING YOUR LOST PLATOON BACK!

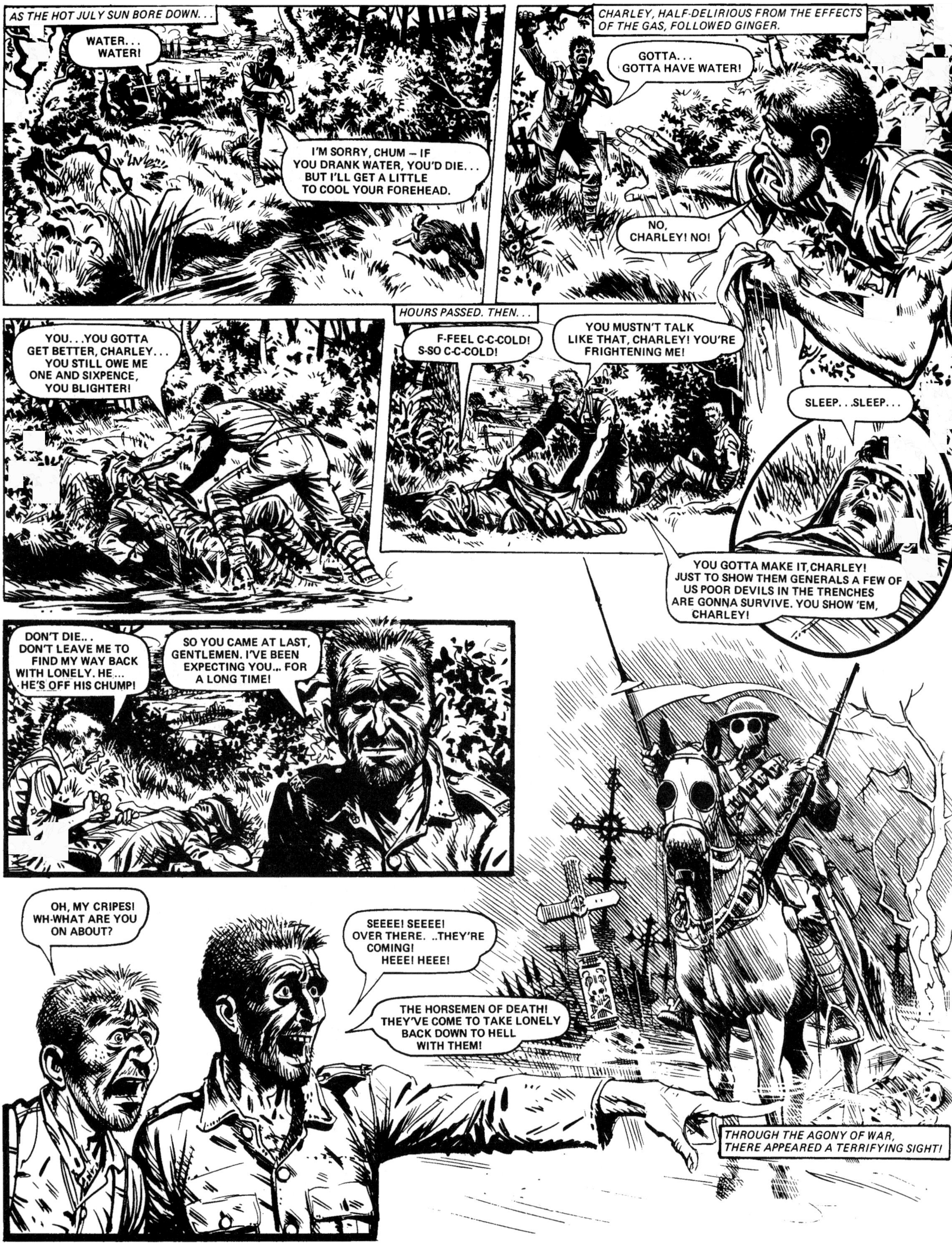
AS THE HOT JULY SUN BORE DOWN. . .
WATER. . . WATER!
I'M SORRY, CHUM – IF YOU DRANK WATER, YOU'D DIE. . . BUT I'LL GET A LITTLE TO COOL YOUR FOREHEAD.
CHARLEY, HALF-DELIRIOUS FROM THE EFFECTS OF THE GAS, FOLLOWED GINGER.
GOTTA. . . GOTTA HAVE WATER!
NO, CHARLEY! NO!
YOU. . .YOU GOTTA GET BETTER, CHARLEY. . . YOU STILL OWE ME ONE AND SIXPENCE, YOU BLIGHTER!
HOURS PASSED. THEN. . .
F-FEEL C-C-COLD! S-SO C-C-COLD!
YOU MUSTN'T TALK LIKE THAT, CHARLEY! YOU'RE FRIGHTENING ME!
SLEEP. . .SLEEP. . .
YOU GOTTA MAKE IT, CHARLEY! JUST TO SHOW THEM GENERALS A FEW OF US POOR DEVILS IN THE TRENCHES ARE GONNA SURVIVE. YOU SHOW 'EM, CHARLEY!
DON'T DIE... DON'T LEAVE ME TO FIND MY WAY BACK WITH LONELY. HE... HE'S OFF HIS CHUMP!
SO YOU CAME AT LAST, GENTLEMEN. I'VE BEEN EXPECTING YOU... FOR A LONG TIME!
OH, MY CRIPES! WH-WHAT ARE YOU ON ABOUT?
SEEEE! SEEEE! OVER THERE. ..THEY'RE COMING! HEEE! HEEE!
THE HORSEMEN OF DEATH! THEY'VE COME TO TAKE LONELY BACK DOWN TO HELL WITH THEM!
THROUGH THE AGONY OF WAR, THERE APPEARED A TERRIFYING SIGHT!

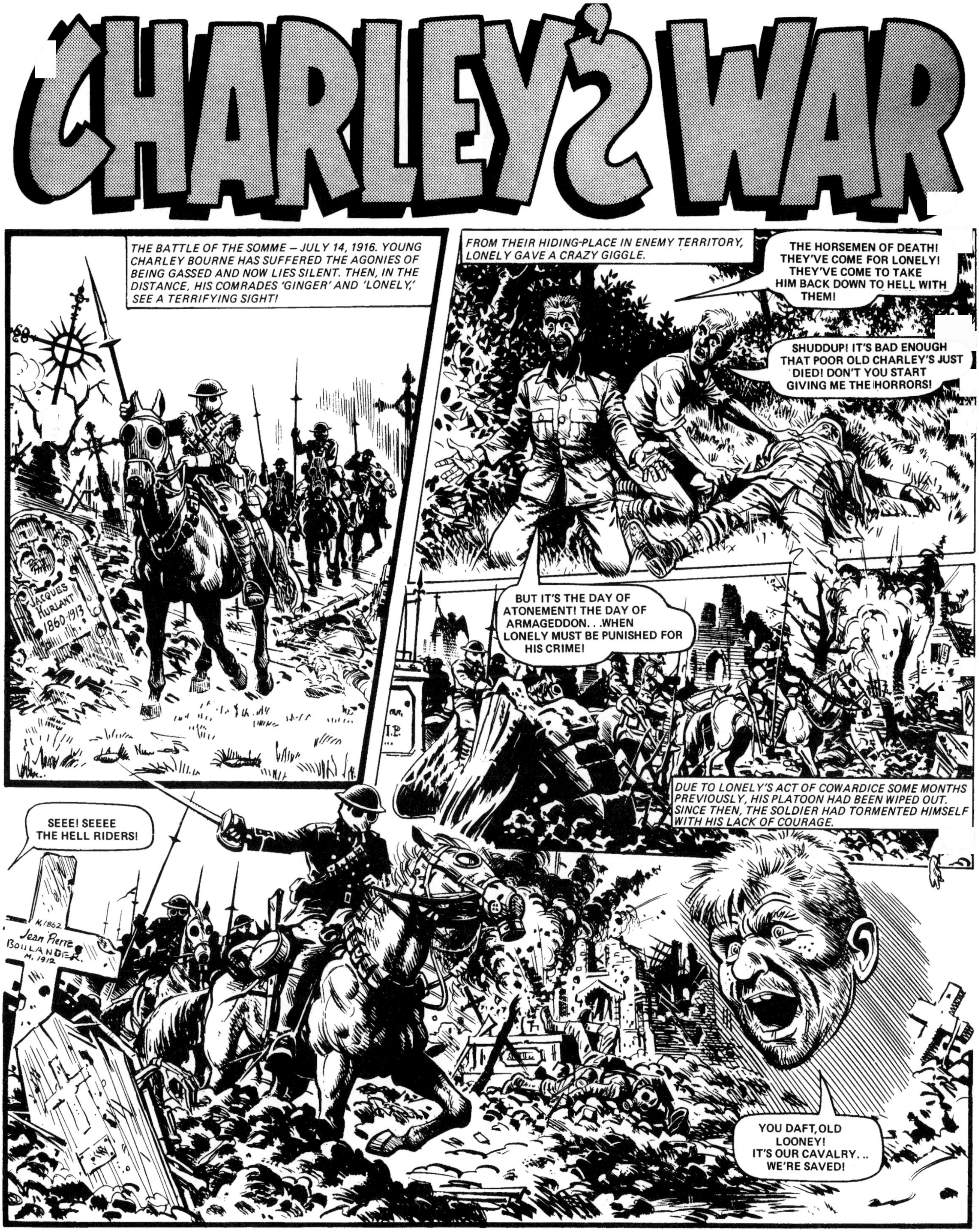
CHARLEY'S WAR
THE BATTLE OF THE SOMME – JULY 14, 1916. YOUNG CHARLEY BOURNE HAS SUFFERED THE AGONIES OF BEING GASSED AND NOW LIES SILENT. THEN, IN THE DISTANCE, HIS COMRADES 'GINGER' AND 'LONELY,' SEE A TERRIFYING SIGHT!
JACQUES HURLANT 1860-1913
FROM THEIR HIDING-PLACE IN ENEMY TERRITORY, LONELY GAVE A CRAZY GIGGLE.
THE HORSEMEN OF DEATH! THEY'VE COME FOR LONELY! THEY'VE COME TO TAKE HIM BACK DOWN TO HELL WITH THEM!
SHUDDUP! IT'S BAD ENOUGH THAT POOR OLD CHARLEY'S JUST DIED! DON'T YOU START GIVING ME THE HORRORS!
BUT IT'S THE DAY OF ATONEMENT! THE DAY OF ARMAGEDDON. . .WHEN LONELY MUST BE PUNISHED FOR HIS CRIME!
DUE TO LONELY'S ACT OF COWARDICE SOME MONTHS PREVIOUSLY, HIS PLATOON HAD BEEN WIPED OUT. SINCE THEN, THE SOLDIER HAD TORMENTED HIMSELF WITH HIS LACK OF COURAGE.
SEEE! SEEEE THE HELL RIDERS!
N.1862 Jean Pierre BOULANDER M.1912
YOU DAFT, OLD LOONEY! IT'S OUR CAVALRY. .. WE'RE SAVED!

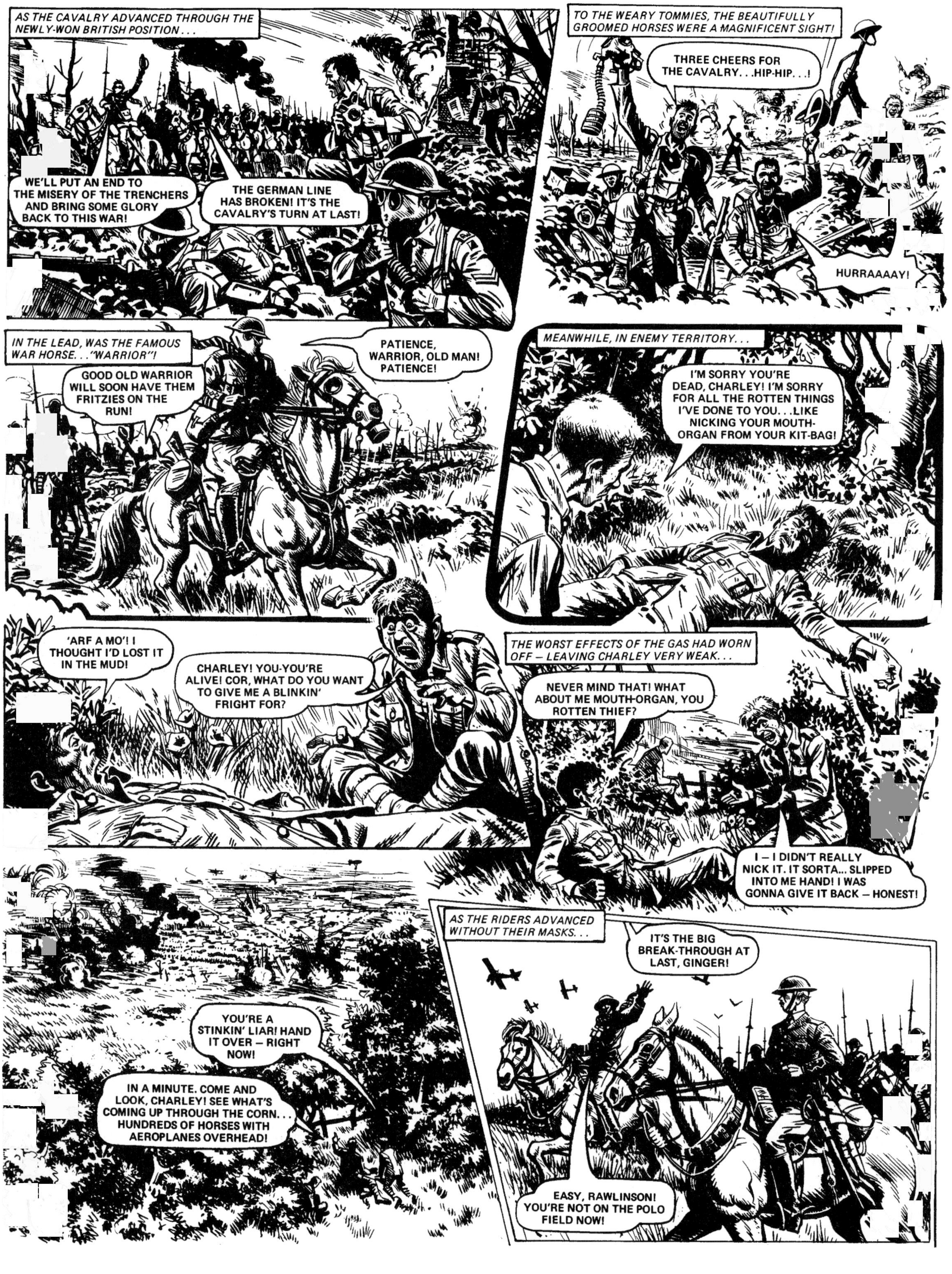
AS THE CAVALRY ADVANCED THROUGH THE NEWLY-WON BRITISH POSITION...
WE'LL PUT AN END TO THE MISERY OF THE TRENCHERS AND BRING SOME GLORY BACK TO THIS WAR!
THE GERMAN LINE HAS BROKEN! IT'S THE CAVALRY'S TURN AT LAST!
TO THE WEARY TOMMIES, THE BEAUTIFULLY GROOMED HORSES WERE A MAGNIFICENT SIGHT!
THREE CHEERS FOR THE CAVALRY...HIP-HIP...!
HURRAAAAY!
IN THE LEAD, WAS THE FAMOUS WAR HORSE..."WARRIOR"!
GOOD OLD WARRIOR WILL SOON HAVE THEM FRITZIES ON THE RUN!
PATIENCE, WARRIOR, OLD MAN! PATIENCE!
MEANWHILE, IN ENEMY TERRITORY...
I'M SORRY YOU'RE DEAD, CHARLEY! I'M SORRY FOR ALL THE ROTTEN THINGS I'VE DONE TO YOU...LIKE NICKING YOUR MOUTH-ORGAN FROM YOUR KIT-BAG!
'ARF A MO'! I THOUGHT I'D LOST IT IN THE MUD!
CHARLEY! YOU-YOU'RE ALIVE! COR, WHAT DO YOU WANT TO GIVE ME A BLINKIN' FRIGHT FOR?
THE WORST EFFECTS OF THE GAS HAD WORN OFF – LEAVING CHARLEY VERY WEAK...
NEVER MIND THAT! WHAT ABOUT ME MOUTH-ORGAN, YOU ROTTEN THIEF?
I – I DIDN'T REALLY NICK IT. IT SORTA... SLIPPED INTO ME HAND! I WAS GONNA GIVE IT BACK – HONEST!
YOU'RE A STINKIN' LIAR! HAND IT OVER – RIGHT NOW!
IN A MINUTE. COME AND LOOK, CHARLEY! SEE WHAT'S COMING UP THROUGH THE CORN... HUNDREDS OF HORSES WITH AEROPLANES OVERHEAD!
AS THE RIDERS ADVANCED WITHOUT THEIR MASKS...
IT'S THE BIG BREAK-THROUGH AT LAST, GINGER!
EASY, RAWLINSON! YOU'RE NOT ON THE POLO FIELD NOW!

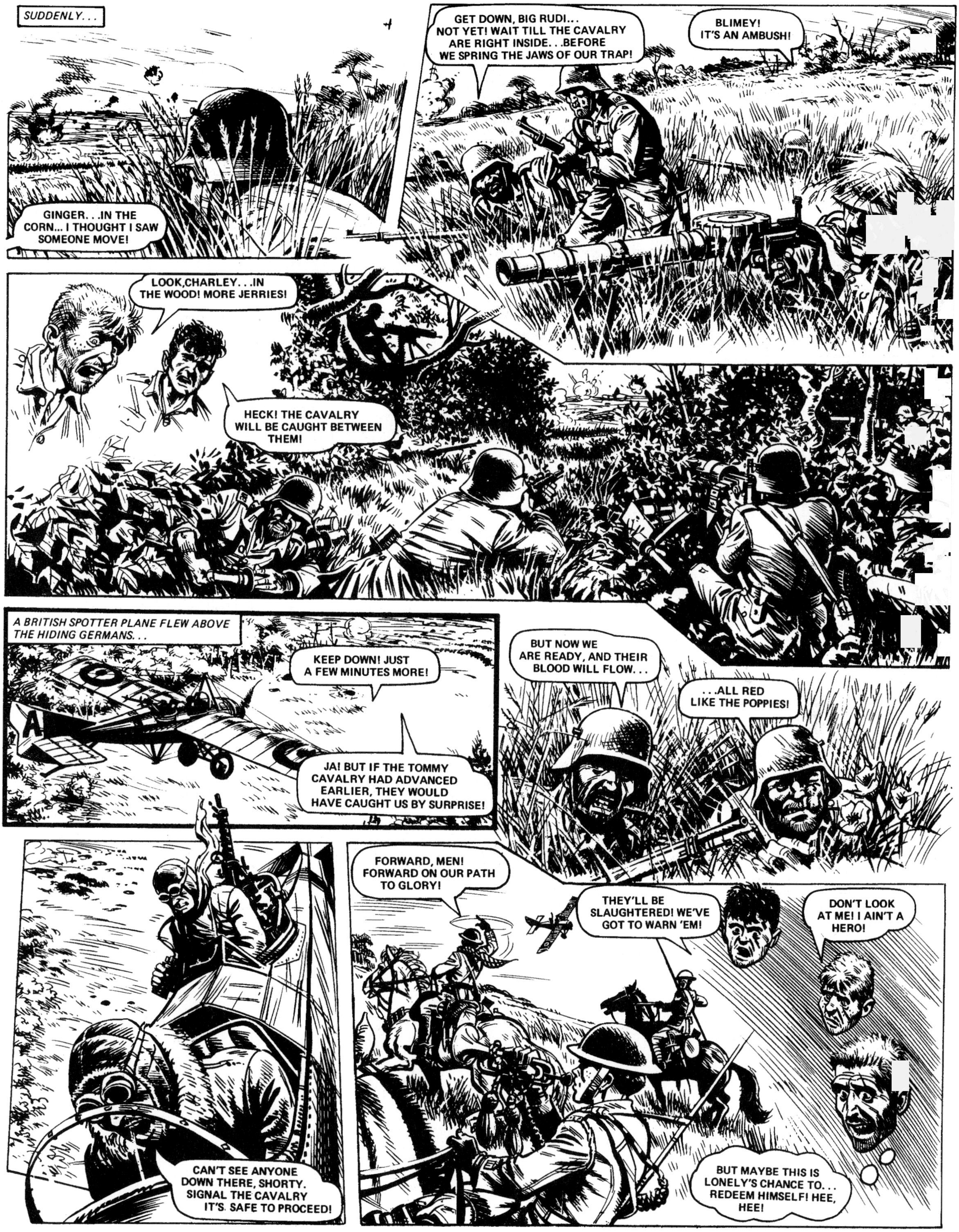
SUDDENLY. . .
GINGER. . .IN THE CORN... I THOUGHT I SAW SOMEONE MOVE!
GET DOWN, BIG RUDI. . . NOT YET! WAIT TILL THE CAVALRY ARE RIGHT INSIDE. . .BEFORE WE SPRING THE JAWS OF OUR TRAP!
BLIMEY! IT'S AN AMBUSH!
LOOK,CHARLEY. . .IN THE WOOD! MORE JERRIES!
HECK! THE CAVALRY WILL BE CAUGHT BETWEEN THEM!
A BRITISH SPOTTER PLANE FLEW ABOVE THE HIDING GERMANS. . .
KEEP DOWN! JUST A FEW MINUTES MORE!
JA! BUT IF THE TOMMY CAVALRY HAD ADVANCED EARLIER, THEY WOULD HAVE CAUGHT US BY SURPRISE!
BUT NOW WE ARE READY, AND THEIR BLOOD WILL FLOW. . .
. . .ALL RED LIKE THE POPPIES!
CAN'T SEE ANYONE DOWN THERE, SHORTY. SIGNAL THE CAVALRY IT'S SAFE TO PROCEED!
FORWARD, MEN! FORWARD ON OUR PATH TO GLORY!
THEY'LL BE SLAUGHTERED! WE'VE GOT TO WARN 'EM!
DON'T LOOK AT ME! I AIN'T A HERO!
BUT MAYBE THIS IS LONELY'S CHANCE TO. . . REDEEM HIMSELF! HEE, HEE!

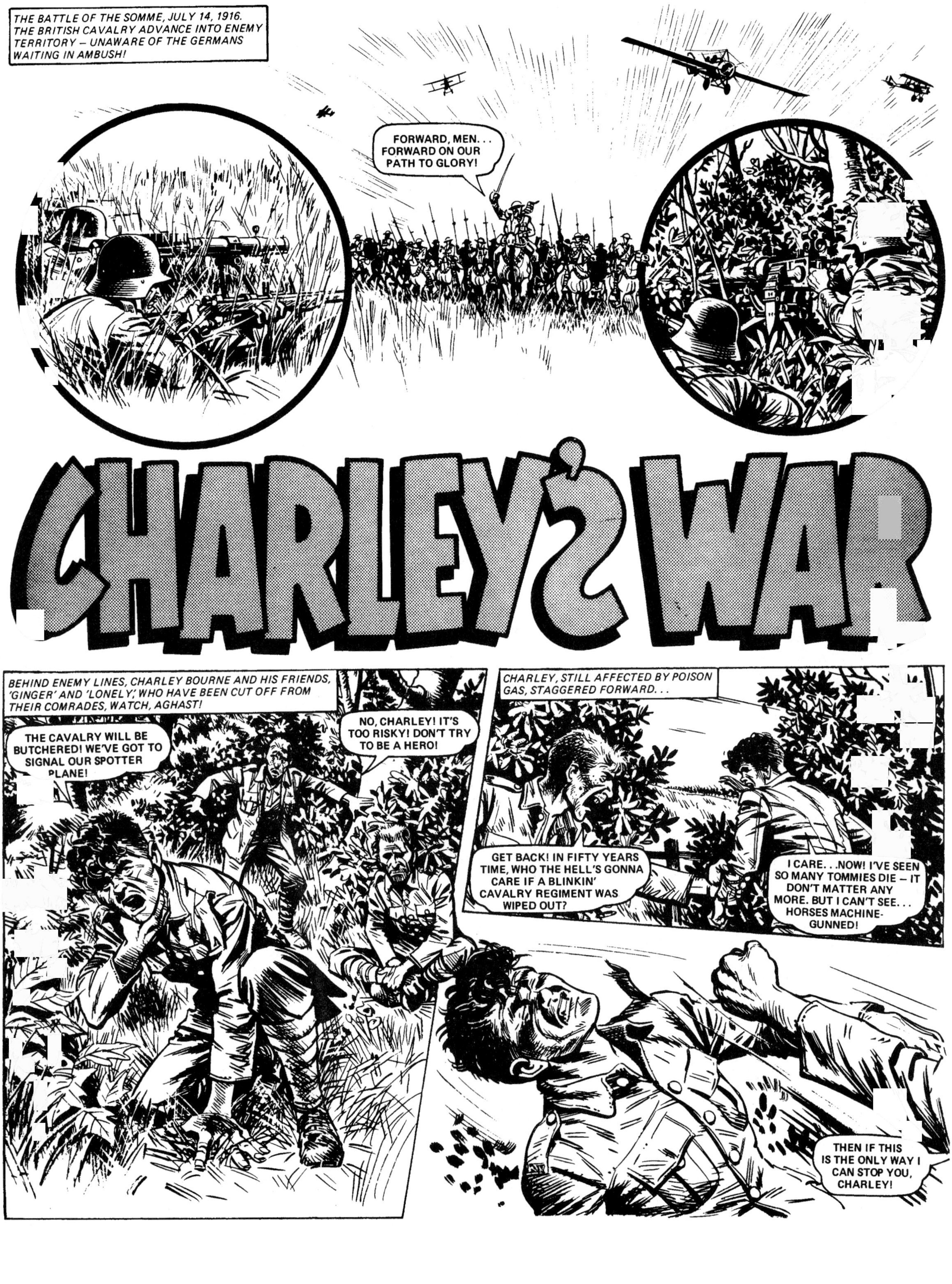
THE BATTLE OF THE SOMME, JULY 14, 1916. THE BRITISH CAVALRY ADVANCE INTO ENEMY TERRITORY – UNAWARE OF THE GERMANS WAITING IN AMBUSH!
FORWARD, MEN... FORWARD ON OUR PATH TO GLORY!
CHARLEY'S WAR
BEHIND ENEMY LINES, CHARLEY BOURNE AND HIS FRIENDS, 'GINGER' AND 'LONELY,' WHO HAVE BEEN CUT OFF FROM THEIR COMRADES, WATCH, AGHAST!
THE CAVALRY WILL BE BUTCHERED! WE'VE GOT TO SIGNAL OUR SPOTTER PLANE!
NO, CHARLEY! IT'S TOO RISKY! DON'T TRY TO BE A HERO!
CHARLEY, STILL AFFECTED BY POISON GAS, STAGGERED FORWARD...
GET BACK! IN FIFTY YEARS TIME, WHO THE HELL'S GONNA CARE IF A BLINKIN' CAVALRY REGIMENT WAS WIPED OUT?
I CARE...NOW! I'VE SEEN SO MANY TOMMIES DIE – IT DON'T MATTER ANY MORE. BUT I CAN'T SEE... HORSES MACHINE-GUNNED!
THEN IF THIS IS THE ONLY WAY I CAN STOP YOU, CHARLEY!

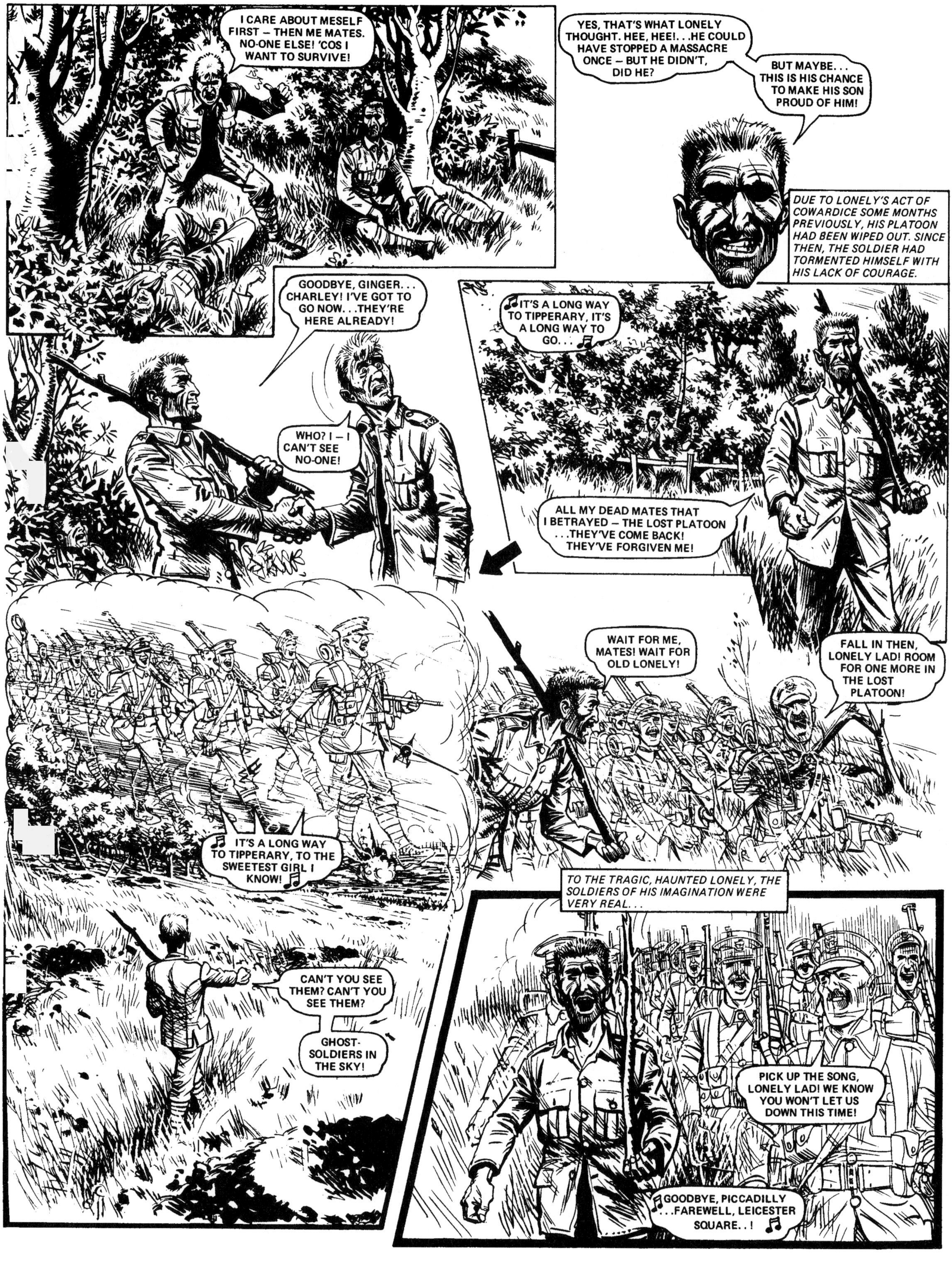
I CARE ABOUT MESELF FIRST – THEN ME MATES. NO-ONE ELSE! 'COS I WANT TO SURVIVE!
YES, THAT'S WHAT LONELY THOUGHT. HEE, HEE!. . .HE COULD HAVE STOPPED A MASSACRE ONCE – BUT HE DIDN'T, DID HE?
BUT MAYBE. . . THIS IS HIS CHANCE TO MAKE HIS SON PROUD OF HIM!
DUE TO LONELY'S ACT OF COWARDICE SOME MONTHS PREVIOUSLY, HIS PLATOON HAD BEEN WIPED OUT. SINCE THEN, THE SOLDIER HAD TORMENTED HIMSELF WITH HIS LACK OF COURAGE.
GOODBYE, GINGER. . . CHARLEY! I'VE GOT TO GO NOW. . .THEY'RE HERE ALREADY!
WHO? I – I CAN'T SEE NO-ONE!
IT'S A LONG WAY TO TIPPERARY, IT'S A LONG WAY TO GO. . .
ALL MY DEAD MATES THAT I BETRAYED – THE LOST PLATOON . . .THEY'VE COME BACK! THEY'VE FORGIVEN ME!
WAIT FOR ME, MATES! WAIT FOR OLD LONELY!
FALL IN THEN, LONELY LAD! ROOM FOR ONE MORE IN THE LOST PLATOON!
IT'S A LONG WAY TO TIPPERARY, TO THE SWEETEST GIRL I KNOW!
TO THE TRAGIC, HAUNTED LONELY, THE SOLDIERS OF HIS IMAGINATION WERE VERY REAL. . .
CAN'T YOU SEE THEM? CAN'T YOU SEE THEM?
GHOST-SOLDIERS IN THE SKY!
PICK UP THE SONG, LONELY LAD! WE KNOW YOU WON'T LET US DOWN THIS TIME!
GOODBYE, PICCADILLY . . .FAREWELL, LEICESTER SQUARE. . !

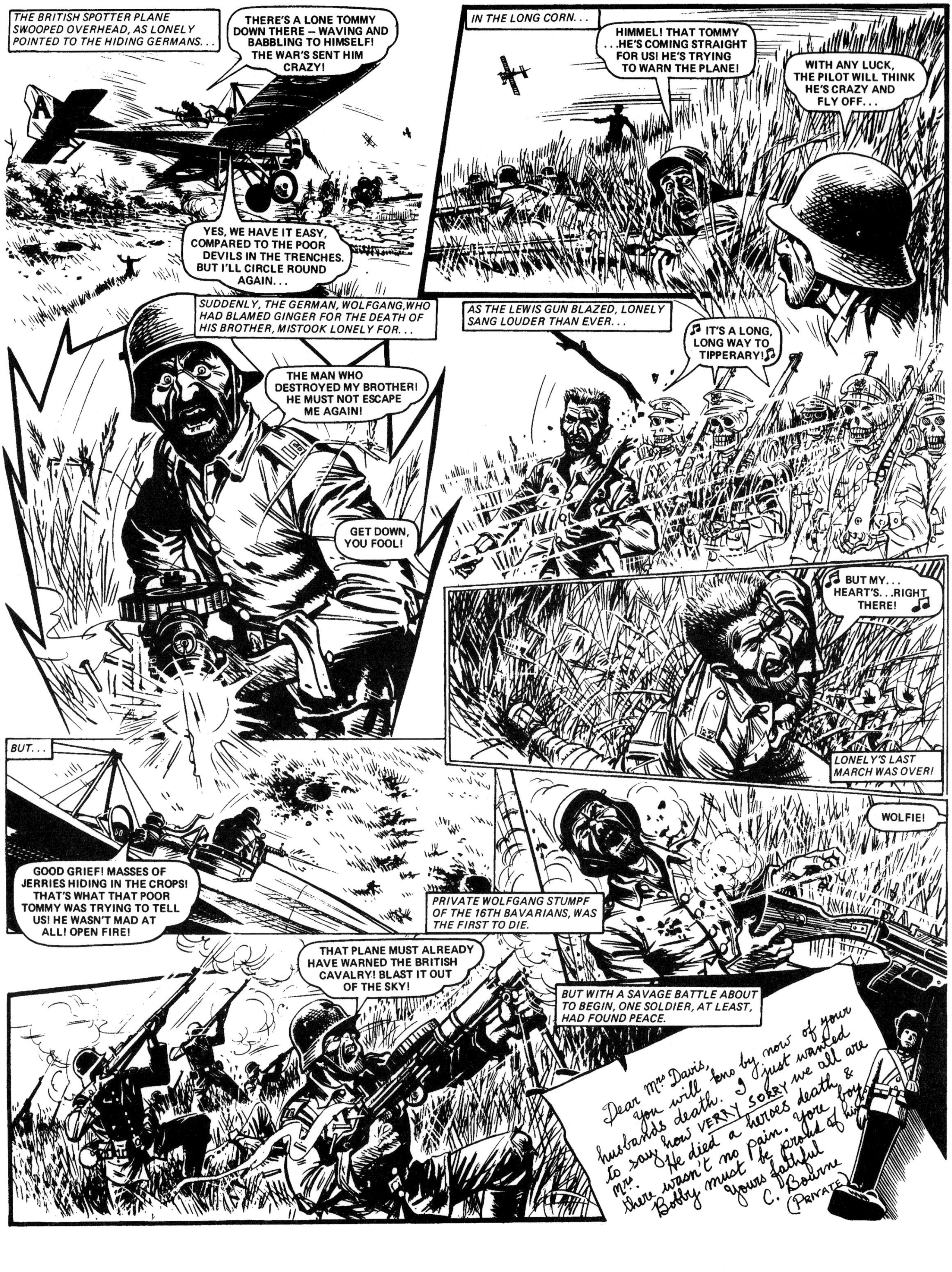
THE BRITISH SPOTTER PLANE SWOOPED OVERHEAD, AS LONELY POINTED TO THE HIDING GERMANS...
THERE'S A LONE TOMMY DOWN THERE — WAVING AND BABBLING TO HIMSELF! THE WAR'S SENT HIM CRAZY!
YES, WE HAVE IT EASY, COMPARED TO THE POOR DEVILS IN THE TRENCHES. BUT I'LL CIRCLE ROUND AGAIN...
IN THE LONG CORN...
HIMMEL! THAT TOMMY ...HE'S COMING STRAIGHT FOR US! HE'S TRYING TO WARN THE PLANE!
WITH ANY LUCK, THE PILOT WILL THINK HE'S CRAZY AND FLY OFF...
SUDDENLY, THE GERMAN, WOLFGANG, WHO HAD BLAMED GINGER FOR THE DEATH OF HIS BROTHER, MISTOOK LONELY FOR...
THE MAN WHO DESTROYED MY BROTHER! HE MUST NOT ESCAPE ME AGAIN!
GET DOWN, YOU FOOL!
AS THE LEWIS GUN BLAZED, LONELY SANG LOUDER THAN EVER...
♪ IT'S A LONG, LONG WAY TO TIPPERARY! ♫
♪ BUT MY... HEART'S...RIGHT THERE! ♫
LONELY'S LAST MARCH WAS OVER!
BUT...
GOOD GRIEF! MASSES OF JERRIES HIDING IN THE CROPS! THAT'S WHAT THAT POOR TOMMY WAS TRYING TO TELL US! HE WASN'T MAD AT ALL! OPEN FIRE!
WOLFIE!
PRIVATE WOLFGANG STUMPF OF THE 16TH BAVARIANS, WAS THE FIRST TO DIE.
THAT PLANE MUST ALREADY HAVE WARNED THE BRITISH CAVALRY! BLAST IT OUT OF THE SKY!
BUT WITH A SAVAGE BATTLE ABOUT TO BEGIN, ONE SOLDIER, AT LEAST, HAD FOUND PEACE.
Dear Mrs Davis,
You will kno by now of your
husbands death. I just wanted
to say how VERRY SORRY we all are
Mrs.. He died a heroes death &
there wasn't no pain. Yore boy
Bobby must be proud of him
Yours fathful
C. Bourne
(PRIVATE)

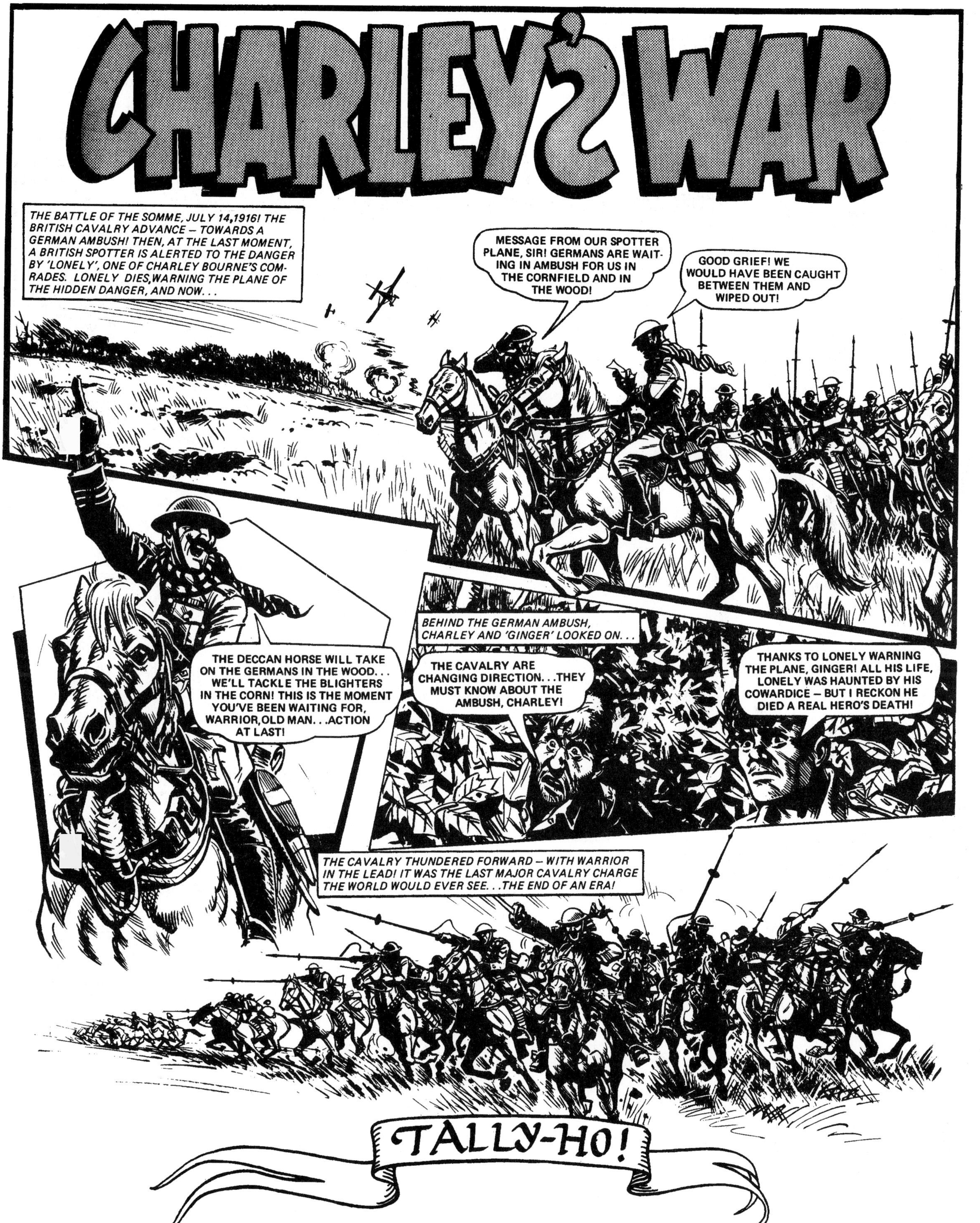
CHARLEY'S WAR
THE BATTLE OF THE SOMME, JULY 14,1916! THE BRITISH CAVALRY ADVANCE – TOWARDS A GERMAN AMBUSH! THEN, AT THE LAST MOMENT, A BRITISH SPOTTER IS ALERTED TO THE DANGER BY 'LONELY', ONE OF CHARLEY BOURNE'S COMRADES. LONELY DIES,WARNING THE PLANE OF THE HIDDEN DANGER, AND NOW. . .
MESSAGE FROM OUR SPOTTER PLANE, SIR! GERMANS ARE WAITING IN AMBUSH FOR US IN THE CORNFIELD AND IN THE WOOD!
GOOD GRIEF! WE WOULD HAVE BEEN CAUGHT BETWEEN THEM AND WIPED OUT!
THE DECCAN HORSE WILL TAKE ON THE GERMANS IN THE WOOD. . . WE'LL TACKLE THE BLIGHTERS IN THE CORN! THIS IS THE MOMENT YOU'VE BEEN WAITING FOR, WARRIOR,OLD MAN. . .ACTION AT LAST!
BEHIND THE GERMAN AMBUSH, CHARLEY AND 'GINGER' LOOKED ON. . .
THE CAVALRY ARE CHANGING DIRECTION. . .THEY MUST KNOW ABOUT THE AMBUSH, CHARLEY!
THANKS TO LONELY WARNING THE PLANE, GINGER! ALL HIS LIFE, LONELY WAS HAUNTED BY HIS COWARDICE – BUT I RECKON HE DIED A REAL HERO'S DEATH!
THE CAVALRY THUNDERED FORWARD – WITH WARRIOR IN THE LEAD! IT WAS THE LAST MAJOR CAVALRY CHARGE THE WORLD WOULD EVER SEE. . .THE END OF AN ERA!
TALLY-HO!

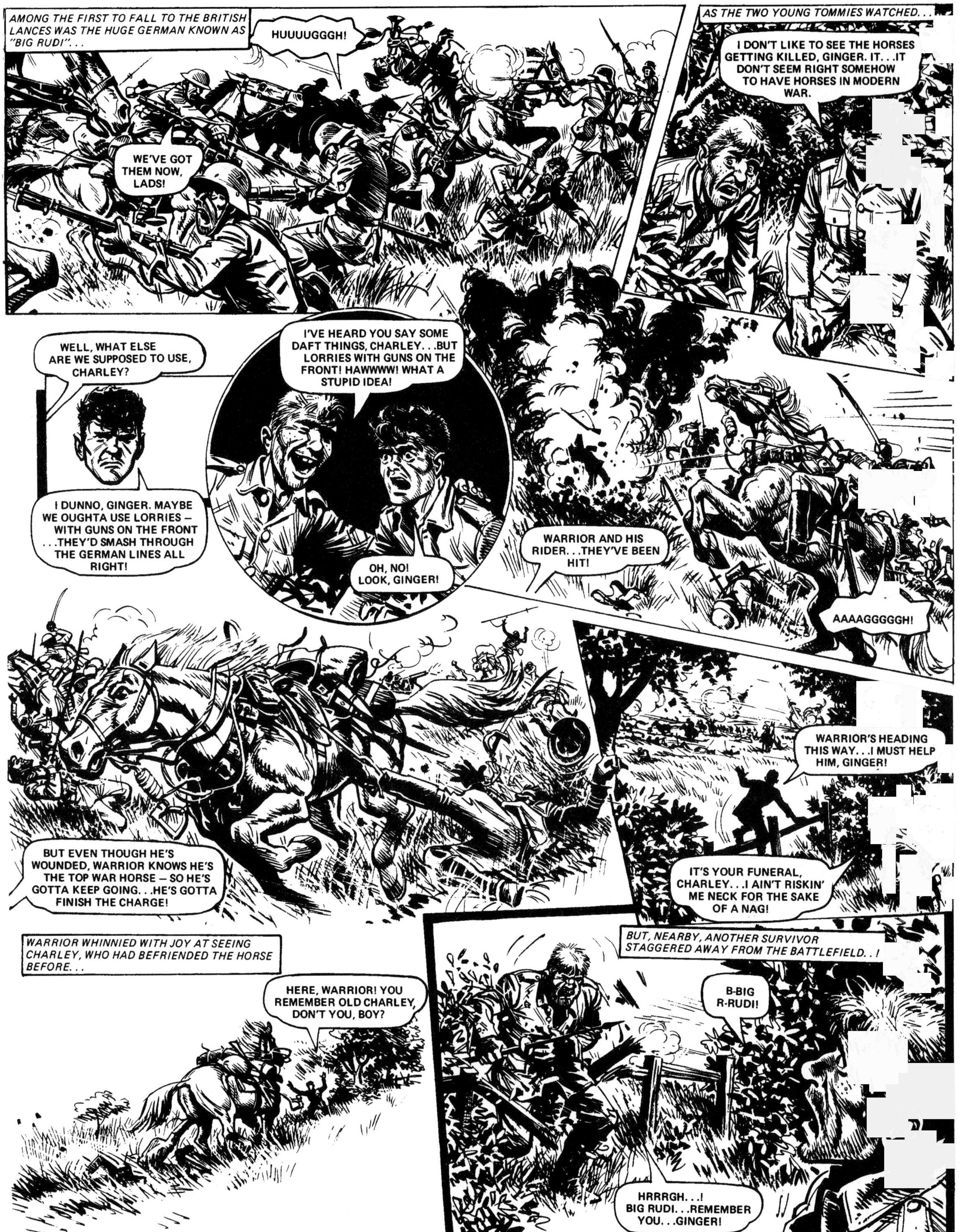
AMONG THE FIRST TO FALL TO THE BRITISH LANCES WAS THE HUGE GERMAN KNOWN AS "BIG RUDI"...
HUUUUGGGH!
WE'VE GOT THEM NOW, LADS!
AS THE TWO YOUNG TOMMIES WATCHED...
I DON'T LIKE TO SEE THE HORSES GETTING KILLED, GINGER. IT...IT DON'T SEEM RIGHT SOMEHOW TO HAVE HORSES IN MODERN WAR.
WELL, WHAT ELSE ARE WE SUPPOSED TO USE, CHARLEY?
I DUNNO, GINGER. MAYBE WE OUGHTA USE LORRIES – WITH GUNS ON THE FRONT ...THEY'D SMASH THROUGH THE GERMAN LINES ALL RIGHT!
I'VE HEARD YOU SAY SOME DAFT THINGS, CHARLEY...BUT LORRIES WITH GUNS ON THE FRONT! HAWWWW! WHAT A STUPID IDEA!
OH, NO! LOOK, GINGER!
WARRIOR AND HIS RIDER...THEY'VE BEEN HIT!
AAAAGGGGGH!
BUT EVEN THOUGH HE'S WOUNDED, WARRIOR KNOWS HE'S THE TOP WAR HORSE – SO HE'S GOTTA KEEP GOING...HE'S GOTTA FINISH THE CHARGE!
WARRIOR'S HEADING THIS WAY...I MUST HELP HIM, GINGER!
IT'S YOUR FUNERAL, CHARLEY...I AIN'T RISKIN' ME NECK FOR THE SAKE OF A NAG!
WARRIOR WHINNIED WITH JOY AT SEEING CHARLEY, WHO HAD BEFRIENDED THE HORSE BEFORE...
HERE, WARRIOR! YOU REMEMBER OLD CHARLEY, DON'T YOU, BOY?
BUT, NEARBY, ANOTHER SURVIVOR STAGGERED AWAY FROM THE BATTLEFIELD..!
B-BIG R-RUDI!
HRRRGH...! BIG RUDI...REMEMBER YOU...GINGER!

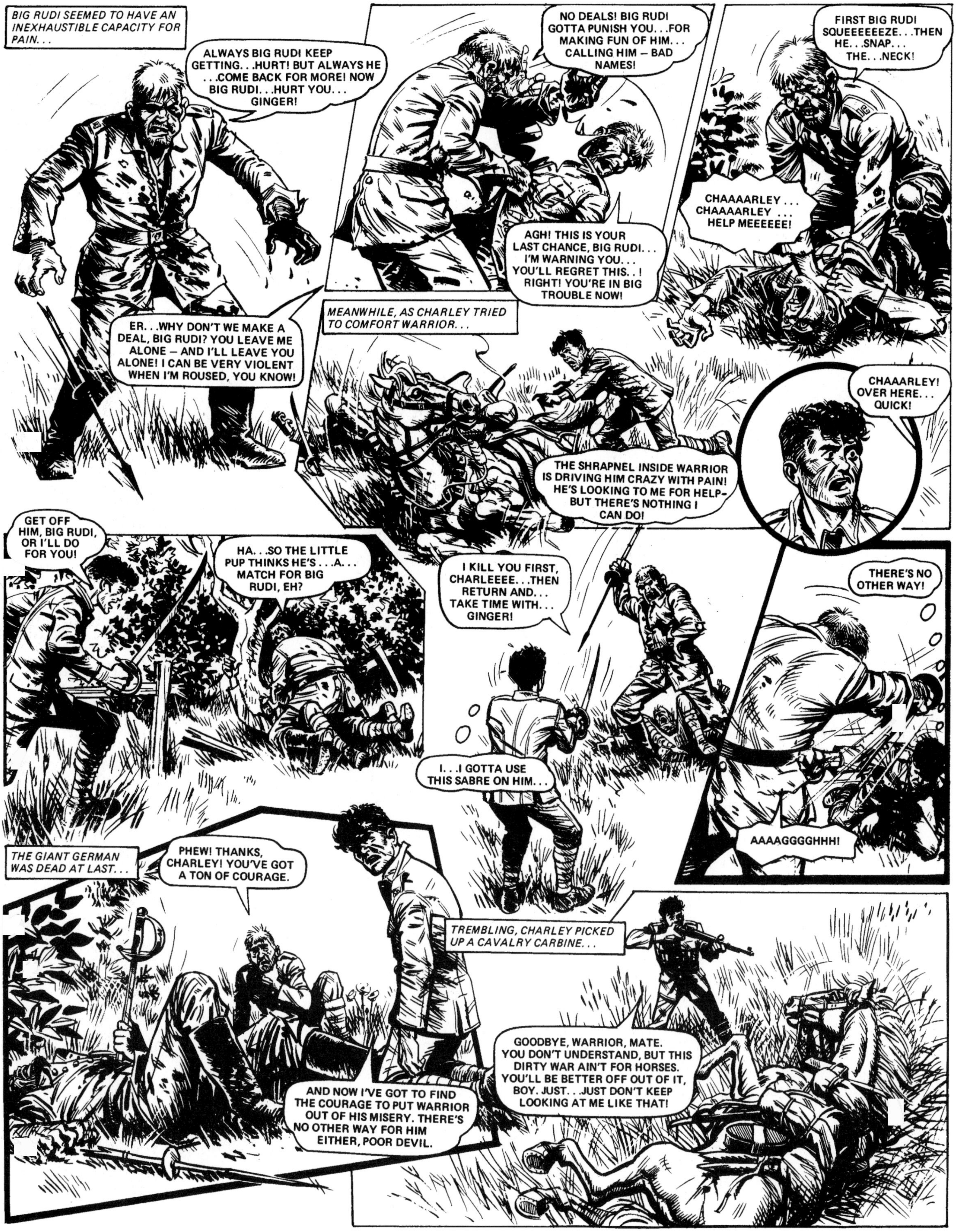

BIG RUDI SEEMED TO HAVE AN INEXHAUSTIBLE CAPACITY FOR PAIN...
ALWAYS BIG RUDI KEEP GETTING...HURT! BUT ALWAYS HE ...COME BACK FOR MORE! NOW BIG RUDI...HURT YOU... GINGER!
ER...WHY DON'T WE MAKE A DEAL, BIG RUDI? YOU LEAVE ME ALONE – AND I'LL LEAVE YOU ALONE! I CAN BE VERY VIOLENT WHEN I'M ROUSED, YOU KNOW!
NO DEALS! BIG RUDI GOTTA PUNISH YOU...FOR MAKING FUN OF HIM... CALLING HIM – BAD NAMES!
AGH! THIS IS YOUR LAST CHANCE, BIG RUDI... I'M WARNING YOU... YOU'LL REGRET THIS..! RIGHT! YOU'RE IN BIG TROUBLE NOW!
FIRST BIG RUDI SQUEEEEEEZE...THEN HE...SNAP... THE...NECK!
CHAAAARLEY ... CHAAAARLEY ... HELP MEEEEEE!
MEANWHILE, AS CHARLEY TRIED TO COMFORT WARRIOR...
THE SHRAPNEL INSIDE WARRIOR IS DRIVING HIM CRAZY WITH PAIN! HE'S LOOKING TO ME FOR HELP-BUT THERE'S NOTHING I CAN DO!
CHAAARLEY! OVER HERE... QUICK!
GET OFF HIM, BIG RUDI, OR I'LL DO FOR YOU!
HA...SO THE LITTLE PUP THINKS HE'S...A... MATCH FOR BIG RUDI, EH?
I KILL YOU FIRST, CHARLEEEE...THEN RETURN AND... TAKE TIME WITH... GINGER!
I...I GOTTA USE THIS SABRE ON HIM...
THERE'S NO OTHER WAY!
AAAAGGGGHHH!
THE GIANT GERMAN WAS DEAD AT LAST...
PHEW! THANKS, CHARLEY! YOU'VE GOT A TON OF COURAGE.
AND NOW I'VE GOT TO FIND THE COURAGE TO PUT WARRIOR OUT OF HIS MISERY. THERE'S NO OTHER WAY FOR HIM EITHER, POOR DEVIL.
TREMBLING, CHARLEY PICKED UP A CAVALRY CARBINE...
GOODBYE, WARRIOR, MATE. YOU DON'T UNDERSTAND, BUT THIS DIRTY WAR AIN'T FOR HORSES. YOU'LL BE BETTER OFF OUT OF IT, BOY. JUST...JUST DON'T KEEP LOOKING AT ME LIKE THAT!

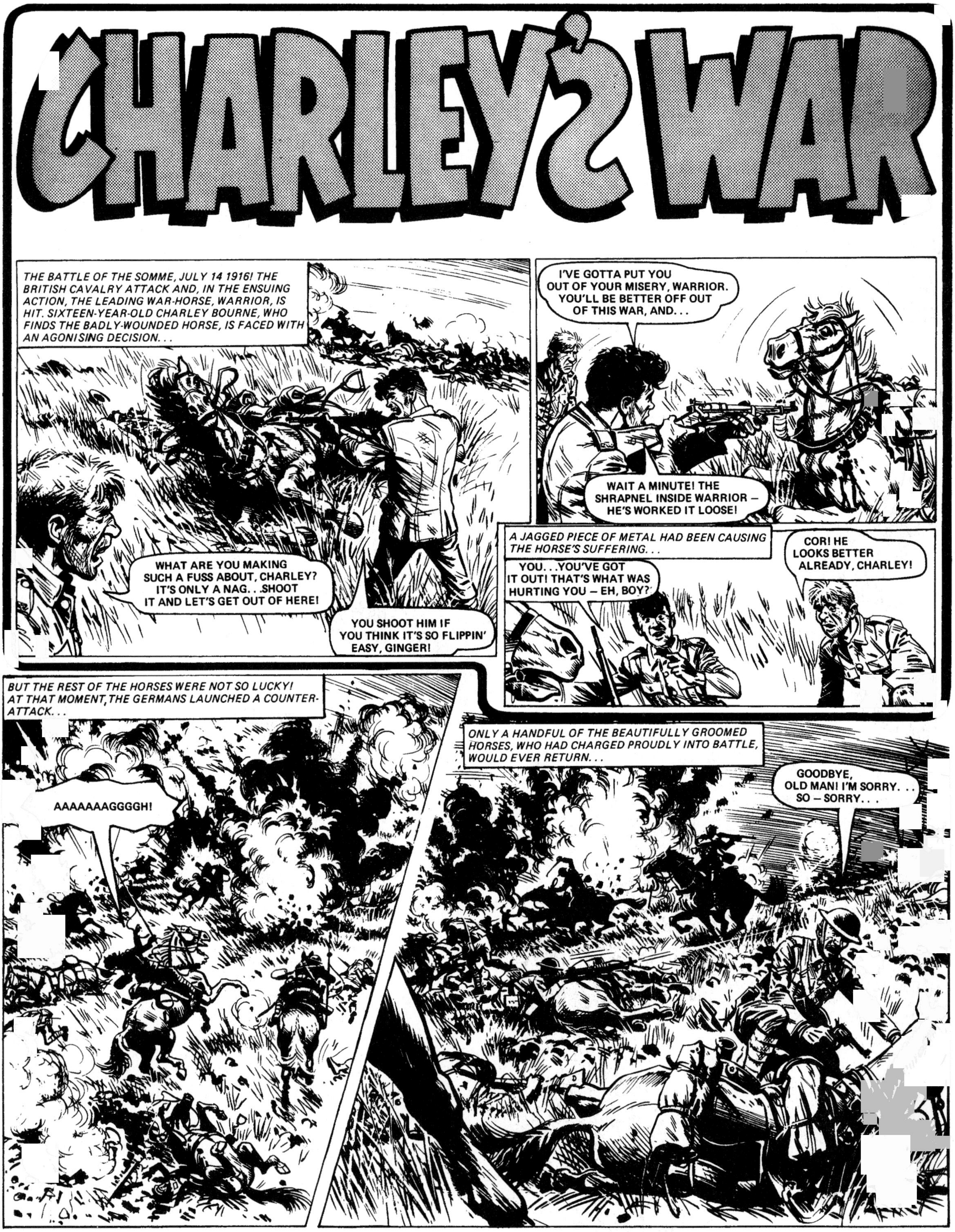
CHARLEY'S WAR
THE BATTLE OF THE SOMME, JULY 14 1916! THE BRITISH CAVALRY ATTACK AND, IN THE ENSUING ACTION, THE LEADING WAR-HORSE, WARRIOR, IS HIT. SIXTEEN-YEAR-OLD CHARLEY BOURNE, WHO FINDS THE BADLY-WOUNDED HORSE, IS FACED WITH AN AGONISING DECISION. . .
WHAT ARE YOU MAKING SUCH A FUSS ABOUT, CHARLEY? IT'S ONLY A NAG. . .SHOOT IT AND LET'S GET OUT OF HERE!
YOU SHOOT HIM IF YOU THINK IT'S SO FLIPPIN' EASY, GINGER!
I'VE GOTTA PUT YOU OUT OF YOUR MISERY, WARRIOR. YOU'LL BE BETTER OFF OUT OF THIS WAR, AND. . .
WAIT A MINUTE! THE SHRAPNEL INSIDE WARRIOR – HE'S WORKED IT LOOSE!
A JAGGED PIECE OF METAL HAD BEEN CAUSING THE HORSE'S SUFFERING. . .
YOU. . .YOU'VE GOT IT OUT! THAT'S WHAT WAS HURTING YOU – EH, BOY?
COR! HE LOOKS BETTER ALREADY, CHARLEY!
BUT THE REST OF THE HORSES WERE NOT SO LUCKY! AT THAT MOMENT, THE GERMANS LAUNCHED A COUNTER-ATTACK. . .
AAAAAAAAGGGGH!
ONLY A HANDFUL OF THE BEAUTIFULLY GROOMED HORSES, WHO HAD CHARGED PROUDLY INTO BATTLE, WOULD EVER RETURN. . .
GOODBYE, OLD MAN! I'M SORRY. . . SO – SORRY. . .

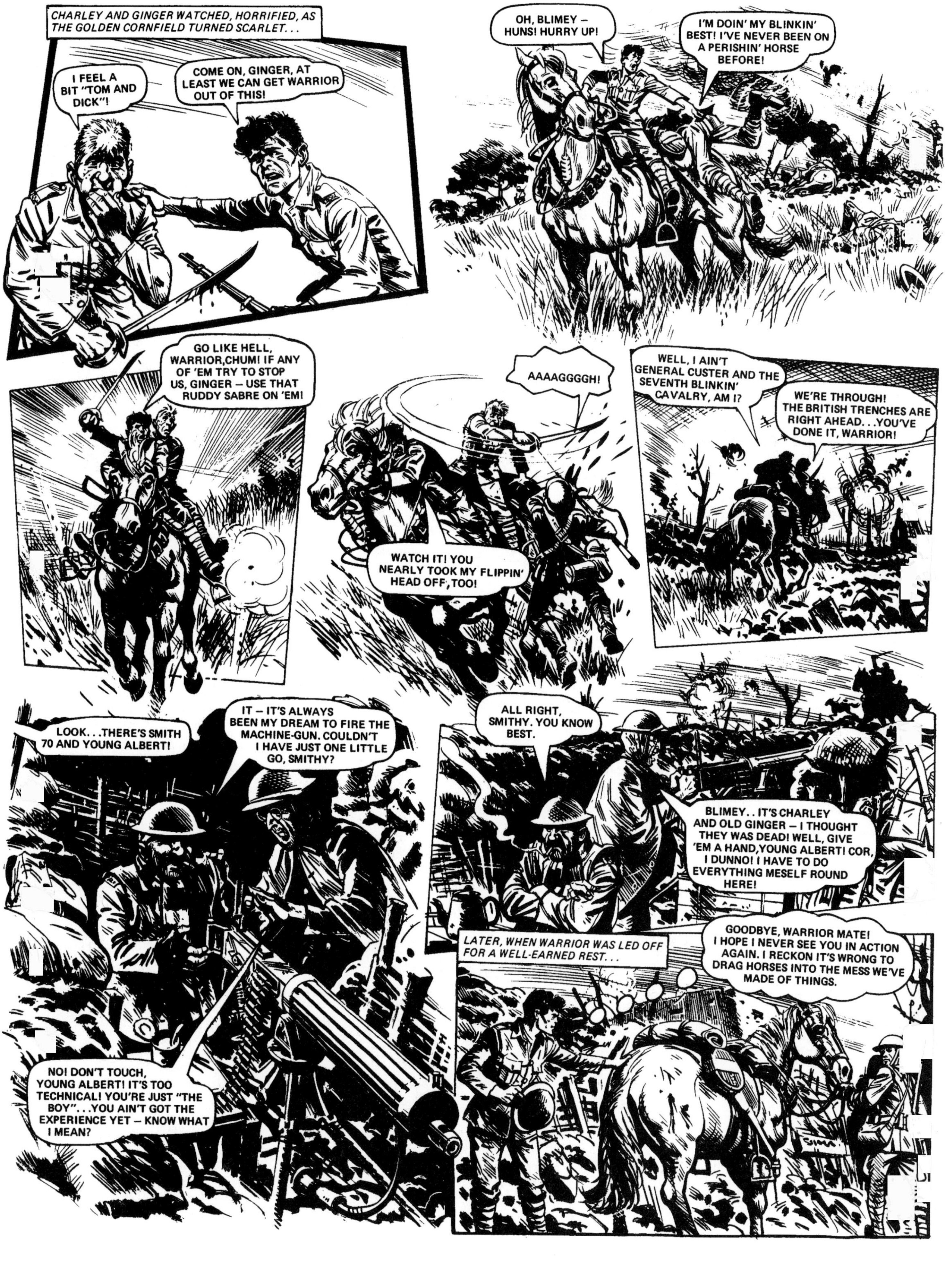
CHARLEY AND GINGER WATCHED, HORRIFIED, AS THE GOLDEN CORNFIELD TURNED SCARLET...
I FEEL A BIT "TOM AND DICK"!
COME ON, GINGER, AT LEAST WE CAN GET WARRIOR OUT OF THIS!
OH, BLIMEY – HUNS! HURRY UP!
I'M DOIN' MY BLINKIN' BEST! I'VE NEVER BEEN ON A PERISHIN' HORSE BEFORE!
GO LIKE HELL, WARRIOR,CHUM! IF ANY OF 'EM TRY TO STOP US, GINGER – USE THAT RUDDY SABRE ON 'EM!
AAAAGGGGH!
WATCH IT! YOU NEARLY TOOK MY FLIPPIN' HEAD OFF, TOO!
WELL, I AIN'T GENERAL CUSTER AND THE SEVENTH BLINKIN' CAVALRY, AM I?
WE'RE THROUGH! THE BRITISH TRENCHES ARE RIGHT AHEAD...YOU'VE DONE IT, WARRIOR!
LOOK...THERE'S SMITH 70 AND YOUNG ALBERT!
IT – IT'S ALWAYS BEEN MY DREAM TO FIRE THE MACHINE-GUN. COULDN'T I HAVE JUST ONE LITTLE GO, SMITHY?
NO! DON'T TOUCH, YOUNG ALBERT! IT'S TOO TECHNICAL! YOU'RE JUST "THE BOY"...YOU AIN'T GOT THE EXPERIENCE YET – KNOW WHAT I MEAN?
ALL RIGHT, SMITHY. YOU KNOW BEST.
BLIMEY.. IT'S CHARLEY AND OLD GINGER – I THOUGHT THEY WAS DEAD! WELL, GIVE 'EM A HAND,YOUNG ALBERT! COR, I DUNNO! I HAVE TO DO EVERYTHING MESELF ROUND HERE!
LATER, WHEN WARRIOR WAS LED OFF FOR A WELL-EARNED REST...
GOODBYE, WARRIOR MATE! I HOPE I NEVER SEE YOU IN ACTION AGAIN. I RECKON IT'S WRONG TO DRAG HORSES INTO THE MESS WE'VE MADE OF THINGS.

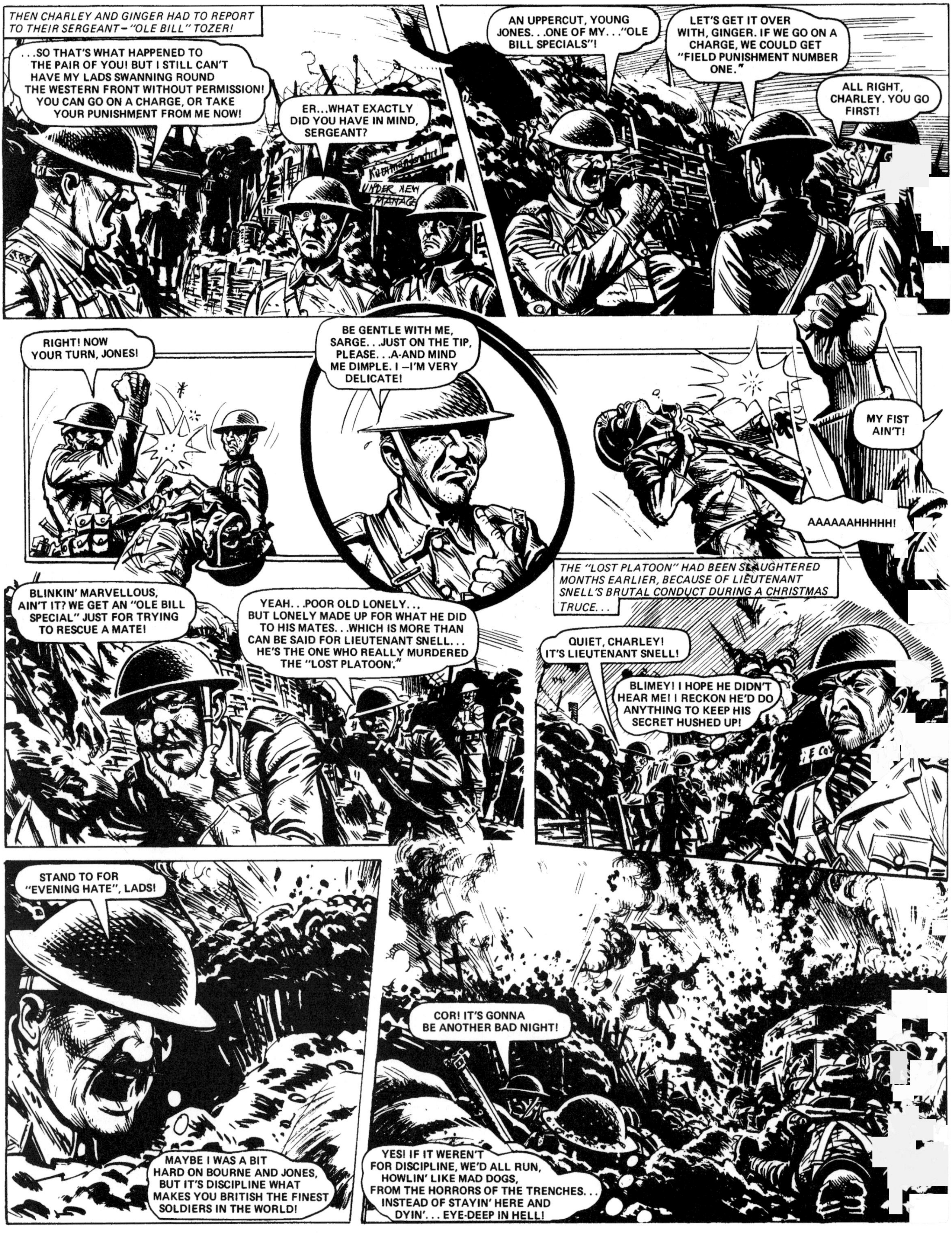
THEN CHARLEY AND GINGER HAD TO REPORT TO THEIR SERGEANT – "OLE BILL" TOZER!
...SO THAT'S WHAT HAPPENED TO THE PAIR OF YOU! BUT I STILL CAN'T HAVE MY LADS SWANNING ROUND THE WESTERN FRONT WITHOUT PERMISSION! YOU CAN GO ON A CHARGE, OR TAKE YOUR PUNISHMENT FROM ME NOW!
ER...WHAT EXACTLY DID YOU HAVE IN MIND, SERGEANT?
UNDER NEW MANAGE
AN UPPERCUT, YOUNG JONES...ONE OF MY..."OLE BILL SPECIALS"!
LET'S GET IT OVER WITH, GINGER. IF WE GO ON A CHARGE, WE COULD GET "FIELD PUNISHMENT NUMBER ONE."
ALL RIGHT, CHARLEY. YOU GO FIRST!
RIGHT! NOW YOUR TURN, JONES!
BE GENTLE WITH ME, SARGE...JUST ON THE TIP, PLEASE...A-AND MIND ME DIMPLE. I –I'M VERY DELICATE!
MY FIST AIN'T!
AAAAAAHHHHH!
BLINKIN' MARVELLOUS, AIN'T IT? WE GET AN "OLE BILL SPECIAL" JUST FOR TRYING TO RESCUE A MATE!
YEAH...POOR OLD LONELY... BUT LONELY MADE UP FOR WHAT HE DID TO HIS MATES...WHICH IS MORE THAN CAN BE SAID FOR LIEUTENANT SNELL... HE'S THE ONE WHO REALLY MURDERED THE "LOST PLATOON."
THE "LOST PLATOON" HAD BEEN SLAUGHTERED MONTHS EARLIER, BECAUSE OF LIEUTENANT SNELL'S BRUTAL CONDUCT DURING A CHRISTMAS TRUCE...
QUIET, CHARLEY! IT'S LIEUTENANT SNELL!
BLIMEY! I HOPE HE DIDN'T HEAR ME! I RECKON HE'D DO ANYTHING TO KEEP HIS SECRET HUSHED UP!
STAND TO FOR "EVENING HATE", LADS!
MAYBE I WAS A BIT HARD ON BOURNE AND JONES, BUT IT'S DISCIPLINE WHAT MAKES YOU BRITISH THE FINEST SOLDIERS IN THE WORLD!
COR! IT'S GONNA BE ANOTHER BAD NIGHT!
YES! IF IT WEREN'T FOR DISCIPLINE, WE'D ALL RUN, HOWLIN' LIKE MAD DOGS, FROM THE HORRORS OF THE TRENCHES... INSTEAD OF STAYIN' HERE AND DYIN'... EYE-DEEP IN HELL!

CHARLEY'S WAR

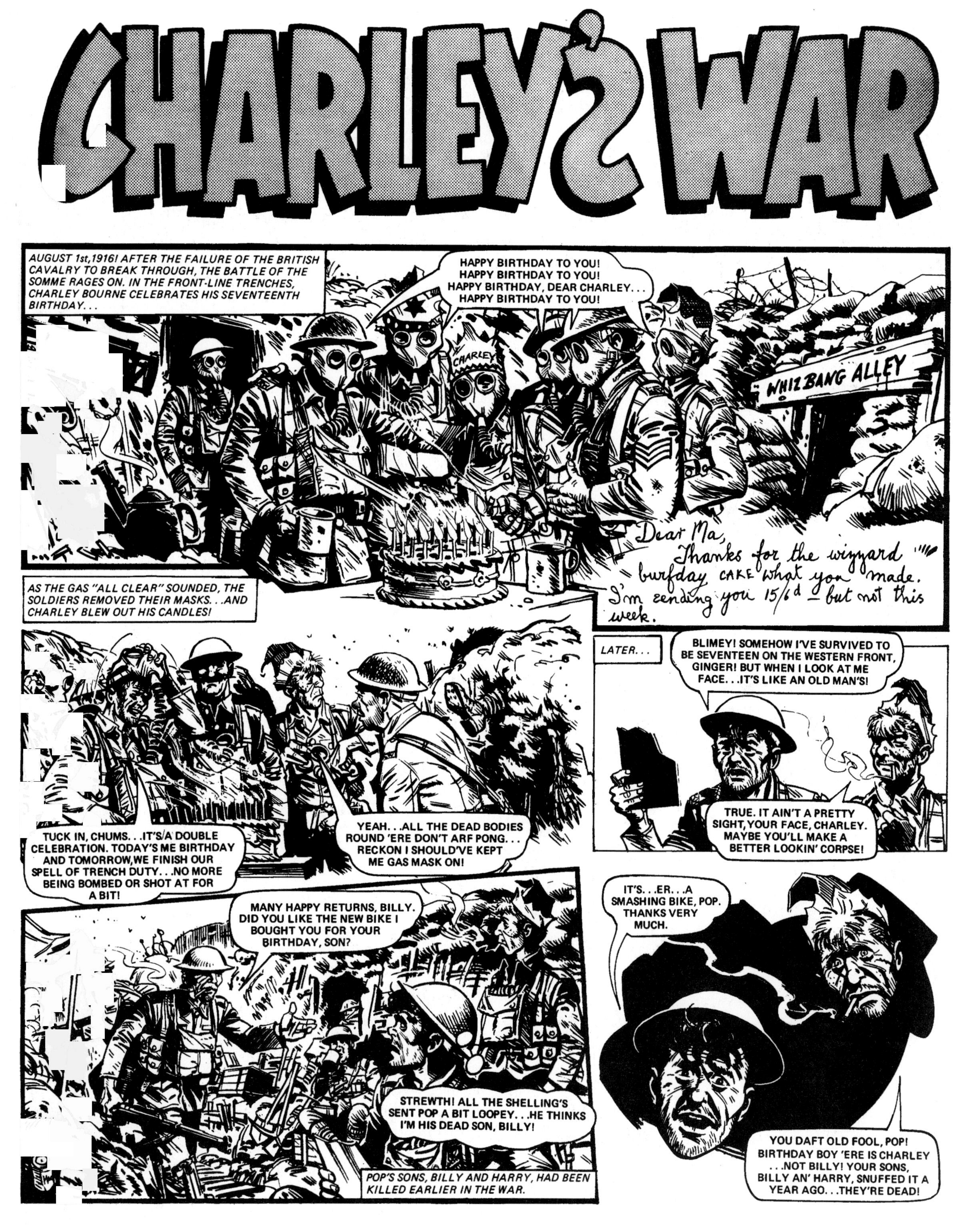

AUGUST 1st,1916! AFTER THE FAILURE OF THE BRITISH CAVALRY TO BREAK THROUGH, THE BATTLE OF THE SOMME RAGES ON. IN THE FRONT-LINE TRENCHES, CHARLEY BOURNE CELEBRATES HIS SEVENTEENTH BIRTHDAY...
HAPPY BIRTHDAY TO YOU! HAPPY BIRTHDAY TO YOU! HAPPY BIRTHDAY, DEAR CHARLEY... HAPPY BIRTHDAY TO YOU!
CHARLEY
WHIZ BANG ALLEY
Dear Ma, Thanks for the wizzard burfday CAKE what you made. I'm sending you 15/6d — but not this week.
AS THE GAS "ALL CLEAR" SOUNDED, THE SOLDIERS REMOVED THEIR MASKS...AND CHARLEY BLEW OUT HIS CANDLES!
TUCK IN, CHUMS...IT'S A DOUBLE CELEBRATION. TODAY'S ME BIRTHDAY AND TOMORROW,WE FINISH OUR SPELL OF TRENCH DUTY...NO MORE BEING BOMBED OR SHOT AT FOR A BIT!
YEAH...ALL THE DEAD BODIES ROUND 'ERE DON'T ARF PONG... RECKON I SHOULD'VE KEPT ME GAS MASK ON!
LATER...
BLIMEY! SOMEHOW I'VE SURVIVED TO BE SEVENTEEN ON THE WESTERN FRONT, GINGER! BUT WHEN I LOOK AT ME FACE...IT'S LIKE AN OLD MAN'S!
TRUE. IT AIN'T A PRETTY SIGHT, YOUR FACE, CHARLEY. MAYBE YOU'LL MAKE A BETTER LOOKIN' CORPSE!
MANY HAPPY RETURNS, BILLY. DID YOU LIKE THE NEW BIKE I BOUGHT YOU FOR YOUR BIRTHDAY, SON?
STREWTH! ALL THE SHELLING'S SENT POP A BIT LOOPEY...HE THINKS I'M HIS DEAD SON, BILLY!
POP'S SONS, BILLY AND HARRY, HAD BEEN KILLED EARLIER IN THE WAR.
IT'S...ER...A SMASHING BIKE, POP. THANKS VERY MUCH.
YOU DAFT OLD FOOL, POP! BIRTHDAY BOY 'ERE IS CHARLEY ...NOT BILLY! YOUR SONS, BILLY AN' HARRY, SNUFFED IT A YEAR AGO...THEY'RE DEAD!

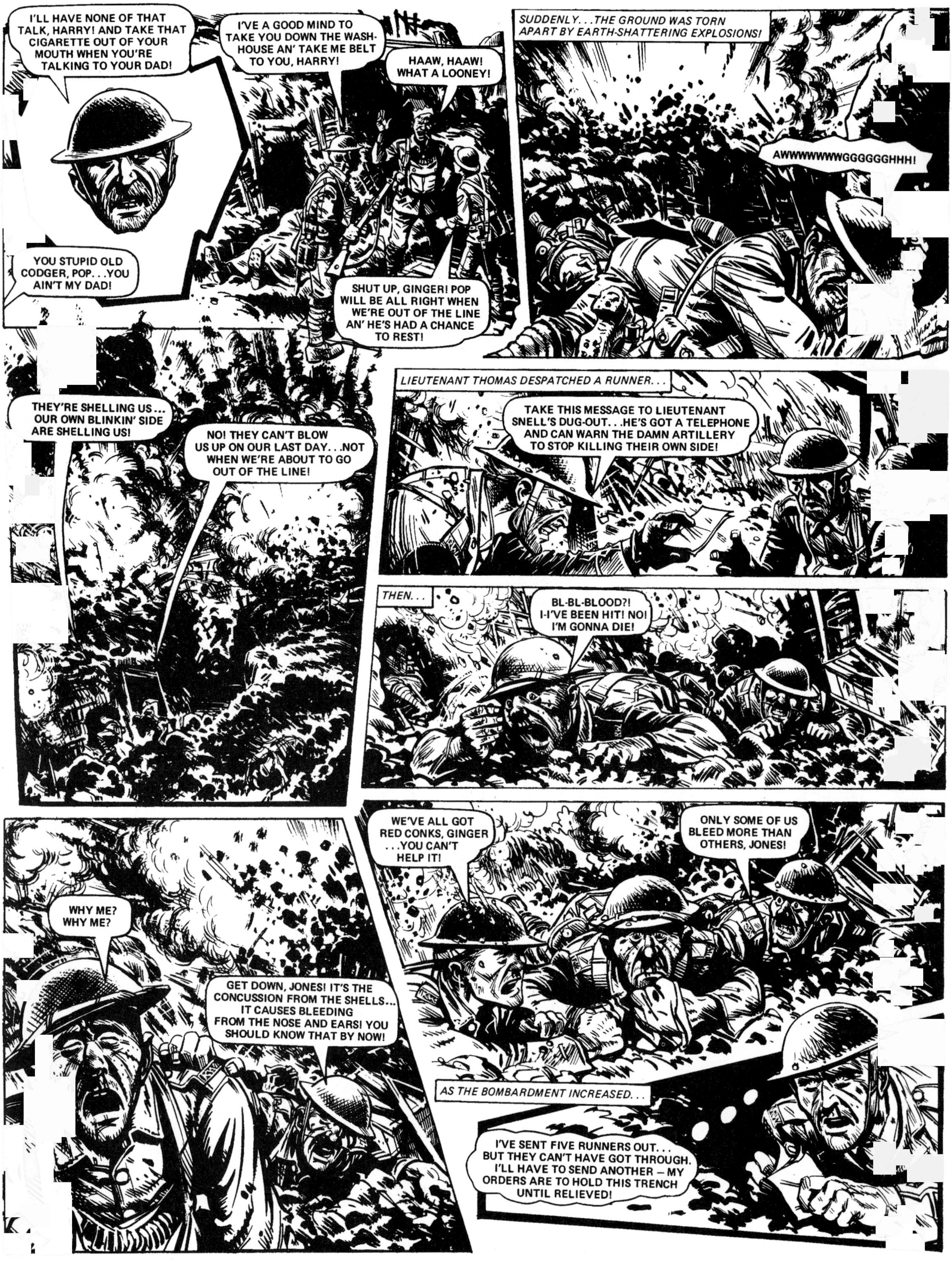
I'LL HAVE NONE OF THAT TALK, HARRY! AND TAKE THAT CIGARETTE OUT OF YOUR MOUTH WHEN YOU'RE TALKING TO YOUR DAD!
YOU STUPID OLD CODGER, POP. . . YOU AIN'T MY DAD!
I'VE A GOOD MIND TO TAKE YOU DOWN THE WASH-HOUSE AN' TAKE ME BELT TO YOU, HARRY!
HAAW, HAAW! WHAT A LOONEY!
SHUT UP, GINGER! POP WILL BE ALL RIGHT WHEN WE'RE OUT OF THE LINE AN' HE'S HAD A CHANCE TO REST!
SUDDENLY. . . THE GROUND WAS TORN APART BY EARTH-SHATTERING EXPLOSIONS!
AWWWWWWWGGGGGGHHH!
THEY'RE SHELLING US . . . OUR OWN BLINKIN' SIDE ARE SHELLING US!
NO! THEY CAN'T BLOW US UP ON OUR LAST DAY. . . NOT WHEN WE'RE ABOUT TO GO OUT OF THE LINE!
LIEUTENANT THOMAS DESPATCHED A RUNNER. . .
TAKE THIS MESSAGE TO LIEUTENANT SNELL'S DUG-OUT. . . HE'S GOT A TELEPHONE AND CAN WARN THE DAMN ARTILLERY TO STOP KILLING THEIR OWN SIDE!
THEN. . .
BL-BL-BLOOD?! I-I'VE BEEN HIT! NO! I'M GONNA DIE!
WHY ME? WHY ME?
GET DOWN, JONES! IT'S THE CONCUSSION FROM THE SHELLS. . . IT CAUSES BLEEDING FROM THE NOSE AND EARS! YOU SHOULD KNOW THAT BY NOW!
WE'VE ALL GOT RED CONKS, GINGER . . . YOU CAN'T HELP IT!
ONLY SOME OF US BLEED MORE THAN OTHERS, JONES!
AS THE BOMBARDMENT INCREASED. . .
I'VE SENT FIVE RUNNERS OUT. . . BUT THEY CAN'T HAVE GOT THROUGH. I'LL HAVE TO SEND ANOTHER – MY ORDERS ARE TO HOLD THIS TRENCH UNTIL RELIEVED!

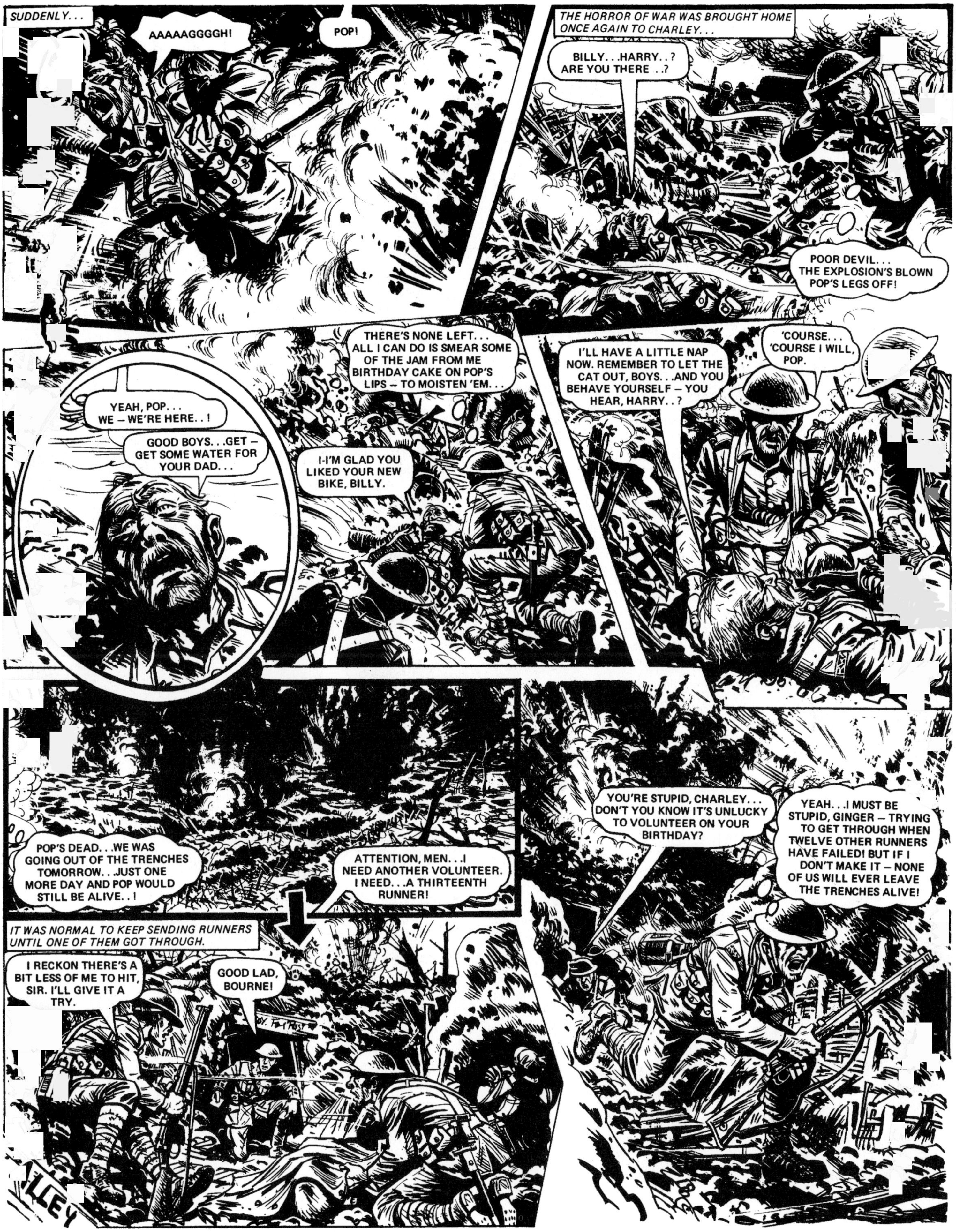
SUDDENLY...
AAAAAGGGGH!
POP!
THE HORROR OF WAR WAS BROUGHT HOME ONCE AGAIN TO CHARLEY...
BILLY...HARRY..? ARE YOU THERE ..?
POOR DEVIL... THE EXPLOSION'S BLOWN POP'S LEGS OFF!
YEAH, POP... WE – WE'RE HERE..!
GOOD BOYS...GET – GET SOME WATER FOR YOUR DAD...
THERE'S NONE LEFT... ALL I CAN DO IS SMEAR SOME OF THE JAM FROM ME BIRTHDAY CAKE ON POP'S LIPS – TO MOISTEN 'EM...
I-I'M GLAD YOU LIKED YOUR NEW BIKE, BILLY.
I'LL HAVE A LITTLE NAP NOW. REMEMBER TO LET THE CAT OUT, BOYS...AND YOU BEHAVE YOURSELF – YOU HEAR, HARRY..?
'COURSE... 'COURSE I WILL, POP.
POP'S DEAD...WE WAS GOING OUT OF THE TRENCHES TOMORROW...JUST ONE MORE DAY AND POP WOULD STILL BE ALIVE..!
ATTENTION, MEN...I NEED ANOTHER VOLUNTEER. I NEED...A THIRTEENTH RUNNER!
IT WAS NORMAL TO KEEP SENDING RUNNERS UNTIL ONE OF THEM GOT THROUGH.
I RECKON THERE'S A BIT LESS OF ME TO HIT, SIR. I'LL GIVE IT A TRY.
GOOD LAD, BOURNE!
YOU'RE STUPID, CHARLEY... DON'T YOU KNOW IT'S UNLUCKY TO VOLUNTEER ON YOUR BIRTHDAY?
YEAH...I MUST BE STUPID, GINGER – TRYING TO GET THROUGH WHEN TWELVE OTHER RUNNERS HAVE FAILED! BUT IF I DON'T MAKE IT – NONE OF US WILL EVER LEAVE THE TRENCHES ALIVE!

STRIP COMMENTARY

by Pat Mills

EPISODE ONE

The letters home in the strip were inspired by real correspondence from World War One. I found the genuine letters as emotional as World War One poems. Their limited, terse vocabulary is actually an asset that creates a powerful response in the reader. Therefore, to me, they qualify as poetry. For example, one soldier wrote home:

"There are times out here when we would rather be gone than put up with conditions… when the Germans are bombarding and the boys get knocked over one by one and can't hit back… The boys come along crying like children and shaking like old men still the shells burst in the air… and is a man is not thinking then 'bing' go a bullet and maybe catch that man. And when you are not fighting you are working and it just seems you will get the dirt. But never mind, dear girlie, you are far braver than us, for you have to take what is given… If we go under we are gone… Don't let it spoil your Christmas for Bert would not like it if he was there."

My neighbour, a Cambridge Don, disagreed with me. "The letters from the trenches can't be categorised as poetry because they weren't intended as poems," he loftily informed me. A *Punch* cartoon by Reading put the issue another way. As two 'Tommies' go over the top into an artillery barrage, one says to the other, "I shouldn't really be here. I don't write poetry." However, a national poet commented recently that I should actually be pleased the letters home haven't been categorised as poems because then they might end up in some sterile 'A' Level literature curriculum.

EPISODE TWO

The sniper appears at the end of this episode, dressed in medieval armour. Some readers questioned the credibility of this, and even World War Two veterans were sceptical and thought I'd made it up. Of course it was authentic, alongside other strange images in future episodes like gas masks on horses and dogs, and the bizarre early tanks. These images give World War One the feeling of a nightmarish science fiction war. And this is a scary point. We tend to think

of apocalyptic war as happening 'manana' – at some terrible and distant time in the future. It's chastening to think we are now living nearly a century after a science fiction war.

EPISODE THREE

The detail on the photo of Charley's family is remarkable. Every one of the Bournes looks a warm and wonderful character. This photo inspired me to develop the family in future episodes. Thus Charley's mother becomes a 'canary' – her skin turned yellow by the shells she was making in an armaments factory. Because of this skin condition, she was socially ostracised and treated as if she were a leper. This was often the fate of the 'canaries' in World War One.

THAT'S YOUNG WILF — ME BROTHER, A RIGHT TEARAWAY — AN' THERE'S ME BIG SISTER, DOLLY.

SHE LOOKS A SMASHER, CHARLEY!

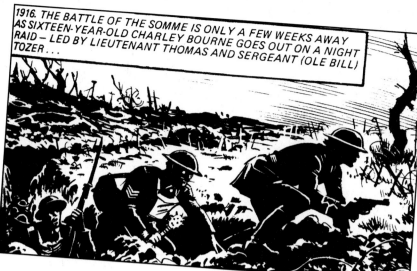

1916. THE BATTLE OF THE SOMME IS ONLY A FEW WEEKS AWAY AS SIXTEEN-YEAR-OLD CHARLEY BOURNE GOES OUT ON A NIGHT RAID – LED BY LIEUTENANT THOMAS AND SERGEANT (OLE BILL) TOZER...

much of his time arresting deserters. He objected strongly to such hateful work and so he joined the army and served as a cook in the trenches. When the war was over, he returned to his job in the police force. I only learnt of this in more recent years, long after he was dead. It's an example of how the 'Tommies' in the trenches were true to the emotive words of the World War One song, 'We'll Never Tell Them.' How many other unsung heroes there must have been whose stories have never been recorded.

EPISODES NINE – TWELVE

Finally Charley and his mates go 'over the top'. The script still works for me, but I should have given Joe far more space to draw it. There are too many pictures on the page and such a battle needs really large images. Joe did a truly fantastic job here, but really I asked too much of him. I think I was overwhelmed by the horror of it all and I didn't have the skills to pace this better and expand the whole sequence. The bright sunshine of July 1st also makes the pages very white, so we don't get the powerful black and white contrasts of early night scenes.

Turning to the subject matter, I know Joe was sad drawing such a terrible event. He cautiously told me he "shed a tear or two". It's a tribute to his artistic genius and temperament that he could depict this relentless conflict for so many years.

EPISODES FOUR – SIX

As Lieutenant Thomas suggests here, the British High Command must have known the impregnable state of the German trenches. Therefore to send soldiers over the top to attack them was a war crime – a clear act of mass murder. Recently, there is a trend amongst historians to justify the actions of the World War One generals. No doubt they would dismiss as naïve the view best expressed in the American post-World War One classic, *War is a Racket* by Brigadier General Smedley D. Butler. "Only those who would be called upon to risk their lives for their country should have the privilege of voting to determine whether the nation should go to war."

That sounds rather sensible to me. After all, if General Haig and politicians like Lloyd George actually had to go 'over the top' themselves would they have made more effort to minimise casualties; or even declared war in the first place? The answer is obvious and as relevant to our leaders today as it was then.

EPISODE SEVEN

The tension continues to mount in preparation for the most shameful day in British military history when 60,000 of the 'Best of British' would be sacrificed. I tried wherever I could to use authentic postcards from the period and the Bruce Bairnsfather card, 'If you knows of a better 'ole', is a classic. His other cartoons and cards also honour the ordinary soldier.

The presentation of the letters was inspired by a story in a romantic teenage paper called *Romeo*, entitled 'The Private War of Nicola Brown'. Despite its unlikely home, this story was actually rather superb. It was drawn by the legendary Estaban Maroto and written by John Cornforth. In stark blacks and whites it showed the horrors of the Crimean War, with diary entries from nurse Nicola Brown. In fact, I think the diary entries worked better graphically on Nicola Brown than the letters on *Charley's War*. Eventually I stopped using them because I felt, as a dramatic device, they were running out of steam. However, I'm not sure everyone would agree with me.

My writing partner at the time, John Wagner, the writer/creator of *Judge Dredd*, was equally impressed by 'The Private War of Nicola Brown' and used similar diary entries in his *Battle* story 'Darkie's Mob' in a very powerful way.

EPISODE EIGHT

A soldier is about to shoot himself in the foot in Episode Eight. Self inflicted wounds, desertions and executions were commonplace on the frontline. My grandfather was a policeman at the beginning of World War One and was called upon to spend

BATTLE ACTION

They knew they were cannon-fodder for the hungry German guns... but they obeyed the order...

OVER THE TOP!

READ 'CHARLEY'S WAR'

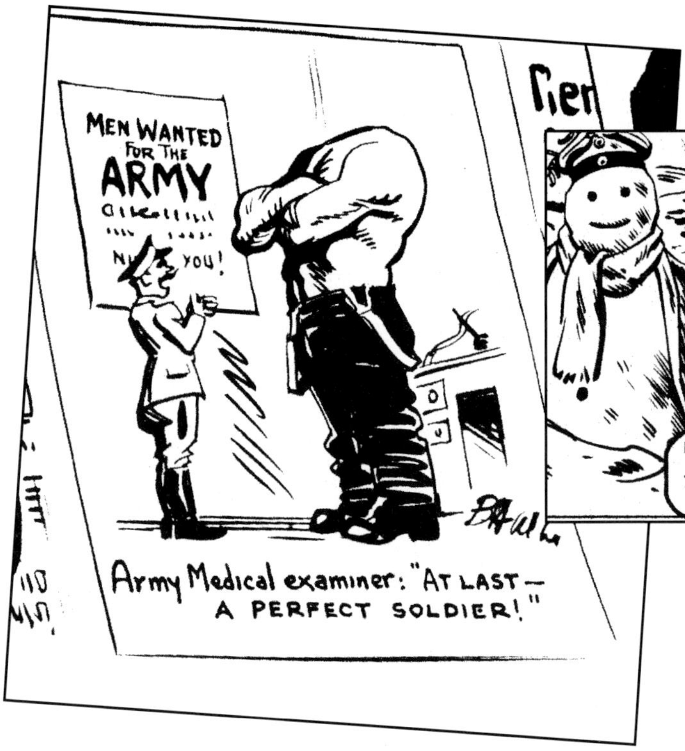
MEN WANTED FOR THE ARMY
YOU!
Army Medical examiner: "AT LAST – A PERFECT SOLDIER!"

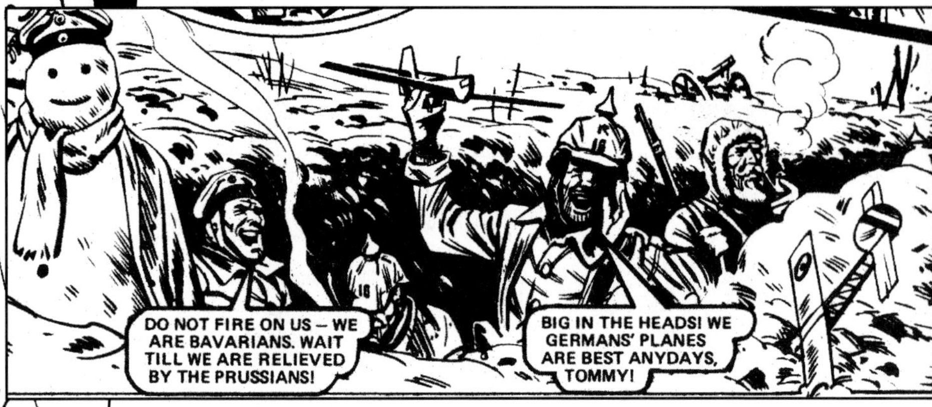
DO NOT FIRE ON US – WE ARE BAVARIANS. WAIT TILL WE ARE RELIEVED BY THE PRUSSIANS!
BIG IN THE HEADS! WE GERMANS' PLANES ARE BEST ANYDAYS, TOMMY!

EPISODES THIRTEEN – FOURTEEN

Once again postcards are used to good effect. This military 'form' postcard is one of my favourites. I used it as a satirical device in the style of *Oh, What a Lovely War*. This film had a deep effect on me as a teenager. I saw it at least six times in one year and also watched the stage play. I was impressed by the use of visual metaphors and I tried to use the postcards in a similar way.

Oh, What a Lovely War is a true anti-war film, unlike some of the 'war is hell' variety. So I tried to ensure *Charley's War* was in the same ilk and could never glorify war. This was an important point to me. I once interviewed a soldier who fought in Northern Ireland about his experiences there and in a military prison – before writing about them in another radical comic series I created entitled *Third World War*, centred on the USA and UK's control of the Third World. He told me he joined the army for two reasons; firstly, because he loved the outdoor life; and secondly, because he read war comics as a kid. As I was one of the two creators of *Battle*, I felt some sense of responsibility here. It was one of the reasons why I needed to write *Charley's War*.

EPISODES FIFTEEN – SIXTEEN

Finally the first day of the Somme is over. Everything that needed to be said is said in that final text panel.

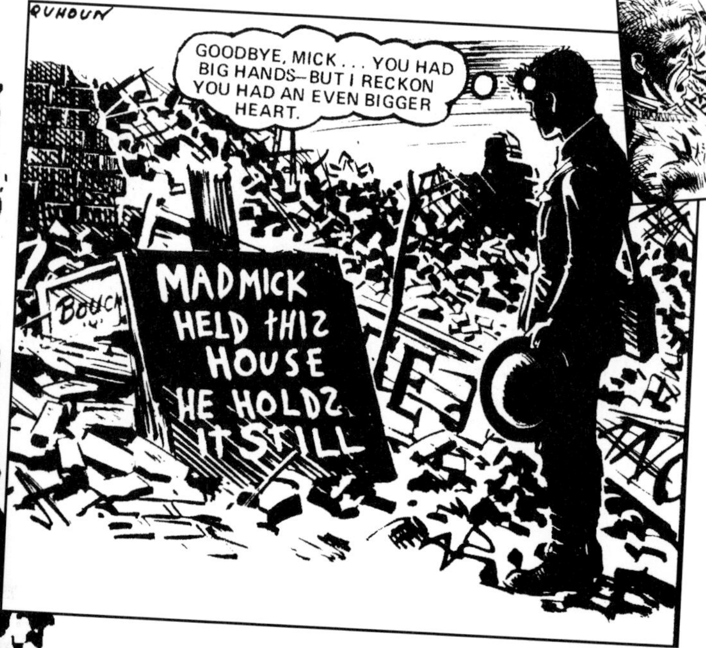
GOODBYE, MICK . . . YOU HAD BIG HANDS– BUT I RECKON YOU HAD AN EVEN BIGGER HEART.
MAD MICK HELD THIZ HOUSE HE HOLDZ IT STILL

EPISODES SEVENTEEN – NINETEEN

A new sequence begins, setting the scene for the last great cavalry charge. It also features a Christmas truce. The famous truce of 1914 is well known, but there were others that have barely been recorded because the Generals fiercely opposed the truces and laid down artillery barrages whenever the British and German soldiers were likely to fraternise.

EPISODE TWENTY

Lonely goes home to a hero's welcome. Joe's detail on the home front is mesmerising as ever. We really feel we are there. When I look at Joe's artwork, it is like going to the movies. You can hear and almost smell the scenes. Because I was familiar with most of the reference source material available, I'm pretty certain Joe actually drew many of these scenes out of his head. This means he had an almost magical artistic gift.

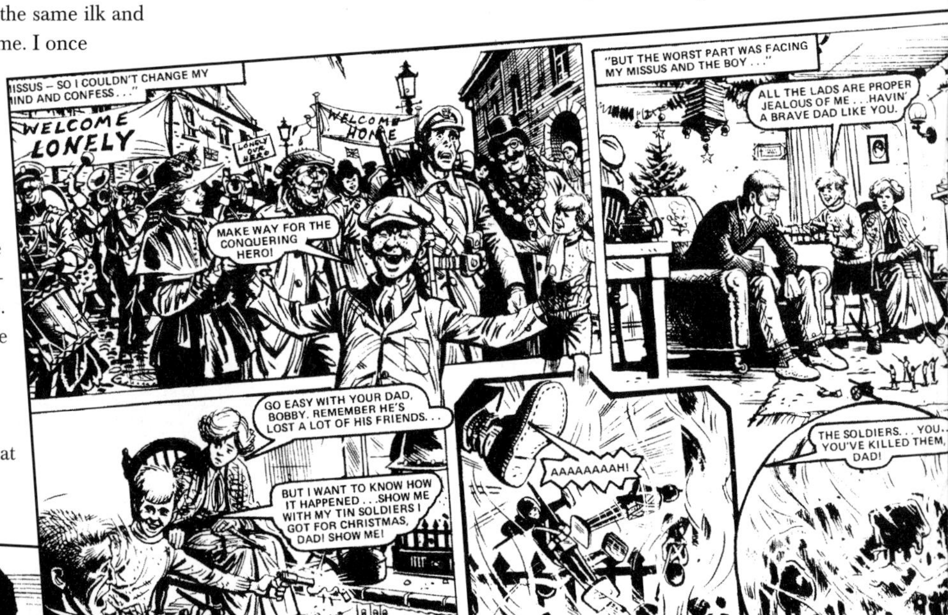
ISSUS – SO I COULDN'T CHANGE MY IND AND CONFESS . . ."
WELCOME LONELY
WELCOME HOME
MAKE WAY FOR THE CONQUERING HERO!
"BUT THE WORST PART WAS FACING MY MISSUS AND THE BOY . . ."
ALL THE LADS ARE PROPER JEALOUS OF ME . . . HAVIN' A BRAVE DAD LIKE YOU.
GO EASY WITH YOUR DAD, BOBBY. REMEMBER HE'S LOST A LOT OF HIS FRIENDS. . .
BUT I WANT TO KNOW HOW IT HAPPENED . . . SHOW ME WITH MY TIN SOLDIERS I GOT FOR CHRISTMAS, DAD! SHOW ME!
AAAAAAAAH!
THE SOLDIERS. . . YOU. . . YOU'VE KILLED THEM, DAD!

You might imagine that Joe and I spent hours on the phone talking over such scenes. Surprisingly, this is not the case. I never met him and we talked on the phone maybe five times in all the years we worked together. This was the traditional way comics were produced and, on this occasion, it worked.

It's a measure of Joe's professionalism that he never once asked for script changes; he drew everything that was put in front of him without comment or complaint. Yet, by the very nature of the creative process,

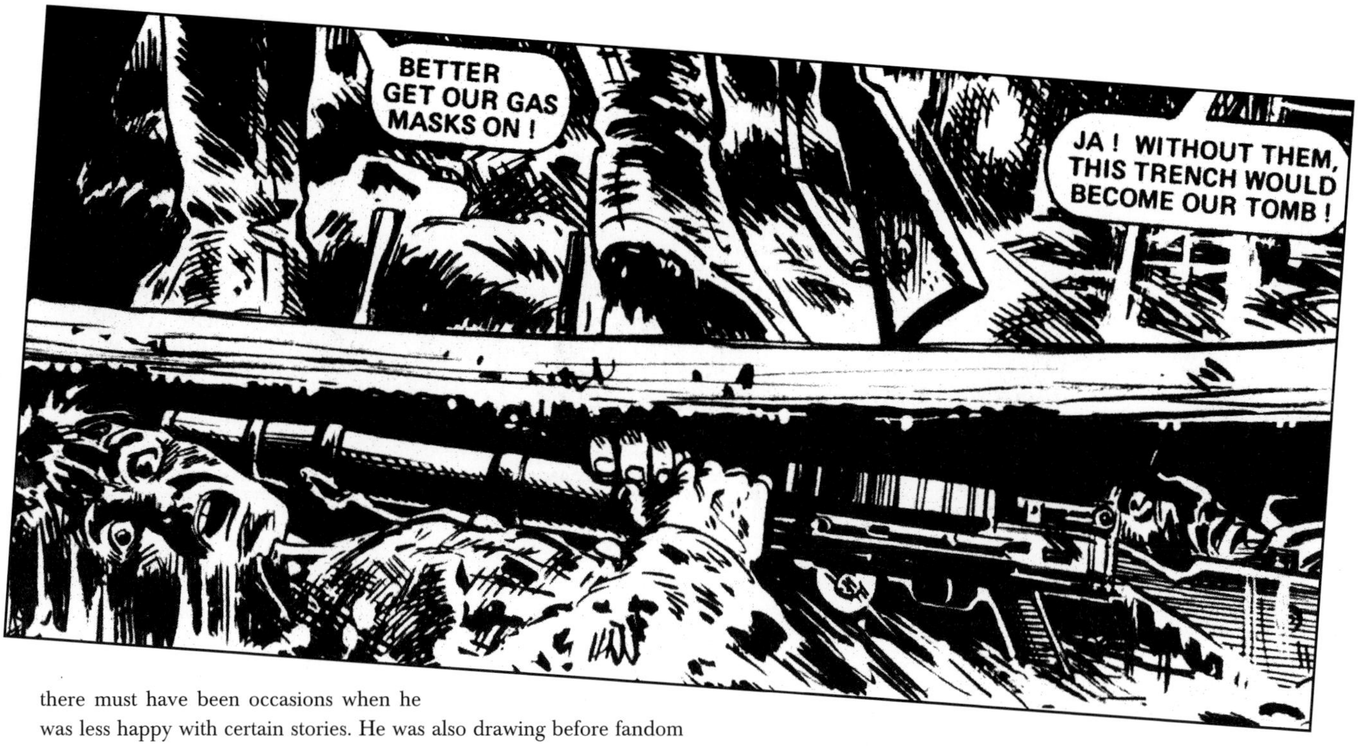
BETTER GET OUR GAS MASKS ON !
JA ! WITHOUT THEM, THIS TRENCH WOULD BECOME OUR TOMB !

there must have been occasions when he was less happy with certain stories. He was also drawing before fandom became a significant force in UK comics; he never received any awards for his work, and the fees he received were barely adequate. So I reached the conclusion that he was drawing not for the fans, not for the money, but purely for the pleasure of it. I decided to use him as my role model in my own approach to my work and it's fair to say he had a significant affect on my life.

EPISODE TWENTY-ONE

Ginger and Charley are under the duckboards at the bottom of a trench. I think this is an interesting example of exploring inner space in comics, rather than outer space. Too often in our medium, we feature vast and meaningless galactic empires, whereas a claustrophobic small space can be far more dramatic, as in this example. Colourful and fantastic science fiction terrains can lead to bad writing habits and quick fix, easy dramatic solutions. The limited possibilities in the trenches forced me to write to a higher standard.

EPISODES TWENTY-TWO – TWENTY-FOUR

It was a little uncomfortable having Charley and Ginger out of their usual bitter trench environment. There was a danger of it becoming a ripping yarn, like the first World War One novel I read as a boy, which rejoiced in the title *Dick Daring in the Dardanelles.* But it was absolutely essential so they could be present at the last great cavalry charge. I also feel the plotting pays off when we see at the end of Episode 24 the nightmarish figure of a gas masked horse and rider appear – surely a scene straight from Hell.

I would also feature poison gas later in *Charley's War*, notably at Verdun (a tale told by Charley's French Foreign Legion friend, Blue). Although the Germans used gas first, our record is by no means as clean as some would have us believe. Thus the British used poison gas against the Bolshevik Russians during their invasion of Russia in 1919 but the wind was wrong, so the weapon was ineffective.

I also discovered that, during the 1920s, the British RAF bombed Iraq with poison gas, wiping out several villages. Britain had occupied Iraq in order to obtain its oil and the Kurds were being 'difficult tribesmen'. Our use of poison gas was in contravention of a League of Nations treaty banning such weapons of mass destruction. Churchill was in favour of gas, regarding it as a 'scientific weapon'. My intention was to have Wilf, Charley's younger brother who served as a gunner in the RFC, fight in that conflict. Unfortunately, details were minimal so, with considerable regret, I shelved those plans.

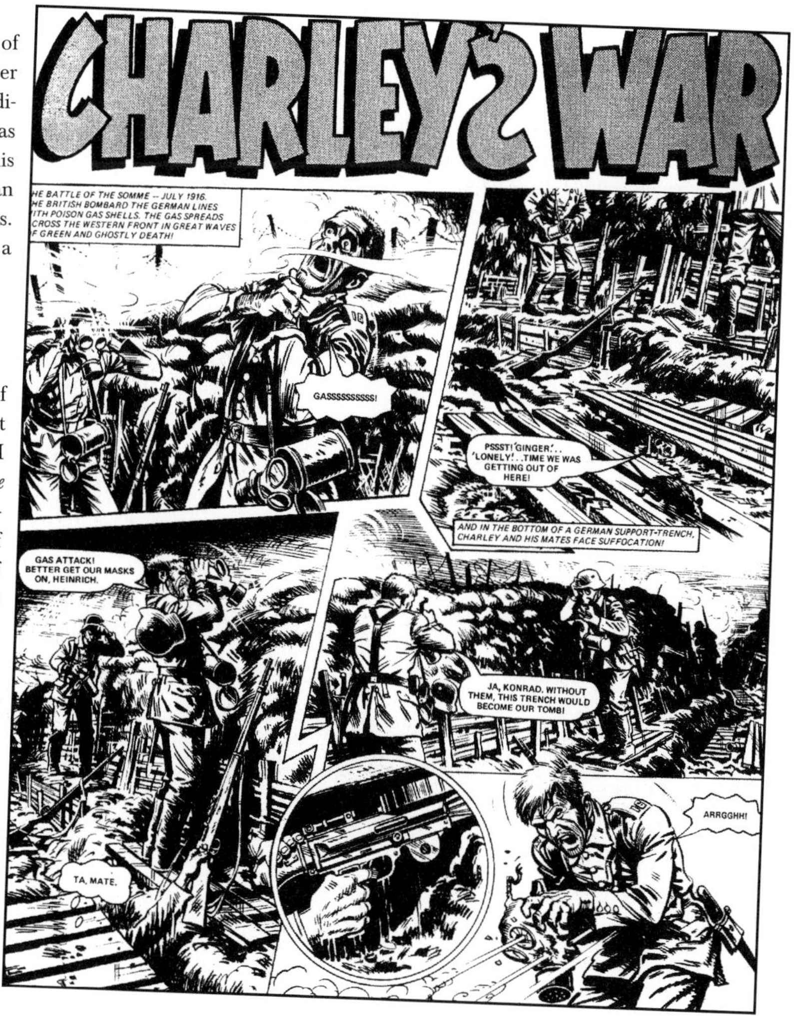
CHARLEY'S WAR
HE BATTLE OF THE SOMME -- JULY 1916. HE BRITISH BOMBARD THE GERMAN LINES ITH POISON GAS SHELLS. THE GAS SPREADS CROSS THE WESTERN FRONT IN GREAT WAVES F GREEN AND GHOSTLY DEATH!
GASSSSSSSSSS!
PSSST! 'GINGER'.. 'LONELY'. .TIME WE WAS GETTING OUT OF HERE!
AND IN THE BOTTOM OF A GERMAN SUPPORT-TRENCH, CHARLEY AND HIS MATES FACE SUFFOCATION!
GAS ATTACK! BETTER GET OUR MASKS ON, HEINRICH.
JA, KONRAD. WITHOUT THEM, THIS TRENCH WOULD BECOME OUR TOMB!
ARRGGHH!
TA, MATE.

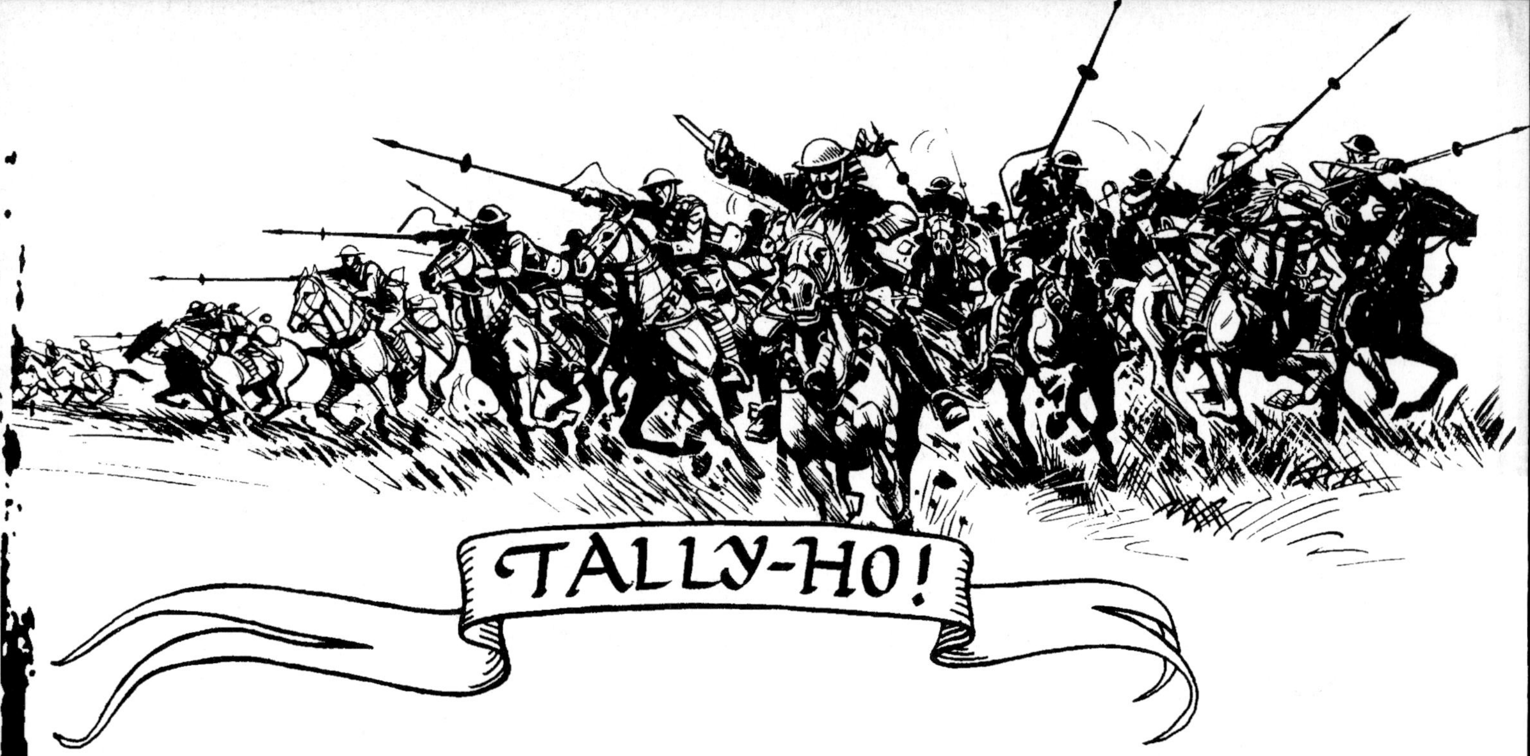
TALLY-HO!

EPISODES TWENTY-FIVE – TWENTY-SEVEN

There was very little information I could find on the physical aspects of the cavalry charge. And I think it shows a little in this sequence. With the benefit of hindsight, I should have researched an earlier cavalry charge, e.g. the Franco-Prussian War or the American Civil War, to dramatise this more effectively.

Research was always a problem on *Charley.* I enjoyed the process, but I had to set myself some time and financial limits, otherwise I'd have gone broke writing it. Ultimately, this problem of research would lead to me ending the serial.

Originally I intended to continue the saga into World War Two, with Charley's son, also named Charley. This was because it's become convenient to isolate World War One and see it as a 'bad' war, and World War Two or later wars as 'good' wars, a viewpoint I strongly disagree with. But, again, research difficulties made it impossible.

EPISODE TWENTY-EIGHT

Charley is about to shoot Warrior here, but the horse makes a recovery, which was actually just as well. Editorial weren't keen on mercy killings, no matter the justification. Thus, in a later sequence, a soldier is drowning in mud and begs Charley to shoot him. Charley does so. Although it was authentic, editorial changed it to Charley rescuing the soldier, which was far too convenient for my taste.

The only other censorship changes I can recall were the deletion of a reference to Charley using barbed wire to fish for rats. This was seen as a bit 'offensive'. And later, in 1918, when the Americans join the war, some white US soldiers behave in a racist way towards black US soldiers and threaten them with the justice of the Ku Klux Klan. This was deleted on the grounds that 'it might offend people', presumably the KKK?

Given some of the content of *Charley's War,* I think I got off lightly. It's why I let all these minor changes go because I was also writing about such controversial subjects as the British army mutiny at Etaples. This was a tragic and shocking event which even today little is known about apart from its dramatisation in the BBC TV series, *The Monocled Mutineer.*

EPISODE TWENTY-NINE

Looking back on the opening picture of the soldiers singing in gas masks, it's visually extremely effective. But I doubt it was authentic and I don't think I would write such a scene today.

This book concludes with Charley becoming the 'Thirteenth Runner'. Messengers in war had a high mortality rate and things really don't look good for our hero as he heads off down the trench. ✢

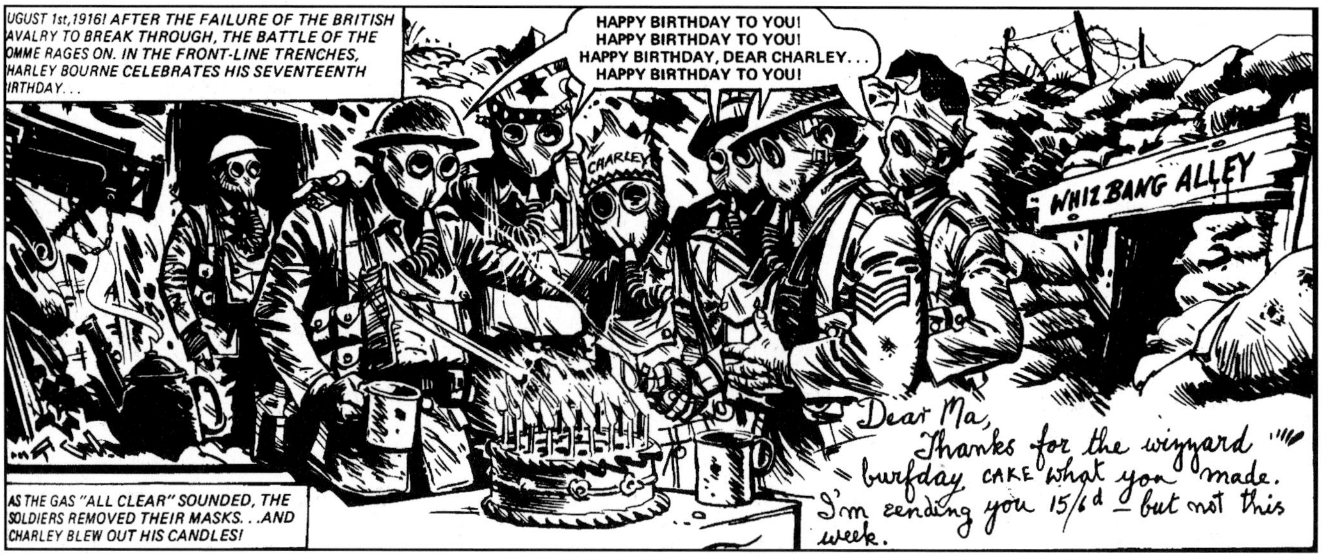
UGUST 1st,1916! AFTER THE FAILURE OF THE BRITISH AVALRY TO BREAK THROUGH, THE BATTLE OF THE OMME RAGES ON. IN THE FRONT-LINE TRENCHES, HARLEY BOURNE CELEBRATES HIS SEVENTEENTH IRTHDAY...
HAPPY BIRTHDAY TO YOU! HAPPY BIRTHDAY TO YOU! HAPPY BIRTHDAY, DEAR CHARLEY... HAPPY BIRTHDAY TO YOU!
CHARLEY
WHIZ BANG ALLEY
AS THE GAS "ALL CLEAR" SOUNDED, THE SOLDIERS REMOVED THEIR MASKS...AND CHARLEY BLEW OUT HIS CANDLES!
Dear Ma, Thanks for the wizzard burfday CAKE what you made. I'm sending you 15/6d – but not this week.

THE BATTLE OF THE SOMME

Putting *Charley's War* in Context

by Steve White

Charley's War is set against the backdrop of the Battle of the Somme. Enshrined not just in military history but scoured onto the British psyche, the Somme was intended to be a decisive knockout blow that would crush German resistance on the Western Front.

The French Commander-in-Chief, Joseph Joffre, originally conceived the assault. He had intended it to be a largely French affair but the German offensive against Verdun drew Joffre's troops into action there, leaving the British to provide the bulk of the forces for the coming battle. Principally designed to inflict crippling loses on German manpower, the plan was also intended to help relieve pressure being exerted on the French at Verdun and the ailing Russians. British Prime Minister David Lloyd George remained unconvinced; he believed the German push on Verdun was faltering. The Russians were also more or less defeated, torn apart not just by the attacking Germans but from within by the anarchy that led to the Russian Revolution in 1917.

The pressure at Verdun was such that the French insisted the attack be brought forward a month from 1 August. The allied plan as developed by the British Expeditionary Force commander, Sir Douglas Haig, called for the British to attack on the morning of 1 July 1916 with eleven divisions along a 24-kilometre (15 miles) front north of the River Somme. Sir Henry Rawlinson's Fourth Army was to strike towards the town of Bapaume, whilst to the north Rawlinson was supported by units from the Third Army. Five French divisions of the Sixth Army were to attack from the south towards Combles.

For a week prior to the start date, allied artillery pounded the German lines with 1.6 million shells in the expectation that it would soften up if not destroy the enemy positions. However, the bombardment, whilst gruelling for the Germans, failed. Many shells did not explode but, more importantly, the Germans had fortified many of their trenches, and dug a network of underground tunnels and positions. When the shells began whistling in, the Germans simply retired underground to sit out the bombardment.

On the morning of 1 July, the shelling lifted and the Germans emerged from their bunkers. They rightly assumed that the allied attack, whose clearly visible preparations they had been monitoring, and which was the source of much gossip in French cafes, was about to begin. Such was the high expectations in the success of the artillery preparations that General Haig ordered his units to 'walk' towards the German trenches. He also believed that, "The machine-gun is a much overrated weapon."

The start of the attack was signalled by the detonation of seventeen huge mines. These were positioned in tunnels dug beneath key points in the German lines by special engineering units, many taken from mining towns in England and Wales. The mines included the 27,216 kilos (60,000 pounds) of explosive that left the 'Lochnager Crater' still visible today just south of the village of La Boisselle. However,

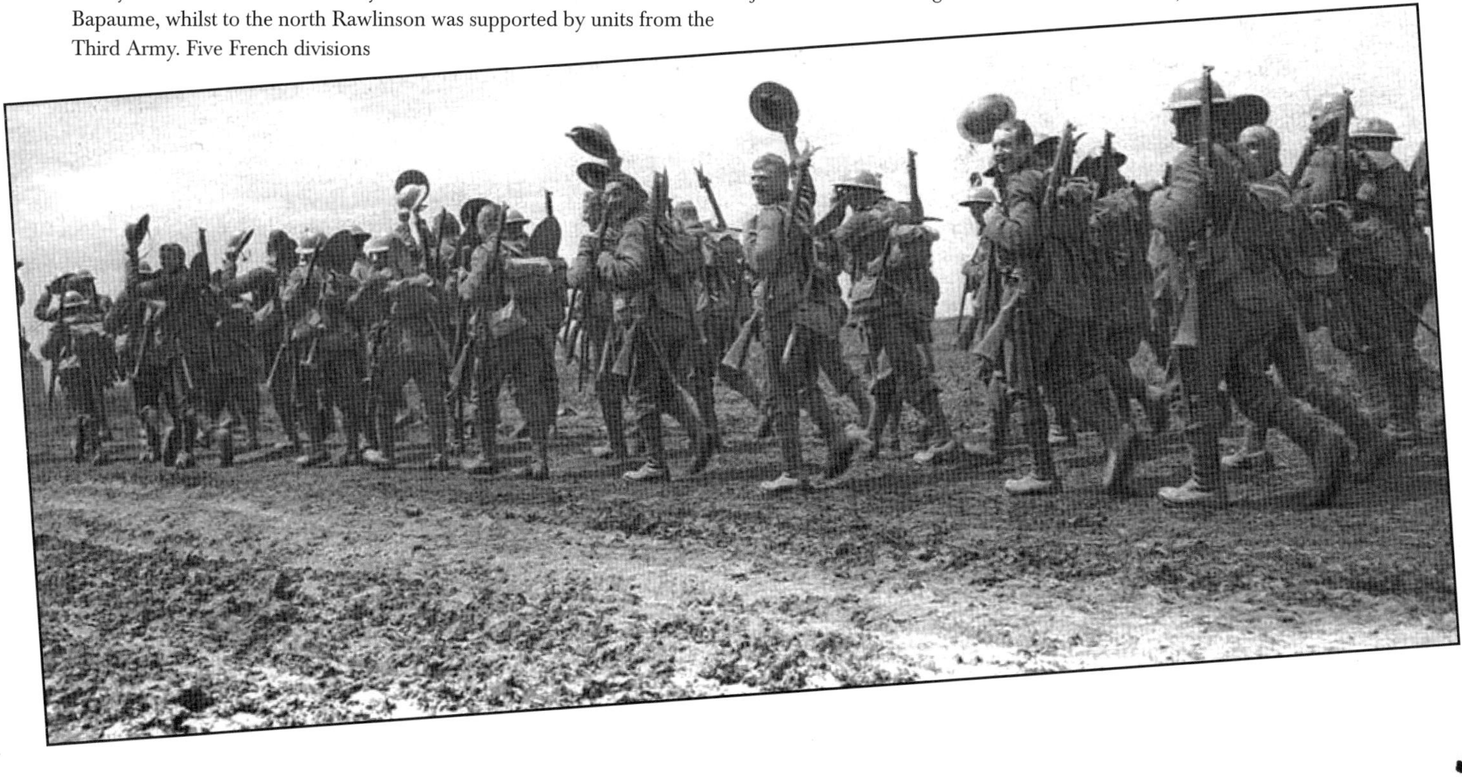

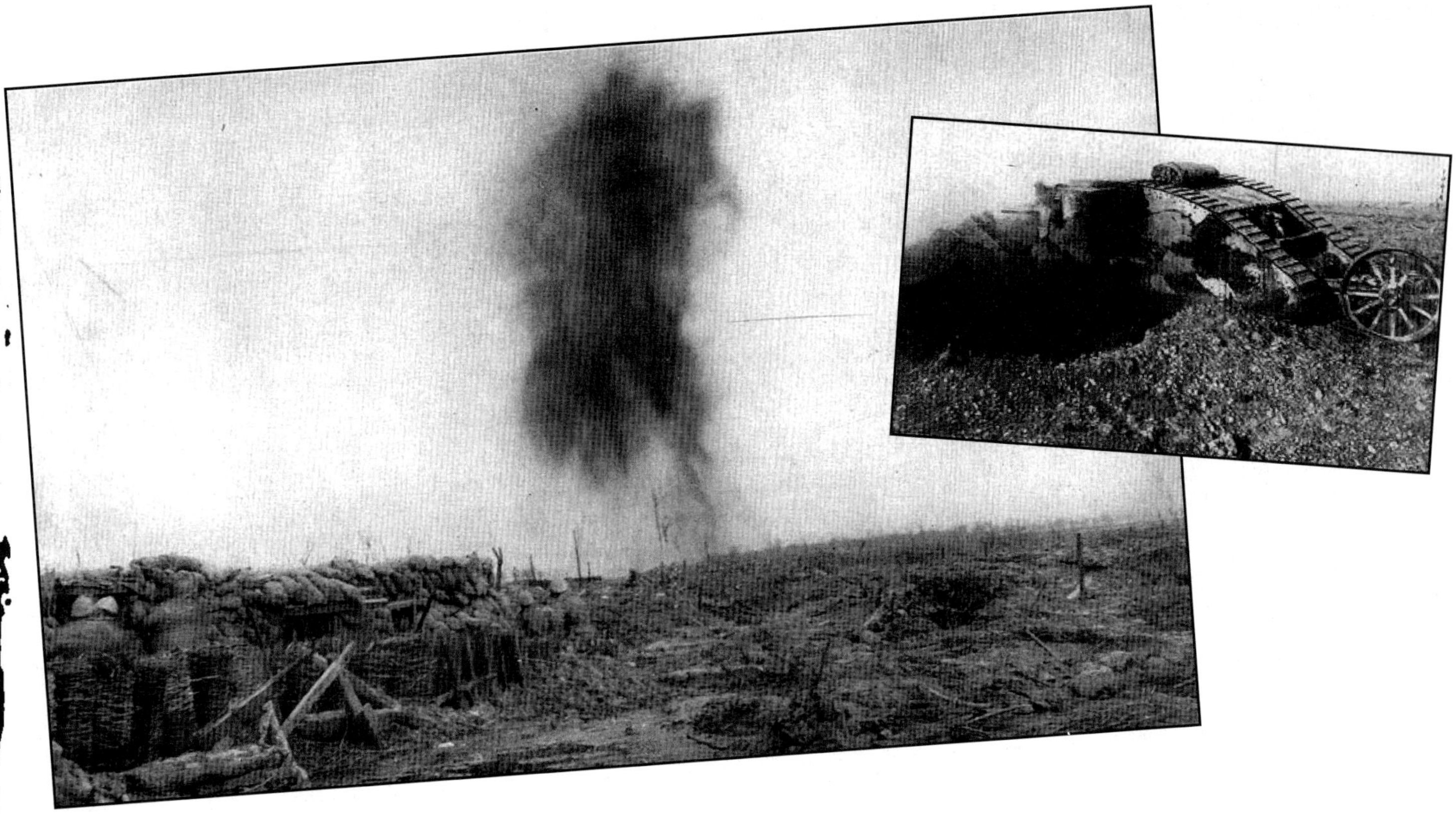

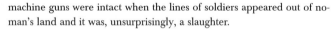

the most famous and dramatic was the massive detonation that left the 'Hawthom Crater'. Despite exploding ten minutes early, it was captured on camera and is now one of the most famous pieces of film from World War One.

At 7.30, British whistles sounded to signal the advance. Laden with heavy packs, the infantry, many from new units about to receive their baptism of fire, lined up neatly and went 'over the top', setting off at a steady walk into murderous German machinegun fire. The Machinengewehr 08 (or MG08), the German's principal machinegun, could fire over 400 rounds of 7.92mm ammunition a minute and its effective employment had already put paid to the almost Napoleonic infantry tactics of the British. Despite the furious artillery barrage, most German machine guns were intact when the lines of soldiers appeared out of no-man's land and it was, unsurprisingly, a slaughter.

"It was a magnificent display of trained and disciplined valour, and its assault only failed… because dead men can advance no further."

These words were written by Major-General Sir Beauvoir de Lisle, commander of the British 29th Division, describing the annihilation of the Canadian 1st Newfoundland Regiment as it tried to take the German fortifications at Beaumont Hamel. Its destruction took just thirty minutes. When the half-hour was up, the regiment had sustained 700 casualties, including all the officers. Only 68 men escaped injury.

This was not a unique experience. The British Army of 1916 included a number of 'pals' battalions, made up of workmates, school friends and neighbours who took up Lord Kitchener's call for a volunteer army at the outbreak of World War One. Kitchener's rallying cry was 'join up with a chum' and the men and boys of many communities jumped at the opportunity to enlist together, giving these units a character, identity and vocabulary very much their own.

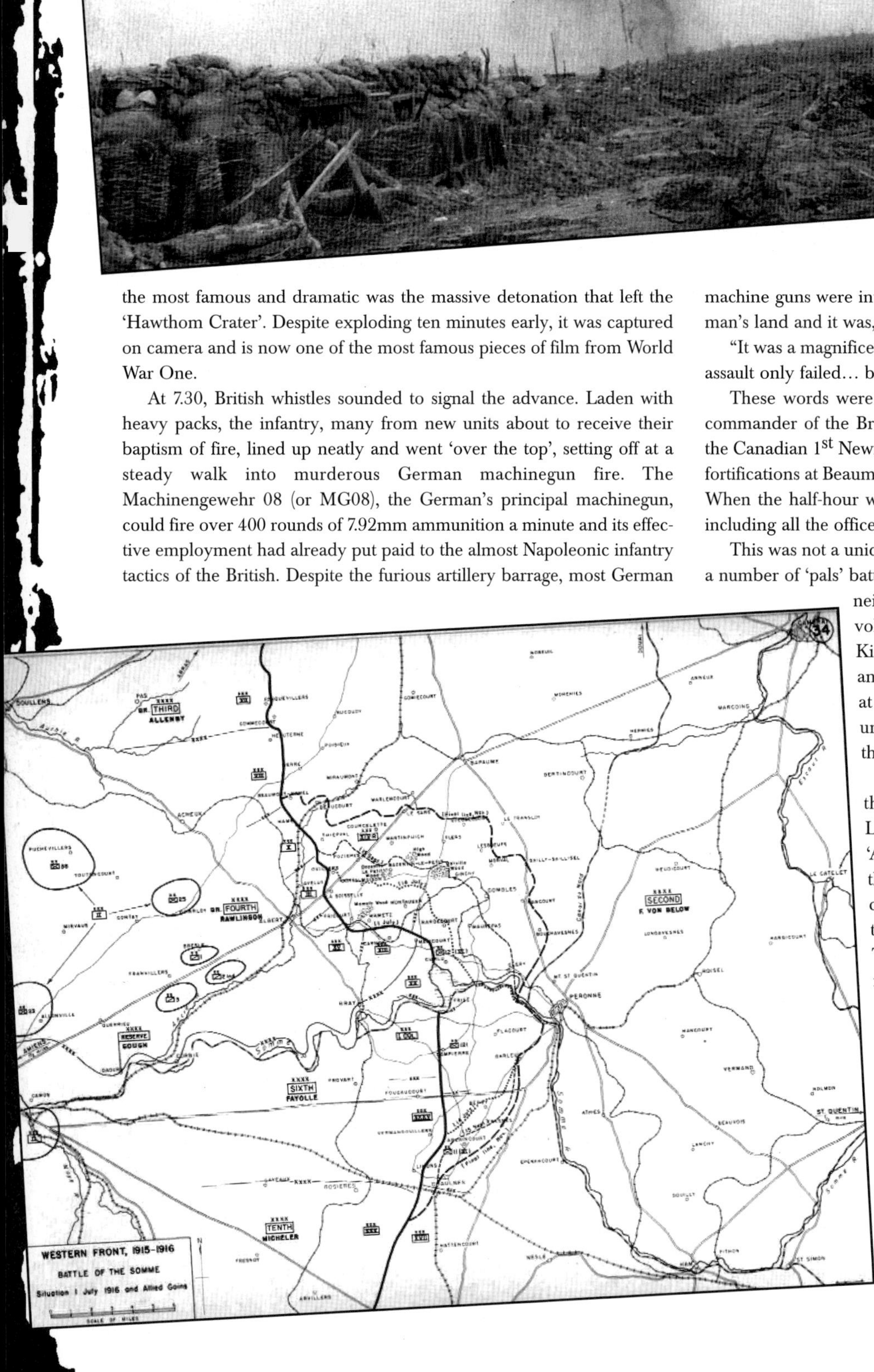
THIRD
ALLENBY
FOURTH
RAWLINSON
SECOND
F. VON BELOW
RESERVE
GOUGH
SIXTH
FAYOLLE
TENTH
MICHELER
PERONNE
WESTERN FRONT, 1915-1916
BATTLE OF THE SOMME
Situation 1 July 1916 and Allied Gains
SCALE OF MILES

One of the most famous of the 'pals' units was the 11th (Service) Battalion (Accrington), East Lancashire Regiment, better known as the 'Accrington Pals'. On the first day of the Somme, the battalion lost 584 men out of 720. When the casualty lists were released, Accrington, like many towns throughout Great Britain, was devastated. The magnitude of these losses are hard to grasp, representing as they did such a toll on the manhood of many towns and villages, factories and universities, that the men who fought in World War One became known as 'the lost generation'.

Such appalling losses were further exacerbated by the medical facilities at the time. Getting injured off the battlefield was itself problematic. There were thirty-two stretcher-bearers – sixteen stretchers – serving a British regiment of generally 900 men and they were expected to recover wounded whilst often under fire themselves. If

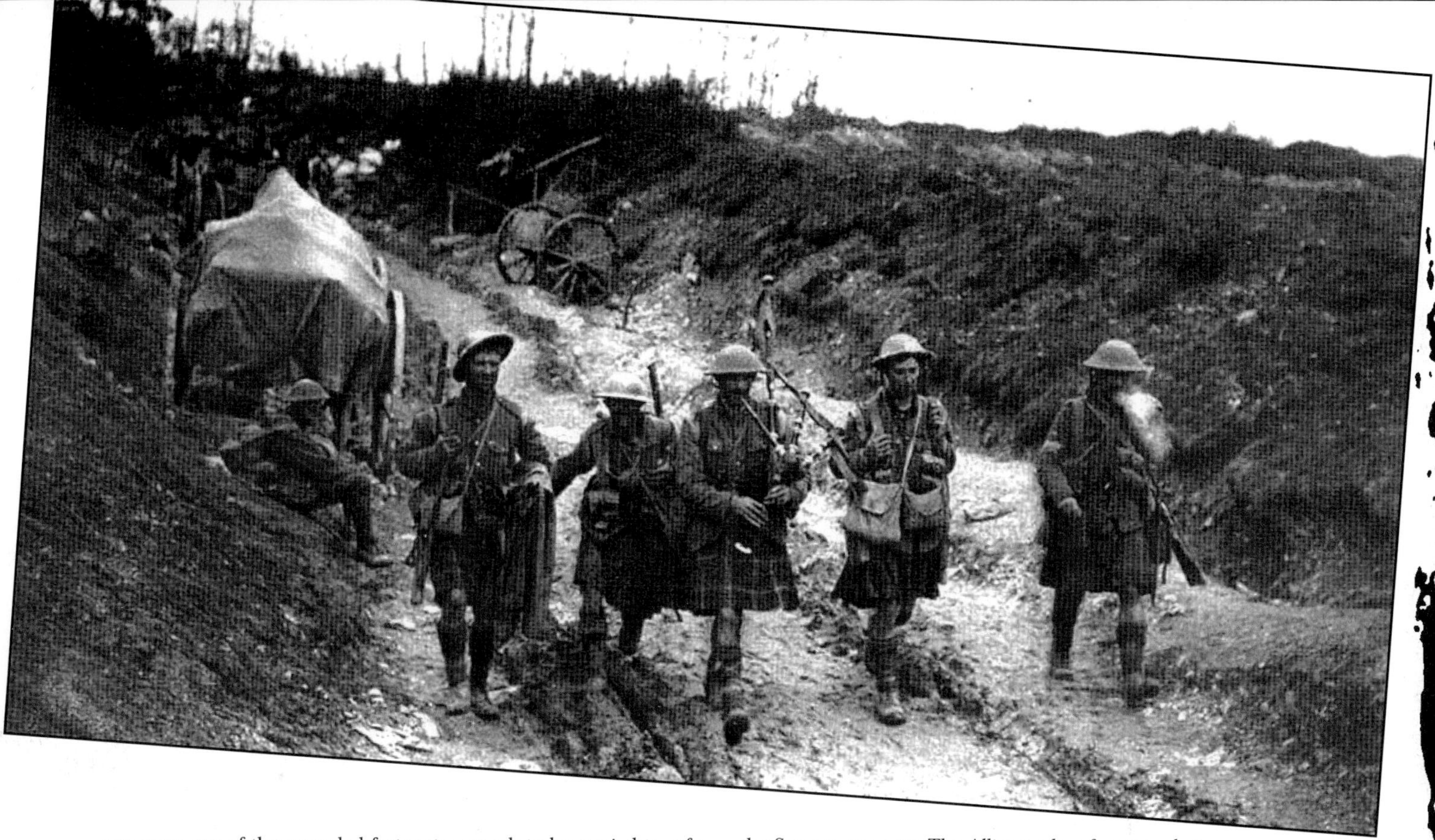

you were one of the wounded fortunate enough to be carried to safety, you found yourself in aid stations that, on 1 July, were overflowing with wounded, attended by too few nurses and doctors, many exhausted and traumatised, to cope with the scale of the disaster.

20,000 British soldiers, including 60% of the officers that led them, were killed on 1 July, another 40,000 injured. It remains the single bloodiest day in the history of the British Army. As author John Buchan wrote in his pamphlet on the battle:

"The splendid troops shed their blood like water for the liberty of the world."

Amazingly, some British troops did reach the German lines, but were far too few to hold their gains and were eventually forced to retreat back to the start line.

A statement issued by the British Army on the 1 July noted that, "The first day of the offensive is very satisfactory."

To the south, the French were more successful and made solid advances into the weaker German sector they attacked. However, the failure of the British attack left them unable to consolidate their successes and they too were forced to withdraw to their previous positions.

The carnage of the July 1 ended any hopes of the vaunted breakthrough. Haig instead concentrated his attacks on the weaker German lines to the south, but even here any successes were fleeting and the battle degenerated into a bloody stalemate. Haig tried again on 15 September, this time using 50 of the new wonder weapon, tanks, as part of the Battle of Flers-Courcelette. The tanks – heavy Mark 1s – met with initial success, surprising German troops who panicked at the site of these clanking behemoths. But the tanks also showed they were not only unreliable, breaking down with monotonous regularity, but were extremely tough on their crews; appallingly noisy and choked with fumes, they were also blisteringly hot. However, they did play crucial roles to a lesser or greater degree in several engagements, such as the critical arrival of four tanks in the advance on Flers, where a lone vehicle helped secure the village. But successes proved to be transitory and the ground they gained was soon given up to the Germans when most of the tanks broke down or became mired in the tangle of trenches.

The weather more of less ended the fighting in October, torrential rain turning the Front into a sea of mud. By November, heavy snow drove the British from their gains at Beaumont Hamel and the Battle of the Somme was over. The Allies made a few gains but never penetrated deeper than twelve kilometres (7.4 miles). These paltry successes cost the British 420,000 casualties, the French 200,000. The Germans, however, lost around half a million men, so in one respect – the destruction of German manpower – the Allied operation had been a success.

But the legacy of the Battle of the Somme is as a symbol of the pointless destruction of the flower of English youth. As the British Official History of the War wrote:

"For the disastrous loss of the finest manhood of the United Kingdom and Ireland there was only a small gain of ground to show..."

The Somme has also become a byword for the seeming indifference of the British High Command, Haig in particular, to the appalling casualties they seemed willing to inflict, a view now ingrained into British culture. ✛

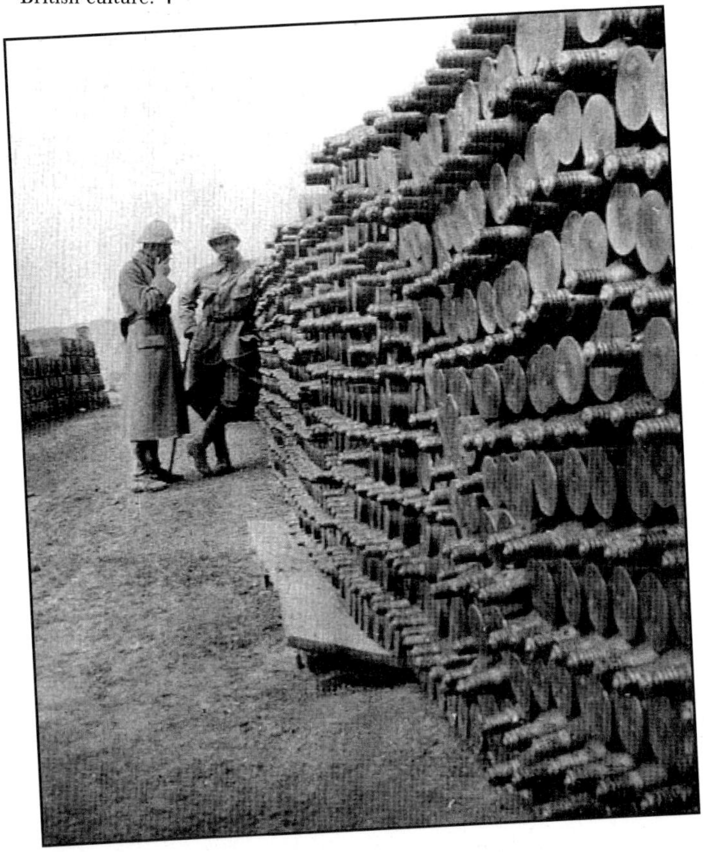

“The old Lie: Dulce et Decorum est
Pro patria mori.” *
Wilfred Owen

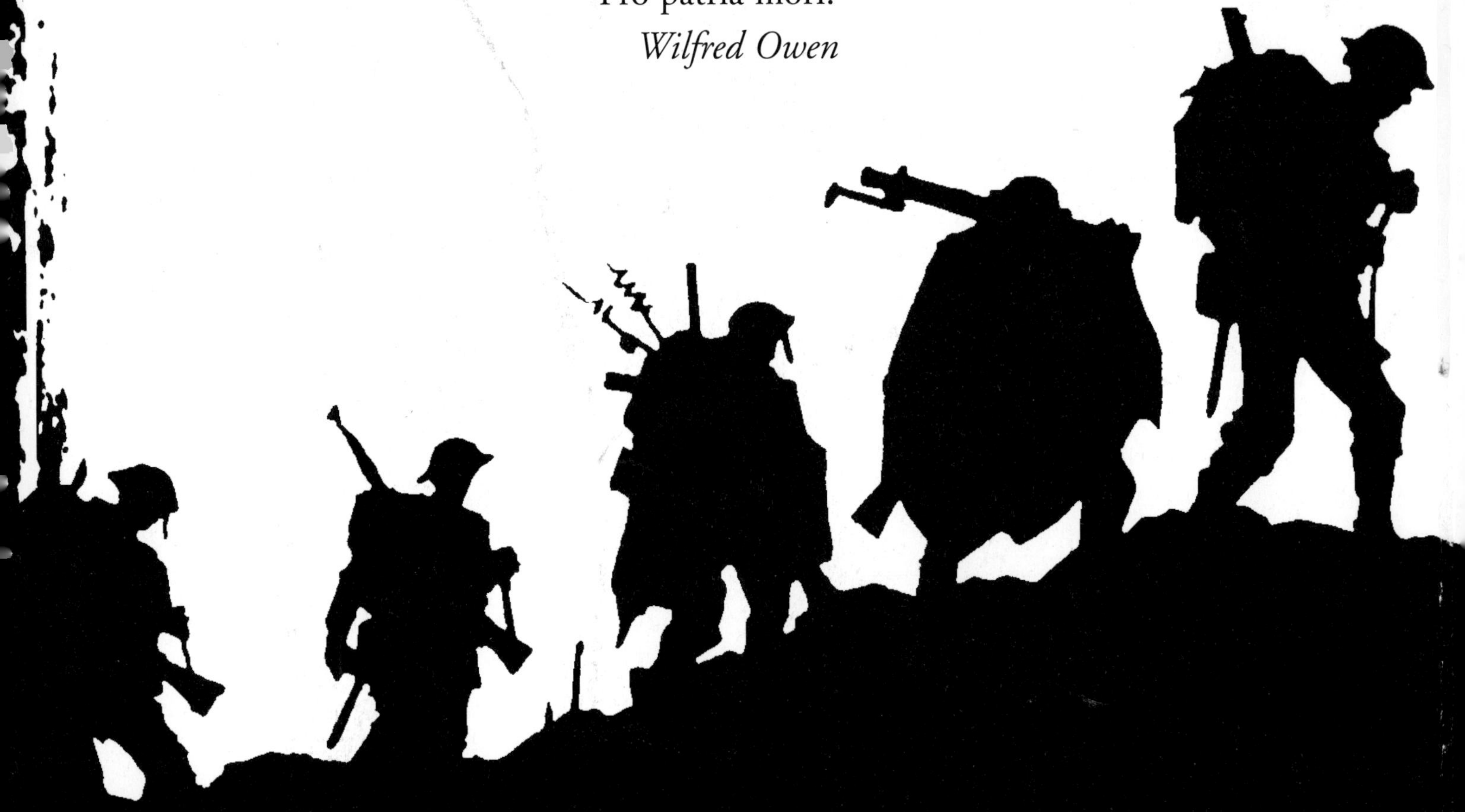

CHARLEY’S WAR

1 August 1916 – 17 October 1916

ISBN: 1 84023 929 8

* “It is sweet and fitting to die for one’s country.”